D0093231

MYTHS AND LEGENDS
SERIES

ROMANCE & LEGEND
OF CHIVALRY

A R HOPE MONCRIEFF

CHARLEMAGNE

MYTHS AND LEGENDS SERIES

ROMANCE & LEGEND OF CHIVALRY

A R HOPE MONCRIEFF

WITH ILLUSTRATIONS
FROM DRAWINGS AND
FAMOUS PAINTINGS

CRESCENT BOOKS
NEW YORK

Previously published by Gresham Publishing Co

This edition published 1986 by Crescent Books
distributed by Crown Publishers Inc.,
225 Park Avenue South
New York, New York 10003

Copyright © BRACKEN BOOKS 1985

All rights reserved. No part of this publication
may be reproduced, stored in a retrieval system,
or transmitted, in any form or by any means, electronic,
mechanical, photocopying, recording or otherwise,
without the prior permission of the copyright holder.

ISBN 0-517-259133

Printed and bound in Great Britain
by Clark Constable, Edinburgh and London

h g f e d c b a

PREFACE

This volume deals with the prose or verse tales styled Romances, as told in one of the Romance languages, being mainly indeed of French origin. Some of them based upon poetic legends that often seem a distortion of historical events, others more consciously woven to pattern from mingled strains of fact and fancy—they all come under a general definition as stories which, with knights for their heroes, illustrate the manners and ideas of mediæval chivalry.

The book is divided into two parts, the first giving an account of the character and development of Romance, which in the second and larger division is represented by typical tales from its various schools. The choice of these has been no easy task, not through any want of material. Among a bewildering abundance of stories, and versions of the same story, it seems best to select such as are at once representative and not without appeal to the sympathy of our generation, with an eye, also, to more variety of interest than much concerned older readers. In some cases it is necessary to pick out a complete episode from a tangled history long enough to fill more than one volume like the present. With certain reservations, it has been attempted here to include all the leading features of romantic fiction, while making the reader better acquainted with its most famous scenes and personages, chiefly known to us through allusions in modern literature.

CONTENTS

Part I—HISTORY OF ROMANCE

Part II—STORIES OF CHIVALRY

vii

CONTENTS

LIST OF ILLUSTRATIONS

LIST OF ILLUSTRATIONS

LIST OF ILLUSTRATIONS   xi

PART I

HISTORY OF ROMANCE

CHARACTER OF
CHIVALRIC ROMANCE

FIVE hundred years after this date some New Zealand University Extension lecturer can tell how our generation had for its favourite reading the novels which to his age may seem tiresome and absurd, as spinning out the same story over and over again, introducing the same characters — the heart - conquering captain, the heroine who hardly knows her own mind, the scheming mother-in - law, the fox - hunting squire, the young man about town, the comic old aunt, the detective of preternatural sagacity, the unscrupulous speculator who commits suicide, and so forth, and so forth—always ending at the altar with what ought to be a happy marriage. Five hundred years ago our forbears delighted in romances which we are apt to consider insufferably tedious, and which even in the day of Cervantes had fallen into such disrepute that most of them were pronounced fit to be tossed out of window by the priest and the barber of Don Quixote's village. So taste changes from century to century; and the pages over which the Middle Ages wept and smiled are for us like the "snows of yester-year". Few but students of the past know more than

the chief names, once familiar to young and old, of
those—

> British and Armoric knights,
> And all who since, baptized or infidel,
> Jousted in Aspramont or Montalban,
> Damasco, or Morocco, or Trebizond.

The history of these heroes had been songs sung by
minstrels kept at the court of great lords, or wandering
from castle to castle to entertain knights who for the
moment were not engaged in the business of slaughtering
man or beast. Still earlier they might have been legends
or myths drifting about the world with the transmigra-
tions of its peoples. Much vain controversy has been
waged as to whether the tales of chivalry were in origin
classical, Scandinavian, Arabian, or what not. The more
we look into the matter by the light of comparative mythology the more we find constant resemblances in all
popular fiction, resemblances too many and too close to
be always accidental. As Achilles had his vulnerable
heel, so on Siegfried's horn-armoured hide a leaf lighted
to make one spot that could be pierced by steel. In all
lands we have the Delilah who betrays her husband, or
is false to her father for love of an engaging captive.
One of the family of Cinderella turns up as a scullion
boy in King Arthur's kitchen. The Knights of the
Round Table seem but Jack the Giant Queller in mail,
whose magic sword, shoes of swiftness, and cap of darkness made common properties for legend and romance.
The adventures of Christian peer and paladin were long
before outlined in the exploits of Theseus and Hercules,
and in that ancient quest of the Golden Fleece. The
Introduction to our companion volume, *Classic Myth and
Legend*, deals with the cloudy genesis of primeval fables,

THE GOLDEN AGE OF THE TROUBADOUR

In May, 1324, Troubadours from all the world over gathered at Toulouse in a beautiful and spacious garden, there to recite poems and hear poems read. The chief prize, a golden violet, fell to a French competitor.

"IN MANUS TUAS, DOMINE!"

in which phenomena of nature are shaped by savage awe into gods, that as demi-gods come upon earth to be often confused with ancestral heroes and not altogether mythical adventurers, their memory looming through the mists of time.

We here take up these fictions, with sometimes a core of fact, as they flourished during the Middle Ages in chivalric trappings, when the king's sons of Eastern fable and the *Degen* and *Recken* of German minstrelsy had become Christian knights, more or less courteous, but never lacking in courage. Chivalry, which found an organization in the feudal system and a consecration in the wars of the Crusades, had its origin in the martial manners of that robust Teuton stock that mainly overspread the downfall of the Roman Empire. Various barbaric dialects, blending with degraded Latin, formed the *Romance* languages, with which in name and in nature this kind of fiction is closely connected, their medley of speech confusing the ideas and traditions of different races. The most marked elements of romance, meeting in the north of France, which was its cradle, seem to come from the Celtic Armoricans on the one hand, and from the Teuton invaders on the other. The amalgamation of speech took two main forms in the breaking up of Gaul. To the south prevailed the more Latinized *Langue d'Oc*, in which sang the *Troubadours* of Provence, whose strains seem to have been lyrical rather than epic. The northern *Langue d'Oil* was used by the *Trouvères*, to whom chiefly we owe the romances for which they found material at hand in the history of that region, and in what was there vaguely known of the world's history. "All the poetic lore of the world flowed to us," says Michelet, speaking of these early French authors. "While the hills of Wales and Brittany distilled Celtic traditions, as the rain murmuring in the green oaks of my own Ardennes, from the Pyrenees fell a cataract of Carlovingian romance. So also from the mountains of Swabia and Alsace, a flood of *Nibelungen* poured to France through Austrasia. The erudite poetry of Alexander and of Troy overflowed the Alps from the old classic world. And even from the distant East, opened by the Crusades, flowed to us, in fables, tales, and parables, the regained rivers of paradise."

Nuggets of shining gold turn up in early romance, but for the most part it works on ore that might have been more skilfully crushed and smelted. Its common produce is a jumble of monotonous adventures, loosely strung and full of vain repetitions, as told on long dark winter evenings when the idle audience could not have too much of a familiar theme. Their action would be set in a misty arena, where the realities of life were as much ignored as in our Christmas pantomimes. The characters, plots, and machinery of these stories show little variety. The bold knight errant, the distressed damsel, the sage enchanter, the wicked and gigantic oppressor, who is so easily knocked on the head as soon as the hero stands up to him, appear as regularly as the personages of the pantomime ; and the castles, forests, and tournament lists which form the scenery are as like one another as a stage room and street. Like our friend the clown, the knight errant has no business but meddling with other people's. No matter how great peril environs him, he gets off scot free by help from some harlequin enchanter or some magic sword, while the villain of the piece comes to grief as surely as the pantomimic policeman. Attended by his faithful dwarf or giant, as the clown by the pantaloon, our hero roams the world doing what he pleases, utterly released from the cares of ordinary prosaic existence, and without any visible means of support. So there are no exploits too marvellous to be confidently entered upon by such a fortunate being; and no faithful reader of romance need be the least astonished at his success. An adventurer of later days, whose name was Munchausen, seems veracious and dealing in matter of fact beside some of those heroes so much admired by the would-be knight of La Mancha.

Do but see what it is he wonders at—the stopping of a mill-wheel! Before heaven, your worship should read what I have read, concerning Felixmarte of Hyrcania, who with one backstroke cut asunder five giants through the middle, as if they had been so many bean-cods of which the children make puppet-friars. At another time he encounters a great and powerful army, consisting of about a million six hundred thousand soldiers, all armed from head to foot, and routed them as if they had been a flock of sheep. But what will you say of the good Don Cirongilo of Thrace? who was so stout and valiant, as you may there read in the book, that once as he was sailing on a river, seeing a fiery serpent rise to the surface of the water, he immediately threw himself upon it, and getting astride its scaly shoulders squeezed its throat with both hands with so much force that the serpent, finding itself in danger of being choked, had not other remedy but to plunge to the bottom of the river, carrying with him the knight, who would not quit his hold; and when they reached the bottom, he found himself in such a fine palace and beautiful gardens, that it was wonderful; and presently the serpent turned into an old man, who said so many things to him that the like was never heard!

Don Quixote (Jarvis's translation).

Scenes like these are sometimes changed with bewildering rapidity, for, as in the pantomimes, romancers got into the way of mixing up separate stories without much regard to unity of plot. Such involved construction should be familiar to us in Spenser's *Fairy Queen*, an

elaborate phantasmagoria where it demands no small effort
to keep in mind the different heroes successively passing
out of view. Hence, perhaps, so few modern readers
are "in at the death of the Blatant Beast", that, by the
way, is not run to death at the end of the Sixth Book—
which looks as if even Macaulay's attention had flagged
here for once.

History and geography are made such wild work of
as to be ludicrous in the eyes of our school children.
Charlemagne's reign is by one romancer gravely fixed at
A.D. 103. Lucius, Emperor of Rome, with whom Arthur
wars, has in his army kings of Ethiopia and Egypt; and
here appears a Sultan of Surrey, by which we may understand Syria. A Saracen king leads on the Moabites to
battle. Scotland also we find governed by Saracens, for
the Mahommedans, who play the part of bogey in so
many romances, are often confused with Saxons and other
unbelieving enemies of Christendom. Constantine is
converted from the faith of Mahommed, who deceived
his followers out of spite at not being chosen Pope.
Constantinople, we learn, is on the way between Ireland
and England. Denmark is near Lombardy. Sir Bevis
of Hampton sails from the Greek sea to Cologne. The
Damsel of Denmark takes ship from Scotland to reach
Great Britain. Alexander the Great, making a pilgrimage from the East to a certain shrine of Venus, is wrecked
on the British coast. This ancient hero figures in
mediæval romance as a knight errant, duly killing dragons,
founding orders of chivalry, and presiding at tournaments. Biblical and classical personages are thus freely
invested with arms and customs of chivalry unknown even
in the reigns of Arthur or Charlemagne.

As for morals, they vary with the author's age; but
in general there is much of that glorification of barbarous

manners which so much offended Roger Ascham and other moralists. But whatever their faults of omission and commission, the knights were always consistent in their regard for the doctrines and rites of the Church. Nothing seems more absurd to us than the way in which these heroes mix up devotion with manslaughter, and their zeal for the conversion of infidels whose religion they so ill understood that a Christian knight is frequently seized by a passion for destroying the idols of "Mahound", a name by which he reviled the prophet who so fiercely denounced idolatry. An episode, most gravely related, is that of such interludes in combat as when Sir Roland and Sir Ferragus lay down their arms to engage in a long-winded controversy on the mysteries of the faith. When taken by surprise at Roncesvalles the French peers do not set on till they have knelt for confession and absolution from Archbishop Turpin. The least insult to his creed has always to be wiped out by a good knight in the blood of scores or hundreds of Saracens.

Our ideas of the courtesy of knights and the purity of their mistresses are mainly taken from the more refined works of a later age, when writers like Spenser spiritualized the exploits of chivalry, and Chaucer had gilded the character of such a one as—

> Though that he was worthy he was wise,
> And of his port as meek as is a maid.
> He never yet no villainy ne said
> In all his life, unto no manner wight:
> He was a very perfect gentle knight.

The knights of older story were far from perfect and but seldom gentle. Those of us who know the adventures of Charlemagne's peers and of the Round Table

Knights only as they are told by Tasso or Tennyson might be astonished to learn how often the originals are disfigured by coarseness, brutality, and sensuality. In later versions we find circumstances introduced to palliate the crimes seen in a clearer light, as the spirit of romance became sublimated along with the ideals of chivalry. The early *Chansons de Geste* do not always bear out the aspirations breathed by the charge given to Tristram's son when knighted at the tomb of Launcelot: "Knight, be cruel to thine enemies, kind to thy friends, humble to the weak, and aim always to sustain the right and confound those who do wrong to widows, poor ladies, maidens, and orphans; and love the poor always with all thy might, and withal love always the Holy Church".

It was by a process of evolution from the rude loyalty and ruthless bravery of Rolands and Olivers that Don Quixote came to understand how "in slaying giants we must destroy pride and arrogance, we must vanquish envy by generosity, wrath by a serene and humble spirit, gluttony and sloth by temperance and vigilance, licentiousness by chastity and inviolable fidelity to the sovereign mistresses of our hearts, indolence by travelling the world in search of every honourable opportunity of gaining renown as knights and Christians". Love especially takes on a refinement at last reaching the point of the ridiculous, while all along romancers have much to say of that commerce between the brave and the fair that makes such a figure in the price-lists of poetry.

> Nought under heaven so strongly doth allure
> The sense of man, and all his mind possess,
> As beauty's lovely bait, that doth procure
> Great warriors oft their rigour to repress,
> And mighty hands forget their manliness,
> Drawn with the power of a heart-robbing eye,

And wrapped in fetters of a golden tress,
That can with melting pleasance mollify
Their hardened hearts, inured to blood and cruelty.

There is slight sense of humour in most authors of romance, whose themes lent themselves rather to tragic sentiment, not to say the grim and gruesome. Such buffoonery as turns up here and there is apt to be of a simple and coarsely grained type. In the romance of Ferumbras we have some rough clowning that strikes us as not more grotesque than the theological matter with which also the story is spiced. The Saracen king's son Ferumbras, engaging in single combat with Oliver, is won over, by blows rather than arguments, to the true faith, and when recovered from his convincing wounds, makes no difficulty about serving Charlemagne against his own parent. His sister Floripas also plays false to her father for the sake of his Christian captives, a stock incident in such tales since the days of Ariadne and Medea; and she hardly commands our sympathy when, to free her new friends from their dungeon, she first pushes her duenna into the moat, then knocks out the jailer's brains with his own keys, as may have seemed an excellent joke to her generation. The laugh is not always on the side of the Christians, for a Saracen lord, who pays the prisoners a visit, sets them on the childish amusement of blowing at a live coal, and in this playing with fire slily contrives to burn Duke Naymes's long beard. But the angry peer gets the best of the fun, for he throws that practical joker bodily into the fireplace, and holds him down with a pitchfork till he is burnt up. In the happy ending of the piece the Saracen king, captured and condemned to baptism, behaves in a most improper manner at the "Vat", spitting in it and calling the bishop

names, for which he is duly punished in this world and
the next.   The ruder tales readily take unbelievers as
approved butts for such rough wit.   A certain amount of
farce also is supplied by giants, usually represented as
stupid in proportion to their bulk, and often as not ill-
natured.   In the course of the friendly conversations
relieving the combat of Roland and Ferragus, the latter,
forty feet of simple-mindedness and candour as he was,
is good enough to let his adversary know the only spot
at which his hide may be pierced—information of which
Roland rather unchivalrously takes advantage.   There
seemed no doubt a very comic touch in a foe's thus
betraying himself to destruction.   But the most common
and effective jest is nothing more artful than the cleaving
to the chine of any felon, paynim, or caitiff that stands
in the hero's way.   Even thus in our old ballad—

> The never a word had Dickie to say,
> So he ran the lance through his fause bodie!

Nor need we look for refinement of character and
motive in most personages of romance.   The drawing
is bold black and white, the black very black, and the
white meant to be spotless.   In certain groups of tales
we have the same characters appearing repeatedly, as in
Thackeray's and Trollope's novels, and presenting con-
sistently some prominent virtue or defect: Sir Launcelot
is always chivalrous, Sir Gawayne courteous, Sir Galahad
pure, Sir Kay boastful; Roland is bound to be rash,
Oliver loyal, and Ganilon a traitor.   But as a rule it
might seem enough to label the actors a good knight or
a wicked knight, as the case may be, and our sympathy
thus engaged on the right side we know at once which
is likely to get the best of the encounter.   Not always
so, indeed, for tragic effect is sometimes given by a crush-

ing defeat, as in Arthur's last great battle, and the massacre of Roland's force, treacherously taken at overwhelming odds. In such stories of disaster the romancer may have been bound by tradition, while a quite imaginary hero like Amadis is pretty sure to be brought safe and glorious through the most appalling adventures.

Southey tells us how in his schooldays there was no book except the *Fairy Queen* which " he perused so often or with such deep contentment as *Morte d'Arthur*". His taste no doubt might he a little more discriminating than that of the average youngster. But the romances of chivalry were in fact the literature of Europe's unschooled boyhood, and may be compared with our own boys' books, glorifying virtues that are specially dear to a robust age not yet troubled by the pale cast of thought, or by a taste for heterogeneous motive. The boyish reader's imagination, meeting the author's more than halfway, requires little but a lay figure, to be clothed by the readiness of his own sympathies or antipathies. His stereotyped hero is the bold honest lad he would himself willingly be, who goes through all hazards without turning a hair, to set young John Bull a pattern of such qualities as he can appreciate. British pluck and prowess is his favourite theme; and a picturesquely superficial and patriotically coloured view of history hits the interest of readers who never fail to welcome much the same story in different disguises.

In the "penny dreadful" periodicals of our time there was a hero named Jack Harkaway, who for years went through various rounds of adventure to the entire satisfaction of admirers by the million, just as did Amadis of Gaul and his descendants for hobbledehoyish minds of Europe. Such a modern hero was but a vulgar type of the romantic knights, plus a certain enforced respect for police regulations, but minus an elevating influence brought to bear by the Church upon the manners and morals of chivalry, minus also that characteristic of exalted gallantry towards ladies which came to be evolved by chivalric sentiment.   Else, the stories dear to our idle apprentices, if only embroidered by supernatural prodigies, would display much the same threadbare patterns of gaudy extravagance and conventional figures as pleased mediæval lords and ladies.   And, as youth grows out of relish for Jack and the Beanstalk to take more interest in the adventures of such a less-shadowy Jack as that one above - mentioned, then perhaps comes to require the higher craftsmanship that frames a story like Mr. Jack Easy's, so we can trace a certain development, not always an improvement, in the fiction that won most favour from century to century.

For example of the features that make the ground-work of chivalric romance, let us sketch the old Breton and Welsh tale of Peredur, which, if told at length, might have to be turned into burlesque to catch the interest of considerate readers, so full is it of wild impossibility and monotonous repetition.   The hero is seventh son of a count who with the six elder sons is killed in battle.   Then his widow resolves to bring up her Benjamin in seclusion, out of the way of temptations to peril.   She retires to a wilderness, accompanied only by women, children, and weaklings, who know nothing of arms.   The boy grows up ignorant of war; yet he is such a chip of the old block that daily he goes into the woods to amuse himself by throwing sticks and stones. One day he falls in with three knights, who so excite his admiration that he asks his mother who such personages may be.   She tells him that they are angels; as in an older religious romance a tutor's cue is to set his pupil

against the charms of woman, seen for the first time, by
calling her a devil, or a *goose* in Boccaccio's ungallant
variant of the same story. Peredur, exclaiming that he
wants to be an angel, runs off to join the knights, who
are good-natured enough to acquaint him with their real
vocation, and explain to him the uses of their arms and
equipment. He goes back to his mother, declaring that
he means to be a knight, at which fatal news she swoons
away. Without taking much notice of her distress, he
picks out the best of her cart horses, saddles it with a
sack, and with twisted branches imitates the harness of
the knight's chargers. Thus prepared to take the field,
he asks his mother's permission, which she gives unwillingly along with parting counsels to be generous,
devout, and courteous. She also recommends him to
seek the court of Arthur, as there he will find the best
and bravest knights in the world. Somewhat incon-
sistently with her pacific principles, she further recommends him to help himself whenever he is not offered
meat or drink, and not to be at all backward in making
love to ladies : in short, he must *se faire valoir* among all
sorts and conditions of men.

With no better weapons than a handful of sharpened
sticks, the youth sets out for Arthur's court, where he
arrives just after an exciting intrusion, no reason for
which appears unless to give our hero an opportunity of
distinguishing himself. A rude knight has burst into
the hall to snatch a golden cup, flinging the contents
into Queen Guinevere's face, at the same time giving
her a most ungallant box on the ear. Then off he goes
untouched, with the remark that if anyone cares to
avenge that insult and dispute the cup, he will be found
waiting in an adjacent meadow. All Arthur's doughty
knights stand still in dread of such a challenge when

Peredur enters, looking for the king. By ill luck he addresses himself to the malicious Sir Kay, an unsympathetic character, as stewards are apt to be in romance, perhaps as not over-bountiful to wandering minstrels. Sir Kay scouts the desire of this young scarecrow to become a knight, and mockingly packs him off to prove his manhood by tackling the queen's insulter. That bully, rather amazed to see what sort of champion is sent against him, would have let the youth off with a whack of his spear on the shoulder, which Peredur returns by piercing his eye with one of his improvised javelins. Meanwhile the more gracious Sir Owen rebukes Sir Kay for sending the lad on a hopeless errand, and goes after him to see how he has fared. He finds the supposed young clown standing over the knight's dead body, which he is awkwardly trying to strip.

"What are you doing there?" asked Sir Owen.

"I can't manage to get off this coat of iron," said Peredur. "All my strength is in vain, and my trouble thrown away."

Pulling off for him the knight's arms and clothes, Sir Owen said: "See here, my good soul, a horse and armour better than your own; take them and come with me to Arthur that he may dub you knight, for in sooth you are worthy of being one."

Peredur, however, refused to go back to a court where he had been so slightingly treated; but sent a message to Sir Kay, promising not to forget his scornful behaviour; and, now duly provided with horse and harness, set out in quest of adventures. Before long he meets another knight, who unfolds himself as a hater of Arthur and all his men. Whereupon the stripling puts lance in rest at once to unhorse this reviler, whose life he spares on condition of his promising to present

himself before Arthur as vanquished. Sixteen knights
he serves alike in the course of a week, and when all
those unfortunates arrive one by one at Arthur's court,
Sir Kay begins to think he has made a mistake in braving
the vengeance of that formidable varlet.

But our hero is not yet a fully accomplished knight.
When he presently arrives at the castle of a white-haired
and lame old lord, after dinner this host asks him if he
knows how to use a sword.

"I do not," said Peredur; "but I shall know when
I have been shown how."

"Whoever," said the old man, "knows stick and
target play knows also how to wield a sword."

He set Peredur playing at stick and target with one
of his sons, whose head the hero was quick to break.
Then the old man, delighted to see his own blood so
deftly spilt, revealed himself to Peredur as a hitherto
unknown uncle, and invited him to remain at the castle,
that he might learn good manners and customs, and be
dubbed a knight when the rust of his boorish education
had been rubbed off. In spite of this useful invitation,
the new-found nephew set off again next morning, to
arrive at another castle, where he proved his lately ac-
quired swordsmanship by cleaving an iron post fixed in
the pavement, and thereupon learnt from the admiring
lord that he also was an uncle, brother of his last night's
host. This house had some gruesome mysteries which,
beyond trying the hero's nerves, seem for the present to
play no part in the story, but will figure significantly in
its *dénouement*. Into the hall came two young men bearing a long lance with the point dripping blood, a sight
that set all present weeping and lamenting except the
master of the castle, who went on talking with Peredur,
and offered no explanation of this woe. Next came two

young girls bearing a basin on which a man's head was swimming in blood. Not everyone would have slept sound after such entertainment; and perhaps Peredur did as well to leave his uncle's house next morning.

His next meeting was with another connection hitherto unknown. As he entered a wood he heard lamentations in the distance, and saw a beautiful brown-haired woman and a saddled charger, and beside it lay a corpse which she was vainly trying to lift on to the horse.

"Why do you weep?" asked the youth.

"What is that to you, accursed Peredur?"

Peredur might well ask why he was accursed, and how she knew his name. She informed him that his mother had died of grief after his departure; that she herself was his own foster-sister; that the dead man was her husband, who had just been slain by a knight still lurking in the wood. She advised Peredur not to go near him, but of course her advice was thrown away. As soon as he had buried the body for her he sought out the slayer, overthrew him at the first encounter, and granted his life on condition of taking the widow in marriage, over and above the usual stipulation of presenting himself at Arthur's court and repeating his own defiance to Sir Kay. When so many beaten knights arrived at his court, the king's curiosity was so much stirred by the unknown youth's prowess that he proposed to travel all over the wild parts of Britain till he could fall in with Peredur and see whether he or Kay were the better man.

While he is being searched for by all the Round Table, our hero pursues his course of solitary adventures. His next is the relief of a damsel in much distress, since she was wooed by a hateful lord who would press his suit by cutting off her supply of victuals. Peredur faced this lord and all his myrmidons, overthrowing them day by day, and forcing them to send larger and larger supplies of provision to the castle, finally making the oppressor pay homage and tribute to its mistress. On leaving this scene he was joined by another distressed lady, whom, through the somewhat bold manners enjoined on him by his mother, he had brought into suspicion with a jealous husband, but was now able to make her amends in proving her innocence by force of arms. At his next night's lodging he had to do with more ghostly enemies in the shape of nine sorceresses, one of whom he handled so roughly that she recognized his birth and admiringly carried him off to the "palace" of her uncanny sisterhood, where he stayed three weeks, being here fully instructed in chivalry and the management of arms.

Now comes a rather puzzling incident in the story. It appears that its hero has not yet fixed his affections definitely on any of the ladies whose charms must have wiped out one another's impression on his mind. None the less, like Don Quixote, he is bound to have a Dulcinea in fancy if not in the flesh. As he rides along over snow-clad ground, he sees a crow pecking at a teal that has been killed by a falcon; then he must needs compare the whiteness of the snow, the blackness of the crow, and the red blood to the skin, hair, and cheeks of his imaginary fair one. Lost in reverie over her possible perfections, he comes in sight of Arthur, who sends some two dozen of his retinue in turn to ask who he is and what he is about. For answer Peredur unsaddles them one by one. But when Sir Kay appears to put the same question in a most offensive tone, he is hurled down with such violence as to lie like a dead man. Sir Gawaine coming forward to make enquiries more politely, the would-be lover explains how he does not like being disturbed in his dream of beauty; but, on hearing that it is Sir Kay on whom he has at last taken vengeance, he agrees to present himself before Arthur. Received as his exploits deserve, he goes back with the king to Caerleon, where on the first evening of his stay at court he beholds a damsel seeming to realize his dreams of perfection, her name Angarad with the Golden Hand.

"By my faith," was his proposal, "so please you, I will love you above all other women."

"By my faith," was her answer, "I do not love you and never will."

"Well then," cried the pressing suitor, "I take heaven to witness that I will speak not a word to Christian soul till you have come to love me above all men."

To show himself worthy of her affection, he sets out upon a fresh course of adventures, in which, with the usual ease, making his way into a castle in spite of the lion that stands porter at its entrance, he vanquishes a terrible tyrant backed by a company of giants, and orders them to present themselves before Arthur. It is a relief to him to find that these are pagans, who have need also to be baptized, since thus his conscience need not prick him for breaking his vow to speak to no Christian soul. Henceforth he keeps it strictly, the result being that in lonely wanderings he pines away, for love of his lady, let us hope, rather than from want of gossip. He grows so worn and dejected that when again met with by Arthur's knights none of them recognize him, and his vow hinders him from saying who he is. Unknown, he returns with Arthur to Caerleon; and still this "Young Mute", as they call him, wins such glory by silent feats of arms that one day the haughty Angarad makes him a proposal in turn.

"How sad," cried she, "that you cannot speak, for if you could I should love you above all other men; and in truth, whatever you can or cannot do, I do love you above all!"

"And I love you," exclaimed Peredur, now revealing himself in his true name to those dull-eyed comrades.

Thus fortunate in love as in war, one might think the hero had now nothing to do but marry and live happy ever afterwards; but that is not the formula of this school of fiction. His appetite for adventures is by no means satiated; and he has a mysterious destiny still to accomplish. When out hunting with Arthur, he strays away to reach a castle, in the hall of which he finds some bald and sunburnt young men playing at chess. Throughout this tale there is frequent allusion to the hair and complexion of its actors, contrasted as fair and brown, which looks as if the author's mind ran upon " battles long ago " between rival races. A Breton ballad, containing the same experiences as those of Peredur's boyhood, appears to have for hero an authentic Armorican Wallace, who withstood the power of Charlemagne's son Louis. The untrained youth who suddenly blossoms out as a matchless champion is a common feature in Celtic romance. To have done with our present hero's exploits, hitherto presented in an abridged form, let us take a specimen more closely translated.

And when he entered he saw three young maidens sitting on a bench, and they were all dressed in the same way, as becomes great ladies. And he came up to them and sat down near them on the bench; and one of the damsels looked at him sadly and began to weep. Peredur asked her why she wept.

"For grief to think that a fine young man like you is about to be slain."

" Who will slay me?" asked Peredur.

" If you are bold enough to pass the night here, I will show you."

" What is the great danger of resting here?"

" This palace belongs to my father," said the damsel, "and he kills whoever comes here without his leave."

" What man, then, is your father to kill people so?"

" One who vexes and oppresses his neighbours, and does justice to no one," answered she.

Thereupon he saw the young men get up and sweep away the chessmen from the board, and he heard a great noise, and upon this noise came a tall black man having only one eye; and the damsels rose to greet him; and they disarmed him, and he sat down; and after a moment of consideration he cast his eyes upon Peredur to ask who might be this stranger.

" My lord," said one of the damsels, " it is the most comely and noble young man you have ever seen in your life. For the sake of God and for your own honour, behave well towards him."

" For your sake I will so do, and grant him his life for this one night."

Then Peredur came to join them before the fire, and to take his part of the meat and drink; and he fell to talking with the ladies; and, excited by wine, he said to the black man:

" I am astonished at one thing: strong as you give yourself out to be, who can have knocked out one of your eyes?"

" Whoever asks me that question," answered the black man, " does not leave my house with his life, unless he make me a free gift or pay me a ransom: that is one of my laws."

" Lord," said the damsel to the black man, " whatever he may say to you in jest and heated by wine, keep the promise you have made me."

" I willingly consent for your sake," he answered; " I grant him his life for this night."

And so they passed the night. And next morning the black man got up and donned his armour, saying to Peredur:

" Up, young man, and make ready to die!"

" You must do one of two things, black man," answered Peredur. " If you wish to fight with me, either take off your armour or give me the like, that the match may be fair between us."

"Ah, young man, would you fight if you had arms?" said he. "Then take what arms you please."

Then the damsel brought to Peredur what arms he wished, and he fought with the black man, and forced him to cry for mercy.

"Black man, I grant you grace, if only you will tell me who you are and who has knocked out your eye."

"My lord, I will tell you: I lost my eye in fighting with the Black Dragon of the Cairn. There is a mountain called The Mount of Sorrows, and on this mount there is a cairn, and inside the cairn there is a dragon, and at the tail of the dragon is a precious stone; and the virtue of this stone is such that whoever takes it in one hand, at that very moment has in the other as much gold as he can wish. It is in fighting with this monster that I have lost my eye. And they call me the Black Tyrant; and the reason they call me the Black Tyrant is that not a single man around has not been oppressed by me, and that I have never done justice to anyone."

"Well!" said Peredur. "And the mountain of which you speak, is it far from here?"

"The same day as you leave us you will arrive at the palace of the sons of the King of Tortures?"

"Why are they so called?"

"Because every day the Monster of the Lake kills his sons. When you come away from there you will arrive at the court of the Lady of Exploits."

"What exploits does she?" asked Peredur.

"She has three hundred men in her palace, and to every stranger that arrives they relate the exploits of her warriors. And so it is: the three hundred men sit down at table by the lady, not in want of respect for her guests, but to be able to relate the exploits of the place. And the day you leave her, you will arrive at the Mount of Sorrows; and all around the mount, in three hundred tents, dwell the guardians of the dragon."

"You have been too long the scourge of the world," said Peredur; "I am going to bring that to an end."

Then he killed him.   Then the damsel came in and set to talking with Peredur.

"If you were poor when you came here," said she, "henceforth you will be rich with the treasure of him you have just slain.   You have seen all the lovely damsels who are in this court; well, you can have of them which you wish as your wife."

"Madam, I have not come from my country to get a wife; but marry yourself whomever you like best of the goodly young men I see here.   I do not desire your riches; I have nothing to do with them."

Peredur's adventures, we foresee, are by no means at an end.   But doubtless the reader has had enough of this farrago of improbabilities and impossibilities, obscured and confused by an utter want of sense of proportion and by the author's readiness to bring in all the stereotyped scenes of his art, whether or no they help on the story. It culminates, rather hazily, with the hero's arrival at the Castle of Marvels, where he hears more about that bleeding lance and basin he had seen in the house of his uncle, which now turn out to be the main machinery of the plot.   It is vaguely explained how the gory head was that of a cousin slain by sorceresses, also to blame for laming his uncle—the same weird sisterhood as had been good enough to perfect Peredur's chivalrous education, most unaccountably and unselfishly on their part, since the mission with which destiny had charged him was nothing less than avenging on them the injuries of his kindred. The tale then ends by Arthur and his knights exterminating that college of magic, with Peredur in the forefront of the achievement.

This story seems to date from the beginning of the twelfth century, if not earlier.   When, two or three generations later, such wild fantasy came to be re-

fined by Chrétien de Troyes and other Trouvères into
the romance of Percival-le-Gallois, the gory lance and
basin, here appearing as machinery of rude witchcraft, had
been transmuted into the glorious mystery of the Sangreal, round which the whole story took on a more religious and romantic cast. A mere hint from a hermit to
Peredur, that he ought not to be riding about in arms on
Good Friday, is elaborated in Perceval's story into a long
disquisition on the history of the Christian faith and a
complete penance performed by the hero in recognition of
the Truce of God, by which on holy seasons the Church
sought to calm the bellicose passions of its unruly sons.
For another hint of development, a mysterious dwarf in
the older story has become a court-fool in that of Perceval.
Later on, we shall find some of Peredur's experiences
more elaborately dressed in such artificial romances as
Amadis of Gaul.

What still bears marks of the rough-hewn folktale
has been here dwelt on at some length to show the be-
ginnings of romance, whose early wildness may yet be
found richer in poetic feeling than are some of its more
sophisticated forms. The historical sketch, illustrated by
examples, next to be presented, will make clear how freely
those stories were handled from generation to generation
by their often anonymous authors, each trimming well-
worn themes to suit the taste and morals of his time and
his own sense of artistic fitness. The same freedom has
been used in dressing out the stories to be put forward
as characteristic types of the whole mass. The present
author has chosen them from all the cycles and provinces
of romance except where its main interest is mediæval
ideas of love, the work of the Troubadours rather than
of the Trouvères, that seems not to the purpose of this
volume. He has abridged and toned them, always with

an eye to the truth of their spirit, if not the whole truth, of which sometimes the less said the better. He has veiled coarsenesses, pared down absurdities, done away with vain repetitions, and in Southey's phrase "consolidated" a good deal of slaughter by way of relieving the plethora of combats. On occasion he has even ventured to cover up a rent or a tatter with a patch taken from the original stuff; nor has he scrupled here and there to recolour a morality that does not always harmonize with our idea of the chivalrous. There are many books nowadays treating romance from the scholar's point of view. The aim here is merely to reproduce for our generation some of the interest it had for an audience anything but critical, less humane and more greedy of marvels, prodigies, and bloodshed. What scholars may miss is the real charm they find in some of the older stories, where dew-laden blossoms often bedeck what seems a thorny scrub entangled into labyrinths of narrative.

GROWTH OF ROMANCE

I. The Metrical Romances

In the remotest times, we hear of great men's feasts
cheered by minstrels celebrating the exploits of their real
or supposed ancestors. Such a chant it was that stirred
the heart of Jason to the quest of the Golden Fleece, and
drew tears to the eyes of Ulysses when the Phæacian
bard sang the tale of Troy. Macaulay's *Lays* are spirited
imitations of what such minstrelsy may have been at
Rome. A Greek ambassador, visiting the rude court of
Attila, reports how his drunken banquet ended with
songs in praise of the chief, moving the young to fierce
excitement and the old to tears. By so flattering historians, that ruthless " Scourge of God " was handed
down to figure as no discreditable knight in the " Etzel "
of early northern epics, dealt with in another volume of
this series. After these Gothic imaginations, that seem
a prelude to romance, the tales of chivalry first come to
our knowledge as French *Chansons de Geste*, by which
minstrels naturally sought to tickle the pride of their
patrons. The matter of their songs was *given*, as the
French say, by tradition ; and their hearers might resent,
like children, the omission of any single incident, the

more familiar the better.   They could not have too much
of bold bloodshed; so their favourite poet was bound to
dwell on combats, as later stories would expatiate also on
the pains of love.   To kill time being an object, night
by night the tale was spun out in *fyttes*, or cantos, each of
which should end so as to leave a desire for its "continuation in our next".   There was plenty of room for
the refrains, the characterizing epithets, and other vain
repetitions that punctuate heavy-winged flights of invention, here and there soaring lark-like into the poetic
ether.   The bard and his audience alike took the tale for
true, none the less if it transcended the experiences of
common life: the more wonderful the better.   It was
a pleasing story rather than what we count as history that
most concerned those exaggerating chroniclers.   Scott,
with the keen eye of an accomplice for the tricks of their
trade, saw how the Waverley novel of that period came
by its interest.

The simple tale of tradition had not passed through many
mouths, ere someone, to indulge his own propensity for the
wonderful, or to secure by novelty the attention of his audience,
augments the meagre chronicle with his own apocryphal inven-
tions.   Skirmishes are magnified into great battles; the champion
of a remote age is exaggerated into a sort of demi-god; and the
enemies whom he encountered and subdued are multiplied in
number, and magnified in strength, in order to add dignity to his
success against them.   Chanted to rhythmical numbers, the songs
which celebrate the early valour of the fathers of the tribe become
its war-cry in battle, and men march to conflict hymning the
praises and the deeds of some real or supposed precursor who had
marshalled their fathers in the path of victory.   No reader can
have forgotten that, when the decisive battle of Hastings com-
menced, a Norman minstrel, Taillefer, advanced on horseback
before the invading host, and gave the signal for onset, by singing
the Song of Roland, that renowned nephew of Charlemagne, of
whom romance speaks so much, and history so little; and whose

fall, with the chivalry of Charles the Great, in the pass of Roncesvalles, has given rise to such clouds of romantic fiction.

By and by, romance undergoes a transformation described by German scholars in their distinction between
the *Volks-Epos* and the *Kunst-Epos*. The half-historical
hero is let loose on a wider range of scene and adventure,
growing to be a knight errant whose origin and exploits
can owe more to imagination. Romantic exploits always
inclined to fit an Odyssey rather than an Iliad. But even
before new personages are brought out, the old ones may
be taken in hand by another kind of author, less respectful of time-honoured tradition, and having a clearer eye
for a good story. He does not scruple to improve the
old tales after his own taste, making up for such licence
by pretending very much to believe in their truth, and
using various artful devices to set them off with airs of
verisimilitude. Pen in hand, he takes the popular songs
of doughty deed as groundwork on which he trains finer
flowers of fancy, weeding out redundancies and absurdities and trimming too exuberant growths with some little
regard for proportion and dramatic effect. By what may
be called a topiary treatment, he cuts the wild imagination of his predecessors into quaint shapes, which may
still too much overshadow the garden of romance. The
simpler cultivators of this art " have left their work but
not their name ". Then the names of certain Trouvères
flit out against an obscurity in which their work still
remains doubtful so long as any author holds himself
free to handle the same story with more or less variation,
and we cannot be sure how much they borrowed from or
lent to forgotten rivals ; while it appears that successive
Trouvères worked at expansions of one theme. The least
obscure of these twelfth-century authors seems to be

Chrétien de Troyes, who worked up the Arthurian legends in the reign of our Henry II, when his Plantagenet inheritance brought France and England into intimate relations.

The theological counsels and disquisitions so freely woven into the web of chivalrous deed suggest that churchmen must have had a part in lengthy compositions for which the cloister afforded plenty of leisure. A recent German theory suggests that romances were adapted by monks for the entertainment of their guests on the great pilgrim routes. Besides writing lives of saints whose feats of austerity matched the daring and suffering of the knights, the clergy, long our readiest writers, may well have made a palimpsest of lewd and rude *Gestes*, on which to set forth more edifying fiction or to point a moral hitherto often to seek. The brutalities of half-heathen heroes are softened down, thrown into the background, or decently veiled by some excuse; and if their sins of the flesh stand out too boldly for palliation, these can always be wiped off by due penance, and the story brought to an orthodox end in retirement to monastery or hermitage. When Hildebrand had made a suppliant emperor wait three days barefoot in the snow at his gate, the Church could better set its badge on warriors who during the Crusades learned to look on themselves as devoted champions of the Cross, or at least, so Gibbon puts it, "they neglected to live but they were prepared to die in the service of Christ".

Intercourse with the East, promoted by the Crusades, brought new ornaments into European fiction. Older stories are darkened by the gloom of their native forests and haunted by the weird mythology of the North. Now dawns a glow of Oriental imagination, lighting up romance with sparkling gems, powerful talismans, magic unguents and balsams, graceful fairies, rich palaces, and enchanted gardens. Such conceptions had no doubt been already infiltrating into romance through the Moors of Spain; and it is suggested that the Jews must have had much to do with spreading Eastern tales through Europe. One of our earliest storybooks is the *Clerical Discipline* of Peter Alfonso, a converted Spanish Jew in the time of the first Crusade, who evidently drew his materials from Oriental sources. But there can be little doubt that the Crusades helped to import this new machinery of fiction, brought back by enquiring pilgrims and by the minstrels who, like Blondel, followed their lords into uncouth lands. The knights themselves learnt to know their Saracen adversaries better, then to respect them as worthy of Christian steel, while the Sultan Saladin is said to have so much admired chivalry as to seek knighthood at the hands of an emperor; and Crusaders settled in Palestine even came to fight by the side of their Moslem neighbours against a common foe.

Such a better understanding can be detected in later romance; but contemporary metrical chroniclers of the early Crusades are still found loud as ever in insulting and exulting over the hated foe of Christendom. France took the first lead in the Crusades, English and German knights striking in later on, so it was natural that they should be celebrated by French minstrels; and as they were the chief authors of romance, it is not surprising that their strains dwell a good deal on crusading exploits.

One of this class should be specially interesting to us as having for hero our King Richard Cœur de Lion, a sobriquet he won, we here learn, by the feat of thrusting his arm down a lion's throat to pull out its heart. There is no trace of refinement in this metrical chronicle, with its love of bloodshed and brutal horseplay. The poet simply revels in the slaughter of Saracens by the myriad—sixty thousand at least is his favourite number to kill in a battle, and once the butcher's bill comes to two hundred thousand. One truly British feature is a certain amount of sea-fighting. Richard leads a large fleet to the Holy Land, and, as ammunition for his " mangonels " and " arrowblasts ", he has a dozen ships or so loaded with beehives, which he throws into Acre, to the sore discomfiture of the garrison, as the first Crusaders historically bombarded Antioch with human heads. For a specimen of the humour of this poem: the king, falling sick, has a strong desire for pork, a viand naturally scarce in Moslem lands; but his steward gets over the difficulty by taking " a Saracen young and fat ", and when " slain and sodden was the heathen shrew ", the dish could be served to the king under the name of pork, a meal of which brought about his complete recovery. Later on, he plays on Saladin's ambassadors the trick of dishing up to them the heads of his chief prisoners, jovially informing them that this is the favourite fare of Englishmen. In his other dealings with the Sultan neither of them are so chivalrous as represented in Scott's *Talisman*. Saladin offers to decide the controversy of the Christian faith against " Jupiter " in single combat with Richard, and, feigning a desire for fair play, sends his adversary a marvellous charger, a gift not of generous courtesy but of pagan cunning, for this horse is foal to the Sultan's own steed, of diabolic breed, trained to lie down as soon as it hears its mother's neigh, thus putting its rider at the mercy of his foe. But through the night Richard is visited by an angel, who discloses the Moslem guile, which the Christian hero can baffle by stopping that horse's ears with wax; so of course Saladin was duly set to flight for all his treachery. In the end

THE VIGIL

BENEDICTIO NOVI MILITIS

our lion-hearted sovereign proposes to stake the issue of
the war on a duel between himself and five-and-twenty
knights picked out from the Sultan's army. This challenge so appalled the Saracens that, without more ado,
they agreed to a three-years' truce, whereupon—

> King Richard, doughty of hand,
> Turned homeward to England.
> King Richard reigned here
> No more but ten year.
> Sithen, he was shot, alas!
> In castle Gaillard there he was.
> Thus ended Richard our king:
> God give us all good ending!

This doggerel, based on a French original almost contemporary with the events it professes to record, reflects
the ignorant ferocity of the first Crusaders, who massacred
helpless Jews in the German cities through which they
passed towards the Holy Land, and, when they took
Jerusalem, could boast of riding up to their horses' knees
in blood. Yet the Crusades did breathe a higher spirit
into rude forms of European chivalry. At the Council
of Clermont, Pope Urban's call to the first Crusade raised
a wave of enthusiasm that seemed to uplift men out of
the quasi-barbarism of the Dark Ages. The Truce of
God was invoked to sheathe neighbours' weapons for half
the week, and other measures were taken to restrain the
licence of private war, the estates and families of the
absent Crusaders being put formally under the protection
of the Church. At the same time it was decreed that
every nobly born youth should be called on for an oath
that, when admitted to knighthood, he would fulfil such
generous duties as came to be associated with that rank.

In the days of Charlemagne, kings would gird on the
sword of a promising young warrior, who took rank above

the mass by riding on horseback.   So far back as the beginning of the tenth century, there is a story of Henry the Fowler defining the virtues of knighthood as loyalty to Church and King, truth in speech, and gentleness to women, as well as courage; but it is to be feared that this standard was too high for his age.   With the Crusades, we find knighthood taking on a more definitely religious and moral character, when aspirants should be consecrated to knightly arms by fasting, vigil, and solemn rites.   The two most famous orders were the Knights of St. John of Jerusalem and the Templars, on whom the war for the Holy Land had such exalting effect that they took upon themselves monastic vows of celibacy, purity, poverty, and obedience, in their self-chosen tasks of tending poor and sick pilgrims and of defending them on the way to Jerusalem.   The *Knechts*, servants of the king, by becoming servants of the Church, had been erected into a nobility which kings themselves were proud to share. Originally, this rank could be conferred by any knight, the more illustrious the better; so Francis I was proud to be dubbed by Bayard, and in *Amadis de Gaul* Galaar chooses to be knighted by his doughty brother rather than by the King of Great Britain; but in time the granting of knighthood became a prerogative of kings or of their lieutenants in war.

In romances of the crusading period we meet clear indications of new external features shaped by the growth of chivalry.   At this time armour took a development from the old chain and ring mail to more protective hauberks and helmets, gradually elaborated into the plate armour that cased a knight cap-à-pie.   It is supposed that the heat of Oriental suns prompted the covering of this metal shell with a surcoat which lent itself to blazonry. Heralds and heraldry now make their appearance.   Some sort of martial badge had always been in use among warriors, from the broom sprig of the Plantagenets back to the eagles of Rome, and thence to the lion's skin of Hercules and the bulls that made an ornament for Cretan palaces. Totemism, to which so much attention has been called in our time, may have provided ancient clans with crests representing some supposed beast ancestor, such as were tattooed on Cooper's Red Indians. But it was in the great gatherings of knights from all European nations, mixed together in the East, that there grew up a systematic method of identifying one another by heraldic devices. The story goes that a Milanese noble named Otto Visconti, having defeated a Saracen champion under the walls of Jerusalem, took from him a helmet encircled seven times by the figure of a viper, to which Otto gave an eighth turn in punning allusion to his own name, and assumed it as his crest. This viper, or "dragon", has been claimed as parent of that monstrous brood of wyverns, griffins, lions rampant or couchant, and other such fearful wild-fowl, among which any mushroom family may nowadays choose a becoming device for itself at will; but in the Middle Ages knightly bearings were a serious matter of privilege, carefully guarded and licensed under charge of the heralds, who by their science worked out hieroglyphic patterns on shields and coats-of-arms. In early romances heraldic devices appear as not yet stereotyped, the knights changing their badges and colours at will, while the newly dubbed youth goes forth in white armour with a blank shield that may be adorned by his achievements. The fabulous beasts of heraldry seem to have been much borrowed from Eastern imagination. Another often-unsuspected survival of the Crusades is when an officer in saluting raises his swordhilt to his lips, as a knight did to kiss

the straight crosspiece that for him made the sacred
ensign of his faith.

The twelfth and thirteenth centuries, in which crusading enthusiasm exhausted itself, were the palmy days of
metrical romance, that duly reflects various changes going
on over the feudal world.   The stones and clubs with
which older heroes might crush their adversaries at a
pinch, are quite laid aside for heavy lances, swords of
proof, and showy armour becoming a perfect knight.
Tournaments, said to have been introduced in France
before the twelfth century, are now proclaimed as most
fitting scene for such encounters as still may come off
without ceremony in any forest glade or mountain pass.
More and more the rites, punctilios, and pageantry of
accomplished knighthood are insisted upon.   Courts appear more brilliant, and their frequenters more courteous.
Above all, we find the *preux chevalier* bound to set more
by ladies' favours.

It would not be from the East that there came a
development of chivalry in gallantry to the fair.   That
must have been fostered rather by lovesick lyrics of
Provençal Troubadours, importing a fresh interest into
the sanguinary chronicles of the Trouvères.   Mars and
Venus have always been on intimate terms ; but the
heroes of the *Chansons de Geste* were apt to treat its
heroines more cavalierly than chivalrously, when even
a peerless knight like Roland did not seem much to
mind several years' absence from his betrothed, for whom
he has no dying thought when he fondly recalls his
prowess, his kinsmen, his great sovereign, and his dear
native land.   We saw how, in the story of Peredur,
Arthur's queen was rudely insulted in her husband's hall;
and it takes all the art of Tennyson to cloak for us
Geraint's brutality to his patient wife Enid.   A heroine

was once not indispensable to a story, so long as its hero found some other excuse for fighting. But times changed, and heroes with them. Romance had to follow real life in providing a knight with a Dulcinea, sometimes indeed with more than one, to whom it behoved him to profess idolatrous devotion, shrinking from no risk to deserve her favour, ready to quarrel with whoever cared to question her perfections, and not ashamed to go out of his wits for love.

Scenes of slaughter were now chequered with vows and ordeals of courtship, in time pushed to the extravagant freaks imitated by Don Quixote. Romancers had to glorify suffering as well as doing when they appealed to the interest of both sexes. It was through poring together over the seductive pages of *Lancelot* that Paolo and Francesca came to their famous doom in Dante's *Inferno*. Such romances, if now written for women also, are still written by men, as we can guess from the frequency with which their heroines appear proud, wilful, or false, and, if good, so very good as to be dolls of impossible virtue. Bad or good, their part is to set man fighting and travelling on foolhardy errands for their smiles; and one glance from his lady-love's eyes is enough to rouse the chosen knight to victorious effort at the very point of defeat. Then, if wounded almost to death, he may find his else coy and disdainful mistress able to play the ministering angel, skilled as she should be in the leechcraft of the period, which had enchanters and fairies also as its most celebrated practitioners. There is a good deal in the morality of romance, at this stage, hardly to be recommended for a young lady's reading nowadays; but the spirit of gallantry had on the whole an elevating influence. It became much a good knight's business to quell tyrants, to hunt dragons, to rescue dis-

tressed damsels, to put down wicked customs, or by
other such worthy services to justify his profession of
chivalry.

This development is carried on into the fourteenth
and fifteenth centuries, when it takes a more marked
form in the prose tales of chivalry that then overlaid the
metrical chronicles. The date of a romantic author may
often be fixed by the costumes and customs of his own
age, which he usually reproduces without scruple, as
Georgian actors played Hamlet or Macbeth in wig and
laced waistcoat. Unlike Homer, who seems to have
archaized with the design of giving his *Iliad* some colour
of its time, the minstrel shows us what he saw at the
court of his patron, rather than what belonged to the
generation he undertakes to depict. It proves less easy
to date these stories by their manners and morals, sometimes involved with the plot and personages of an older
version. Another source of confusion is the way in which
their authors, not content with careless adaptation, did
not stick at stitching together separate traditions to stretch
out narratives already too prolix.

One of the least-forgotten romances is *Guy of Warwick*,
told in so many forms down to our own day. It gives
the reign of Athelstan as date for the events of what is
probably an old English legend, possibly grown up out
of some real personality. But its first recorded form in
England is as a translation from the Anglo-Norman; and
a French habitat has even been claimed for the hero, as
one Guido of Tours. If it be English in origin, the
French minstrels, who had almost a monopoly of this
manufacture, have evidently added a good deal of material to make a volume as long as *Paradise Lost*. Could
we come by its complete history, it might prove that the
patiently romantic courtship which for us makes the main

interest did not play such a leading part in the original form. So famous a tale cannot be left out of our specimens; but here, as in other modern versions, the reader will find only the distilled extract of its spirit. The story as thus told gives but an incomplete account of the old metrical chronicle that lumbers along after its hero in a very wide course of adventure involving exploits of other knights pieced on to his own; then a sequel is provided by those of his son, Rainburn, a favourite device for drawing out records that to our taste seem already too long. As this really independent narrative, now little known, is illustrated by several of the *clichés* of romance, an outline of it may be taken for fair sample of such versified chronicles.

Rainburn, born during his father's long pilgrimage, was put in charge of Guy's friend Heraud, or Harrowd, an accomplished knight who, when at home, lived at Wallingford. To his house here came certain merchants from Russia, in one version defamed as " Saracens ". At all events, these were unscrupulous traders, that, admiring Guy's child, when they saw him " play in the hall so wanton and wild ", reckoned him a valuable article in their way of business. By corrupting the porter they kidnapped the boy for sale in Russia; but their vessel was wrecked on the African coast, and they thought well to placate the local king by making him a present of their young captive. There he fell on his feet; for this king, Argus by name, had a daughter of the same age, with whom young Rainburn was brought up as a pet or companion, and grew to be a valiant knight in the service of his kind patron.

Meanwhile Harrowd had in vain searched far and wide for the lost child. To embitter his grief, ill-wishers at Athelstan's court spread a scandal that he had treacherously

sold his own ward. Thus stung to further exertion, he
embarked on a voyage of discovery, to be cast away, like
Rainburn, and, by a very long arm of coincidence, upon
the same coast. But he fell into the hands of a less-
friendly potentate, a most miscreantish "Admiral", who
had no better usage for Christian captives than harsh
imprisonment.

Many years Harrowd pined in a dungeon, till the
Admiral found himself hard pressed by his neighbour
and enemy, Argus, whose forces were carrying all before
them under no other than young Rainburn, promoted to
be this king's "constable", a title now rather come down
in the world. From Harrowd's loud lamentations over
happier days the jailer learned how he had been a knight
of prowess, and reported this discovery to his master.
The Admiral had such faith in knighthood that he proposed to release and equip the prisoner on condition of
his leading an army against Argus. As a matter of course,
the sword of a single hero turns the scale of conquest.
After much hot fighting, Harrowd, though long out of
practice, would have overthrown King Argus, but for the
succour of a gallant youth who engages the old knight in
single combat. Both prove themselves so worthy op-
ponents that many hard blows move them to ask each
other's names; then, to the amazement of Harrowd, the
youth tells him—

> I was born in England,
> In Warwick, as I understand.
> Sir Guy my father was:
> A better knight never was.

His long-lost guardian in turn reveals himself; and
both the old and the young hero swoon away for joy
of this unlooked-for reunion. They were naturally

bent on going homewards together; and the Admiral's gratitude to his champion could not hinder them from taking their departure, at first by sea, but as soon as might be they got on land, where they felt more at home.

On the way they let themselves be delayed by turning aside for adventures, including the deliverance of an old friend of Guy's from "elvish" captivity, by means of an enchanted sword that comes to hand in the nick of time. In passing through Burgundy they are warned to keep out of the way of a doughty young knight who holds a pass in the hills to take life or toll from all comers; but Rainburn of course exults in this chance of trying his mettle. The encounter is so vigorous and well kept up that Harrowd, standing by as umpire, declares he never saw such a good fight; and Guy's son is fain to confess that for once he has met his match. He proposes to swear eternal friendship with so good a foe; but the stranger will have nothing less than his death, before taking on the old knight in turn. After a good deal of fencing, in words as well as blows, they come to exchanging names; then the experienced reader of romance need not be so much surprised as the heroes to learn that this young fire-eater is no other than Harrowd's son Asslake, who, after long search for his father, has hit on the plan of keeping a pass to ask tidings of him, at the sword's point, from everyone coming by—

> But heard I never man speak with mouth,
> That ought of him tell couth.
> Therefore oft was I wrath,
> And many a man I have done scaith—

as seems rather hard on innocently ignorant wayfarers. In these tales one of the stock incidents is two friends, or brothers, or father and son, fighting fiercely unknown, their faces hidden by the *nasal*, *ventaille*, or *beaver* that guarded and obscured them.

Another joyful recognition now takes place; when Asslake does not seem so much concerned to think he has been on the point of attempting parricide, as to know that he has plied his sword on the son of his father's friend. He falls at Rainburn's feet, who raises him up with tears and kisses. The Earl of Burgundy invites all three to enter his service, which might give occasion for further episodes of adventure. But the poet seems now to be out of breath, or parchment, or tradition, for in a page or so he hurries his heroes to London, whence, after hearty welcome from the king, they pass on to Warwick and Wallingford, to be received with joy by the friends and vassals of Guy, dead and buried some way back in his chronicle.

By this time romancers must have lost all illusion as to the marvels they piled up with an eye to dramatic effect, and more discriminate readers may be suspected of yawning a little over tales that could not find some new spice of interest. The lays of chivalry were even burlesqued by the vulgar, as in *The Tournament of Tottenham*, a poem so old that it can hardly be quoted without a glossary. Chaucer, we remember, in his *Sir Thopas* mocked the rhyming of romance with jog-trot parody, till mine host of the "Tabard" would hear no more of it.

> His merry men commanded he
> To makë him both game and glee;
>   For needës must he fight
> With a giant with headës three
> For paramour and jollity
>   Of one that shone full bright.

CHAUCER AT THE COURT OF EDWARD III
READING HIS CANTERBURY TALES

The central figure seated on the steps is a Troubadour from the south of France;
on either side of him are his minstrels

FOREST LOVERS

"Do come," he saidë, "my minstrales
And gestours for to tellë tales
   Anon in mine arming,
Of romances that be royals,
Of popës and of cardinals,
   And eke of love-longing."
They fetch'd him first the sweetë wine,
And mead eke in a maseline (*drinking-bowl*)
   And royal spicery;
Of ginger-bread that was full fine,
And liquorice and eke cumin,
   With sugar that is trie (*refined*)
He diddë, next his whitë lere (*skin*)
Of cloth of lakë fine and clear (*lawn*)
   A breech and eke a shirt;
And next his shirt an haketon (*cassock*)
And over that an habergeon,
   For piercing of his heart;
And over that a fine hauberk,
Was all y-wrought of Jewës werk,
   Full strong it was of plate;
And over that his coat-armour,
As white as is the lily flower
   In which he would debate (*combat*)
His shield was all of gold so red,
And therein was a boarë's head,
   A charboucle beside (*heraldic device*)
And there he swore on ale and bread,
How that the giant should be dead,
   Betide whatso betide.

In this doggerel Chaucer is understood to be slily hitting at the popular romance *Sir Bevis of Hampton*, which looks to be an old English story, though, as in the case of *Guy of Warwick*, we have it translated from the Anglo-Norman. The hero of a string of prodigies very open to satiric attack, has, like Hamlet, a wicked step-father, but, unlike Hamlet, his native hue of resolution is so unsicklied that at the age of seven he strongly objects to his mother's marriage with the murderer of his father. The unnatural parent proposes to get rid of her inconvenient child; but, instead of seeing to this business herself, put it upon his uncle, Saber, who, being a good uncle, sent her in proof of compliance his nephew's garments sprinkled with the blood of a pig, while he kept the boy safe and sound till manhood should bring him an opportunity of revenge. But this seven-year-old fire-eater had too high a spirit for Hamlet's delays. Disguised as a shepherd on the downs, he was so moved by sounds of revelry, amid which the guilty pair played Macbeth in drowning the memory of their crimes, that he burst into the hall and, "with a mace", laid his step-father senseless before the whole company.

If so terrible with a stick, we may guess what feats such a hero would perform when he grew big enough to wield a sword. The mother was so much displeased by his violence to her husband, that she punished the pre-cociously brave child by sending him to be sold in slavery to a Saracen soldan named Ermyn, whose daughter Josyan, as romantic matter of course, at once fell in love with the young captive. The soldan, for his part, re-cognizing the youth's quality, was willing to take him as son-in-law and heir on condition of his abjuring Christianity. But the knights of old were as orthodox as valiant. Bevis, hardly yet in his teens, uplifted such bold testimony against the paganism of "Mahound" that Ermyn was fain to drop the subject, for the present taking him on as page, with promise of further advance-ment. No evil communications with unbelievers could corrupt the youngster's faith. At the age of fifteen, some Saracen knights rudely venturing to abuse his religion, he slew them all, three score or so, on the spot.

Their master forgave him for this once, and Josyan, with kisses and salves, soon cured him of his wounds; then, in gratitude, he rid them of a fierce wild boar that had long been a local bugbear.

Such petty exploits served as the work of our hero's prentice hand: the time was now come for him to be dubbed knight, presented on the occasion with his irresistible sword "Morglay" and the best horse in the world, by name "Arundel". Thus equipped, he did good service to Ermyn as his champion against the King of Damascus, who was pressing a violent suit for Josyan's hand. The lady so much admired his prowess that, in somewhat unmaidenly manner, she now proposed to her Christian knight; but Bevis would give her no encouragement unless on condition of her renouncing the Moslem creed. The Soldan's patience comes to an end when he hears how his daughter is being converted. Not daring to use open violence, he sends the wooer on a treacherous embassy to his late adversary, the King of Damascus. At Damascus, Bevis loses no time in getting himself into trouble by knocking over a Saracen idol, an act that brings the fanatical population upon him, odds too great even for such a prodigy. Overpowered for once, he is thrown into a dungeon with two dragons, which he has no difficulty in killing after twenty-four hours' combat; but hunger proved a sorer enemy. Here come two still-familiar lines of this long poem, preserved for us by quotation in *King Lear*:

> Rats and mice and such small deer
> Were his meat for seven long year.

Escaping, after seven years, he goes off to Josyan, whom, though still faithful to him at heart, he finds wedded to a heathen king, and has to obtain access to her in disguise of a palmer. The couple elope together, and he celebrates his honeymoon by such exploits as killing a brace of lions at one blow, and overthrowing a giant named Ascapard, who saves his life by becoming Bevis's squire.

It was now high time for the hero to think of dealing with his wicked stepfather. Passing by Cologne, where an uncle of his happened to be bishop, he took the opportunity of having Josyan and Ascapard christened, and left his wife in the charge of this uncle, while with a hundred knights he landed on his native soil. There the villain caitiff, Sir Murdour, is duly tricked and discomfited. In vain calling to his aid hosts both from Scotland and Germany, he could expect no better fate than to be boiled into dogs' meat in a great cauldron of pitch, brimstone, and lead, after which his wicked wife had nothing for it but to throw herself from the top of a high tower; then the delivered citizens of Southampton were free to hail their true lord.

This is but a cursory account of adventures which are by no means yet at an end. It is common for romancers to take second wind for a long appendix of fresh exploits; and so our author again carries Bevis abroad on a triumphant career of slaying, conquering, and baptizing the heathen. The conclusion of his story seems hardly historical. In his absence his earldom and estates had been confiscated by King Edgar, a wrong that brought Bevis to London, where, now backed by two sturdy sons, he could easily kill sixty thousand of his enemies in a battle fought about Ludgate Hill, and thus turned the king to a gracious mood. One of his sons, marrying King Edgar's daughter, succeeded to the crown of England; the other was provided with a kingdom abroad; and Bevis himself ruled his foreign dominions till he, Josyan, and Arundel came to die almost at the same minute.

> Thus ended Bevis of Hampton,
> That was so bold a baron.

Readers who could relish Chaucer would hardly care for this wild fiction. And the minstrels themselves had been falling into discredit as well as their songs. Once attached to great houses, as trumpeters of family pride, they had taken to wandering about to inns, fairs, and popular gatherings, as well as to castles; so their strains, at first addressed to "seigneurs" and "barons", became tuned to catch the ears of the vulgar. Few of them were like Goethe's singer who disdained all reward but a cup of wine in a golden beaker. Their tales, as preserved for us in manuscript, are sometimes interrupted by hints of breaking off for want of *largesse*, a mediæval equivalent of passing round the hat; and they are found sharply pointing the moral that all worthy people should treat *jongleurs* well, with money and clothes and good suppers. This title, from the Latin *josulator*, reflects the history of a brotherhood that in its wandering life had a ready chance to fall into bad ways. The jongleurs or gleemen became jugglers, mixed up with conjurors, tumblers, bear leaders, and other more or less disreputable vagrants, among whom they lost their character while increasing in numbers. Long before the date which Scott fondly gives for the *Lay of the Last Minstrel*, Stubbs, in the *Anatomy of Abuses*, can complain that "every town, city, and country is full of these minstrels to pipe up a dance to the devil". So far had their quality decayed from the days of Rahere, said to have been our Henry the First's favourite minstrel, who founded St. Bartholomew's Hospital as well as the adjacent Priory, still showing its chapel as one of the noblest of London's old churches.

The lion-hearted Richard had prided himself on being a bit of a minstrel *à ses heures*, and could we have his own story of the war with Saladin it might be more complimentary to that gallant foe than were the fierce revilings breathed by professional singers at a safe distance from Saracen steel. The chronicle that bears his name makes little for his fame. But the reader must not forget that the romances here held up rather for ridicule are by no means the most favourable specimens of their kinds, such as should be reserved for worthier treatment in the body of this volume. Among much that is absurd, dull, and tedious to our discriminating mind, we have to recognize some of those forgotten minstrels for true poets.

II. Romance in Prose

As minstrels went out of fashion, romance took a new lease of life in the form of prose, hitherto held more appropriate for matter in which " there be some mirth or some doctrine ", as Chaucer has it. He perhaps meant compilations like the *Gesta Romanorum*, wherein old stories were fitted with a monkish moral, and tales of what may be called tavern mirth, passing from mouth to mouth. Short tales of such vulgar comedy, as well as more sentimental ones, had been turned into *lais* and *fabliaux* by Trouvères, among whom occurs the name of a woman, Marie de France ; and too many of these illustrate the coarse manners of an age for which the same kind of fable soon began to be elaborated in prose by Italian novelists. Chaucer's own example, in tales which he is said to have been sorry for on reflection, shows too plainly what tickled the laughter of his Canter-

bury pilgrims. But the tales of chivalry in their best
days, though their morality is not ours, seem notably
free from the ribaldries and indecencies that do intrude
into the lays of some of their last minstrels. *Aucassin
and Nicolette*, dealing with love rather than war, has
admirers to pronounce it the most beautiful story ever
written. This novelette of the romantic age, coming
down to us in a thirteenth-century manuscript, but
perhaps of earlier date, is peculiar as written in a mixture
of prose and verse, the prose itself rhythmical, as M.
Gaston Paris points out, intended for recitation, even for
being acted, rather than read by the eye. Here we have
a transition between the two forms.

The prose romances, beginning before Chaucer, over-
lap the metrical chronicles they supplanted,[1] and like
them underwent a course of development, which had
reached its height when printing came to give them wider
currency. There was also a process of winnowing at
work, for more romances in verse have survived than in
prose, and only a proportion of the latter got into print.
The fourteenth and fifteenth centuries were the flourishing time of authors, or adaptors, who seem to have been
often employed by princely and lordly patrons to translate
the songs of the minstrels into prosaic form. They took
a larger canvas, to work on a less confined scale, and, no
longer bound to end every canto with a " curtain ", like
the minstrel when he ran out of breath, they were more
free to attend to a sustained plot and unity of design.
But, to make a longer story of it, they might, as the
poets had done in the end, weld two or three chronicles
together, sometimes with a result still showing an im-

---

[1] The high authority of M. Paulin Paris maintains that some prose romances of
the Round Table date from the middle of the twelfth century, preceding the verse
of Chrétien de Troyes. But there is still much obscurity as to their dating.

perfect sense of proportion.   Malory's *Morte d'Arthur*, for example, the book of the kind best known to us, is an attempt at fusing several romances, so carelessly carried out that the story of Beaumains, in the seventh book, and that of La Cote Male Taile, in the ninth, seem merely variations of the same theme.   Those who could read them had so few books to read that the longer the better was the rule even before early printers brought folios into fashion.

So, while the prose scribe sometimes discriminately pared down the tedious absurdities of their originals, we find them rather concerned to pad out the story with conversations, reflections, and episodes, often very loosely strung upon the main thread of interest, notably also with descriptions of the customs and manners of chivalry, valuable to students of the period who can make allowance for the writer's idea of artistic effect.   M. Langlois, for instance, has compiled an interesting view of *La Société française au XIIIme Siècle* from half a dozen of its fictions, metrical ones, to be sure, yet somewhat artificial in treatment.   The older romances were more in the way of taking the manners of the age as matter of course, and dwelling on the exploits rather than the equipment of their heroes.   In the later ones there is less wholesale slaughter, but more detailed account of ceremonious combats and fantastic enterprises of gallantry.   The knights-errant flourish in this period, inspired not so much by religious bigotry and love of brutal bloodshed as by devotion to their mistresses, thirst for glory, or not seldom by a mission to do good in the world according to their lights.   This nobler aspect of chivalry we catch in such true chronicles as Froissart's ; and the romantic storytellers of the same age took care to make the best of it.   They evince a rising consciousness that homicide

should be justified by a good cause, were it but the
smiles of beauty or some nice point of honour, whereas
once on a time any excuse had been enough for a fight.
Scott took his half-barbarous "Robert of Paris" from a
pugnacious Frank mentioned in the memoirs of the Princess Anna Comnena as boasting to her father the Emperor
—"where three roads meet in the place from which I
came, there is an ancient church in which whosoever has
the desire to measure himself against another in single
combat, prays God to help him therein, and afterwards
abides the coming of one willing to encounter him. At
that spot long time did I remain, but the man bold
enough to stand against me I found not." In later
romance we still find knights making themselves a
nuisance by holding a pass, a bridge, or a ferry against
all comers out of mere churlish defiance; but the lime-
light is thrown chiefly on the champions that come to
break down such obstructiveness. A solitary post of
challenge was no longer needed when every court offered
opportunities of public distinction at the stately tournaments that became a favourite mediæval spectacle—

> Where throngs of knights and barons bold,
> In weeds of peace high triumphs hold,
> With store of ladies, whose bright eyes
> Rain influence, and judge the prize
> Of wit, or arms.

The wonder is that, what with tournaments, perilous
quests, and chance encounters, any of these knights could
ever reach a good old age, who, for all their martial
vigour, seem to have been much given to swooning away,
to shedding floods of tears, and to going mad under
stress of sorrow. The wonder for Middle-Age readers,
or hearers, was abated by their own familiarity with

tournaments and duels, not so deadly as the prowess in which romantic heroes used to cut down paynims by the hundred. Our British Solomon, King James, sagely remarked of armour that it hindered the wearers from doing much harm to one another as well as from being harmed. When the equipments of chivalry grew more elaborate, for both steed and rider, the chief danger a knight ran was of being smothered or trampled to death if unhorsed. Chaucer describes such a wounded hero as " carven out of his harness " before he could be put to bed. Spenser compares a knight unarmoured to a falcon freed from its jesses. After the battle of Pavia, we learn, French knights who had the ill luck to be overthrown lay helpless as lobsters on the ground, till the peasants hacked them out of their shells with pickaxes. So Don Quixote's first fall exposed him to having his own lance broken to splinters on him by an ill-tempered muleteer. Such humiliation might prove a sore one in the hands of mere plunderers ; but among men of means, the expectation of ransom went a good way towards sparing life in mediæval battles, where the most sweeping carnage would be of the "rascal many", such penniless and half-naked villains or churls as are seldom thought worth mention in romance. But its Rolands and Olivers, its Lancelots and Tristrams, after courteously assisting each other to don their complete panoply, might well hack away at shield, hauberk, and helmet for a whole day and still live to be friends, or at least to fight another day. Like schoolboys, such heroes sometimes began their friendship by a good fight.

In the exercise of tilting, it is well known, certain rules came to be observed that, as in our own prize ring and football field, might secure the maximum of excitement to the spectators with the minimum of peril to the

THE SOLEMN JOUST ON LONDON BRIDGE

Between David de Lyndsays, Earl of Crawford, and Lord John de Welles,
Ambassador of King Richard II, 1390

A MEDIÆVAL KNIGHT

performers. "Arms of courtesy" were commonly used—
headless spears, and blunted swords; blows should be
aimed above the belt, and other restrictions barred indis-
criminate hacking and hewing as not playing the game.
So we read of a tournament described in Chaucer as
permitted by "Duke Theseus" of Athens, how "an
herald on a scaffold" made proclamation—

> "The lord hath of his high discretión
> Considered that it were destructión
> To gentle blood to fighten in the guise
> Of mortal battle now in this emprise:
> Wherefore to shapë that they shall not die,
> He will his firstë purpose modify.
> No man therefore, on pain of loss of life,
> No manner shot, nor poleaxe, nor short knife
> Into the lists shall send, or thither bring.
> Nor short sword for to stick with point biting
> No man shall draw, nor bear it by his side.
> And no man shall unto his fellow ride
> But one course, with a sharp y-grounden spear."

It was in exceptional cases of bitter enmity that combats were fought *à outrance*, for life or death, as in war;
while in real life, as in romance, some hot-blooded gallant
might accept a defiance to ride into the press clad in no
better mail than his lady's shift. The romance *Palmerin
of England* describes an unusually spirited tournament,
where "Such was the uproar of the lance-breaking that
it seemed as if all London were falling in ruins"; yet the
banquet and "ball royal" that followed could be attended
by most of the competitors. There is an account of an
actual tournament held in Spain, A.D. 1434, which lasted
a month, more than seven hundred courses being run and
several scores of lances broken, but only one champion
lost his life, and that through the accident of a spear

piercing his eye. A like fatal accident to Henri II of France, in the sixteenth century, is said to have gone far to putting tournaments out of fashion. In later romances tilting tends to become a mere pastime, as when the giant Dramuziando is on such friendly terms with his captive, Prince Duardos, as to favour him with first turn in jousting against the very knights who come, one by one, to deliver him. Eventually it dwindled down to tilting at a ring, as in the contest undertaken at Saragossa by Don Quixote in Avellanedo's imitation of Cervantes.

There are hints, in history if not in romance, of certain knights attending tournaments not so much from a thirst for bloodshed as with an eye to business in horse flesh, since the chargers of the vanquished became the property of the victor; and a horse strong enough to carry the weight of its heavily mailed master, as well as its own housings and platings, must have been worth fighting for. Perhaps out of regard for such prizes, it was counted not quite "playing the game" to injure an adversary's steed. In those days, the "great horse" used in war was distinguished among the *sommiers, roncins,* and palfreys of everyday work; and the trappings alone of a knight's *destrier,* as sometimes described in romance, must have made a valuable prize. The horses of romantic heroes, by the way, often play a hardly less heroic part than their masters; so Renaud's "Bayard", Ogier's "Broiffort", and Roland's "Veillantif" have name and fame in the story, like the "Durandal" and other resistless swords with which those worthies were endowed.

"Villainous saltpetre", of course, was now undermining the institutions of chivalry, whose arms would grow rusty in lordly halls as they ceased to shine in romance. Even the crossbow of William Tell, and the longbows of English archers, had foiled mail-clad men, soon to find their prestige vanishing like a bubble at the cannon's mouth. There are some curious allusions to gunpowder by the romancers, little suspicious how it would blast their trade. In the *Orlando Furioso* we hear of a deadly fire reed invented by Satan, which the hero with unusual prudence has thrown into the sea. In the late romance *Palmerin of England*, a castle defends itself by "bombarding" its assailants as a last resource. But we cannot be sure if Sir Mordred was much before his age when he besieged Queen Guinevere with great "guns", that may have been such "engines" as were brought by the Crusaders, and by Alexander the Great in his day, against the walls of Antioch and Jerusalem, where, besides catapulting huge stones, they "blew wild fire through trumpes of gin", as one rhymer has it. That destructive Greek fire, the exact composition of which is now unknown, had been used in early wars between the Eastern Empire and the Caliphs. Shakespeare was certainly not well prompted when he introduced cannon in *Hamlet* and *King John*. Such artillery appears to have been tried at Cressy (A.D. 1346), but it was not till the next century that it played much part in war. Even before this, however, the ill-disciplined valour of knights was found not always serviceable, and their place in battle began to be taken by men-at-arms or "lances", each a centre of some half-dozen lighter-armed followers, making units to be ranged in companies and battalions. In the crusading wars we hear much of *sergeants*, whose name (servants) had the same meaning in French as Teuton *Knechts* that took superior rank on horseback. St. Louis was one of the first French kings to have an army at his command, apart from feudal levies; and these paid soldiers are called by de Joinville either sergeants or crossbowmen. Under his successors, we hear of *knights-at-law* as well as men-at-arms; while in England to our own time lasted the style of *sergeants-at-law*, and the title of "Sir" was once given to priests as to knights.

And before knights ceased to be formidable, they had begun to lose the character borne by them in romance. The Templars, who set out with such professions of pious humility, had in less than two centuries waxed so rich, haughty, and insolent that they became feared and suspected by the kings of Europe, among whom their Grand Master held his head as high as any. With the Pope's licence, and much popular applause, they were cruelly robbed and tortured out of existence, a few survivors joining the Order of St. John of Jerusalem, which kept itself longer in moral health by chivalrous exercise against the Saracens. There were many robber knights as well as champions of the oppressed; and the castles of Germany notably made dens for mail-clad brigands who sallied forth to take toll from the traders of rising commercial cities. St. Louis, on his way to the last great Crusade, turned aside to destroy one such nest of vultures that preyed upon pilgrims passing down the Rhone valley. Dunlop, in his *History of Fiction*, quotes an old author as abusing knights errant for arrant knaves, and another who, so far back as the twelfth century, complained that these heroes rode loaded "not with iron but with wine, not with spears but with cheeses, not with swords but with bottles, not with darts but with spits". At all times, it is to be feared, it was only in the pages of romance that knights commonly lived up to their romantic character, for even in sympathetic chronicles like Froissart's and Joinville's there is too much evidence of a seamy side to the chivalry which they exhibit in such showy colours.

In Scott's "Essay on Chivalry" he has quoted from the late romance *Le Petit Jehan de Saintré*, which is understood to have been based on fact, and which, written in the middle of the fifteenth century, he takes as a valuable document for the manners of its time. A short sketch of this tale will show how far its author had turned his eyes from old models to fix them on his own surroundings, not always squaring with our ideas of the chivalrous period, now indeed on its decline. It will serve also as an example of how prose romance had been growing more realistic, more self-conscious, more artificial and artful, till this one reads almost like a modern novel. It can hardly have been in Don Quixote's mind when he exclaimed: " What knight errant ever paid custom, poll tax, subsidy, quit rent, porterage, or ferry boat? What tailor ever brought in a bill for making his clothes? What governor that lodged him in his castle ever made him pay for his entertainment? What king did not seat him at his table? What damsel was not enamoured of him?" In fact, however, the need of money sometimes does peep out even in older romances, when now a king cannot go to war without paying soldiers, and again a poor knight is hard put to it for means to make a creditable appearance, when the crowd in the street may mock at him if his equipment be out of fashion.

The little Jehan de Saintré, we are told, began his career in the train of a renowned knight, his father's neighbour, bound for the court of France. There, by his good manners, good looks, and good horsemanship, the boy attracted the king's notice, who made him one of his own pages. He became a favourite with the master of the pages, as well as with his comrades, and soon took the fancy of a young widowed princess, the Dame des Belles-Cousines, living at this court. Her

first mark of favour was handing him a plate of sweets
as he waited at the royal table, where the blushing youth
paid special attention to her; then she took to watching
from a balcony the sportive exercises in which he was
trained to feats of arms.   Before either of them quite
knew what they would be at, each began to be all eyes
for the other.

One day the lady carried Jehan off from a game of
tennis to amuse herself by teaching him the art of love,
in which, though only half a dozen years his senior, she
seems to have been a past mistress.   The fifteen-year-old
boy, pressed to name his sweetheart, gave his mother and
his sister as the ladies he loved best; but already he was
too conscious of a hotter passion.   The dame professed
to scorn him as unworthy of her regard, and fit for nothing
till he should devote himself to some fair one; whereon
the shamefaced lad, abashed by her reproaches, fell on his
knees before her, as, at a sign from their mistress, did her
maids of honour, praying her to give him another chance.
Affecting to relent, she commanded his presence another
evening, when again Jehan was so overwhelmed with confusion that he could do nothing but sob and hang his
head; then in desperation named as the mistress of his
heart a child ten years old.   One of her ladies, suggesting that the shy youth might better unbosom himself if
left alone with the princess, she led him into her cabinet
to be further catechized.

"Alas, madame," she forced him to confess, "even if
I dared form the first vows of my life, could I flatter
myself that they would be listened to?   What lady
would deign to cast her eyes on a poor stripling without
name or fame?"

"Why so distrustful of yourself?" replied the
princess.   "Are you not nobly born?   Are you not

handsome, well made, and marked among your comrades ?"

"Madame is very good, but I feel that the honour of serving a lady with true devotion cannot yet be my happy lot."

"You are too modest, Saintré," quoth she. "Have you not a heart to love her, eyes to see her, a mouth to tell her so, courage to serve her? If by chance you pleased some lady, would she have to humiliate herself by being the first to make a declaration?"

"Ah," cried Jehan, "if this lady were like you, she would have little difficulty in making me fall at her knees!"

"Well, if it were I that had deigned to cast my eyes on you, would you dare to swear eternal fidelity to me, to have no other wishes but mine, and to die rather than betray me?"

"Ah, would I not swear it!" he exclaimed, and pressed a kiss upon her hand.

She answered by kissing his fevered brow; and now that their relation to each other was understood, the young widow proceeded to give her pupil a long lecture on religion, morality, gallantry, and chivalry, which oration, including several score of quotations from the classics, would fill a considerable part of this volume, so it may here be taken as read.

For Jehan's outward man his instructress was not less solicitous than for his education in knightly duties. She found his clothes oldfashioned and in bad taste, so, counting out twelve gold crowns, she bid him have himself dressed afresh by the king's own tailors. The tailors did their work so well that he astonished the governor of the pages by the smart figure he cut next Sunday, which he accounted for by telling a fib, that his mother had sent him some money to keep himself clad as became his position.

"See, you scamps," said the governor to his fellow pages, " was I not right in holding up Saintré to you as a pattern? None of you would have spent your money so well; it would have gone to the wine shop, or in some other wastefulness. You are a good lad, Saintré, and I shall bring you to the king's notice."

The Dame des Belles-Cousines, while affecting to give Jehan up as hopelessly ungallant, was delighted by the improvement in his appearance. Even the queen observed it, and gave her cousin a commission to find out for what lady's eyes the page had decked himself out so finely. On this excuse the princess invited him into her oratory, where she examined his new clothes with the admiration of a connoisseur; and for his still further adornment gave him sixty crowns more in a purse woven from her own hair. She also trusted him with a key by which he might visit her apartments secretly. In public she would pretend indifference to him, and he must imitate her example; but a pin placed between her teeth was to be invitation to a rendezvous, to which he should reply by rubbing his right eye. With this secret understanding between them, the sly widow dismissed him in presence of her ladies with a haughty command not to appear before her again, unworthy of her favour as he proved.

Apparently crushed to the ground by her disdain, but joyful at heart, the lucky page gave himself to love's young dream and to the spending of the sixty crowns. Now he went finer than ever in a robe of blue cloth trimmed with costly lambskin and a hood lined with fur from Siberia. Few lords of the court were so well dressed, and none became their finery so well. The queen cast her eyes upon him as she went to church, and

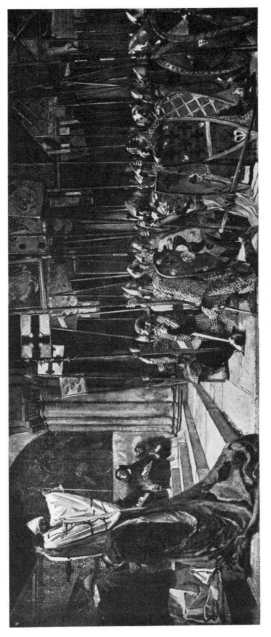

THE DEPARTURE

DON QUIXOTE AND SANCHO PANZA

again charged her cousin to find out how this youth came
to be such a dandy. The Dame des Belles-Cousines
arranged with Jehan to report that his parents sent him
money which he laid out thus in the hope of being promoted from page to esquire-carver at the king's table.
The queen obtained this favour for him, so at seventeen
our hero got a good position in the royal household, with
three horses and two servants of his own, whom he was
able to equip in rich liveries through the ever-increasing
generosity of his mistress.

So several years passed, during which young Jehan
kept rising in esteem with the king and all his court,
winning honours and graces at balls as at tourneys, and
looked on coldly by the Dame des Belles-Cousines alone,
in public that is, yet often the signal of the pin to her
teeth told him another story. There came the time when
he might aspire to knighthood. The custom then was,
we learn, for an aspirant to prove his valour by some
notable enterprise abroad; and Jehan's patroness was
bent on his doing so with all éclat. When advanced to
be chamberlain in the royal household, he knelt at the
king's feet, declaring his ambition and praying for a
"letter of arms" that should be his licence to distinguish
himself in foreign courts. The king granted his wish,
giving him a bounty of two thousand crowns, to which
the queen added one thousand out of her own purse;
and all the princes and princesses bestowed on him rich
presents by way of fitting him out to advantage. His
sly charmer, for her part, pretended to grudge him a gift,
only on the queen's request providing a bracelet that was
to be the badge of his undertaking; but secretly she
lavished the contents of her coffers to equip her would-be
knight with the fieriest steeds from Andalusia and Arabia,
with the finest armour, and with a train of richly ap-

parelled attendants. By her advice he sent his "heralds" in advance to the four greatest courts of Europe to announce his appearance; and when all was ready for setting forth he presented himself before the royal family to be passed in review. In full armour, with his vizor raised and his right hand drawn out of its gauntlet, he threw himself at the king's feet, renewing his oath of fidelity and kissing the hand from which he took his commission or letter of arms. The Dame des Belles-Cousines, coldly, but with an air full of nobleness and dignity, attached to his wrist the rich bracelet which he wore as her favour. Kissing respectfully the hem of her dress, Saintré thanked her, and took farewell of the lords and knights. Then, leaping lightly on his steed, he left Paris by the road to Spain.

As he passed through France his magnificence and liberality excited general admiration. The passes of the Pyrenees were held by Catalan knights, whom the young stranger so overcame by his arms, his gifts, and his courtesy, that one after another they followed in his train to escort him to Pampeluna, where the court of Aragon had its seat. His reputation having gone before him, the Spanish knights disputed among themselves the honour of encountering such a paragon; and this fell to a lord named Enguerrand, the king's nearest kinsman. The conditions of the encounter were set out in Jehan's credentials. On the first day they broke five lances, and the Frenchman had slightly the advantage. After an intervening day spent in festivities, they met again on foot, with swords, daggers, and axes. Both fought so vigorously that often time had to be called to let them take breath and to repair their armour, till at last both had their axes struck out of their hands, when Saintré deftly recovered his own, setting his foot upon his adversary's weapon. Thus disarmed, Emguerrand threw himself on Saintré, and, clutching him closely, tried in vain to throw him down, while the Frenchman, using his left arm to hold him off, raised his axe in the right hand, but without striking a blow. The King of Aragon, seeing the combat brought to such a perilous point, threw down his baton as sign for it to cease; and the knights were parted, to engage in a fresh dispute of generosity.

"Noble Frenchman," cried Enguerrand, raising his vizor, "you have vanquished me for the second time!"

"Ah! my brother, what do you say?" answered Saintré; "am I not rather conquered by your hand, since my axe fell first?"

Brought before the king for the heralds to proclaim his victory, Saintré would have interrupted them by offering his bracelet to the Spanish knight, who refused to receive it, presenting him his own sword by the hilt. But the king decided that this prize was Saintré's by right, and he received moreover a valuable ruby pledged against it by his competitor, as well as a diamond necklace which the queen took from her own neck when he courteously offered her the bracelet. The king himself helped to disarm the two knights. Seeing blood upon his opponent's arm, Saintré bent down to kiss the wound he had made, bathing it in tears. But Enguerrand's hurt, after all that striking and thrusting, was not severe enough to keep him from the feasts given in honour of the foreign champion who had now proved himself well fit to sit at royal banquets.

As soon as might be, he tore himself away to carry back his trophies to Paris, where also he was hailed with all honour. The king embraced him, the queen smiled upon him, and even his lady relaxed her wonted air of indifference when he presented her with the diamonds he brought in exchange for her bracelet. But to his disappointment she did not invite him by the signal of a pin to a private meeting. This was only because she chanced not to have a pin about her; so, pretending to admire a jewel worn by the queen, the artful widow stealthily drew what she wanted out of the royal stomacher, not, however, without being noticed.

"Dear cousin," remarked the queen, "are you not afraid of spoiling your fine teeth by that bad habit of putting a pin to them I have marked in you for some time past?"

"You are right, madame," she replied in confusion. "I was not thinking what I did: it is hard to cure oneself of bad habits!"

Fêted by his old comrades, as by all the court, and admitted to the presence of his mistress, Jehan was soon to win fresh laurels. Here Scott refers to this romance for an illustration of the fantastic manners of knighthood. The copy we have in hand tells the story a little differently, but bears out his account of "deliverance" from a chivalric vow.

The hero, with nine companions at arms, four of whom were knights and five squires, vowed to carry a helmet of a particular shape, that of the knights having a visor of gold, and that of the squires a visor of silver. Thus armed, they were to travel from Court to Court for the space of three years, defying the like number of knights and squires, wherever they came, to support the beauty of their mistresses with sword and lance. The emblems of their enterprise were chained to their left shoulders, nor could they be delivered of them until their vow was honourably accomplished. Their release took place at the Court of the Emperor of Germany, after a solemn tournament, and was celebrated with much triumph. In like manner, in the same romance, a Polish knight, called the Seigneur de Loiselench, is described as appearing at the Court of Paris wearing a light gold chain attached to his wrist and ankle for five years, until he should find some knight or squire without reproach, by encountering with whom he might be delivered (such was the phrase) of his vow and enterprise. Lord Herbert of Cherbury mentions, in his memoirs, that when he was made Knight of the Bath, a tassel of silken cordage was attached to the mantle of the order, which, doubtless, had originally the same signification as the shackle worn by the German champion. The rule was, however, so far relaxed, that the knot was unloosed so soon as a lady of rank gaged her word that the new Knight of the Bath would do honour to the order; and Lord Herbert, whose punctilious temper set great store by the niceties of chivalrous ceremony, fails not to record, with becoming gratitude, the name of the honourable dame who became his security on this important occasion.

Our French author, for his part, has no high opinion of English knights. Twelve of them had crossed the sea to Calais, and in an uncourteous way were challenging the French king's champions on ground which they claimed as their own sovereign's. Those rude islanders, it is stated, had so much practice at tilting on the plains of Camelot that they now overthrew all the knights venturing against them, till Saintré was sent to vindicate the honour of France. An exhibition of French shields, reversed and trailed in the dust, so enraged him and his comrades that they charged home to bring the insulting Britons to their knees, Saintré laying five of them low with his own hand. He disdained to take their horses, as was his right, but kept their banners and shields for trophies, sending the beaten knights back to Calais, while he undertook to remain three days at the same spot in case any of their countrymen cared to try another ordeal of battle.

Only after this signal exploit, it appears, was our hero duly dubbed knight by the king, when, according to our author, he must have been about thirty years old. He chose the Dame des Belles-Cousines to buckle on his gilt spurs; and henceforth, one might suppose, there need be no reason for their amours remaining hidden.   But that very fact would seem to have damped the lady's ardour. When Jehan set out for the East, where fresh glory waited him, absence did not make her heart grow fonder. She presently fell ill of vague symptoms, for which the court physician could find no better name than " the vapours", and no more artful prescription than country air.   So the widow left the court for a castle she possessed in Touraine.

Here she should have had Saintré for neighbour, whose father's death had now made him lord of a town in these parts.   But before he came back from the wars his fickle fair one had cast eyes on another swain.   This was, shame to say, the abbot of a rich monastery, still in the prime of life, and answering to the description of Chaucer's monk.

> A manly man, to be an abbot able;
> Full many a dainty horse had he in stable . . .
> He gave not of the text a pulled hen,
> That saith that hunters be not holy men,
> Nor that a monk when he is cloisterless,
> Is like to a fish that is waterless.

The worldliness of this athletic churchman is described with a good deal of sly humour, for however respectful romancers were bound to be to the Church, they are often found taking a fling at the clergy, a trick of the old opposition between monks and minstrels.

When Jehan came home, rich in honours and rewards, his first thought was to set off in his finest clothes for the lady's castle, where he heard that she was out hunting in the forest.   The cheery noise of horn and hounds soon put him on the track, to come up with the princess looking more beautiful than ever on horseback, her eyes and cheeks glowing in the excitement of the chase. But she started and frowned at the sight of him, even turned away her head. Leaping from his horse to salute her, he stood confounded by this cold welcome, still more so when there dashed up a goodly rider in the dress of a monk, calling on her to lose not a moment if she would be in at the death of the stag. Off she galloped by his side, without deigning another look at her lover, who turned to her ladies for some explanation of this displeasure.

"Ah, brave de Saintré, times are changed!" sighed one of those old friends, and, as they followed the hunt, briefly let him know how their mistress seemed infatuated by her new acquaintance, the abbot. They came up as he was gallantly presenting the stag's foot to that dame, for him all smiles; but she answered shortly and stiffly to Saintré's stammering enquiries after her health.

"I have never been better and happier than now," she said, turning her eyes away to the abbot, who, on learning Saintré's name, came forward to greet him.

"My lord, we are neighbours, and we should be friends." Then, with a familiar air, he asked the lady: "Madame, shall I not beg the Lord de Saintré to sup with us?"

"As you please," she replied; "but you need not tear his cloak to hold him if he care not to come."

Putting constraint on himself, Saintré thanked him and followed to the abbey. As he rode behind he could hardly hide the rage with which he saw how this presumptuous monk played the cavalier, whispering often in the princess's ear, as if jesting on the newcomer who had appeared to spoil their sport. When they reached the gate the knight would have helped the lady from her horse, but it was the abbot from whom she accepted this service. Saintré was minded to leave her here, but for his anxiety to understand the strange change in her demeanour.

He was still more surprised, on entering the abbey, to find a table laid out with rich food and wine, as if for the wedding of a great lord rather than the frugal fare of monks vowed to poverty. The abbot did the honours of this banquet like a man of the world, conversing gallantly with the ladies and freely with the knight, who gave him but short answers. When he had quaffed several goblets of wine, the host's mirth grew louder and bolder, till, egged on by the glances and whispers of his fair guest, he even ventured to rally Saintré on his silent humour.

"What ails you, my good lord, with your fare and your company? Do you find my wine sour, or is the pittance of us monks too poor for one used to eat with kings?"

Saintré assured him that nothing could be better than his good cheer, and that in any case the presence of such a great lady would dignify the meanest hovel. The monk, taking offence at a phrase that seemed to belittle his hospitality, replied with a sneer at knights, who in running about the world, he said, would often find themselves lucky to be entertained in such vile hovels. The lady, giggling and pressing the abbot's knee, encouraged him to carry on the jest.

"You must own, sir," he exclaimed, "that few of those fellows in armour are led by pure love of glory. Idling at the court, they look about for some woman to befool by deceiving her as well as themselves. One of their duperies is undertaking for a lady what they call

adventures of love. Wearing some token on arm, neck,
or leg, they make these poor women believe that for their
sakes they are ready to run all sorts of risks. It being
a custom of courts to encourage such enterprises, their
master's bounty bestows on them means of jaunting
about the world and amusing themselves as they please.
When tired of travelling, they return with a lying varlet
at their backs, dressed up as a herald-at-arms, whom they
set to brag of their exploits even louder than they do
themselves, and thus gain renown they have ill deserved.
What do you say of it, madame?" added the impudent
abbot.

"I think that you are not far wrong," said the princess, with a laugh that went to Saintré's heart.

"Ah," he cried, "is it possible that a king's cousin
should let chivalry thus be reviled with so much falsehood and audacity?"

"Nay," chuckled the monk, "I have told nothing but
the truth of those people who cover themselves with iron,
but would feel their hearts fail them if they fell in with
any real danger."

"Lord abbot," said the knight sternly, "respect an
order which protects you in possession of the wealth you
abuse. Could you support by deeds the rash words you
have uttered, you should soon suffer due punishment!"

"Faith," cried the abbot lightly, "I am ready to support them against anyone, so it be on equal terms. All
very fine for a man whom it would be difficult to prick
with a needle through his armour to defy a poor monk
that has nothing but his frock and his rosary; but if you
were to produce a champion who would maintain your
cause by wrestling with me, for example, madame should
soon see which of us is in the right!"

The lady had kept screaming with laughter during

this dispute, applauding the abbot and urging him on to fresh insolence. As if to provoke her former lover, she cried mockingly:

"My lord, do you risk such a challenge when the knight happens to be without his panoply and is sure to accept it?"

"I will not go back from my word," said the abbot. "If the sport please the gentleman, I am his man, the more readily if madame will consent to be judge of the contest and to crown the victor with her own fair hand."

Provoked by his insolence, and by the lady's sneering smile, Saintré sprang to his feet. His high spirit could not bear to be thus defied by the boastful monk; and, though wrestling was a sport to which he was little used, he said with a scornful glance at the princess:

"This, madame, is indeed the only combat you merit to have undertaken for you!"

The abbot exultingly led the way to a meadow in which he was accustomed to run, to jump, and to wrestle with the younger monks. The ladies took their seats under leafy trees, and the monks made a circle in which the two rivals stripped for their contest. It was with some misgiving that Saintré noted the brawny limbs of the abbot, more fit for a soldier than for a churchman, but with good grace he presented himself to his opponent's grasp. Warily they locked arms and legs to wrestle together with firm-set lips and strained sinews. They bent, they writhed, they tottered, and for a little it seemed as if neither could overthrow the other. But the monk was well practised at this game, and before long laid the knight on the grass. Burning with vexation he sprang up for another tussle, only to be again thrown, amid the laughter and applause of the spectators, loudest of all that lady's jeering voice:

"Spare him, Saintré! Do not hurt the poor monk!"

Her maids had some difficulty in persuading her to retire from this unseemly scene. They went back into the hall, Saintré hiding his chagrin under an affected air of indifference. Some of the older monks, long scandalized by their superior's ways, ventured to remonstrate with him, representing that more respect was due to this young lord, whose ancestors had been rich benefactors to the abbey. The abbot agreed that he might have pushed his pleasantry too far, and tried to make up by politely complimenting Saintré for his condescension in sharing their country sports. To this the knight replied in the same tone that it seemed a pity so athletic a man should be thrown away on a peaceful life, when he might bear arms with credit in the service of the king.

"I might perhaps," said the abbot, with feigned modesty, "have been worth something in arms, had I the fortune to serve as squire to such a knight as my Lord de Saintré."

When they thus seemed to be reconciled, Saintré invited the whole party to dine with him next day at the castle. The invitation was accepted, and he rode home to make preparations for their entertainment.

The party arrived in good time for dinner, where the host dutifully waited on the princess; but all her smiles were for the abbot, whom he took care to ply with food and wine. Laughing and talking loudly, this proud churchman bore himself as if he were the chief guest, while the lady seemed to have entirely forgotten her old lover. After a time, however, they thought it civil to take some notice of their entertainer, complimenting him on his repast, or the stateliness of his castle, and especially on the standards, suits of armour, and other trophies with which the banqueting-hall was decorated. Saintré pointed

out to them a heavy suit of mail taken from a sultan by
his own hands, and remarked how few men were strong
and tall enough to wear it.

"If any of us could," he added, "I believe it would
be a man like you, my lord abbot; for the sultan who
wore these arms was the most terrible Turk with whom
I ever had to do."

The Dame des Belle-Cousines, duped by Saintré's
flattering speech, and curious to see how this fine armour
would become the sturdy limbs of her favourite, urged
the abbot to try it on. By no means unwilling, the vain
monk laid aside his frock, and Saintré offered himself to
act as squire to this holiday knight. He laced the helmet
and hauberk on tightly, and closed the rivets with a
hammer so that the wearer would not easily rid himself
of such unaccustomed array. When armed from top to
toe, the abbot took to strutting up and down with an
absurdly complacent air, proud to display himself thus
before the ladies; but Saintré had slipped away to an
adjoining chamber, where his squire stood ready to equip
him.

That burly churchman was still swelling himself like
a turkey-cock, and gobbling up the flattery of the foolish
princess, when the knight returned, clad in full armour,
followed by a herald in his livery carrying two shields,
two swords, two battleaxes, and two daggers. Behind
them the doors of the hall were filled with armed men,
who crossed their weapons so as to bar all exit.

"What means this, Saintré?" demanded the princess,
turning pale, while the abbot fumbled with the vizor of
his helmet, unable to see clearly through its bars. "What
would you do?"

"Yesterday," said the master of the house sternly,
"this abbot of yours provoked me to a combat at which

he was long practised. To-day, in turn, I challenge him
to meet me with my weapons."

At the same time the herald offered the abbot his
choice of arms, which he pitiably refused, backing off and
looking around in vain for some way of escape.

"Saintré, Saintré!" cried the lady beseechingly; and
as he turned away without heeding her, she changed her
tone. "Forbear, sir, or fear my high displeasure!"

"Perfidious dame, you have shamed your rank and
your beauty; and I no longer own you as the mistress
of my heart or the cousin of my king. And thou,
presumptuous wretch," he cried with a stride towards
the quailing abbot, "defend thyself like a man, or I
will have thee hurled from the window into the castle
moat."

The monk saw that he was taken in a trap. Trusting
in his great strength, he chose a battleaxe and a dagger
from the arms presented him, and Saintré did the like.
The abbot, taller than his opponent by a head, ran
straight upon him to crush him at a single blow. But
Saintré deftly parried the stroke, and, without returning
it, clapped the spike of his axe to the bars of the abbot's
helmet, bearing him backwards several paces till he
stumbled and fell heavily, so that the hall rang with the
crash of his heavy armour. Unable and unwilling to
rise, he lay still under the uplifted axe of the knight, who
seemed about to cleave off his head, when the Dame des
Belle-Cousines shrieked out:

"Stay! Oh, Saintré, spare him for pity's sake!"

"Fear not; his base blood is unworthy to be shed by
my hands." With this he raised the vizor of the abbot,
lying breathless and speechless at his feet. As he quaked
and gasped, Saintré caught his tongue, dragged it out,
and slit it with his dagger. "Be thus chastised for the

reviling words thy false mouth has vomited out against the sacred order of knighthood and those who profess it!"

At this sight the princess fainted away among her trembling and weeping attendants. From her senseless form Saintré untied the blue girdle which loving ladies were then wont to wear as a badge of fidelity. Looking on her face with a hard smile, he strode out of the hall and galloped away from his own castle, where the abbot and the dame were left to console each other as best they could.

Saintré thought to see her no more. But once again these parted lovers met at the court, where one day the queen set her favourite friends to amuse her by telling stories. When it came to Saintré's turn, he told one of which he laid the scene in Hungary and pretended to have heard it on his travels. But it was the tale of his own courtship and its reward. The queen and the princesses spoke with horror of that faithless loved one, suggesting the most shameful and cruel punishments for her as well deserved. The Dame des Belle-Cousines alone sat silent, till Saintré asked her:

"And you, madame, what do you think of that lady?"

She did not dare to defend his heroine, but falteringly blamed the knight for carrying his vengeance too far. He silently let her see an end of the blue girdle, making haste to hide it from all other eyes. That was the end of their long love.

Since the specimens that are to make the bulk of our volume have been mainly chosen as characteristic, the reader need not grudge the space given to this one by way of contrast. We have here come a long way from the grotesque exploits of Peredur, as formerly related. Another half-century and this realistic author might have anticipated Cervantes. As it is, one hardly feels sure whether he means to water or to weed out the blooms of chivalrous fiction. But at this very time it was striking fresh root in the rich soil of Spanish imagination, to flourish more exuberantly than ever under the forms that would be most familiar to Don Quixote. His favourite authors will be dealt with later on, when we come to consider the subjects and characters of romance.

III. Later Romance

By the sixteenth century the romance of decayed chivalry was falling into ruins, to be used as a quarry for the construction of two different styles of edifice. On the one hand it was vulgarized as chap-books, that continued to appeal to unschooled readers. On the other it became, first by Italian authors, elevated with choice and conscious art into world-famous poetry. It may have been some pride of classic culture that had made Italy herself no fruitful soil for such wilder growths of romance as long satisfied Gothic taste, content with the entertainment provided by gleemen and jongleurs when Dante and Boccaccio were at work on masterpieces of literature. The feudal system, also, that made a frame for *Chansons de Geste*, was in Italy earlier broken up by communes and republics, whose militia became strengthened by hired soldiers of fortune, like that Sir John Hawkwood said to have begun his career as a London tailor's apprentice— heroes not so likely to furnish stuff for chivalrous legend. Then the great Italian trading ports were in touch with the East, whence they imported exotic dyes of fiction to colour their imagination. At Venice more than one of the *Arabian Nights* stories were current long before these seem to have been known to the rest of Europe.

Pulci and Boiardo, Ariosto and Tasso, adopted the French romances as raw material for a series of romantic poems, spangling these rude originals with gracefully sportive fancy, fitting them with more elaborate machinery, and inventing new personages, such as the Saracen leaders Agramante and Rodomonte, the Amazons Bradamante and Clorinda, the beautiful princess Angelica, the Scottish prince Zerbino, the Moorish king Mambrino, and other phantoms that haunted Don Quixote's disordered imagination along with the old quasi-historical shades. Roland thus came to fresh renown in Boiardo's *Orlando Innamorato* and Ariosto's *Orlando Furioso*, though the latter's real hero seems rather to be the Ruggiero glorified as fabulous ancestor of the poet's patron house of Este. In his *Jerusalem Delivered* Tasso also compliments his patrons through their ancestry and invents fictitious characters to fill the Saracen ranks, but he keeps closer to history by throwing Tancred and Godfrey of Bouillon into the foreground. In general it may be said that these poets owed little to old romantic chroniclers but a few names, traditions, and conventions, transmuted by their genius into modern poetry, or sometimes alloyed by burlesque.

In England, such poets as Spenser and Sidney followed Italian example in sifting the rubbish heap of old romance to find hints for finer shapes that, as belonging to modern literature, lie outside our field. Here also tales of chivalry were now degraded into chapbook forms like Richard Johnson's *Seven Champions of Christendom*, works apparently well known to that Transatlantic hero, John Smith, whose adventures with Pocahontas and other heroines and caitiffs suspiciously resemble those of the heroes of romance. He is more

than once rescued by a paynim princess; he overthrows
three Turks in succession at a tourney; and he challenges
a Red Indian chief to single combat on an island, after
the precedent of Roland and Oliver, while the practical
side of his character and the needy state of his colony
prompt him to propose that this adversary shall bring
baskets of corn, against which he is to stake the value in
copper, and "our game shall be, the conqueror take all".

Shakespeare, it will be noticed, who drew his plots
from so many sources, made little use of the manners
of chivalry, that in his day began rather to furnish our
stage with targets for satire, as a new style of romantic
novels came into vogue with sentimental readers. The
very year Cervantes brought out *Don Quixote*, London
saw the play *Eastward Ho!* the authors of which were
punished by King James for reflections on Scotland;
and as this king looked to make money by cheapening
knighthood, he may not have relished a speech put into
the mouth of one of the characters. "The knighthood
nowadays are nothing like the knighthood of old times.
They rid ahorseback; ours go afoot. They were attended by their squires, ours by their lackeys. They
went buckled in their armour; ours muffled in their
cloaks. They travelled in wildernesses and deserts; ours
dare scarce walk the streets. They were still pressed
to engage their honour; ours still ready to pawn their
clothes. They would gallop on at sight of a monster;
ours run away at sight of a sergeant. They would
help poor ladies; ours make poor ladies."

A few years later, Beaumont and Fletcher, or one
of them, produced *The Knight of the Burning Pestle*, a
long-drawn farce evidently prompted by Cervantes. Its
hero, the grocer's assistant Ralph, goes off to seek
chivalrous adventures in Epping Forest, attended as

squire and dwarf by two junior apprentices, whom he thus schools in their part. "My beloved squire, and George my dwarf, I charge you that from henceforth you never call me by any other name but the *Right courteous and valiant Knight of the Burning Pestle*; and that you never call any female by the name of a woman or wench but *fair lady*, if she have her desires; if not, *distressed damsel*; that you call all forests and heaths *deserts*, and all horses *palfries*." So the next customer is introduced as "a distressed damsel to have a half-pennyworth of pepper".

Half a century later, English romance seemed to get the *coup de grâce* from a Cavalier poet.

> Sir Hudibras his passing worth,
> The manner how he sally'd forth;
> His arms and equipage are shown;
> His horse's virtues and his own.

It has been said that Cervantes "laughed Spain's chivalry away", but what he did was rather, at the opening of the seventeenth century, to sweep together and pile up with humorous effect what had already been falling into contempt. It was his great-grandfather's rusty armour in which the Knight of La Mancha set out to seek adventures; and the amazed amusement called forth by his array shows how long knight-errantry had been out of fashion. This author, who tried his own hand at serious romancing, was less than some of his contemporaries out of sympathy with the chivalrous spirit, so there are tears as well as smiles in his view of Don Quixote's delusions; and where some see nothing but grinning horseplay others detect a noble resentment against the realities that so meanly disappoint heroic aspirations. This has even been called the most melan-

choly book ever written. Not every reader, indeed, has
ears fine enough to catch the strain of "world-sadness"
under what seems a laughing mask, as was Heine's
fairy gift while still so young that he took a whole
summer to spell through the book which our rising
generation hardly cares to skim in an abridgment.

I could have poured out the bitterest tears when the noble
knight, for all his nobleness, got only ingratitude and beating;
and as I, yet unpractised in reading, spoke every word out loud,
so could birds and trees, brooks and flowers, hear it too; and as
such innocent creatures of nature, just like children, know nothing
of the irony of the world, so they also took all for real earnest,
and wept with me over the sorrows of the poor knight. Even
an old, worn-out oak sobbed, and the waterfall shook more
vehemently his white beard, and seemed to be calling shame on
the baseness of the world. We felt that the heroism of the knight
deserved none the less admiration, though the lion turned its back
to him without caring to fight; and that his deeds were all the
more praiseworthy the weaker and leaner his body, the rustier
the harness which defended him, the more miserable the nag
which carried him. We despised the low people who treated the
poor knight so roughly, but yet more the great people who,
adorned with gay silk mantles, fine fashions of speech, and ducal
titles, made light of a man so much superior to them in strength
and nobility of spirit. Dulcinea's knight rose always higher in
my esteem, and won always on my love, the more I read this
wonderful book, which was every day, in the garden, so that by
autumn I had reached the end of the history; and never will I
forget the day when I read the mournful encounter in which the
knight had to fall so ignominiously. . . . Ah! this shining Knight
of the Silver Moon, who conquered the bravest and noblest man in
the world, was a disguised barber.

The Knight of the Moon, by the way, was not a
barber, but the bachelor Sampson Carrasco—matter of
detail such as your budding poet often treats with a
certain carelessness. It has been suggested as a test for

a discriminating reader that he can, like Heine, catch the pathos of Don Quixote, where the vulgar mind relishes only the tilting at windmills and the tossing in blankets. Other critics are more chary in crediting the author with sentiment. Perhaps the truth is that he was himself a Quixote and a Sancho Panza by turns, who in different moods could appeal to both classes of reader; it is significant that the second part, written in his later years, shows more reflective sympathy with his hero. He was goaded into producing this continuation by the doubly fictitious sequel of Avellaneda, who makes the knight more of a pantaloon, shows him followed by a rabble of street boys, and at the end leaves him in a lunatic asylum.

Cervantes certainly seems no mere mocker at knight-errantry, whose own life was full of chivalrous adventure, and it was in a soured spirit of romance that he dipped the shafts of his ridicule. Nor had that spirit altogether gone sour in his heart. Chivalry was dead, but not so romantic fiction, which had now taken a new form, or rather an old one revived from ancient models. At the height of their popularity were then the so-called pastoral romances, in which simple shepherds came to be strangely companied with gallant knights and sentimental princesses. This kind of story, as beseemed its classical origin, arose in Italy, but the most famous example of it was the *Diana* of Montemayor, that appeared in Spain about the middle of the sixteenth century, to be imitated all over Europe—by Cervantes himself in his *Galatea*, in France by D'Urfe's *Astrea*, and in England by the *Arcadia* of Sir Philip Sidney, who on his part confesses to a soldierly weakness for the heroes of chivalric romance, even as "evil apparelled in the dust and cobwebs of that uncivil age".

Pastoral romance passed for more elegant than rude

tales of bloodshed; and the elaborate conceits with which
it was stuffed had a high flavour for the taste of a
generation that swallowed this kind of fare greedily,
while turning up its delicate nose at the absurdities
retailed by minstrels to the vulgar. Don Quixote's niece
and housekeeper had some reason to fear that he would
next propose to turn shepherd, as indeed he did, when
vanquished by the Knight of the White Moon. "What
a life shall we lead, friend Sancho! what a melody we
shall have of bagpipes and rebecks!" quoth the Don.
"One circumstance will contribute much to make us
perfect in our new profession, which is my being, as thou
well knowest, somewhat of a poet, and the bachelor
Sampson Carrasco an excellent one. Of the priest, I
will say nothing; yet will I venture a wager that he too
has the points of a poet; and Master Nicholas the
barber, also, I make no doubt: for most or all of that
family are players on the guitar and songmakers. I
will complain of absence; thou shalt extol thyself for
constancy; the shepherd Carrascon shall complain of
disdain; and the priest Curiambro may say or sing whatever he pleaseth: and so we shall go on to our heart's
content."

The romance of stilted and bedizened shepherds, preserved for us by the poetry embodied in it, had a long
run, for at least in abridgments such fiction found a
certain favour up to Horace Walpole's condemnation of
it as "tedious, lamentable, pedantic", and too much even
for the "patience of a young virgin in love", who
would soon have the woes of *Pamela* and *Clarissa
Harlowe*, and the mishaps of *Evelina* to weep over, as
French eyes were moistened by those of Marianne and
Manon Lescaut. In France, to be sure, pastorals *à la
Watteau* still found favour far on in the eighteenth

century, when Florian adapted the *Galatea* of Cervantes for the decade that danced in the Reign of Terror.

In the France of Richelieu's time, Charles Sorel did for shepherds what Cervantes had done for knights, by his burlesque, *Le Berger Extravagant*, which more heartily holds up for ridicule the tawdry and threadbare patterns of romance, ancient and modern. Yet, like the great author he imitated, Sorel was himself a bit of a romancer, with "the fatal eye of an accomplice" for the weak points of such handiwork. His best-known story, however, is *Francion*, belonging to an order that sprang up in Spain before Don Quixote, and flowered in the *Gil Blas* of Le Sage. This, from a Spanish word for rascal, was named the *picaresque* romance, detailing the usually unedifying tricks of some sharp and needy scamp such as the *Lazarillo de Tormes* and the *Guzman de Alfarache* that set headlines for it in the Peninsula, copied in England by Nash's *Jack Wilton* and other books more worthy to be forgotten. In Germany, later on, it produced Grinmelshausen's *Simplicissimus*, a book by no means forgotten, imitated by *The Hungarian Simplicissimus*, that in our time has supplied material for one of Jokai's novels. The author of *Simplicissimus* seems a literary kinsman of Defoe, who is sometimes taken as the father of the modern novel, by the stories in which he wove realistic detail and improving lessons into the texture of picaresque adventure.

Side by side with the homespun of rascally tricks and matter-of-fact experiences, highly embroidered fiction got one more " boom " in the French Heroic Romances, whose well-deserved nickname was *Romans de la Longue Haleine*, for they were long-winded in every sense. The parents of this brood were the pastoral romance and a romance of Moorish life that won admiration about the same time as Don Quixote; while for remoter ancestry they had post-classical Greek novels, which may all along have helped to colour mediæval fiction, and clearly came into the hands of Renaissance storytellers. The cradle of heroic romance was the Hotel de Rambouillet, rendez-vous of those *Précieuses* satirized by Molière. Its chief authors were Mademoiselle de Scudéry, with her brother and M. La Calprenède. The characters were Moorish, classical and chivalric as labelled, but all rigged out in a French full dress in which to go through involved episodes of suffering and of adventure conceived from the old romances, with inflated gallantry as the main interest, replacing supernatural marvels and prodigies of valour. Romantic courtships were here drawn out to a length that delighted that leisurely age, for which special relish was sometimes added in a supposed identification of the puppets of the piece with living personages. The most famous title of this library was the Scudérys' *Grand Cyrus*, published in ten successive parts about the middle of the seventeenth century; and perhaps its best-remembered feature is the *Carte du pays de Tendre*, illustrating *Clelia*, another ten-volumed romance of the same authorship. This map of the Love Country, which strikes us as rather a heavy joke, excited serious admiration by its conceits, "The River of Inclination", "The Lake of Indifference", "The Mountain of Pride", the villages of *Petits Soins, Jolis Vers, Billet Doux*, and the like. A satire after the manner of Lucian, in which Boileau attacked the heroic romances, suggests that these places are on the way to *Petites Maisons*, translatable for us as Bedlam. He represents Pluto as condemning the whole crew of heroes and heroines to be carried to the banks of Lethe, and there thrown head foremost into the deepest part of the river "with their billets doux, their gallant letters, their passionate verses, and all the many volumes or rather piles of ridiculous paper covered by their histories ". A skit of the next century, the Jesuit father Bougeant's *Marvellous Journey of Prince Fan-Feredin in Romantia*, makes great fun of this region, whose inhabitants live on air, whose rocks can be softened by tears, and where nothing but the very finest phrases are used, swelling out into a volume what might be said in a page, so that the chief epidemic here is one of yawning.

The vogue of these books was as phenomenal as their length. In vain for a time were they laughed at by Molière on the stage, by Boileau in his famous satire, and in novels like Scarron's *Roman Comique* and Furetière's *Roman Bourgeois*, which preluded a new school of realism. In England, also, the long-winded romances were translated, admired, and imitated, as we learn from the *Spectator*; and Fielding seems to take a fling at them in his *Tom Thumb*. Richardson's novels, so doted on by soft hearts of the eighteenth century, are but a version of the French heroics transposed into a lower key and harmonized with British morality. Matrons and maids, the most eager readers of *Clarissa Harlowe* as of heroic romance, are apt to have less relish for humour than for sentiment, however cloying. But humour now was acting as a solvent even upon feminine sentiment. When Fielding mocked Pamela in his *Joseph Andrews*, Mrs. Lennox, hailed by Johnson and Goldsmith as their peer, brought out *The Female Quixote* to tilt at the high-horsed romance of love. The same enterprise, with an eye to Mrs. Radcliffe's stories of mysterious intrigue, was more wittily undertaken by Jane Austen in her *Northanger Abbey*. Books with a like purpose are Barrett's *Heroine*, lately reprinted, and Paget's *Lucretia* in our own time, which at length hardly needs such a lesson, now that it has no

patience with romance unless refined by art or sublimated
by genius.

When the Heroic Romances had been laughed or
yawned out of credit, a sort of revival of the old tales of
chivalry was attempted for the generation that rhymed
and jested above the first volcanic rumblings of the French
Revolution.   Powdered heads, soon to be shorn by the
guillotine, were bent over a *Bibliothèque des Romans* ex-
tending to a hundred and twelve double volumes, which
contained many of those rusty-dusty stories polished and
varnished in the Louis XVI style.   Some of them were
even degradingly sophisticated by writers like De Tressan,
pandering to the loose morals of French society.   For
the common folk, also, romance was cheapened in the
abridgments of the *Bibliothèque Bleue,* answering to the
chap-books once much hawked by pedlars in England,
a popular literature still not extinct on the Continent.
But the Napoleonic wars for a time threw chivalric fables
into shade beside the dazzling exploits of a modern
Charlemagne, who with his peers came to be overthrown
by an authentic Arthur.   It was the nineteenth century
that set France, England, and Germany on earnestly
unearthing their treasures of old romance, not only to
be exhibited in literary museums, but often recoined by
appreciative pens for a fresh currency.   It may even be
claimed that its true beauties are better known to us than
to its fondest admirers.   " When ", says J. M. Ludlow,
" in the sixteenth century the immortal chronicler of the
hidalgo of La Mancha proceeds to burn the huge pile
which by this time has grown up of prose romantic
fiction, he shows no symptom of having ever suspected
the presence of the lovely corpse that lay smothered
beneath."

This sketch has gone beyond the bounds of our

proper subject, which is the tales of chivalry while chivalry was still in arms. One word in conclusion on the movement of modern literature that has been christened romanticism in opposition to classicism, a distinction easier to realize than to define. Goethe surely went beyond the mark in taking the latter for health and the former for disease. The contrast may be typified by setting the Parthenon beside Westminster Abbey: on the one hand, lucidity, regularity, solidity, entire proportion, and clear-cut form; on the other, a natural ruggedness, an intricacy of jutting outlines lending itself to mysterious shadows and broken lights, comparative neglect of symmetry and finish, room for fanciful caprice and wild exuberance, indulgence even for the quaint and the grotesque, amid aspirations towards what cannot be attained on earth—characteristics also of an authorship that no longer kept its eye fixed on classical models. It is significant that Gothic architecture flowered in what were the flourishing days of chivalric romance.

ROMANTIC HISTORY

LET us now turn from the development of romance in time, to distinguish its different departments of scene and personages, which claim separate examination. Its "matter" is the technical term applied by French minstrels to their diverse subjects. These, again, can be subdivided into "cycles", clustering round the figure of this or that hero, whose exploits, as variously chronicled, are sometimes marked off in "branches".

One class may be briefly dismissed as almost forgotten, and not worth remembrance. A once-popular school of romance was drawn from the classics for an age so little critical that it could accept the fairy prince Oberon as son of Julius Cæsar, when it found no fault with Huon of Bordeaux's experience of Saracens keeping the feast of St. John, nor with a tournament, in all due form, being held at the Court of the "Grand Turk". All periods, regions, and religions were freely confused by romancers, who found the heathen mythology convenient for cloaking their ignorance of Islam, made to worship "Jupiter" or "Apollo" among other miscreancy, and to swear as readily by "the red Mars omnipotent" as by "Termagant" and "Mahound". Chaucer's *Knight's Tale* seems the most respectable example of the way in which poets took licence to mix the manners of different ages.

The learning of that day was, of course, nothing if

not classical. The *Gesta Romanorum* collection includes the stories of Codrus, of Atalanta, of the Minotaur, of Androcles and his lion, of Argus tricked by Mercury, of Achilles hiding among women, of the Sword of Damocles, of Damon and Pythias, with many other ancient figures gravely dressed up in mediæval guise, as puppets for pulpit display, while Virgil, strangely degraded into a magician, plays a frequent part in this edifying fiction, when Aristotle had a similar fate.

It seems natural enough that incidents from classical legend should be adapted by monkish authors; but the same source was drawn on by less-moral fablers. The romance of *Partenopex de Blois* is an evident adaptation of the Cupid and Psyche story. William of Orange takes Nimes through a stratagem apparently suggested by the Trojan Horse. The tale of *Sir Tristram* is full of such instances: the hero slays a monster, like Perseus; he is wounded by a poisoned arrow, like Philoctetes; he is recognized in disguise by his dog, like Ulysses; he deserts his bride, like Paris and too many another gallant in tale or history; then his death comes about by such deception as drove Ægeus to despair, a ship having to hoist a white or a black sail according to the fate of its errand.

The Tale of Troy and the exploits of Alexander were favourite themes for metrical chronicles, making strange work with them in the darkness of ages that took these stories mainly through the medium of Ovid, Virgil, and inferior Latin writers, preserved during the mediæval neglect of Greek. Hercules, Jason, and Perseus were heroes obfuscated alike in chivalric trappings. Orpheus is made to figure as Sir Orpheo in his quest of Eurydice. Vespasian and Titus undertake a Crusade to avenge the death of Christ. The fabulous history of Alexander seems to have come from Eastern romance through a chronicle falsely attributed to the king's philosophic attendant Callisthenes. The triumphs of Julius Cæsar and the tragedies of Thebes were treated with the same freedom as did not let Alexander weep for more worlds to conquer.

> Then had king Alisaunder y-meant,
> By all his baronage consent,
> The sea to have y-passed again,
> And warren upon French men,
> Alemans, and eke English,
> Bretons, Irish, and Denmarkish.

The revival of Greek letters must have gone to expose the absurdity of the pseudo-classic romance. It almost entirely died out before Don Quixote's day, or now lives only on the dustiest shelves of antiquarian lore. One relic it has left us in the title of Alexandrine verse, taken from a once-famous chronicle of Alexander written in this metre. Another is the use made by Chaucer and Shakespeare of the Trojan war and its heroes, as handed down to them through romancers, from the same sources as supplied Britain with Brutus as an imaginary ancestor. The Pastoral Romance of the sixteenth, and the Heroic Romance of the seventeenth century also derived much from the classics; but these, as has been shown, were more artificial products of riper scholarship.

Still more absurd, in our eyes, are romantic fictions in which Biblical characters appear without shocking the robust faith of the age. Pilate, for example, is made to figure as a felon knight, jousting with a champion whose name may not now be lightly spoken. Joseph of Arimathea is arrayed in chivalric arms through his connection with the legend of the Sangreal. In fiction so ill informed as to make Joshua contemporary with Solomon, Joseph

and his kinsmen are made to act the part of conquering
missionaries in Britain and to become ancestors of the
Round Table heroes.   A German minstrel anticipated
Milton in versifying the fate of Adam and Eve, em-
bittered by some incidents that seem quite unscriptural :
our first parents are set to do separate penance by several
weeks freezing immersion in the Jordan and the Tigris.
Goliath and David are as easily adapted to romantic history as Hero and Leander

Unconsciously old Christian storytellers drew their
materials from farther afield than Palestine.   The seventh-
century Greek romance of Barlaam and Josaphat, parent
of a long line of religious fiction, is now detected as the
legend of Buddha, which seems to have been also adapted
to Jewish and to Moslem tenets.   The once very popular
tale of the Seven Wise Masters betrays an Eastern origin,
to be suspected in many other mediæval favourites.   These
indeed are hardly romances of chivalry.   But chivalry and
orthodoxy have full play together in chronicles of the
Crusades, of which some specimen has already been presented.

It is, by the way, a significant hint of how ill defined
were once the boundaries of fact and fiction, that the title
of romance could be applied to a true crusading chronicle
by William of Tyre, who has been styled " the father of
modern history ".   At the same time poetic invention
gave itself airs as historical authority.   Caxton enumerates
the nine famous worthies of the world, fittest to be heroes
of romance, as three pagans, to wit, Hector of Troy, Alexander the Great, and Julius Cæsar ; three Jews, Joshua,
King David, and Judas Maccabeus ; three Christians,
Arthur, Charlemagne, and Godfrey of Bouillon.   One of
the *Chanson de Geste* minstrels divides romance into three
classes : " matter of France " ; " matter of Britain, or Brit-

KING ARTHUR

THE ROAD TO CAMELOT

tany"; and "matter of Rome", in which he means to include all other history sacred and profane.

In a bewildering mass of stories, our survey may be mainly confined to those still so far alive as to supply plots, characters, scenes, or allusions for modern literature. Leaving in their deserved neglect the outrages on ancient history above-mentioned; also setting apart certain local legends such as *Guy of Warwick* and the Scottish *Sir Eger Sir Grime and Sir Graysteel*, which fit into larger cycles only by similarity of sentiment and incident, we may take the most famous romances in prose and verse as grouped under three heads—

I. Those of Arthur and the Round Table.
II. Those of Charlemagne and his Peers.
III. Those of the Spanish Peninsula.

This classification ignores the German stories that are not in the strictest sense romance, but often give a Teutonized version of the French romances, to which they may indeed sometimes stand in the position of originals.

I. Arthur and the Round Table

The romances of Arthur are naturally the most familiar to us, and to most of us through Tennyson's *Idylls of the King*, not an appropriate title, as these are rather epical fragments. Milton, we know, meditated an epic on this theme, which he abandoned for one more congenial. William Morris, Matthew Arnold, and other poets of our time have drawn freely on the same storehouse of legendary incident. From shadowy traditions cherished by the kindred peoples of Wales and of Brittany, sung by bards and put in writing by churchmen, Geoffrey of

Monmouth, in the twelfth century, worked up a Latin
chronicle of the supposed descendants of one Brutus,
grandson of Ascanius, who, after the example of his great
ancestor Æneas, sailed to the south of Britain to found
a new kingdom. The tale of Troy was at this time a
fashionable topic in romance. Geoffrey's chronicle of
Brutus and his supposed descendants, Arthur and Cad-
wallader, was presently versified by Robert Wace and
other minstrels, who at the court of our Norman kings
may well have been encouraged to dwell on themes that
went to glorify the past history of their English conquest.
But till the ill will between conquerors and conquered
died out, such themes, not appealing to Saxon sentiment,
would hardly be popular in the vernacular, while the long
connection of the Plantagenet sovereigns with France
helped to give them a vogue on the Continent.

The metrical romances of Arthur, by this time turned
into prose, came to be translated in English about the
period of the York and Lancastrian wars, when the Normans and Saxons had been welded into one people, cap-
able of common pride in a national hero, real or fictitious.
In Malory's compilation, under the title of *Morte d'Arthur*,
several Arthurian romances were imperfectly fused into
something like connected history. This, made in the
reign of Edward IV, was one of the first books printed by
Caxton, as bidding fair for a popularity evinced down
to our own day by numerous editions. Then, indeed,
Arthur's name was not so familiar in England as that of
the Saxon Robin Hood, while the British king's memory
would be better kept in Wales.

Caxton, in his preface to the *Morte d'Arthur*, has to
lament that this hero " is more spoken of beyond the sea,
more books made of his noble acts than there be in England, as well in Dutch, Italian, Spanish, and Greekish,

as in French ". And yet this editor indignantly declares that Arthur's tomb might still be seen at Glastonbury, and the impression of his seal in Westminster Abbey, as well as Gawaine's skull in the castle of Dover, with other relics, on consideration of which " can no man reasonably gainsay but there was a king of this land named Arthur. For in all places, Christian and heathen, he is reputed and taken for one of the nine worthy, and the first of the three Christian men ". Neither Caxton nor Malory could guess how future writers would explain away their hero as originally a Celtic god, who may have become identified with the tradition of some faintly remembered chief or chiefs, as the reader will find explained at large in a former volume of this series, Mr. Squire's *Celtic Myth and Legend*.

We need not here go further into the origin of these legends, nor into the more dubious question of whether Arthur ever lived. Some of his exploits seem to belong to the historical fame of Alfred; and where or when Arthur ruled, if ever he did rule, must be left to imagination. All over Britain, from Arthur's Seat to Tintagel, various localities are haunted by his name. Even in the romances it is not made clear whether his chief seat was in England, Scotland, Wales, Cumberland, Cornwall, or in the legendary land of Lyonnesse, believed to have been submerged beneath the sea that now foams round our Scilly Islands. His capital is not less hard to fix. In the great hall of Winchester Castle is preserved a titular " Round Table ", on which four-and-twenty rainbow rays shoot out from the centre, each lettered with the name of one of Arthur's famous knights, and somewhat defaced by the bullets of Cromwell's soldiers. This relic is mentioned as far back as Henry VI's time; but is suspected of adaptation from a " wheel of fortune ", recorded earlier among Winchester's treasures. The Arthur of romance figures both at Winchester and London, cities which at the time of the Conquest shared the prestige of being England's capital; but he is also found seated at Caerleon on Usk, at Carlisle, and at other places, notably the Camelot for identification with which there are various candidates among renamed towns. Cadbury Camp—one of three so named in the county—near the Somerset villages of East and West Camel, is called *Camalet* by Camden, who makes it the scene of a great battle between Arthur and the Saxons. A central mound here, claimed also as a Roman prætorium, is popularly known as "King Arthur's Palace", near "King Arthur's Well"; and "King Arthur's Causeway" is an overgrown track leading towards Glastonbury, along which on stormy nights rustic imagination hears the sweep of the king's phantom hunt, where another German-like legend makes the inside of the hill a treasure house of fairy gold. The crooked Cam that names these villages means, as at Cambridge, a winding stream. There is another Camel River in Cornwall, where, near Camelford, Slaughter Bridge, corrupted into Slovens Bridge, pretends to commemorate the battle in which King Arthur fell, and a stone is even shown as marking his grave. The sonorousness and metrical adaptability of Camelot and Tintagel have given these names a larger place in poetry than in the old chronicles, where we find Arthur's abode shifting like a mirage. His geography must be pronounced still more hazy than his history; and puzzling hints as to the scenes of his knights' adventures lead us all over the British Isles.

The fabled records of this reign may be summed up as follows, on the authority of Malory and his sources of information.

At the death of King Uther Pendragon, Britain stands in peril of usurpation and anarchy till Arthur comes, unwitting, to take his own. It seems almost necessary to the character of a complete romantic hero that he should be of mysterious or irregular birth, so the boy Arthur, though the son of King Uther, has been brought up in secret as the supposed child of a lord named Sir Ector. In good time the wizard Merlin arranges for the production of the right heir by getting the Archbishop of Canterbury to call the lords and gentlemen of the realm together in the greatest church of London, where in the churchyard stood a marble stone bearing up a steel anvil in which stuck a naked sword, having written about it, in letters of gold: "Whoso pulleth out this sword of this stone and anvil is likewise king born of all England". No knight could stir the sword till the lad Arthur, as yet unconscious of his noble birth, draws it out with ease, is declared, by Merlin, Uther's son, and has to be recognized as king, not without some grudging on the part of certain knights, so old is our spirit of parliamentary opposition.

Once well seated on his throne, the young king shows himself the right man in the right place. No adversary can stand against him when he draws his sword Excalibur, which "was so bright in his enemies' eyes that it gave light like thirty torches". The idea of the magic sword, only to be drawn out by a destined knight, recurs in Malory's story; and according to a conflicting statement, which he does not concern himself to reconcile, Arthur again got this wonderful blade from a mysterious patroness, The Lady of the Lake, allegorized by Tennyson as representing the Church. She, rather a shadowy personage in Malory, elsewhere is identified with the Vivienne that beguiled Merlin. However he came by it, the

THE ROUND T

KING ARTHUR

king plied Excalibur so well that "all men of worship
said it was merry to be under such a chieftain that would
put his person in adventure as other poor knights did".
He restored peace around him, quelled heathen neighbours, conquered Scotland and Wales, and had a great
indecisive battle with eleven kings, who were drawn off
by news of the Saracens ravaging their territory.   Merlin
stands by his side as sage counsellor, not always a sound
one, for we find him leading the Christian king to copy
the statecraft of Herod.   Aware by his arts that Arthur
should perish through one born on May-Day, Merlin
puts him at gathering together, for no good, all children
born on that day, and setting them on board a ship, lost
in a storm; but among those young castaways the king's
nephew, Mordred, is saved by a kindly wrecker, who
rears him up to become the agent of fate.

On another matter, in which young men are seldom
open to wise advice, Arthur does not listen to Merlin.
His barons urging him to marry, he chooses Guinevere,
daughter of his ally, King Leodegrance of Cameliard;
and in vain Merlin warned him that "she was not wholesome for him to take to wife".   As dowry, along with
a hundred knights, she brought him the famous Round
Table, at which there was room for a hundred and fifty
champions; but as yet Arthur could find no more than
thirty of his own followers worthy of such an honour,
and long one seat remained vacant, the "Siege Perilous",
to be filled in time by the pure knight, Sir Galahad.

These heroes wander about the country, like police
constables, alone or in knots, ever ready to assist fair
ladies and oppressed folk, according to their vow and
duty.   They do good service in subduing felon knights,
cutting giants in two, and putting down bad customs.
On their return from adventures, they are sworn to tell

the truth of such exploits to heralds, through whom their prowess becomes known and estimated ; then, when no other fighting was on hand, the king takes every opportunity to "let cry" a tournament, in which his knights can keep their hands in by tilting with each other and with all comers. As usual in romance, some young knight, untried and unknown, is apt to distinguish himself by blossoming out at once into a flower of chivalry.

While ruling masterfully at home, Arthur has also a vigorous foreign policy. Lucius, Emperor of Rome, sends ambassadors to demand homage in right of Julius Cæsar as conqueror of Britain. In answer, the king declares war before a parliament at York, assembles his fleet at Sandwich, and invades the Continent for an early demonstration of the doctrine that one Briton is equal to at least three foreigners. "Sir Lucius", though backed by nineteen kings, including those of Egypt and Ethopia, and having a bodyguard of fifty fiend-born giants, was totally defeated and slain by Arthur's own hand, along with a hundred thousand of his men. The British king passed into Germany, but returned to Italy to subdue Lombard and Tuscan cities, and took a turn at successful war with the Saracens, whose leader, "Sir Priamus", was conquered, baptized, and made a knight of the Round Table. By such acts of prowess, of course, Arthur is decked in the romantic and historical plumes of Charlemagne.

But at the height of all this glory we see how the ruin of the Round Table is being prepared by guilty passion, a hint of which has cast its shadow from the first. The valour, so invincible by mortal arms, is tainted by a sin. Lancelot, bravest of Arthur's knights, well sees the source of his weakness, and struggles against his disloyal love for the queen—struggles in vain. Their guilt is too black to be washed out save by noblest blood. Slowly and surely, like the fate of a Greek tragedy, the end draws on, till at last that goodly fellowship is dissolved in treachery and wrath.

There was ill blood between Guinevere and her husband's fairy sister, Morgan, the "sea born". Prompted by this kinswoman, the envious Mordred and his brother Agravaine spy upon the queen's secret meetings with Lancelot, and betray them to Arthur, who now cannot but open eyes long blinded by his own loyal nature. Guinevere, doomed to be burnt at Carlisle, is rescued by Lancelot, and he carries her off to his castle of Joyous Gard, variously identified with Berwick and Bamborough. Here he is besieged by Arthur, with Gawaine now as his right hand. In their enmity there are still gleams of that high-mindedness that marked their friendship; but the breach is too wide for Arthur and his best knight to meet save as mortal foes. Lancelot contents himself with standing on his defence; and when the king calls him forth to single combat, for once he shrinks from such an ordeal.

"God defend me," said Sir Launcelot, "that ever I should encounter with the most noble king that made me knight."

"Fie upon thy fair language," said the king, "for wit you well, and trust it, I am thy mortal foe and ever will to my death day, for thou hast slain my good knights, and full noble men of my blood, that I shall never recover again: also thou hast dishonoured my queen, and holden her many winters, and sithen like a traitor taken her from me by force."

"My most noble lord and king," said Sir Launcelot," ye may say what ye will, for ye wot well with yourself I will not strive, but there as ye say I have slain your good knights, I wot well that I have done so, and that me sore repenteth, but I was enforced to do battle with them, in saving of my life, or else I must have suffered them to have slain me. And as for my lady queen Guenever, except your person of your highness and my lord Sir Gawaine, there is no knight under heaven that dare make it good upon me, that ever I was traitor unto your person. And where it pleaseth you to say that I have holden my lady your queen years and winters, unto that I shall make a large answer, and prove it upon any knight that beareth the life, except your person and Sir Gawaine, that my lady queen Guenever is a true lady unto your person, as any is living unto her lord, and that will I make good with my hands; howbeit, it hath liked her good grace to have me in charity, and to cherish me more than any other knight, and unto my power I again have deserved her love, for ofttimes, my lord, ye have consented that she should be burnt and destroyed in your heat, and then it fortuned me to do battle for her, and or I departed from her adversary they confessed their untruth, and she full worshipfully excused. And at such times, my lord Arthur, said Sir Launcelot, ye loved me, and thanked me when I saved your queen from the fire, and then ye promised me for ever to be my good lord, and now me thinketh ye reward me full ill for my good service; and, my good lord, me seemeth I had lost a great part of my worship in my knighthood, and I had suffered my lady your queen to have been burnt, and insomuch she should have been burnt for my sake. For sithen I have done battles for your queen in other quarrels than in mine own, me seemeth now I had more right to do battle for her in right quarrel, and therefore my good and gracious lord," said Sir Launcelot, "take your queen unto your good grace, for she is both fair, true, and good."

"Fie on thee, false recreant knight!" said Sir Gawaine, "I let thee wit my lord mine uncle king Arthur shall have his queen and thee, maugre thy visage, and slay you both whether it please him."

"It may well be," said Sir Launcelot, "but wit ye well, my lord Sir Gawaine, and me list to come out of this castle, ye should win me and the queen more harder than ever ye wan a strong battle."

The Pope interferes, sending a bishop with "bulls under lead" to make peace, on which persuasion Arthur takes back his queen, and Launcelot goes into woeful banishment across the sea, where, like the Plantagenet

princes, he has territories in France. Arthur and
Gawaine follow with an invading army, but are presently
recalled by news that the king's nephew Mordred had
turned traitor, calling a Parliament, having himself
crowned at Canterbury, and even proposing to marry his
uncle's wife. But Guinevere, who " for fair speech nor
for foul, would never trust to come in his hands again",
threw herself into the Tower of London, to which the
traitor laid siege in vain, though he made many assaults
" and shot great guns". Unfortunately, " the most party
of all England held with Sir Mordred, the people were
so new-fangle", so that he could venture to oppose
Arthur's landing at Dover, but was defeated and drew
back into the west country, whither Arthur followed him
for that last great battle in Lyonnesse, which Tennyson
has famed for us—

> A land of old upheaven from the abyss
> By fire, to sink into the abyss again;
> Where fragments of forgotten peoples dwelt,
> And the long mountains ended in a coast
> Of ever-shifting sand, and far away
> The phantom circle of a moaning sea.
> There the pursuer could pursue no more,
> And he that fled no further fly the King;
> And there, that day when the great light of heaven
> Burn'd at his lowest in the rolling year,
> On the waste sand by the waste sea they closed.

" Never was seen a more dolefuller battle in Christian
land." Treachery prevails over loyalty, though the
traitor falls by Arthur's hand. But the king's own wound
is mortal; nor does he care to live. His last follower, Sir
Bedevere, bore him to a chapel nigh, " a broken chancel
with a broken cross", between the ocean and a great
water lit by the full moon. We remember how he bade

KING ARTHUR AT THE COURT OF AVALON

THE MERCIFUL KNIGHT

("Of a Knight who forgave his enemy when he might have destroyed him, and how
the image of Christ kissed him in token that his acts had pleased God")

Bedevere throw his sword Excalibur into the mere; how the knight grudged to lose a so precious blade; then how, at the king's angry entreaty, he flung it into the dark water, to be caught and drawn down by an arm clothed in white samite, a rich stuff like satin or velvet. Arthur is taken into a dusky barge by three weeping queens, who carry him away—

> To the island valley of Avilion;
> Where falls not hail, or rain, or any snow,
> Nor ever wind blows loudly; but it lies
> Deep-meadow'd, happy, fair with orchard lawns
> And bowery hollows crowned with summer sea.

There he may be at rest and heal him of his grievous wound. But on earth he leaves all dark behind him. Two more tragic scenes conclude the story. The guilty lovers, who have brought about so doleful ruin, hide their shame and remorse, the one in a convent, the other in a hermitage—and to both comes the end that comes to all human sin and sorrow.

In this snatching from death all Arthur's mind "is clouded with a doubt", and the story too presents some confusion as to what became of his body. Next morning Sir Bedevere finds a new-made grave at a hermitage, where he spends the rest of his life in prayer and in mourning for the past. For—

> Now the whole Round Table is dissolved
> Which was an image of the mighty world,
> And I, the last, go forth companionless,
> And the days darken round me, and the years
> Among new men, strange faces, other minds.

Glastonbury was taken for the site of a tomb, on which romantic history inscribed: *Hic jacet Arthurus Rex quondam Rexque futurus.* According to popular tradition the great king is nowise dead, but lives in Avilion, and will come back again to help England in her hour of need. Don Quixote tells us how the English in his time expected Arthur's appearance every day; but we managed without him to make head against the Don's countrymen. In other stories Arthur is understood to be in charge of Morgan-le-Fay, that Madame Tussaud of romance, in whose realm he was joined by Ogier the Dane, a Rip Van Winkle from another cycle of fabulous history, where we find an amusing description of the introduction of these two heroes by the fairy queen, with compliments interchanged between them quite *à la française*. This is, of course, an idea common to romance and to romantic history, that looks for the coming again of Frederick Barbarossa, James IV of Scotland, Sebastian of Portugal, and other vanished monarchs, who sometimes, in more senses than one, were dear to their people.

With the story of Arthur, Malory has interwoven others in a way that does not always make for clearly consecutive narrative. Merlin, that sage of supernatural birth and gifts, who appears in so many romances, and is also connected with such quasi-historic princes as Vortigern and Hengist, has important functions in the early part of this reign. He knows the past and the future; he can become invisible or change himself into a stag as easily as into a dwarf; and his counsel is invaluable to a young king as to hot-blooded knights. But his wisdom saves him, no more than Samson nor Hercules, from the wiles of woman; so in his dotage he is "assotted" by the false charms of a water-nymph —always a dangerous character from the days of the Sirens—who steals from him the spell by which she shuts him up under a rock, or, as some have it, in a hawthorn bush, or a tower woven out of air, but according to

Tennyson in a hollow oak, "lost to life and use and name and fame". This on the whole benevolent enchanter was adopted as a congenial figure in more artificial romances, such as Spenser's *Fairy Queen* and the Italian poems. In Italy also became naturalized Arthur's sister, Morgan-le-Fay, who, as the *Fata Morgana*, has given her name to a meteoric mirage seen on the Sicilian and Calabrian coasts. Arthur himself grew to be familiar on the Continent, as may be guessed from his effigy on Maximilian's tomb in the Hofkirche of Innspruck.

The story of Tristram's adventures makes another interpolation, a tale more moving than edifying. Tristram, by means of a love potion, becomes inconveniently enamoured of the fair Yseult of Ireland, betrothed to his uncle, King Mark of Cornwall, who is to him throughout "a little more than kin and less than kind". Uncles, no more than stepmothers, are favoured by old writers of fiction. But Mark had cause for ill will against his nephew, whose offence sympathetic romancers seek to tone down by making this uncle cowardly and treacherous. Tristram's first acquaintance with Yseult came through her curing him of a sore wound. When again hurt by a poisoned arrow, he places himself in the surgical care of another lady doctor of the same name, distinguished as "Yseult of the White Hands", who practises in Brittany as her rival in Ireland. Being cured by this Yseult, Tristram feels bound to marry her, but deserts her, returning to singe his wings in the illicit love of his uncle's wife. After many misfortunes and exploits, including a fit of madness, he dies of a broken heart, a more romantic version of the story than Tennyson's, which makes him treacherously murdered by the jealous husband. Then, the guilty queen dying also of grief, both of them are buried in one tomb, shaded under a tree that, as often as it was cut down, next morning would be found flourishing greenly as ever. Tristram also passed with great acceptation into foreign romance, carrying with him his renown as harper, hunter, and lover. In Malory, he and Lancelot are the two greatest knights in the world, who well know each other's worth, and strive to rival one another in courtesy as in glory. But here we do not find all the story of Tristram's life, which some have judged the most beautiful of chivalric romances. It has peculiar features and marks of high antiquity. There are bows and arrows in it, and dogs, elsewhere rather overshadowed by the horses of chivalry. By his name the hero seems to have anticipated Cervantes' "Knight of the Sorrowful Countenance", for *Tristram* has some implication of a destiny to sorrow. It was given to the youngest son of Louis IX, as born in the darkest days of his Crusade.

Lancelot, who so often takes a hand in the adventures of other knights, is always the most towering figure, that not immaculate hero that wins our hearts above the blameless virtues of the king, so trustful, so noble, so easily deceived. The whole history of Lancelot, a French contribution to the British legend, does not come into the *Morte d'Arthur*, but is told in romances where he plays the title rôle. In them is celebrated his friendship with Sir Galahaut, a name once so famous as to appear in Dante, but Malory makes little of it. Son of King Ban, in childhood he was benevolently kidnapped by a mysterious lake fairy, who reared him in her watery palace, whence he had the cognomen Lancelot of the Lake. He comes to own the castle of Joyous Gard in the north, originally the Dolourous Gard, but it changed its name when he destroyed the baneful enchantments that beset the place. There are even hints of his being a Scottish laird on a large scale, while Malory bestows on him great dominions in France, of which the capital (*Benoic*) is Anglicized as Benwick in the *Morte d'Arthur*. Brought in youth to the court of King Arthur, he gets the name of the "Handsome Lad" at once, as is the way with other young unknown knights, proving his quality to general recognition, and drawing on himself the bright eyes of Guinevere. Their secret love, made more of by the French romancers than by Malory, is the rift that will break up that goodly fellowship of the Round Table. But for long Arthur remains unsuspicious of its chief member, who has intrigues with other ladies to excite the queen's jealousy. In some stories Guinevere has a double, who complicates the scandals of this court. Through a period of years that, accurately counted, would have brought him to decrepit age, Lancelot stands out as the flower of chivalry, the knight without fear or reproach, but for that one sin, the champion whose fearlessness we never forget in the most debasing circumstances. In his guilt, in his penitence, in the madness that comes upon him as on so many other heroes, he is always great. And when at last his brother, having sought him seven years through England, Scotland, and Wales, finds him lying dead in the choir of his castle church, our hearts cannot but throb with the cry that makes his noble epitaph. "Sir Launcelot, there thou liest, that were never matched of earthly knight's hand; and thou were the courtiest knight that ever bare shield; and thou were the truest friend to thy lover that ever bestrode horse; and thou were the truest lover of a sinful man that ever loved woman; and thou were the kindest man that ever strake with sword; and thou were the goodliest person ever

came among press of knights; and thou was the meekest
man and the gentlest that ever ate in hall among ladies;
and thou were the sternest knight to thy mortal foe that
ever put spear in the rest."

Malory's story is spiritualized by the Holy Grail,
flitting like a will-o'-the-wisp through scenes dark with
peril and bloodshed. Out of older mythology, pious
legend recast this as the cup from which Christ drank at
the Last Supper, treasured by Joseph of Arimathea,
and brought to Britain to work miracles, not always
worthy of the sacred blood that filled it. Even in
Malory its metal is sometimes debased, as when, the
Holy Grail passing through Arthur's hall, "it was suddenly filled with good odours, and every knight had such
meats and drinks as he loved best", in virtue of a talisman not more celestial than the horn that fills with wine
at the wish of some enchanter's favourite. But Malory
has passed on to Tennyson lofty imaginations of this
mystery, which makes a test to try the shortcomings of
mere knightly valour. The quest for it is vainly undertaken by any but the pure in heart. When we accompany Sir Lancelot into the Chapel Perilous, through a
shadowy crowd of gigantic black knights filling the
churchyard, and see a corpse lying before a dimly lighted
altar, and feel the earth quaking under us, we recognize
a superstition far more powerful than the enchantments
that turned poor Don Quixote's brain. Against such
tawdry marvels mortal knights can be brave enough; but
the bravest of the Round Table is not lowered in our
eyes by his trembling "right hard when the deadly flesh
began to behold the spiritual things". Lancelot and
his fellows have but tantalizing visions of the Grail; the
quest of it is fully achieved by his son alone, Sir Galahad,
that maiden knight, and by him when near to death.

Since then no man has ever been found worthy of that revelation.

> A gentle sound, an awful light!
>   Three angels bear the holy Grail:
> With folded feet, in stoles of white
>   On sleeping wings they sail.
> Ah, blessed vision! blood of God!
>   My spirit beats her mortal bars,
> As down dark tides the glory slides,
>   And star-like mingles with the stars.

From this glorification of the maiden knight we can guess how monks as well as minstrels had a hand in the elaboration of the old romances. Malory is at his best in such mystic conceptions, where the very vagueness of his narrative heightens the effect of supernatural fancies exhaling like mists among wild mountain scenery to shroud the impressive ceremonies of the Church. This author, or editor, whose archaic style has been praised by Scott for " simplicity bordering on the sublime ", did his best to extract the ore from older materials, to be still further refined by Tennyson and other modern poets. Readers of the *Idylls of the King*, unacquainted with the originals, hardly know what arts of selection and sublimation have here gone to tone those gracious pictures of a past that never was. Moving as Malory proves in parts, it needs a robust youthful appetite for deeds of violence to stomach all the hacking and hewing that fills every second page, and to overlook the monotony, the repetitions, and the anachronisms that did not repel his generation. A whole chapter may be quoted, almost at random, as sample of one main interest so shocking to Roger Ascham in this " crude farrago of incongruous materials ", as J. M. Ludlow qualifies it.

And then they put their spears in the rests, and came together with their horses as fast as they might run, and either smote other in the midst of their shields, that both their horses' backs brast under them and the knights were both astonied, and as soon as they might avoid their horses they took their shields afore them, and drew out their swords, and came together eagerly, and either gave other many strong strokes, for there might neither shields nor harness hold their strokes. And so within awhile they had both grimly wounds and bled passing grievously. Thus they fared two hours or more, trasing and rasing either other where they might hit any bare place. Then at the last they were breathless both, and stood leaning on their swords.

"Now, fellow," said Sir Turquine, "hold thy hand awhile, and tell me what I shall ask thee."

"Say on."

Then Turquine said, "Thou art the biggest man that ever I met withal, and the best breathed, and like one knight that I hate above all other knights; so be it that thou be not he I will lightly accord with thee, and for thy love I will deliver all the prisoners that I have, that is threescore and four, so thou wilt tell me thy name. And thou and I we will be fellows together, and never to fail the while that I live."

"It is well said," said Sir Launcelot, "but sithen it is so that I may have thy friendship, what knight is he that thou so hatest above all other?"

"Faithfully," said Sir Turquine, "his name is Sir Launcelot du Lake, for he slew my brother Sir Carados at the dolorous tower, that was one of the best knights on live; and therefore him I except of knights, for may I once meet with him the one of us shall make an end of other, I make mine avow. And for Sir Launcelot's sake I have slain an hundred good knights, and as many I have maimed all utterly that they might never after help themselves, and many have died in prison, and yet I have three-score and four, and all shall be delivered, so thou wilt tell me thy name, so it be that thou be not Sir Launcelot."

"Now see I well," said Sir Launcelot, "that such a man I might be that I might have peace; and such a man I might be that there should be war mortal betwixt us; and now, Sir Knight, at thy request I will that thou wit and know that I am Launcelot

SIR LANCELOT DU LAKE

CHARLEMAGNE

du Lake, king Ban's son of Benwick, and very knight of the Table Round.   And now I defy thee, do thy best."

"Ah," said Turquine, "Launcelot, thou art unto me most welcome that ever was knight, for we shall never part till the one of us be dead."   Then they hurtled together as two wild bulls, rashing and lashing with their shields and swords that sometimes they fell both over their noses.   Thus they fought still two hours and more, and never would have rest, and Sir Turquine gave Sir Launcelot many wounds that all the ground there as they fought was all bespeckled with blood.

Even more sanguinary appears the career of the French paladins who, on Continental soil, had to carry out such sweeping slaughter of paynim foes, deserving as little courtesy as pity.   But before passing on to this "matter of France", we must remember that Malory by no means exhausts the stories, French or British, of Arthur and his knights, so our selection is to be chosen from various sources.

II. Romances of Charlemagne

For France, Charlemagne and his Peers take the place of Arthur and the Round Table in Britain.   Charles the Great has the advantage of being an historical personage and living in a dawning light of knowledge, yet his story as told by romance is little less misty than Arthur's.   As matter of fact this emperor was a Teutonic prince, speaking a German mother tongue, and having his favourite residences on the Rhine; but French pride soon adopted him as a national hero with his capital at Paris and the glory of a French crown, not yet existent, by which these stories were dignified as "Romances royal".   At the core of his fabled exploits seems to be the fame of his grandfather, Charles Martel, that mighty hammer of the

heathen; and their renown in romance became swollen by
confused memories of separate succeeding Charleses who
from German Frankland shifted the seat of their power
into the modern France.

The earliest authority given for this perverted history
is the chronicle ascribed to one Archbishop Turpinus, or
Turpin, which seems as authentic as the tale of our Dick
Turpin's ride to York.   A clerical origin might be indicated by the fact of a theological as distinguished from
a moral element being more conspicuous here than in the
stories of Arthur.   All Arthur's mind at death is clouded
by a doubt; while the heroes of Charlemagne's court are
apt to expire in a more edifying way, their souls carried
off not by mysterious half-heathen queens but by angels
and archangels.   In these romances the part of fell foes,
duly discomfited, is played by Saracens almost as invari-
ably as Red Indians used to figure in American stories of
adventure.   Saracens do casually appear in stories of The
Round Table, notably the bold Sir Palamides, whom the
fair Iseult, with a rare touch of feeling, is unwilling to
see slain offhand because he has not been christened.
When the powerful Moors of Spain seriously threatened
Christian Europe by their invasions, all unbelievers were
readily included under the name of Saracen, a more formidable one in France than across the Channel.   Charlemagne had to do with veritable turbaned followers of the
Prophet, who actually came near to overrunning southern
France as well as Spain, and who were in some respects
the superiors of the Christian neighbours that held them
in such hateful contempt.   But the real Charlemagne
wars more often with Saxons, whom he forced to be
baptized in troops, and in one case had four to five thousand of them executed as hopeless miscreants.   Vague
traditions of his civilizing massacres between the Rhine

and the Elbe, and of his expeditions for the protection of
the Pope, by whom he was crowned Emperor at Rome,
are magnified through a halo of romance as Crusades in
Palestine, Italy, and most famously in Spain, where in
fact his arms did encounter the Crescent, but with no
such overwhelming victories as legend heaps upon his
name.

Romance represents the great Charles as of supernatural stature and strength, a true king of men, at least
in the earlier part of his legendary career. Yet, as in the
case of Arthur, his own prowess is eclipsed by his peers or
companions ; and in some stories he figures as playing,
like Agamemnon, the tyrant rather than the hero. The
most illustrious exploits are achieved by the twelve peers,
a number no doubt suggested by the Apostles. It would
be vain to give the names of these mostly quite unhistoric
worthies, who vary in different tales, and are killed off in
battle or driven to rebellion so often as to make frequent
vacancies in the order. As most renowned may be mentioned Archbishop Turpin, the supposed chronicler of
the brotherhood ; Duke Naymes, the Nestor of Charles's
court and his wise counsellor ; the traitor Ganilon, or
Gan, who turns out a Judas ; Ogier the Dane, who, as
Holger, has become a national hero of Denmark, but is
suspected of belonging to the Ardennes ; and Oliver, the
Patroclus of Roland, who stands out as Achilles of this
legend.

A piece of Roland's sword is still shown at the church
of Rocamadour, in Guienne; but so could Ipswich point
to the green gate at which Sam Weller encountered Job
Trotter. The most that can be said for the French hero's
fame is that it may not be altogether a myth. His name
flits once across the page of history in the uncouth form
of *Hruodlandus*, whom Eginhard styles " Prefect of the

Breton marches ", when casually mentioning his death at
Roncesvalles in A.D. 778.   Against the Saracens of Spain
Charles had carried a campaign as far as Saragossa, then,
on his return through the gorges of the Pyrenees, a band
of wild Basque mountaineers fell upon his rearguard, cut
it to pieces, and plundered the baggage.   Half a century
later a similar disaster befell a French army in the same
pass, and these acts of unromantic brigandage ran together, perhaps with the memory of other Pyrenean
skirmishes, to make the oft-sung battle of Roncesvalles,
celebrated also, from another point of view, in a Basque
ballad.

"They come! they come! what a hedge of spears!   How
the rainbow-hued banners float in the midst!   What lightning
flashes from the weapons!   How many are there?   Child, reckon
them well!"   One, two, three, four, five, six, seven, eight, nine,
ten, eleven, twelve, thirteen, fourteen, fifteen, sixteen, seventeen,
eighteen, nineteen, twenty!

"Twenty, and thousands more besides!   One should lose
time in reckoning them.   Let us unite our sinewy arms, let us
uproot these rocks, let us fling them from the mountain tops upon
their very heads!   Crush them!   Kill them!

"And what had they to do in our mountains, these men of
the North?   Why are they come to disturb our peace?   When
God makes mountains, it is that men may not cross them.   But
the rocks rolling, they overwhelm the troops; blood streams, flesh
quivers.   Oh, how many crushed bones!   What a sea of blood!

"Flee, all to whom strength remains, and a horse!   Flee,
King Karloman, with thy black plumes and thy red mantle.
Thy nephew, thy bravest, thy darling, Roland, is stretched dead
yonder.   His courage was of no avail."

On such slight foundation seems built up the towering edifice of a fame that loomed so large through
Christendom for centuries, and gave a theme to so many
bards, under whose handling Roland's story grew like

a huge tree from a tiny grain of fact. Eginhard names two other officers as killed in that combat, but neither of them won such renown as somehow gathered about the Latinized name that came again to be Italianized as *Orlando*, and made Spanish as *Roldan*. Rotolando is another resounding *alias*.

How this hero was akin to Charles does not appear in history. The Roland of romance was his nephew as son of his sister Bertha by Duke Milon. The king's domestic affections were so strong that he did not favour marriages in his family, if we are to believe his secretary Eginhard, who may have had some cause to dwell on the point, as in legend he is credited with falling into disgrace by stealing the heart of one of his master's daughters. Milon and Bertha likewise are said to have incurred the king's displeasure by a runaway match, so that they had to wander into exile and poverty with their child Roland. The father being accidentally drowned, the mother found herself reduced to such straits that she sent little Roland to beg for food in the nearest town. Charles sat feasting in his hall, when the boy, dressed in parti-coloured rags, appeared among the guests, not hanging back in shame like a common beggar, but boldly walking up to the king and carrying off the dish that stood before him, by way of making himself quite at home. He returned in the same unceremonious manner to snatch up the royal goblet, amid general astonishment; but his impudence set Charles laughing.

" You behave as if you were in a forest, where dishes of meat may be plucked like berries from a bush, and wine runs in streams like water."

" It is for my mother," was all Roland's explanation.

" She must be the queen of beggars," said Charlemagne, and sent his knights to fetch her.

When she came before him, to fall at his feet without a word, the king loudly reproached himself with having mocked his own blood in the person of this ragged varlet, whose boldness had won his favour; and forthwith all was forgotten and forgiven.

Another story begins Roland's exploits while his father was still alive and not banished from the court. Charles had heard of a giant in the Ardennes, whose shield was set with a marvellous jewel the king desired to possess. Half a dozen of the peers set out on the giant-robbing errand, among them Milon, who took little Roland with him as page. On the way, while his father lay sleeping under an oak, Roland was aware of the giant coming through the forest. The precocious warrior did not trouble to wake Milon, but got on his great horse, taking his shield and spear for the combat. The giant laughed at the sight of such a puny adversary, but he laughed on the wrong side of the mouth when the boy cut off his left hand, and with it went the shield containing that jewel talisman that was the secret of his strength. As the monster ran to pick up his precious shield, Roland brought him to the ground by a cut behind the knees, then was able to hew off his head. Hiding the jewel under his clothes, he washed his hands in a stream and went back to fall asleep beside his father, as if nothing particular had happened. When Milon awoke, he exclaimed bitterly on himself as disgraced; but still the boy did not tell him what had happened during his nap. The other knights, returning from their bootless quest, found the bleeding trunk of the giant and brought home, one his gauntlet, one his sword, one his spear, and one his shield, as trophies by which they each claimed success in the adventure. But the jewel was missing, till it appeared shining like the sun as the boss of Milon's shield, to the amazement of himself as of all the rest, who hailed him vanquisher of the giant.

"Where got you this, boy?" he asked of Roland, who answered: "Don't be angry, father, that I killed the big fellow while you were asleep!"

There are variants of the story of Roland's youth quite inconsistent with each other. In one his father has to support the family as a poor woodcutter; in another he dies gloriously fighting against Breton rebels. One account makes the widow marry Ganilon the traitor, who thus becomes Roland's stepfather; but we may understand that there is no love lost between them. Again, on Charlemagne's return from Rome, we are told, in a certain town his hospitable board is visited by thirty boys, whose leader excites admiration by his strength, smartness, and good appetite. He turns out to be the emperor's nephew, and leads him to his parents' retreat. At the sight of his undutiful sister, Charles is moved to draw blade upon her seducer; whereupon, like a young lion, Roland flies at his uncle, holding his hand in such a violent grasp that blood bursts from under the nails, a feat which turns wrath to pride in the courage of that promising scion.

At all events, the boy was recognized and adopted by Charles, soon to show himself worthy of his favour. On Whitsunday a fierce Moorish ambassador arrives with fell defiance from the Soldan, who declares that, already holding the greater part of Asia, Africa, and Europe, he means to be master of the rest, so demands submission from the Christian king. Charles turns pale with wrath, but, at the prompting of Duke Naymes, restrains himself to answer that he will meet the Saracens in battle at Aspramonte. Before setting out, he bids Turpin shut up Roland in the donjon of Laon, along with four more noble youths, as prisoners, to keep them from sharing the perils of such an expedition. But when they hear the trumpets of the army and the neighing of the chargers, and see the warriors prancing by the windows of their prison, they are wild to follow to the field. In vain the porter bids them go play in the garden. They try first to bribe and coax him; then get loose by the simple method of knocking him down. Falling in with five Breton horsemen, the young fire-eaters go to fisticuffs with them for their horses, upon which these boys take leave to gallop off where glory waits them.

The army has got a good start of them, but in the thick of the battle, just as Charlemagne, like to be overcome by Yaumont, the Soldan's son, cries for help to heaven, up dashes Roland in the nick of time. Like a falcon on its prey he swoops at Yaumont, kills him of course, and from him takes the matchless sword Durandal, which is to serve Christendom so well. Girt with this good blade, Roland is dubbed knight by his proudly grateful uncle; then in the final encounter St. George, with invisible hand on his bridle, leads the young hero on to signal victory.

Thus launched on his career, Roland's next exploit was to serve as his uncle's champion against Oliver, nephew of a disobedient vassal; and the courteous duel ended in their becoming bosom friends for life. To Oliver's sister, Alda, Roland is duly betrothed; but so far as appears they could not have seen much of each other, as the hero is constantly away fighting the Saracens, for seven years at one stretch, in Spain and elsewhere.

The chief exploit attributed to him in these wars is the conquest and conversion of a giant, who, in Pulci's *Morgante Maggiore*, the first of the Italian poems that take Roland for hero, becomes his devoted squire to

follow him on other adventures.   In a ruder legend, the
Moorish Goliath is named Ferracutus.   Elsewhere, he
appears as the Saracen king's son, giving a name to the
romances of Ferumbras and Fierabras, which are practi-
cally the same story.   In them, indeed, Roland does not
play the most noble part, for, having taken offence at
some scolding from his uncle, he refuses to go forth
against the defying Philistine, and leaves this duty to be
done by Oliver.   The champion of the Crescent, for all
his bulk, is of course laid low; but Oliver seems so
hard pressed by a treacherous onset of the Saracens that
Roland spurs to his aid; then, overcome by numbers,
both are taken prisoners.   The same fate falls upon the
rest of the peers whom Charles sends to demand the release of these two; when the Emir claps them all in a
loathsome dungeon as hostages for his captive son and
threatens to put them to a shameful death.   His daughter
Floripas, however, they find a friend in need: it is almost
a matter of course in romance that a pagan princess
should take pity on Christian captives to the point of
tricking and deserting her father.   She leads the prisoners
out of their dungeon into a strong tower, which they hold
against all the Emir's force till Charlemagne's army comes
to their release.   Her gigantic brother, by this time baptized and enlisted in the orthodox service, does good
service against his own father; and Floripas herself ends
by marrying Sir Guy of Burgundy, with whom she had
already fallen in love on happening to witness his prowess
in a tournament at Rome.   The unnatural daughter, well
content with her husband, actually cries out for her
father's execution; but her brother, as becomes a new-
made Christian knight, begs that the Emir shall at all
events be baptized.

    For a time the army has to do without Roland's

services, if we are to believe all the stories. This hero has the defects of his qualities in being rash, outspoken, and impatient; so he sometimes fell into quarrel with his uncle, who on one such occasion strikes him across the face with his gauntlet. Red with anger, he lays his hand on his sword, and would have struck the king but for the consideration: "It was he who nourished me when I was a boy!" Yet this affront drives him from the camp like Achilles; he wanders off to fight for his own hand in far-off lands; he reaches Mecca, interferes forcibly in its local politics, and pushes matters so far as to become governor of Persia. But in all these triumphs he cannot think without tears of Charlemagne, of Oliver, and of France; while the French chivalry, we are told, long to see him again as a mother to see her child. Returning to Europe, after a due visit to Jerusalem, he is luckily shipwrecked on the coast of Spain, and easily rejoins the army, to be received with universal joy. This vagary of his is the cue for later Italian poets in taking him off to lands known and unknown, reached with as much ease as Rome or Saragossa, when knights are assisted in their distant travels by griffins, fairy horses, swans sent from heaven to tow a shipwrecked hero into harbour, and charms which in a moment call a powerful enchanter to his support, a kind of machinery we shall find much used in the romance of Huon of Bordeaux.

Roland's career ends with the ambuscade at Ronces-valles, where valour is undone by the treachery of Ganilon or Gan, in some stories his stepfather, in others a jealous rival. That name was execrated like Judas all over Middle-Age Europe. Dante puts Ganilon in the lowest depths of Inferno; and Don Quixote "would have given his housekeeper, and his niece into the bargain, for a fair chance of kicking the traitor". Sent to arrange a treaty

with the Saracen king, Ganilon suggests his cutting off
the rearguard of Charles's army on its retreat across the
Pyrenees.   Well knew that traitor how Roland's audacity
would claim the post of danger.   The plot is carried out;
with twenty thousand choice warriors the hero falls in
the pass of Roncesvalles.   With his last breath he sounds
his ivory horn for help, so loudly that it is heard on the
other side of the mountains; then Charles returns only
in time to take sore vengeance for the flower of his army
cut down in that fatal gorge.   At the news of her lover's
death, the fair Alda falls lifeless, according to French
stories.   In a well-known German legend, the lady's
name is Hildegunde, and she at the mournful news retires into a convent.   But the news in this case turns out
false : Roland comes back safe and sound to find his
beloved the bride of heaven; then from the castle of
Rolandseck he spends the rest of his life in gazing at the
walls of her cloister, till he sees her bier borne forth, and
never spoke another word, soon dying of a broken heart.

As in the *Morte d'Arthur*, and in the catastrophe of
the *Nibelungenlied*, the romantic glory of this reign ends
with a scene of tragic destruction.   But Milton's history
and geography were alike at fault when he has it that
Charlemagne "with all his peerage fell by Fontarabia",
which is brought so near Roncesvalles by a stretch of
poetic licence.   The emperor lived through another generation, to die in his bed at a good old age, after half a
century's reign.   The romancers make him two hundred
years old ; and even in his early Spanish wars he is represented as having a long white beard.   In many stories he
is degraded below the level of his historic fame, coming
to exhibit himself in old age as obstinate and resentful,
yet weak and easily led by evil counsellors, faults of
which there is some hint even in his prime, but which

should seem to have grown upon him in his dotage. What is thus subtracted from his character is added to the glory of his reign and the extent of his dominions, that include England in romantic history. As at the court of Arthur Queen Guinevere was the weak point, so Charlemagne shows a fatal fondness for his ill-conditioned son Charlot, through whose misdeeds the king gets much into hot water with his peers, provoking them to rebellions in which he does not appear to advantage. This means that a minstrel had to please his patrons, the great barons, by glorifying their real or fabled ancestors ; and in those days the nobility of France were by no means so obsequiously subservient as the courtiers of the Grand Monarch. So a favourite theme of romance is Charlemagne's being foiled and defied by disloyal vassals.

Of these stories the most often told was the long feud between Charlemagne and the Four Sons of Aymon, personages less popular on this side of the Channel than in Germany and France, where a common signboard and a familiar chap-book illustration show all four brothers riding on one horse. Their names were Renaud, Richard, Alard, and Guichard. Their father, Aymon, was Count of Dordogne, and they had for cousin Maugis, an enchanter who practised his black art against Charlemagne out of an old grudge for the death of his own father. He it was who had caught and tamed Bayard, Renaud's most serviceable steed, that figures so largely in their adventures.

Brought up in the Ardennes, the four youths come to court, are knighted by the king, and bid fair for favour till they incur his rancorous wrath. One day, over a game of chess, Renaud quarrels with Charles's nephew Bertolais, and answers an insulting speech by laying him dead with the chessboard. After this he has nothing for

THE KNIGHT ERRANT

"LAUS DEO!"

it but to leap on Bayard's back and gallop off with his
brothers to their father's castle.   But Aymon, though in
his own youth he has been a bit of a rebel, is now too
loyal to the angry king to protect them; and their mother
herself bids them begone for fear of bringing ruin on the
house, of which Renaud takes farewell with tears—a rare
stroke of sentiment in romance.

They wander through the Ardennes; they build a
stronghold for themselves on a rock above the Meuse;
they live by hunting in the forests.   But the troops of
Charles track them to their lair, besieging them till, driven
out by starvation, they again take to the woods, chased
by their own father, who at the price of his sons' blood
would win the king's favour.   They escape, to suffer
sore straits of cold and hunger through the hard winter.
Their armour grows rusty; their clothes fall to pieces;
under hail and rain their skins turn black and hairy like
bears.   All their steeds die except Bayard, that seems to
thrive on withered leaves as common horses on corn, so
it can carry all four brothers at a pinch.

When summer comes they slink to their home, to
throw themselves on their mother's mercy.   She hardly
knows them at first in such a miserable plight, till she
recognizes Renaud by a scar on his forehead made in
childhood.   She cannot refuse to entertain her hungry
sons, but when Aymon comes home, to catch them
devouring like beggars, he breaks out on them with
curses, and orders them from the house.   The mother,
however, is able to clothe and equip her boys before
sending them out into the world; thus now they leave
home at the head of a gallant train.

Falling in with Maugis, they travel south and are
able to do good service to Yon, King of Bordeaux,
against his troublesome Saracen neighbours.   In grati-

tude Yon marries his sister Clarice to Renaud, and lets him build a strong castle named Montauban on a rock overlooking the Garonne. The eldest brother is throughout the principal personage, and in its older poetic forms the story is entitled *Renaud de Montauban*; it is in later prosaic versions rather that it becomes *The Four Sons of Aymon*. In Italian poems, Renaud grew still more famous as the Rinaldo, who made also such a favourite popular hero that the open-air reciters of Naples are said to have got the by-name *rinaldi*.

Charles, coming home from a pilgrimage to the shrine of Compostella, in Spain, catches sight of this new-built castle, and is furious to learn that it belongs to the brothers against whom he has vowed dire vengeance. He summons Yon to surrender them, and on his refusal prepares for war. At this point Roland makes his first appearance in the present story. Coming to court, he is recognized by Charles as a worthy nephew, and to find a horse fit for such a promising knight the king holds races at Paris. Renaud cannot resist the temptation of showing off the paces of his matchless steed. Maugis, by enchantment, changes him to a blooming youth, and disguises Bayard by turning every hair white as snow. Of course Bayard wins the race, so Charles would fain buy him. Renaud, in his pride, refuses to sell the horse, proclaims his name, and gallops off, pursued in vain by fifteen thousand cavaliers. This episode does not in the least help on the story, a matter of no great consequence in romance ; then for a time Charles is so much taken up by other wars that he has to leave the Sons of Aymon alone.

Once more at peace, he gathers against the castle of Montauban his whole host of French, Flemings, Germans, Saxons, Bretons, Normans, and English. But

before coming to blows he tries treachery. Yon is persuaded to yield up the brothers ; and, on pretence of peace
and pardon, he lures them out of their stronghold clad
in scarlet mantles and carrying roses in their hands as if
for a holiday occasion. As they come, singing for joy,
they are waylaid and set upon, and have to stand on their
defence, throwing boulders from a rock on which they
ensconce themselves. But their cousin, Ogier the Dane,
who heads the attack, does not press it very hotly, being
secretly in sympathy with his kinsmen ; and Maugis
comes up to their aid in time to save them. Then begins
a long siege of Montauban, pushed by the obstinate anger
of Charles, while Renaud does all in his power to make
peace. In one encounter his brother Richard is taken
prisoner and condemned by the king to be hanged. One
by one the peers refused to carry out this execution,
Roland most loudly of all, who threatens to go over to
the enemy if his uncle persist in such cruelty. A shame-
less minion is found who consents to put the rope round
Richard's neck. At this moment the intelligent horse
Bayard awakes his master by striking its hoof on his
shield. Renaud starts up, to see his brother on the gallows at a great distance ; he springs on his steed, that
with bounds of thirty feet carries him to deliver Richard
and to slay the executioner. The brothers make several
such sallies ; and when their walls hold out stoutly, it
was agreed to decide the war by a duel between Roland
and Renaud. The scene may be quoted, as characteristic
of what to our ancestors were the titbits of such long
stories.

When the day came, Roland rose and went to mass, then he
had himself armed and mounted his horse.

"Nephew," said Charles, "I recommend you to God, to save
you from death and prison, for you know that Renaud is right

and that we are in the wrong: so I would not for the half of my kingdom that any harm should befall you."

"Sire," said Roland, "your repentance is too late; if you knew you were in the wrong you should not have accepted the ordeal of battle; but since the matter has gone so far I cannot leave it without great dishonour. Now may God in His mercy have me in good and holy keeping!"

He found Renaud awaiting him, and cried: "Renaud, to-day you have to do with me."

"Roland," said Renaud, "it does not become such a knight as you to threaten: will you have peace or war? You shall have it as you please."

"Renaud," said he, "I am not come here for peace; you had best beware of me."

"Guard yourself from me likewise," said Renaud, "for to-day I will abate your pride."

Then they spurred their horses, and rushed together with such a shock that their lances broke, and clashed so roughly on their shields that Renaud had to fall to the earth with his saddle between his legs. He quitted his stirrups, got up hastily, remounted Bayard's bare back, and charged against Roland, to whom he gave such a stroke of his sword that Roland was severely wounded, who drew his own sword and ran at Renaud. The combat between them became terrible, for they broke one another's armour in more than a thousand pieces, so that the barons looking on were in pity for them. When Duke Naymes had watched the combat for a long time, he cried out:

"Ah, Charlemagne, accursed be your cruelty, for by your rancour you will cause the death of the two best knights in the world, and you may have need of them one day!"

Renaud, seeing that neither of them could get the better, said to Roland: "If you agree with me, we will fight on foot, so as not to kill our horses, for we shall never be able to find such good ones."

"You are right," said Roland.

When they had dismounted, they rushed upon one another like two lions. Roland, seeing that he could not overcome Renaud, ran against him and caught hold of him. Renaud called out for a wrestle; they struggled together for a long time and neither could make the other fall. Seeing that it was so, they let go and drew back to take breath, for indeed they were tired out; their shields, hauberks, and helmets were all broken; where they had fought the ground was as trampled up as if corn had been thrashed there.

To abridge an episode that might try the modern reader's patience : when Charlemagne on one side, and the brothers of Renaud on the other, fall on their knees to pray for their respective champions, heaven accords a miracle by sending a cloud to hide them from each other, as Olympus had done for the heroes of the *Iliad*. The blinded combatants take the hint to make friends for the moment, Roland begging Renaud to lead him into his castle; and when the cloud clears away, Charlemagne has the amazement of seeing them go off the field together, apparently on the best of terms; but he follows them to shout out : " Renaud, so long as I live you shall never have peace ! " Then the siege is resumed with fresh vigour.

In another encounter Renaud overcomes Charles himself, but lets him go unhurt, so great is his inbred reverence for that ill-tempered sovereign. More formidable is the enchanter Maugis, who slinks into the king's camp disguised as a beggar, a pilgrim, a leper, or what-not, steals the royal crown and the swords of Turpin, Oliver, Ogier, and Roland, and finally, throwing Charles into an enchanted sleep, brings him bodily within the castle. The amazed king awakes to find himself a prisoner; but the four brothers kneel at his feet, begging him to make peace. "I will give you Montauban; I will give you Bayard; I will leave France; I will set out for the Holy Sepulchre," promises Renaud. But Charles, though at their mercy, still shows himself proudly inflexible, and does not even evince gratitude when the brothers let him free. " Go," said Renaud; " when it pleases God and you, we shall be friends!"

But now the garrison loses its potent ally Maugis, who, repenting of his practice in sorcery, goes off to become a hermit. Assault after assault is ordered by the ungrateful king. Worst of all, food runs short within the walls. The defenders have neither corn, nor oats, nor wine: the children are heard crying for bread, and daily they die of hunger. The knights have to eat their horses; there is even question of butchering the peerless Bayard, as Renaud's wife and children implore him to do, when they have all gone hungry for three days. Renaud draws his sword to slay the faithful beast, but has not the heart to strike when it welcomes him with a joyful neigh. He contents himself with bleeding Bayard and living on its blood for a fortnight, till the poor horse is nothing but skin and bone. All the survivors are in no better state, when an old inhabitant remembers, rather late, a subterranean passage by which they can escape from the castle. So they do, and when Charles enters at last, it is to find nothing but starved corpses.

But the implacable king seeks out his enemies in a new retreat, and there is more fighting, which the modern reader may be glad to have cut short. In turn one of the peers, Richard of Normandy, is captured by the brothers, who send to tell his master that they will hang him unless peace be granted them. Charles refuses their terms, and the condemned prisoner behaves in a manner recalling Barnardine's obstinacy in *Measure for Measure*. Richard, while playing chess with Renaud's son, Yonnet, is summoned to come and be hanged, and at first does not condescend to answer; but when the messengers lay hands on him, declaring that they must be drunk to interrupt him in his game, he kills three of them off-hand, and calls for his servant to throw their bodies out of the window.   Renaud has to come himself before the violent peer will consent to be bound and brought to the gallows, where he seems to remain in suspense all the time necessary for prolonged negotiations with the court.   Hanging, to Middle-Age minds, was always an excellent joke.   But the most comic character in this story is the enchanter Maugis, who, when taken prisoner by Charles, and sentenced to be hanged next morning, appears not in the least put out, but goes to sleep with the utmost coolness, for he knows as well as the reader that, before the hour of execution comes, he will by his arts send the whole army to sleep ; after which, chaining Charlemagne to his bedpost before awakening him, he can load two or three horses with the most precious spoils of the camp and ride off at his ease, the king left to stamp and shout without being able to rouse one of his entranced warriors.

To return to Richard of Normandy, kept waiting so long with the rope round his neck and his game at chess unfinished, his fate depending on an unworthy master's temper.   Another messenger is sent to Charles, whose evil councillors would have him still harden his heart. But now the peers mutiny in a body, moved by the peril of their comrade Richard.   " Sire," exclaimed the in-dignant Roland, " I give up your service without taking leave ! "   Thus pressed, the king grants their wish and, in modern phrase, changes his ministry by sending his chief bad adviser, bound hand and foot, to be at the disposal of the peers.   Then, since so it must be, he consents to make peace with the sons of Aymon, on con-dition that Renaud departs for Jerusalem.   The mar-

vellous horse Bayard is also to be given up to the king,
who has a last fling of spite by throwing it, with a mill-
stone tied round its neck, into the Meuse.   But the good
horse breaks the stone with its hoofs, swims to land, and
gallops off into the forest, where still, on dark windy
nights, it may be heard trampling and snorting through
the valleys of the Ardennes.

There is yet a good deal more of the romance, which
now takes a religious turn, following the fortunes of
Renaud alone.   He goes to fight in the Holy Land,
where he plays the part of Godfrey of Bouillon against
the unbeliever.   He comes back to find his wife dead
and his sons beset by enemies, yet able to take good care
of themselves.   Covered with glory, and settled in peace,
the hero now proposes to retire from the world, devoting
himself to the salvation of his soul.   In poor attire, barefoot, he steals away from his castle, wandering off to
Cologne, where he finds a cathedral in construction.   By
way of pious exercise he hires himself to the masons as
a hodman, carrying the heaviest burdens, with daily bread
for his only pay.   But his fellow workmen are jealous
of his strength ; they kill him with their hammers and
throw his body into the Rhine.   It floats miraculously,
shedding an unearthly light, accompanied by angelic
chants, and wherever it passes the church bells ring of
themselves, the sick are cured, the lame walk and the
blind see, till it comes on shore to be recognized by the
brothers of Renaud, who thus from a hero is transfigured
to a saint.

In another romance, Maugis carries his repentance so
far as to be made Pope, while the three younger sons of
Aymon, falling out again with the king, are smoked to
death in a cave.   Even without this appendix, it will be
seen how the whole story is too long to be told here in

full. There are others like it, turning on Charles's injustice to his peers and paladins, who seem more often in the right of it and play the nobler part, while their rebellion may be strangely chequered by scruples of loyalty to the Lord's anointed. In one legend, both of France and Germany, the great king is put through a singular adventure, awakened at night by an angel, who tells him it is the will of heaven that he go out at once to steal. Furthermore, he is given as companion a real robber, who leads him to a castle where their attempt at burglary leads to Charles overhearing a plot against himself, which by this curious miracle he is enabled to foil, and to hang the conspirators. Those imaginations reflect the troubled history of feudal Europe before his dismembered empire was consolidated into the two realms of France and Germany, powers still in the making during the heyday of romance.

Another cycle of the romance of the peers has for its centre William of Orange, a figure in which again there seems to be some core of historic fact swollen to mythical greatness by the confusion of various personalities. He is represented as one of the four sons of Aimeri, another turbulent imperial vassal. But William's deeds are chiefly ascribed to the reign of Charlemagne's feeble son Louis. His field of activity is the south of France and the north of Spain, so long in dispute with the Moslem. He wins the city of Orange and marries Orable, its Saracen queen, an old sweetheart, of whose people he is the lifelong foe. He got the by-name of William Shortnose, through the loss of his nose in combat with a paynim giant, that feature having been left untouched when the Pope undertook to make him invulnerable by rubbing him over with a holy relic. There is a great deal of rather coarse buffoonery in his legend, notably at the end of it, where, after his wife's death, William becomes a monk but scandalizes the cloister by his rude and masterful manners. The most romantic hero in this cycle is his nephew Vivien, who seems modelled after Roland, and like him dies in a battle against hopeless odds. But this tragic episode leads to a farce in which the chief part is played by an obstreperous young giant named Renouard. He was a Saracen by birth, who, being captured and converted, began his career as a scullion in the emperor's household. Here his enormous appetite and clownish ways make a great joke; but jokers had to be careful how they rallied a young monster who thought nothing of knocking a reviler's brains out upon the nearest pillar or throwing an angry cook into his own furnace. Then he took the field to distinguish himself as a Christian champion, brandishing a mighty club, with which he avenged the slaughter of Vivien's comrades.

Mixed with such fooling there are gleams of poetic beauty in this cycle, once very popular in France and also in a German translation, but it has been rather neglected by the later poets who embalmed the fame of Roland and Charlemagne.[1] Victor Hugo, indeed, inserted in his *Legende des Siècles* one episode from what is now best known as a literary curiosity. It was first put into modern prose by the Dutch scholar Jonckbloet, attracted to this theme no doubt by the romantic origin it attributes to the House of Orange, that by marriage was merged in the Nassau family of the Rhine and the Ardennes.

[1] The William legend is evidently to some extent a *replica* of features in the Charlemagne stories. For instance, when William sets out to rescue Vivien from the Saracens, his young brother Guichardet has to be shut up, like the boy Roland, in a vain attempt to keep him out of danger. The chief scene of each cycle is a massacre of Christians brought on by the rashness of heroes who in either case are favourite nephews of their uncles. Alischans, Vivien's battlefield, is identified with Arles, where Turpin buries the victims of Roncesvalles.

III. Romances of the Peninsula

We now come to the romances best known to Don Quixote, of which it may be said in general that, by style and origin, they form a class apart, only at a few points coming into touch with the legends of France and Britain.

Spain had a romantic hero of the first class in Roderigo Diaz of Bivar, called *par excellence* the "Cid" (lord) and the "Campeador" (champion) on the score of his resounding exploits against the Moors. He is an historical or half-historical personage, flourishing about the time of our Norman Conquest, when the Caliphate of Cordova had gone to pieces, but still over the sundered states of the Peninsula ebbed and flowed a chronic feud between the Cross and the Crescent. His victories are celebrated in a noble poem, as in the prose chronicle translated by Southey, and in popular ballads, all of which show him much like a hero of romance. It is told how in boyhood he challenged and slew a nobleman insulting his father; how out of Christian courtesy he slept with a leper, shunned by all else, who revealed himself as a saint, blessing him with such invincibility that Moorish kings and cities went down before his youthful sword; how he had a lion that followed him as a dog, and, like Roland and Ogier, a spirited horse which none could back but himself, as also two peerless swords, "Colada" and "Tizona"; how he fell into disgrace both with his king and with the Pope, who yet were bound to forgive so doughty a defender of Church and Throne; how at a good old age he died in the besieged city of Valencia, then the Christians sallied out with his dead body fastened upright on his famous steed Bavieca, and at the very sight the Moors fled in dismay. In history, indeed, there are some hints of this hero being a sort of aristocratic Robin Hood, who fought sometimes against the Moors but also, for the nonce, against his own people. In any case, the Spaniards take his fame very seriously, whereas he has not made much figure in fiction beyond the Pyrenees, so we may set him aside as a character rather for epic than for romance. French tragedy has seized upon one dramatic feature in his marriage to Ximena after slaying her father: "A man I slew—a man I give!"

Several more shadowy heroes are commemorated in Spanish ballads, that connect some of them with the Pyrenean wars of Charlemagne and his peers. Most famed among these seems to be Gayferos, whose adventures, exhibited in a puppet show, so much excited Don Quixote that he drew his sword to succour the hard-pressed knight, and made costly havoc among the pasteboard Moors. In Spanish romance he appears as a kinsman of Roland, and husband of Charlemagne's daughter Melisenda, who came to be carried off as a Moorish captive to Saragossa. Her captivity had lasted for the approved romantic term of seven years, before the husband was able to retrieve his bride, and then only when stung to action by the reproaches of her father. Finding him one day idly playing *tric trac* with Guarinos, Admiral of the fleet, Charlemagne said bitterly:

"Were you as ready to handle arms as dice, you would go to the rescue of your wife. Many another sought her hand, and had she wedded a braver man, she would not now be in captivity!"

This insult set Gayferos beside himself; he sprang to his feet uttering cries of rage, and rushed off to find his uncle Roland.

"For God's sake," he begged, "lend me your horse

and your arms! My uncle the emperor hath done me wrong, saying that I am good to play but not to fight. You know the truth, that three years I wandered in search of Melisenda through mountains and valleys, till I had worn the shoes from my feet and the nails off my fingers; but never could l find her. Now I know that she is in Saragossa; but I am without horse or arms, since I have lent mine to our kinsman Montesinos[1], who is gone to a tournament in Hungary.

Roland at first shows himself a little churlish to this carpet knight, who has put off the deliverance of his wife so long. He declares that he has made an oath to lend his arms to no one, nor Veillantif his well-trained charger, which another hand might spoil. Gayferos is not so weaponless but that he has still a sword, which in wrath he would have drawn upon his uncle, had not the other peers separated them. Such an exhibition of spirit so much pleased Roland, that after all he agreed to lend horse and arms, and even offered to accompany his nephew on the perilous errand; but Gayferos, to wipe out all suspicion of his courage, was bent on going alone, and vowed not to return without Melisenda.

He travelled in such haste as to do the fortnight's journey to Saragossa in a week, arriving at the city on a Friday, when its king, Almanzor, was going to the mosque with all his knights. The Moslem sabbath may have availed the stranger to let him enter the gates unchallenged; then he soon came upon a Christian captive who directed him to the palace in which his wife was imprisoned. Looking up, he saw her at a window. And the very sight of him set her weeping; not that she knew him with his vizor down, but because his arms and har-

---

[1] This personage, who figures so largely in Don Quixote's imagination, does not appear in the French legends, but seems to be a purely Spanish hero.

ness recalled to her the twelve peers, the palace of her father, and the jousts and feasts there held in honour of her bright eyes. With sorrowful voice she leant out to call him.

"In the name of heaven I pray you, knight, whether you be Moor or Christian, do not reject a charge for which you will be richly paid! If ever you go to France, ask for Don Gayferos, and tell him it is time he should come to deliver me. But if he have forgotten me for another love, take my message to Oliver, to Roland, to the emperor himself, my father; for if I am not ere long delivered, they will make me turn infidel against my will. Seven Moorish kings torment me for my hand, but I can never forget the love of Gayferos."

"Do not weep so, my lady," answered Gayferos. "Your charge you can well lay on me, for I am no other than Gayferos, lord of Paris, cousin of Oliver, and nephew of Roland, and it is my love that has brought me here."

Melisenda, recognizing his voice, joyfully ran down into the street to embrace her long-lost husband. But when he took her in his arms, a "dog of a Moor", set to guard the Christians, raised such an outcry that orders were given to shut the city gates. Gayferos rode seven times round inside the walls without finding a way out, while the Moorish knights, now coming forth from their devotion, got on horseback with a great crash of arms and clang of trumpets.

"Ah!" cried Melisenda; "if it were Roland's horse Veillantif you rode, I have often heard him say that he had only to loosen the girth, open the breastplate, and drive his spurs into its side, then it would leap across any barrier."

This was indeed Veillantif on which he rode, so

Gayferos sprang off to loosen the girth, leapt on without putting foot in stirrup, to hold Melisenda in his arm as he spurred the good steed, and lo! at a bound it cleared the wall of Saragossa.

Off they sped, soon chased by seven troops of Moors; and when the pursuers drew hard at hand, Gayferos set down his wife in a grove, where she kept lifting prayers to heaven while he turned to face the foe. Then such was the virtue of Roland's sword and of Roland's horse that they fled back to the city, leaving the knight and his bride to ride on towards France.

Night and day they rode, speaking together of love and of no other thing, till they stood again upon Christian soil. There Gayferos found his way barred by a knight in white armour, with whom he made ready to fight. But as they drew to an encounter, he knew his own arms, and his own horse recognized him with a neigh, for this was his kinsman Montesinos come to look for him. Embracing each other with all heartiness, they took their way together, all the knights and ladies they met following in their train, and thus triumphantly Don Gayferos brought back to Paris the daughter of Charlemagne, who could no more reproach him as faint-hearted.

The puppet-show version, so we learn from Cervantes, was duly spiced with comic effect. As from the balcony of her prison the lady is casting wistful looks along the road to France, a sly Moor steals behind to give her a kiss that sets her spitting, wiping her mouth, and tearing her hair. Then, on seeing her husband, she is so impatient to join him that her petticoat catches in one of the rails of the balcony, and she hangs dangling in the air head downmost, till Gayferos cuts her loose. Their flight sets the whole city shaking with the ringing of bells in the mosque steeples, which the critical knight of

La Mancha exclaims against as a gross absurdity, declaring that a Moorish alarm would be given not by bells but by kettledrums. "Signor Don Quixote, if you stand upon these trifles we shall never please you," protested the showman. "Have we not thousands of comedies full of such mistakes and blunders, and yet are they not everywhere listened to, not only with applause, but admiration? Go on, boy, and let these folks talk; for, so that my bags are filled, I care not if there be as many absurdities as there are motes in the sun." That was the rule with most *entrepreneurs* of romance.

The Admiral Guarinos of this story—The *Garin* of French romances—was also hero of a daring escape, as known to us by a spirited if somewhat free translation in J. G. Lockhart's *Spanish Ballads*. At Roncesvalles, where he fell with the rest of the peers according to most French authorities, he was captured by seven Moorish kings, who seven times cast lots for him, and the lot gave him captive to one Marlotes. So highly did Marlotes esteem this prisoner of war that he offered him two of his daughters in marriage on condition of his turning Turk. Of course the hero indignantly refused to be false either to his wife or to his creed, and thereupon was cast into a dark dungeon loaded with fetters. Three times only in the year might he see the light of the sun, to wit, on the Moslem feasts of Christmas, Easter, and St. John's Day, when he was led out to make sport for the Philistines. On the seventh Midsummer Day, as aim of one of the exercises with which it was celebrated, Marlotes had set up a quintain so high and strong that none of the Moorish knights could bring it down with their spears; yet the angry king had vowed not to eat till the feat was accomplished. Then the lean and ragged prisoner offered to try his hand, if given his

rusty arms and set upon his trusty steed, which meanwhile had been sold as a " carrion drudge"; if he failed,
let his life be the forfeit.   His offer was taken; and so—

They have girded on his shirt of mail, his cuisses well they've
  clasped,
And they've barred the helm on his visage pale, and his hand the
  lance hath grasped;
And they have caught the old grey horse, the horse he loved of
  yore,
And he stands pawing at the gate, caparisoned once more.

When the knight came out the Moors did shout, and loudly
  laughed the king,
For the horse he pranced and capered, and furiously did fling;
But Guarinos whispered in his ear, and looked into his face,
Then stood the old charger like a lamb, with a calm and gentle
  grace.

Oh! lightly did Guarinos vault into the saddle-tree,
And slowly riding down made halt before Marlotes' knee;
Again the heathen laughed aloud—"All hail, sir knight!" quoth he.
"' Now do thy best, thou champion proud.   Thy blood I look to
  see"—

With that Guarinos, lance in rest, against the scoffer rode,
Pierced at one thrust his envious breast, and down his turban trode.
Now ride, now ride, Guarinos—nor lance nor rowel spare—
Slay, slay, and gallop for thy life.—The land of France lies there!

Another celebrated escaper was Count Fernan Gon-
salez, who more than once got loose from captivity by
help of his devoted wife.   He was not captive to the
Moor, but to a fellow-Christian prince, one of many who
did much confused fighting among themselves as well as
against the Crescent.   The unbeliever here is not always
the stock villain of the piece as in French romances.   The
two creeds, so long at such close quarters, got into
relations of love as well as of war; and Moorish heroines

play their part in a romance that is not purely Christian. Spanish patriotism, too, came to resent the idea of Charlemagne's supposed conquest across the Pyrenees. The real perpetrators of the massacre of Roncesvalles, as we have seen, appear to have been Basques, who were no more Spaniards than they were French; but in some of the Spanish stories of this affair Roland is slain by the hardly less mythical hero Bernardo Del Carpio, who squeezes the invulnerable peer to death in his arms, as becomes the champion of an imaginary Spanish independence against French aggression. He is even understood to have gone over to the Moors, when driven to rebellion by the perfidy of King Alfonso in promising to restore to him his imprisoned father, a promise fulfilled with a senseless corpse.

Ye swore upon your kingly faith to set Don Sancho free,
But curse upon your paltry breath, the light he ne'er did see;
He died in dungeon cold and dim, by Alfonso's base decree,
And visage blind, and stiffened limb, were all they gave to me.

The king that swerveth from his word hath stained his purple
  black;
No Spanish lord will draw the sword behind a Liar's back!
But noble vengeance shall be mine, an open hate I'll show—
The king hath injured Carpio's line, and Bernard is his foe.

Bernardo seems in his right place as hero of an elaborate Spanish poem after the model of Ariosto. More popular ballads give him youthful experiences very familiar in romantic fiction. He had a wicked stepfather who sought to get rid of him by the hand of a soft-hearted murderer, but was duly deceived by the blood of a dog and other false tokens. The boy grew up in secret, and came home, disguised as a pilgrim, just in time to cut off his stepfather's head, when found ill-treat-

ing his mother. Step-parents of both sexes bear a bad
name with poets of all countries.

From these legendary ballads, in which Lancelot as
well as Roland appears among native heroes, let us go
at a bound to the most famous and characteristic fiction
of the Peninsula, *Amadis de Gaul,* which started a new
school of prose romance for Spain. Its origin is matter
of some controversy. By Southey and most writers it is
taken to be the work of the Portuguese Vasco Lobeira,
written by him towards the end of the fourteenth century.
It has been supposed that he copied a French orginal, in
which case France might claim to be the cradle of almost
all romances. An Italian author has also been put forward. Whoever was the begetter of Amadis, he appears
to owe a good deal to the romance of Lancelot, whose
exploits in the *Val des faux Amants,* for instance, evidently suggested the famous enchantments of Apollidon,
and Urganda the Unknown looks like a replica of the
Lady of the Lake. The French and Spanish translators
of Lobeira's work treated it somewhat freely; then came
a cloud of imitators, among whom we cannot always distinguish definite authorship. At all events, the Amadis
romances may be called representatively Spanish in their
colouring, as in the great popularity they obtained among
the peoples of the Peninsula, then the chief maritime
adventurers of the age, while their character was strongly
tinged by a glow of Oriental fancy, congenial to a nation
in whose poetry, as a poet has well said, the Moorish
cymbals can be heard tinkling with the Spanish guitar.

In these fictions, ships and sea fights figure among
giants, dragons, enchantments and other properties of
romance; and the vogue of Amadis tells as plain a tale
as the popularity of Captain Marryat or of J. Fenimore
Cooper in another tongue. A century later the dis-

coverers of America believed themselves to be realizing the wonders now imagined. Its strange fruits and flowers seemed marvellous as those which hung in the enchanted gardens of Apollidon. Its stupendous volcanoes, its earthquakes and hurricanes were like the work of the malignant Archalaus. Its vast swamps and exuberant forests might well prove the abode of some such mysterious sage as Alquife or Urganda. At the sight of Mexico, the companions of Cortes readily recalled a scene from Amadis; and the name of California was bestowed from the same body of romance which supplied Shakespeare with his Florizel and Spenser with his *Masque of Cupid*. In one of the later Amadis stories the scene is shifted to America, for what seems to be the first and last appearance of a knight errant on that continent.

The author of Amadis boldly cut himself loose from conventional traditions of his predecessors, setting up new dynasties over a history and geography of his own, with a mythology also mainly original. If he have any distant ancestry, this hero derives from Arthur rather than from Charlemagne. The central scene of the story, as far as its first books are concerned, is laid in and about Britain, a choice perhaps suggested by the then fresh fame of the Black Prince both in France and Spain; but it is quite an imaginary Britain. The date is expressly put as very soon after the Christian era, though the laws and customs of chivalry appear in full bloom. London, Windsor, Bristol, and other familiar landmarks turn up among some localities quite strange to us, inhabited by personages natural and supernatural, whose names were once household words to diligent readers of romance. But since few readers of this busy generation give much study to the history of Amadis, even in Southey's abridgment, a short summary may not be amiss.

Garinter, King of Brittany, has two daughters, one of whom marries respectably Languines, King of Scotland, and the other, Elisena, is beloved by her father's guest Perion, King of Gaul, which some take to be Wales. There seems no particular reason for this courtship being a clandestine one, except that a hero's birth should be wrapped in romantic mystery. Amadis was born in secret, and by his shamed mother's *confidante* launched out in an ark, like Moses, upon a stream that carried it into the sea, where it was picked up by the Scottish knight Gandales. He took the babe home to be reared with his own son Gandalin; and the two boys grew up inseparable companions. The "Child of the Sea", as he was called in youth, could be recognized for no ordinary foundling, a parchment scroll round his neck declaring him to be son of a king, and his floating cradle containing tokens by which in due time he might be identified. The king and queen of Scotland, his kinsfolk without knowing it, took a fancy to the promising lad, and brought both him and Gandalin to court as companions for their own son Agraies. At this point comes the most realistic scene in the book, even showing a touch of local colour in what looks like a dominie's *tawse*.

When he was seven years old, King Languines and his queen and household, passing through his kingdom from one town to another, came to the castle of Gandales, where they were feasted; but the Child of the Sea, and Gandalin, and the other children were removed to the back court, that they might not be seen. It fortuned that the queen was lodged in one of the highest apartments of the castle, and looking from her window she saw the children at play with their bows, and among them remarked the Child of the Sea for his shapeliness and beauty, and he was better clad than his companions, of whom he looked like the lord. The queen called to her ladies and damsels: "Come and see the fairest creature that ever was seen!" While they were looking at him, the child, who was thirsty, laid down his bow and arrows, and went to a waterpipe to drink. A boy bigger than the rest took up his bow to shoot with it; this Gandalin would not suffer; the other struck him angrily, and Gandalin cried out: "Help me, Child of the Sea!" He hearing this ran to him, and snatched the bow and crying: "In an ill minute did you strike my brother!" struck him on the head with all his force. They fought a while till the other was fain to run away, and meeting their tutor, who asked what was the matter, replied that the Child of the Sea had beat him. The tutor went towards him with the strap in his hand. "How is this, Child of the Sea," said he, "that you dare beat the boys? I shall punish you!" But the Child fell upon his knees. "I had rather you would strike me," said he, "than that anyone before me should dare to beat my brother;" and the tears came in his eyes. The tutor was moved, and told him to do so no more. All this the queen saw, and she wondered why they called him the Child of the Sea.

Amadis of Gaul (Southey's translation).

Meanwhile King Perion had openly married Elisena, and they had another son called Galaor, who was stolen away from them by a giant named Gandalac. This giant had kidnapped the boy to rear him as the avenger of an injury done to himself, and put him to school with a hermit under whose instruction he grew up a mirror of chivalry, to be in due time restored to his sorrowing parents. Perion had another son, named Florestan, who also comes to fight beside his family, after long separation that has no effect but of entangling the story in knots, to be untied by recognitions and surprises. The three brothers perform many of their exploits together, Amadis being also attended by his foster brother, Gandalin, as faithful squire; but again they go apart, so that, as in the Round Table romances, we are always being switched off, first on one, then on another line of adventures.

Perion comes as a visitor to the court of his Scottish brother-in-law, who has also as guest Lisuarte, King of Great Britain, with his daughter Oriana, our heroine. To her young Amadis is assigned as page, who willingly becomes her devoted squire, and gets her to ask Perion to knight him, as the king does, soon repaid by the prowess of the new knight against his enemy Abies, King of Ireland. Having been identified by the tokens in his cradle as Perion's hitherto unknown son, Amadis is presently able to discover and dub as knight his long-lost brother Galaor; then the story is fairly launched on its main stream of interest.

This is the course of love between Amadis and Oriana, in whose father's service the brothers do doughty deeds, favoured by their fairy patroness, Urganda the Unknown, and foiled by the fell enchanter Arcalaus, an enchanter-at-arms, described as "one of the largest knights in the world who were not giants". For purposes of his own, this miscreant stirs up a rebellion against Lisuarte; who, by the arms of the ever-victorious brotherhood, is brought back in triumph to London, a city stated to be at that date "like an eagle above the rest of Christendom", and seat of the king's "Cortes", while his residence was already at Windsor.

Other episodes in the history of Lisuarte's kingdom at that period have been overlooked by our own historians. Amadis and Galaor are always going apart on separate missions, much hindered by their eagerness to have a shy at any rival adventurer that comes across their path. It would take an actuary to calculate the number of men and steeds put *hors de combat* by these two in their errant journeys, which bring Galaor into the arms of too many charmers, while Amadis remains chivalrously faithful to his Oriana. But she, deceived as to his constancy, writes him such a cruel letter that, at the height of his renown, he renounces friends, arms, fame, and all, going off, under the name of Beltenebros, the " Fair Forlorn ", to do penance upon an island called the Poor Rock, inhabited only by a hermit—an unreasonable course of mortification in which he was imitated by Don Quixote.

When this misunderstanding between the lovers has been duly cleared away, Lisuarte, in turn, is misled into quarrel with his champion, and would have married his daughter to a brother of the emperor, whom, of course, the hero confounds and defeats. He carries off Oriana to the Firm Island, a notable home of enchantments, where both were able to achieve the adventures of the Arch of Lovers and of the Forbidden Chamber, to be entered only by the bravest of knights and by the fairest of ladies. After that there was nothing for Lisuarte to say but " Bless you, my children!"

So ends the proper story of Amadis, filling four books with a closely woven network of the adventures of himself and his contemporaries, to be spun out much further by a long string of sequels. The general idea in these is that the original Amadis has been enchanted along with his friends, and can only be restored to active life by some magic sword or other talisman in the hand of one of his descendants, successively taking after the ways of their great ancestor in love and war. So we have the adventures of his son Esplandian, of his grandson Lisuarte Junior, of his great-grandson Amadis of Greece, and of still more generations. The comparatively commonplace scenes and events of Britain being exhausted, their affairs take them farther afield—to Constantinople, to Trebizond, to Babylon, and to other lands known and unknown. To keep up the interest in this line of knights of " The Sphere ", of " The Serpent ", of " The

DON QUIXOTE AND MARITORNES AT THE INN

SIR GARETH AND THE DAMSEL ON THE WAY TO
CASTLE DANGEROUS

Flaming Sword", and so forth, wonders are piled on
wonders, misfortunes on misfortunes, enchantments on
enchantments, till the modern reader would be apt to fall
into the enchantment of sleep and give up their endless
quest in despair, having lost the clue of allurement supplied in the first books by strands of natural sentiment
and discriminated character.   The present writer has
pushed some way into this rank jungle of entangled
episodes; but perhaps no living reader could stand an
examination in the manifolded history involved through
a couple of dozen books, with some of which the name
of Feliciano de Silva is associated as author.   Counting
French imitations, there are in all about fifty volumes of
the Amadis family; books of the kind continued to be
brought out even after Don Quixote found in them such
lively delight.

What more delightful than to have, as it were, before our eyes
a vast lake of boiling pitch, with a prodigious number of serpents,
snakes, crocodiles, and divers other kinds of fierce and dreadful
creatures floating in it; and from the midst of the lake to hear a
most dreadful voice saying: "O knight, whosoever thou art, now
surveying this tremendous lake, if thou wouldst possess the treasure
that lies concealed beneath these sable waters, show the valour of
thy undaunted breast, and plunge thyself headlong into the midst
of the black and burning liquid; if not, thou wilt be unworthy to
see the mighty wonders enclosed therein and contained in the seven
castles of the seven enchanted nymphs who dwell beneath this horrid
blackness."   And scarcely has the knight heard these terrific words
when, without further consideration or reflection upon the danger
to which he exposes himself, and even without putting off his cum-
brous armour, he commends himself to heaven and his mistress,
and plunges headlong into the boiling pool; when unexpectedly
he finds himself in the midst of flowery fields, with which those
of Elysium can bear no comparison, where the sky seems far more
clear and the sun shines with greater brightness.   Beyond it appears a forest of beautiful and shady trees, whose verdure regales

the sight, whilst the ears are entertained with the sweet and art-
less notes of an infinite number of little birds of various hues, hop-
ping among the intricate branches. Here he discovers a little
brook, whose clear waters, resembling liquid crystal, run murmuring over the fine sands and snowy pebbles, which rival sifted gold
and purest pearl. There he sees an artificial fountain of variegated
jasper and polished marble. Here he beholds another of rustic
composition, in which the minute shells of the mussel, with the
white-and-yellow-wreathed houses of the snail, arranged in orderly
confusion, interspersed with pieces of glittering crystal and pellucid
emeralds, compose a work of such variety that art, imitating nature,
seems here to surpass her. Then suddenly he descries a strong
castle or stately palace, the walls of which are massy gold, the
battlements composed of diamonds, and the gates of hyacinths; in
short, the structure is so admirable that, though the materials where-
of it is framed are no less than diamonds, carbuncles, rubies, pearls,
gold, and emeralds, yet the workmanship is still more precious.
And after this, can anything be more charming than to behold,
sallying forth at the castle gate, a goodly troop of damsels, in such
rich and gorgeous attire, that were I to attempt the minute description that is given in history, the task would be endless; and then
she who appears to be the principal takes by the hand the daring
knight who threw himself into the burning lake, and silently leads
him into the rich palace or castle; and stripping him as naked as
when he first came into the world, bathes him in temperate water,
and then anoints him with odoriferous essences, and puts on him
a shirt of the finest lawn, all sweetened and perfumed. Then
comes another damsel, and throws over his shoulders a mantle
worth a city at least. He is afterwards led into another hall,
where he is struck with wonder and admiration at the sight of
tables spread in beautiful order. Then to see him wash his hands
in water distilled from amber and sweet-scented flowers! To see
him seated in a chair of ivory! To behold the damsels waiting
upon him, all preserving a marvellous silence! Then to see such
a variety of delicious viands, so savourily dressed that the appetite
is at a loss where to direct the hand! To hear soft music while
he is eating, without knowing whence the sounds proceed! And
when the repast is finished, and the tables removed, the knight

reclines on his seat, and perhaps is picking his teeth, when suddenly the door of the saloon opens, and lo! a damsel enters more beautiful than any of the former, who, seating herself by the knight's side, begins to give him an account of that castle, and to inform him how she is enchanted in it, with sundry other matters which amaze the knight and all those who read his history.

Don Quixote (Jarvis's translation).

Another series of Chronicles, quite as high flown but not so long drawn out as those of Amadis, imitates them in the adventures of the Palmerin family, that also won fame in the lists of artificial romance. Its ancestor was Palmerin de Oliva, who, of princely birth, grew up as a peasant's son, and, after many perils endured for her sake, won the hand of the western emperor's daughter, then himself succeeded to his grandfather's throne at Constantinople. His son and grandson succeeded with records of their own, as again the son of his daughter, who married one of our English Edwards, so their child was known as Palmerin of England. That parentage may have gone to make his history popular in an English translation cited in *The Knight of the Burning Pestle* as the book that turned its hero's head, but the passage he reads from it belongs to Palmerin de Oliva.

Then Palmerin and Trineus, snatching their lances from their dwarfs, and clasping their helmets, galloped amain after the giant, and Palmerin, having gotten a sight of him, came posting amain, saying: "Stay, traitorous thief, for thou mayst not so carry away her, that is worth the greatest lord in the world!" and with these words, gave him a blow on the shoulder, that he struck him besides his elephant. And Trineus coming to the knight that had Agricola behind him, set him soon besides his horse, with his neck broken in the fall; so that the princess getting out of the throng, between joy and grief, said: "All happy knight, the mirror of all such as follow arms, now may I be well assured of the love thou bearest me."

The translation of *Palmerin of England* was reprinted,
1807, in four volumes as revised by Southey, who had
a robust appetite for a kind of fiction now caviare to the
general reader. Don Quixote's priest, while handing over
the first of the family to the secular arm, finds *Palmerin
of England* worthy to be preserved as both good in itself
and as having for its supposed author a King of Portugal;
but the first *Palmerin* is said to have been the work of a
woman. Another book he saves from the flames is *Tirante
the White*, a Catalan romance professing to be translated
from the English. The hero of it is a Breton knight,
and the scene of some of his adventures is England,
where he makes the acquaintance of Guy of Warwick in
his hermitage, to be instructed by him upon the customs
of chivalry as set forth in a work called *L'Arbre des
Batailles*. In this story another link with British romantic
history is that the fairy Morgan, having in the course of
centuries changed her name to Urganda, is able to release
King Arthur, who has come to be confined in a cage at
Constantinople. That this is clearly of much later date
than the Arthurian legend, appears from its elaborate
insistence on the rules of chivalry, and by such incidents
as a fantastic duel for a lady's favour between two knights
in their shirts, armoured only with paper shields and helmets of flowers. The priest's not unqualified admiration
of *Tirante the White* seems to have been won by features
novel in romance. " Here we have Don Kyrie-Eleison
of Montalvan, a valorous knight, and his brother Thomas
of Montalvan, with the knight Fonseca, and the combat
which the valiant Tirante fought with the bulldog, and
the witticisms of the damsel Plazerdemivida, also the
amours and artifices of the widow Reposada; and Madam
the Empress in love with her squire Hypolito. Verily,
neighbour, in its way it is the best book in the world :

here the knights eat, and sleep, and die in their beds, and make their wills before their deaths; with several things which are not to be found in any other books of this kind. Notwithstanding this, I tell you, the author deserved, for writing so many foolish things seriously, to be sent to the galleys for the whole of his life."

The priest, we note, was a more considerate critic than those of the Don's household, who held in horror his whole library, amounting to "above a hundred volumes well bound besides a great many smaller ones"; so that the housekeeper was for sprinkling the room with holy water by way of exorcising the enchanters she feared to set scuttling like spiders out of those mischievous tomes. His reverence himself showed patriotic prejudice that discredits him as a judge of older romances. "Here comes Signor Reynaldos de Montalvan, with his friends and companions, greater thieves than Cacus; and the Twelve Peers with their faithful historiographer Turpin. However, I am only for condemning them to perpetual banishment, because they contain some things of the famous Mateo Boyardo, from whom the Christian poet Ludovico Ariosto spun his web, and even to him, if I find him here uttering any other language than his own, I will show no respect. . . . I sentence this, and all other books that shall be found treating of French matters, to be thrown aside and imprisoned in some dry vault till we can deliberate more carefully what is to be done with them, excepting indeed Bernardo del Carpio, and another called Roncesvalles, which, if they fall into my hands, shall pass into those of the housekeeper, and thence into the fire, without any remission."

Amadis, the father, is another book spared by these inquisitors, to whom no great grudge seems owing for their work of destruction. Bishop Percy testified to

Dr. Johnson reading all through *Felixmarte of Hyrcania*, but this folio, along with *The Mirror of Chivalry, Don Olivante de Laura,* and the rest, few readers would now lift a hand to save from the bonfire to which they were condemned in the clearance of Don Quixote's library. Even in Spain they are hardly known at the present day; and some of the romances which that would-be knight cited so enthusiastically seem to have been washed away by the waters of Lethe without help from his house-keeper's broom.[1]

---

[1] Duffield's Translation of *Don Quixote* gives a catalogue, thirty pages long, of the books that might have filled his library.

PART II

STORIES OF CHIVALRY

THE YOUNG UNKNOWN

I

WHEN King Arthur's glory was at its height, his sister, the Queen of Lothian, lived at her lonely castle in the north, where day after day went and came like the waves breaking on the beach or the wind sighing idly among the fir trees. Her husband had been killed in battle, leaving four sons. Three of them had been brought up at Arthur's court, and the eldest, Sir Gawayne, was already famed throughout Christendom as second in renown only to Sir Lancelot of the Lake, the bravest and most courteous of all the knights of the Round Table.

Gareth, the youngest, who was but a child when his father died, alone remained at home. But as he grew up to be a tall, sturdy lad, and heard the tales of his brothers' prowess, he became more and more eager to follow them and seek honour in the service of his uncle. Then the queen, knowing that his father's son would never rest content in ease and idleness, gave him her blessing and sent him to Arthur, equipped and attended as became his birth.

Now as the youth drew near the castle on the marches of Wales, at which the king was holding the feast of Whitsuntide, it came into his mind that there would be no true honour in being well received for the sake of his name and kin; and as his brothers had not seen him since childhood, he bethought himself how, unknown and by his own deeds, he might be able to prove his worth.   He laid aside all marks of rank, exchanged clothes with one of his attendants, and dismissed them, charging them to keep his secret for a time.   Thus meanly attired, he presented himself in the hall where Arthur was banqueting with the knights of the Round Table, and making his way to the dais, bowed before the king, and sought of him a boon.

"Ask and you shall have your asking, for you are the goodliest young man that ever I saw," answered Arthur.   "But fain would I know your name."

"Nay, that I may not tell.   My petition is but to have food and lodging for a twelvemonth, and then will I ask another gift that to you shall be no harm or loss."

"You might have asked a greater thing," said his uncle, feeling his heart drawn towards this stranger, whose looks and bearing seemed to bespeak him of noble blood. "Food and shelter shalt thou have, for that I never denied to friend or foe; but next time I counsel thee to ask better."   Wherewith Arthur called for Sir Kay, his steward, and charged him to see that the young man had fitting entertainment.

"Aye, he shall have meat and drink to his mind, and be as fat as a pork hog by the twelvemonths' end!" muttered the sour-hearted, sharp-tongued steward, who bore ill will to Gareth from the moment he saw the king look upon him with favour.   So he led him to the lowest end of the hall, and gave him a place near the door, among the servants and kitchen boys, saying scornfully: "This is thy proper place, for if thou wert of gentle birth thou wouldst have prayed the king for a horse and armour; but now it may well be seen that thou art a base churl and fit to live with churls, who seek not honour, but meat and drink."

But when Sir Lancelot and Sir Gawayne heard the steward speaking thus they rebuked him, and Lancelot bid him remember how it became a gentle knight to be courteous to every stranger, and warned him that this youth might yet prove himself no churl.

"Let be," snarled Sir Kay. "As he is, so hath he asked. My life on it, the fellow has run away from some abbey where the starveling monks could not give him his fill."

Then Gawayne would have had the boy come to his chamber and eat there, little knowing that it was his own brother to whom he thus showed kindness. But Gareth refused his friendly offers, and humbly took the place appointed him among the meanest of the castle, meekly bearing the steward's taunts, and letting none know who or what he was.

Thus for twelve months he lived at the court unknown, sleeping hard and faring poorly among the serving boys of the kitchen, speaking little to any man, but so ordering himself towards great and small that he displeased none, save only Sir Kay, who ever jeered and flouted him with his lack of spirit. But wherever feats of arms were done, there the youth was looking on to learn how brave knights should bear themselves in battle; and at such games and trials of strength as were open to him he showed himself a right manly lad, and carried away the prize from all his fellows. And Lancelot and Gawayne often spoke kindly to him, and gave him money to spend, and clothes. So the twelve months passed, till Whitsuntide again came round.

Again King Arthur was keeping the feast right royally, when there came another suppliant to his castle.

A damsel, alighting from her palfrey, suddenly appeared in the hall, and kneeling before him, piteously besought his aid.

"For whom, and in what cause?" asked the king.

"Sir, my name is Linet, and because here are said to be the noblest knights of the world, I am sent by the Lady of Lyonnesse to seek succour against a cruel tyrant who wastes her lands and besieges her in her castle this two years past."

"Fair damsel, fear not," said Arthur. "There be knights here, I trow, that will do their power to rescue your lady; but who may this oppressor be?"

"Know ye Sir Ironside, whom men call the Red Knight?"

"Ah!" said Gawayne; "I know him well. He is one of the strongest and fiercest knights alive, and once I escaped full hard from him with my life."

While now the brothers of the Round Table looked on each other before any spoke, Gareth came pressing through the crowd, crying out:

"Sir king, heaven thank thee! Twelve months I have lived here as I desired, and now let me ask another boon. Grant me and none else this adventure, for I will free that lady from the Red Knight's power."

All who stood by were amazed to hear him speak thus; but Arthur's eyes kindled, and his heart told him that this youth's deeds would answer to his words.

"So be it," he said. "This adventure shall be yours, for sure I am that you will prove right worthy of it."

But the damsel was ill pleased, and turned away in anger, when she found her lady was to have no better champion.

"Fie!" she cried. "Would you mock me, that you send none but a serving boy to fight such a knight as

Sir Ironside?" And without another word she hastened from the hall, then mounting her palfrey rode off in high dudgeon, attended by a dwarfish page that had accompanied her to the castle.

Gareth ran out and made after her, crying on her to wait till he might find a horse and armour, but she heeded not. He was gone before any of those who marvelled at his boldness could stay him. But Sir Kay was wrathful, and cast about to humble this upstart. Quickly he equipped Dagonet, the king's fool, with shield and spear, and, mounting him on a poor hackney, sent him after the youth to bring him back shamed and beaten.

Away rode Dagonet mirthfully on his errand; but ere long he came limping back on foot, with a pitiful tale that the youth had pulled him over the horse's crupper, and, not deigning to do him further harm, had taken his horse and arms, and ridden on after the damsel.

"Ha!" cried Sir Kay; "is this my boy of the kitchen? I will ride after him to see if he will know me for his better."

"Best abide at home," counselled the other knights with laughter; but the spiteful steward would not be gainsaid. He made ready and galloped away; and next Sir Lancelot took horse and rode after to see what would befall.

The damsel Linet made the more haste as she perceived her young champion held so lightly at Arthur's court that they sent a fool to have to do with him; but Gareth, urging on Dagonet's beast, was pressing hard upon her flight, and had almost made up with her when he heard a voice behind him, crying:

"Sirrah, dost know me?"

"Yea," he answered, as he turned and saw that it

was Sir Kay, "I know thee for an ungentle knight of the court, who hast done me much despite; therefore look to thyself."

And thereupon they put their spears in rest, running together so fiercely that both came to the ground, for Gareth's sorry steed stumbled and fell, yet not before he had avoided Sir Kay's spear, and hurled him from his saddle, so that he lay sorely hurt and helpless.

Lightly then Gareth rose to his feet, and would have unlaced the fallen man's helmet, when he was aware of another knight who, with his vizor down, had beheld the combat from a thicket hard by. This knight said not a word, but dismounted and came towards him with his sword drawn, proffering to fight. And Gareth did not hold back, but taking Sir Kay's sword and shield, made at him.

No sooner had they crossed swords than Gareth knew right well he had met his match, yet none the less was the other hard put to it to defend himself, so many and mighty blows did the youth deal upon him, and would not give ground an inch. Like two giants they fought, each marvelling at the other's strength, and neither could make an end, till the unknown knight, as he seemed at last like to gain the advantage, drew back and lowered his blade, saying courteously:

"Fair sir, fight not so sore; our quarrel is not such but that we may leave off and think no scorn of each other."

"That is true," said Gareth; "but truly it doth me good to feel your might; and yet, my lord, bear me witness that I did not first cry hold."

"Well," said the other, "I thought to try you, but I promise you I had much ado to keep myself from you unharmed, so doubt not henceforth to face any knight alive." With that he raised his vizor, and revealed himself as who but Sir Lancelot?

Joyful and astounded to learn that he had withstood the most famous knight in the world, the youth eagerly asked if, in Lancelot's judgment, he might hope to quit himself worthily in arms.

"Yea," said Lancelot, smiling. "Do as you have now done, and I will be your warrant."

"Then, I pray you," cried Gareth, falling on his knees, "give me the order of knighthood, for by you and none other have I ever desired to be made a knight."

"Willingly; but first must you tell me your name and kin."

"So be that you will not discover me——"

"Nay, that I promise you, till you see good to make it openly known."

"Then know, sir, that my name is Gareth of Orkney, and that I am sister's son to King Arthur and brother to Sir Gawayne; yet I would not that they know my name till all men shall know my deeds."

"Ah!" cried Lancelot; "I am gladder of you than before, for ever methought that you were of noble blood. Arise, Sir Gareth; I make thee knight; be gentle, valiant, and fortunate."

Having thus bestowed on him the order of knighthood, Sir Lancelot, since the youth was impatient to be gone, took leave of him, wishing him good speed on his adventure, and returned to the court. But we go with the new-made knight, who, on the steward's horse, and having donned his armour, now made all haste after Linet and her dwarfish page.

II

Sir Gareth soon overtook Linet, who, though she now saw him horsed and armed like a knight, seemed nowise more willing to have him as her champion, but welcomed him still with scornful words.

"What doest thou here, ladle washer and turner of spits? Turn again and leave me; thy clothes be foul with grease and tallow!"

"Nay," quoth Gareth; "I will not leave you whatsoever you say, for I have undertaken this adventure, and I will achieve it or die therefore."

"Fie on thee! Thou achieve mine adventure! Soon shalt thou meet one thou darest not look in the face for all the broth that ever thou hast supped."

"Damsel, say what you will, but you shall see if I fear to look any man in the face, so I may come to the aid of your lady."

But Linet yet chid and mocked him, turning away her head and whipping on her palfrey, and thus she rode, he following her, till they came to a gloomy pass overhung by a thunder-blasted thorn tree, from which hung a black banner, and beneath, beside a dark rock, stood a coal-black horse covered with trappings of black, and by it a knight armed in black, with a black shield, who kept this perilous pass against all comers.

"Flee," said Linet, "ere he mount his horse."

But Gareth did not stop or shrink; and as they drew near the Black Knight leaped into his saddle, crying loudly:

"Damsel, is this the knight you have brought from King Arthur to be your champion?"

"Nay," she answered; "this is but a kitchen knave that the king fed for charity. Think not that he is a worshipful knight, because he rideth with me against my will, but I pray you, make him leave following me."

"Why cometh he in such array?" said the Black Knight, casting grim looks on Gareth. "But he is a likely lad and should make a strong man, so I will but set him down and take his horse and harness, for it were shame to me to do him any more harm."

"Sir knight!" cried Gareth, "thou art full free with my horse and harness, but I let thee know that I will pass whether it liketh thee or not, and horse nor harness gettest thou none of me, unless thou win them with thy hands."

"Sayest thou so?" spoke the other with scorn. "Now turn back, for it beseemeth never a kitchen page to ride with such a damsel."

"Thou liest!" said Gareth. "I am a gentleman born, and of higher lineage than thou, and that will I prove on thy body."

"Ha! let us see what thou canst do?" cried the Black Knight, laying his lance in rest.

Then wrathfully both knights spurred their horses and came together, while the damsel rode on with her dwarf, scarcely looking behind to see how the battle went. At the first shock the Black Knight's spear splintered against Gareth's shield, but he sat firm, and his spear pierced through the other's side and broke off, leaving the point still in his body. Nevertheless the Black Knight drew his sword and smote fiercely, and gave Gareth many sore strokes. But his wound weakened him, and his blows became wilder and fainter, and suddenly he fell off his horse in a swoon.

Then Gareth, seeing him to be so well armed and mounted, lighted down and took his horse and his armour, and rode after the damsel, hoping now for a kinder greeting.

"Away!" she cried, as he drew nigh. "Out of the wind, knave, for thou still smellest of the kitchen! Alas! that ever such a one as thou should by mishap overthrow so good a knight. But ere long we shall meet his two brethren, and they will make thee pay dearly for it, unless thou take my counsel and flee in time."

"Fair damsel, give me goodly language," said Gareth, "for always you would have me a coward. It may happen me to be beaten or slain, but I warn you that I shall neither flee nor leave your company for all you say, so it were good for you to cease thus rebuking me, since follow you I will, whatsoever befall, while I can."

Yet would she not be silent nor cease chiding him, and thus they passed on till they came to a great forest, out of which rode a knight all armed and equipped in green, and stood in the way before them.

"Is that my brother the Black Knight that thou hast brought with thee?" he cried to the damsel, as they drew near.

"Nay, nay," said she, "this is but a boy from King Arthur's kitchen that hath overthrown him by mischance, and stolen his horse and armour."

"Alas, that such a good knight should be overthrown thus, and by a poor knave!" cried the knight in green. "But for this, traitor, thou shalt die forthwith."

"I defy thee!" said Sir Gareth; "and know that I fought thy brother knightly, not shamefully."

Without more ado they ran at each other, and at the first encounter the Green Knight was unhorsed. But he rose and drew his sword, and Gareth leaped down to fight with him on foot, and they strove together like two right valiant champions.

"Ah, my lord the Green Knight," cried the scornful damsel, "why, for shame, stand you so long fighting with the like of him? Shame it is to see such a lad match so good a knight, as the weed overgrows the corn!"

Wherewith the Green Knight being stirred to fury, thought to have slain Gareth with one mighty stroke, but Gareth put the sword aside, and dealt the other such a buffet on the helm that he fell to the ground and lay there grovelling. Then as Sir Gareth stood over him with his sword, the vanquished cried him mercy, and besought him:

"Fair knight, spare my life and I will forgive thee for my brother, and become thy man, and serve thee with all that is mine."

"I grant thee thy life," said Gareth, "so that thou wilt go to King Arthur and yield thee to him."

Then the Green Knight kneeled before him and thanked Gareth for his life, but the damsel mocked, saying:

"Fie, fie, that any knight should be obedient to a kitchen knave! And woe is me, Sir Green Knight, for what has befallen you, since of your help I had great need to pass this dreadsome forest."

"Nay, dread you not," said he, "for I will guide you through the forest."

So he rose up and rode with them till they had passed the forest; and much marvelled he to see how Linet bore herself towards her knight, and would never give him good word or look, for all the service he did her. And when the Green Knight had taken leave of them, she again sought to drive Gareth from her, bidding him turn ere he came to harm.

"Damsel," said he, "ever you threaten me that I shall be beaten by the knights that we meet, but ever, for all your boast, they lie in the dust and the mire. When you see me beaten or yielded as recreant, then may you bid me go from you shamefully, but before that will I not leave you, for I were worse than a fool to depart from you all the while that I win honour in your company."

"Well," said she, "you shall soon, whether you will or no."

Thus they rode on till they came to a ford in a stream, and beyond was a fair meadow, where stood pitched a pavilion all of blue silk, and before it a lordly knight, armed in blue.   He, too, when he espied Gareth, took him for his brother the Black Knight, and cried aloud across the stream : "Brother, what do you here?"

"It is not he," said the damsel, "but a knave bred in King Arthur's kitchen, who hath overthrown him foully; also, I saw thy brother, the Green Knight, vanquished by his hands.   Now, be revenged upon him, for I cannot make him cease following me."

Hastily then the Blue Knight took his spear and mounted his horse, and Gareth made ready to meet him. They spurred their horses into the stream and met midway, and both lances were broken in pieces.   Then each drew his sword and hewed and hacked, so that the blood ran down into the water, and it was wonder to see that strong battle.   But at last Gareth struck the Blue Knight from his horse, and he fell into the stream and was like to be drowned had not the other dragged him on land. Then unlacing his helm he made as if he would have smote off his head, but the beaten knight prayed for mercy, saying:

"Slay me not and I yield me to thee with fifty knights that are at my command, and forgive thee all the despite that thou hast done to me and my brothers."

"All that shall not avail thee," said Gareth, "and thou shalt die unless this damsel pray me to spare thy life."

"Out on thee, false kitchen page!" quoth she. "I will ask nothing of such a one as thou; but be not so bold as to slay him."

"Alas! suffer me not to die when a fair word may save me!" cried the Blue Knight, as Gareth again raised his sword and seemed about to strike the deadly blow; and at this entreaty the ungracious damsel said:

"Let him be, for it were pity that such a knight should die by thy hand."

"Damsel," said Gareth, "your will is to me a pleasure, and at your bidding his life shall be saved; therefore rise, sir knight, and thank this lady."

The Blue Knight having given thanks for his life, they crossed the ford, and he led them into his pavilion, where he called on his attendants to serve them and set forth food and wine. But when he would have placed them at the board, Linet cried shame on him. "Are you so uncourteous as to set a kitchen page beside me. It beseemeth him better to stick swine than to sit before ladies."

"Truly," said the Blue Knight, "it were not my part to do him any dishonour, since he hath proved himself a better knight than I am." And, marvelling much at the pride of this lady, he set Gareth at a side table and served him courteously with his own hands.

Then, having rested and eaten, they set forth again; but first Sir Gareth charged the Blue Knight to present himself and all his knights at Arthur's court and do homage to the king. This he promised, on his faith as a knight, and thus they took leave friendly, and Gareth rode on with the damsel.

"And now," said he, "fain would I see this Red Knight that oppresseth thy lady."

"Thou wilt see him time enough," said she, and Gareth again assayed to reason with her.

"Proud damsel, you are to blame to scorn me thus, for I had liefer fight with many knights than be so scorned by a lady."

Linet rode on in silence for a time; then suddenly she said:

"Sir, boldly thou speakest and boldly hast thou done; therefore I pray thee save thyself while thou canst, for both horse and man may well be weary, and I dread lest ye come to harm. We are now but seven miles from the besieged castle. The Red Knight is a man without mercy, and men say that he hath seven men's strength."

"Be that as it may," saith Gareth; "since I am come so near this knight, I will prove his strength ere I turn back; and do not doubt, damsel, that, by the grace of Heaven, I shall deliver thy lady from him."

"Ah me!" cried Linet; "I marvel what manner of man be you, and of what kin you come; for never did woman treat a knight so foully and shamefully as I have done you, and ever gently you have borne with me, and that came never but of gentle blood."

"Lady," said Gareth; "a knight will do little that cannot suffer a woman's tongue. And truly your ill words but furthered me in my battle, for the more you chid me the more I wreaked my wrath on them I had to do with, and all your scorn but sharpened me to show myself what I was. Peradventure, though I had meat in Arthur's kitchen, yet might I have had meat enough in other places; but whether I be a gentleman born or no, fair damsel, I have done you gentleman's service, and will do you better service yet ere I leave you."

"Alas! sir" said she, "forgive me all that I have said and done against you."

"With all my heart!" said he. "Right glad am I that it pleaseth thee to speak me fair, and now meseemeth that there is no knight living but I am able for him."

Of good cheer was Gareth now that the damsel looked friendly on him, and the time seemed long till he should see the face of this Sir Ironside. Thus they rode on together, and came within a little of the besieged castle. But now, because it grew towards evening, they turned aside to a hermitage hard by, and there rested the night with the holy man, while the dwarf went forward to let the lady of that castle know that one of Arthur's knights was at hand to help her.

III

In the morning the dwarf came back from the lady of the castle, bearing her thanks and greetings to the young knight; also she sent wine and bread and baked venison, desiring him to refresh himself, for he would have need of all his strength. So, having risen betimes and gone to prayers with the hermit, Gareth and Linet broke their fast. Then they took their horses and set out towards the castle, which was called the Castle Dangerous.

They passed through a wood, and before the sun was high came to a fair plain by the sea, where they saw the walls and towers of the castle, and many goodly tents and pavilions pitched before it; and there was much smoke and noise, the songs of minstrels and the shouts of mariners; and in a meadow all manner of games and jousts were going forward among the knights and lords who had come to this great siege.

As he drew near, Sir Gareth was amazed to see how on a row of tall trees wellnigh forty knights hung by the neck, all in rich armour, with their shields and swords hanging beside them and gilt spurs on their heels.

"What meaneth this?" he cried.

"Ah! sir," said the damsel Linet, "abate not your cheer at this sight, but encourage yourself, or else you are lost. For all these knights came hither to rescue the Lady of Lyonnesse, and when the Red Knight had overcome them he put them to this shameful death. And in the same wise will he serve you unless you quit yourself better.

"Thus shall he never do to me," said Gareth; "for rather than come to such a villainous end I will die knightly in the field."

"So were ye well, for in him is no courtesy or mercy; and that is pity, for he is a noble knight of prowess and a lord of great lands."

"Truly, damsel," said Gareth, "he may be a knight of prowess and great possessions, but he useth shameful customs, and I marvel that none of Arthur's knights have dealt with him ere this."

"Sir, there is the cause of his tarrying so long at the siege. For two years he hath lain before this castle, and many times he might have had it if he would, but he prolongeth the time to the intent to have Sir Lancelot or Sir Gawayne to do battle with him."

"Well, were he as good a knight as ever was, I shall not fail him," said Sir Gareth stoutly, spurring his horse towards the high pavilion, where he saw the blood-red banner of Sir Ironside, and hard by was a sycamore tree, on which hung a mighty horn of ivory.

Straight to the sycamore tree rode the young knight, and blew the ivory horn so eagerly that the castle towers rang with the sound. They within ran to the walls, and the besiegers looked out of their tents; then Sir Ironside hastily made himself ready to meet the challenge.

"Who is this that cometh to his death, like many another before him?" he cried, coming forth in his blood-red armour; and they buckled on his helmet, and brought him a shield and a red spear shining like fire in the sun. Then he leaped upon his horse, and rode into the open space under the castle walls, that all within and without might behold the battle.

"Now, sir, bear you well," said Linet, "for yonder is your deadly enemy, and there is my lady, Dame Lyonnesse."

"Where?" asked Gareth; and she pointed with her finger, and he looked up and saw the lady of the castle at a window, smiling on him and waving her hand.

"She seemeth the fairest lady that ever I looked on, and I ask no better quarrel to fight in," said he, courteously saluting her.

Then the Red Knight called loudly to him:

"Leave thy looking, sir knight, or look at me, for I warn thee that is my lady, and I have done many a battle for her."

"If thou have so done," answered Gareth, "me-seemeth it was but labour lost; for to love one that loveth not thee is great folly, and she will have none of thy love, as I may understand by thy besieging this castle. And were she not glad of my coming, I should not have come to rescue her or die."

"Sayst thou so?" quoth the grim Red Knight.

"Methinks thou mightst well beware by the knights that thou sawest hanging on yonder trees."

"Fie on thee!" cried Gareth. "In that hast thou shamed thyself and knighthood, and thou mayest be sure there will no lady love thee that knoweth thy wicked customs. And weenest thou that these hanged knights should affright me? Nay, that shameful sight but giveth me more courage and hardiness against thee, than if thou hadst been a gentle and courteous knight."

"Make thee ready, and prate no longer," said the Red Knight wrothfully; while the lady of the castle and all her damsels fell upon their knees to pray for the young knight.

"Do thy worst!" cried Gareth. Then both knights rode back to the edge of the field, and turning round their horses, galloped straightway together with all their might.

Dreadful was the shock of their encounter! So truly did the spears strike the midst of either shield that girths and cruppers burst, and the riders were hurled to the ground with the bridles in their hands. All who saw thought their necks had been broken, but they sprang up and drew their swords and ran at one another. Each gave the other a blow that made him reel backwards; then recovering, they closed again in furious fight, hewing, cutting, slashing, clashing, and thrusting till both were out of breath. Now they drew back and leant panting on their swords; then they hurtled together like two fierce lions. At one time they would fall to the earth and wrestle there; at another time, in the madness of the struggle, each would snatch up the other's sword instead of his own. The Red Knight was a wily swordsman, and taught Gareth to be wily

in turn, but he paid full dear for it with his blood before
he could learn that foe's manner of fighting. Yet the
young knight, too, dealt many a shrewd stroke at him,
and the blood ran down their bodies, and the armour
of each was so hewn that in many places men might see
their naked sides.

Thus for an hour and more they fought, and none of
the beholders could say which of them was like to win
the battle. So weary grew they that by assent of both
they paused a while and sat down, and their pages
unlaced their helms to let them feel the wind on their
faces. But when Gareth's helm was off he looked up
to the castle windows, and caught sight of the fair Lady
of Lyonnesse, and that gave him new heart for the
combat, so that he called on the Red Knight to make
ready forthwith, and they started up at once and fell
to it again with fresh fury, till the ground at their feet
was covered with blood and pieces of broken armour.

Never before had Sir Ironside met a foe who gave
him so much ado. But at last Gareth's strength began
to fail, while the other doubled his strokes and pressed
on him more and more sorely as he bore his shield low
for weariness. His arm waxed fainter, his foot slipped,
his sword was forced out of his hand. Then with one
blow the Red Knight clove his shield, with another he
laid him on the earth, and stood already bending over
him to make an end, when Linet was heard crying
shrilly:

"Ah! knight, where is thy courage gone? Alas!
how my lady weeps to see thee fall!"

These words brought the youth back to life. With
a mighty bound he gained his feet, and nimbly springing
to and gripping his own sword, dealt the Red Knight
such a blow on the head that he now fell to the earth,

and Gareth stooped over him to hold him fast. All in the castle shouted for joy.

"Oh! noble knight, I yield me to thy mercy!" cried Ironside, as the vanquisher would have unlaced his helm. But Gareth bethought him of the forty knights hanging upon those trees; and said, raising his sword above the oppressor's throat:

"Nay, traitor, thy life is forfeit for the shameful deaths thou hast caused so many good knights to die."

"Yet stay," besought the Red Knight; "hold thy hand and thou shalt know why I did thus."

"Say on, and say quickly."

"Sir, I loved once a lady, and she had her brother slain, and she said it was by the hands of Sir Lancelot of the Lake, or else of Sir Gawayne; and she prayed me that, as I loved her heartily, I would promise, on the faith of my knighthood, to labour in arms until I met with one of those two, and that I should do all the villainy I could unto King Arthur's knights. Therefore, all I overcame have I put to a villainous death, to this end that I might have Lancelot or Gawayne come against me to take vengeance upon them. But now I confess and repent me that I have done so foully."

Then as Gareth stood questioning with himself whether or no to strike, the friends and followers of Sir Ironside fell on their knees before him, praying him to spare their lord's life. "For," said they, "by his death you will have no advantage, and his misdeeds that he hath done may not be undone; therefore let him make amends, and we will all become your men and do you homage."

"Fair sirs," said Gareth, "be sure I am full loath to slay this lord, ill though he have done. And insomuch as all that he did was at a lady's bidding, I blame him the less; and so for your sakes I will release him and let him have his life upon this covenant: that he go within the castle and yield him to the Lady of Lyonnesse, and make her amends for the trespass that he hath done against her and her lands, and if she will forgive and acquit him I am well pleased. And also, when that is done, must thou go to King Arthur's court and swear him fealty, and there ask pardon of Sir Lancelot and Sir Gawayne for the evil will thou hast borne against them."

"Sir," said the Red Knight, "all this will I do as you command."

Then Sir Gareth suffered him to rise, and he and all his men paid homage to the young knight. They entered Sir Ironside's pavilion, where he bid his servants bring meat and drink for Gareth, and himself waited on him courteously. Next came Linet, who unarmed him and searched his wounds and stanched the blood; so also did she to the Red Knight. And when their hurts were dressed they all went up to the castle to see the fair Lady of Lyonnesse, that Sir Kay's boy of the kitchen had thus delivered.

IV

Now turn we to King Arthur's court, whither Sir Kay had been brought to be healed of the hurt that he got from Gareth. Small pity on him for this mishap had his fellows of the Round Table; and especially Sir Lancelot and Sir Gawayne rebuked him, telling him it was not the part of a good knight to scorn any young man, who might yet come to put his scorner to shame. All marvelled who this stranger might be, and of what lineage; only Lancelot knew, and he kept the secret.

They marvelled more and more, when there came to the court, first the Green Knight, then the Blue Knight with fifty followers, then the Red Knight, Sir Ironside, with all his men, to tell how each of them had been overthrown by the nameless youth, and that, at his behest, they yielded them to King Arthur and did him homage for their lands.

"Ye are welcome," said the king; "for ye have been long great foes to me and to my knights, but now I trust so to treat you that ye shall henceforth be my friends."

Lastly, came to the castle another guest with a great train of knights and dames. It was the Queen of Lothian, and at the sight of her Sir Gawayne and his brothers, Sir Agravayne and Sir Gaheris, ran and fell on their knees to ask her blessing; they had not seen their mother for many a year. When she had saluted them she cried out to her brother, King Arthur:

"What have ye done with my dear son Gareth, that was my hope and joy? He was here amongst you a twelvemonth, and ye made a kitchen knave of him and fed him like a poor hog—shame to ye all!"

"Oh, dear mother, I knew him not!" cried Gawayne, all amazed.

"Nor I," said the king; "and right sorry am I now for it. But, thanked be heaven, he hath proved himself as good a knight as any now living of his years, and never shall I be glad till I can find him. Fair sister, meseemeth it behoved you to have let me know of his coming, and then if I had not done well to him you might have blamed me. But let all this pass, and be merry, for, if he live within these realms he shall be brought back, and we will do him honour, as he is worthy."

So now the queen abode with Arthur, while Gawayne and his brothers went forth in search of Gareth, but nowhere could they find him. They thought first to hear

news of him at the Castle Dangerous, but the Lady of
Lyonnesse could not tell what had become of her young
champion.   These two had plighted their troth to each
other; then, as soon as Gareth was recovered from his
wounds, he had set out to win honour for himself in
fresh adventures.

Right willing was she to see him again, and when
months passed by and he came not, she devised a plan
for bringing him back.   She sent to invite Arthur and
his knights to a great tournament at her castle next
Whitsuntide, and all over England, Wales, Ireland, and
Scotland she caused this tournament to be proclaimed,
that the best knights in the world might meet there, and,
for the prize, he who proved himself the worthiest was to
wed her and to have her lands.

Once more it was the merry month of May, when
the sun shone hot and bright, and the birds sang in buds
and boughs, and the flowers were springing on the green
meadows.   From east, west, north, and south the knights
came riding to the great jousts at the Castle Dangerous.
Many a duke and lord there came, and many a famous
champion; and, leading kings and princes in his train,
came Arthur with his brotherhood of the Round Table,
who proffered to hold the lists against all comers.

Great array was made by the lady of the castle for
all these noble knights and their followers; lodging and
victual lacked none of them, according to his degree;
there was plenty for high and low who gathered to
behold their great feats of arms.   Nor were heralds
wanting, nor minstrels to sing the deeds that should be
done.   And among the rest came Gareth, but only his
lady knew him, and he strictly charged her to make no
more of him than of the meanest knight there, till it
should be time to disclose himself.

On the appointed day all was astir betimes. The plain before the castle showed gay with lordly pavilions, and glittered with arms and coats of mail. The walls rang with music and minstrelsy, with the clank of steel and the neighing of eager steeds. Around the new-mown meadow set apart for the jousting were raised scaffolds and arbours, from which the dames and damsels might behold the prowess of their knights. High above the rest King Arthur might be known by the golden dragon on his helm, and at his side sat the Lady of Lyonnesse, whose beauty all acknowledged to be worthy of such a festival.

The trumpets sounded, the lists were opened, fair eyes shone bright, brave hearts beat high, as the knights spurred forth, and the lances splintered and the swords clashed, and the blood flowed down. Who but a cunning minstrel can tell aright the jousting of that day? None but a skilled herald can recall what were all the encounters of this great tournament, what goodly forms of man and horse rolled on the grass, what knights, faint and sorry, were borne away from the lists, what mighty strokes called forth cries of wonder among all the beholders, what champions met and how they parted! From noon till evening the battle raged with various chances, till the fresh turf was torn up by the hoofs of the chargers and strewn with broken arms and harness.

But ever, where the press was thickest, rode unhurt a knight in white armour inlaid with gold, upon whom all eyes were fixed, and against whom no shield or weapon could avail, while he himself seemed to bear a magic lance, as if indeed the love of his lady were to him a charm, giving him strength to do marvels. Great and famous champions went down before him one by one; and all men asked in amazement who this might be, but none knew his name. And at last, when Arthur had seen many of the champions of the Round Table thus overthrown, he called on Sir Lancelot, the greatest of all, bidding him assay his matchless might against the unknown.

"Nay," said the chivalrous Lancelot; "this stranger may well be weary after what he hath done, therefore it is no good knight's part to seek to shame him. For me, he shall have all the honour of this day, and win the lady for whose love he hath done such great deeds."

So spoke Sir Lancelot; but Sir Gawayne, second in fame to him only, had already spurred forward, crying:

"Sir knight with the golden armour, well hast thou jousted; now make ready for me!"

They rushed together like thunder. Each was unhorsed; then there was drawing of swords, and a sore battle began between them. Great strokes were given on either side, and loud shouts arose from the throng around; but before the blood began to flow down their armours, a woman's voice was heard high above the din, bidding them hold their hands.

"Sir Gawayne, Sir Gawayne, cease fighting with thy brother!" cried the damsel Linet.

When he heard this, the unknown knight threw away his sword and his shield, and knelt on the ground as if craving mercy of Gawayne, who asked astounded:

"Who are you that just now were so strong and mighty, and yet so suddenly yield you to me?"

"Oh, I am your brother Gareth!" said he, unlacing his helmet, and letting his yellow hair be seen.

Then Gawayne also cast away his sword, and the two brothers ran into each other's arms, and embraced lovingly, hardly able to speak, so full were their hearts. At the sight of her son the Queen of Lothian swooned away for joy, while Dame Lyonnesse wept and smiled in turns; and right glad and proud looked King Arthur to know that it was his own nephew who had borne himself so well that day.

Amidst the rejoicings the brothers generously strove together, each desiring to give the other the prize of the battle and acknowledge himself beaten. But the king, with the assent of all, declared Gareth the victor, and, leading him before the lady of the castle, asked him if he were willing to have her for his wife.

" My lord, I love her above all ladies living."

" Now, fair dame, what say you?"

" Most noble king," said she, " I would rather have him than any king or prince in Christendom, for he is my first love and he shall be my last."

Willingly Gareth's mother gave her consent, and there and then they joined hands, and the day was fixed for their wedding, and throughout all the kingdom Arthur sent to proclaim a great feast in honour of it.

So next Michaelmas they were married at the king's court by the Bishop of Canterbury, with much solemnity, and all manner of revels and games; also there were great jousts for three days, but Arthur would not suffer Sir Gareth to joust because of his new bride. Kings and queens and lords and ladies and all the best knights in the world were guests at that feast, and brought rich gifts to the bride and bridegroom. The bride was attended by a train of maidens and gentlewomen that her chosen knight had delivered from oppression and captivity in the course of his adventures; and he had for his groomsmen and chamberlains Sir Ironside and all the other knights that he had overthrown and made to do homage to him. Moreover, at the marriage, King Arthur received many of these knights, along with Sir

Gareth, into his goodly fellowship of the Round Table, making them vow truly that henceforth they would use their arms only to cast down strong evildoers and to succour the helpless. So all was mirth and gladness, and goodwill towards the Lady of Lyonnesse and her young champion. And long thereafter lived they in honour and happiness.

THE KNIGHT OF THE LION

I

THE brave Sir Ewayne had wed a fair lady, the mistress of goodly castles and wide lands. To the marriage came Arthur and his Knights of the Round Table, and from far and near the people flocked to look upon their great king; so for a week all was feasting and jollity in the lady's castle, where the time was spent in sports, and hunting, and banquets, such as beseemed these noble guests.

But when a week had passed, the king must ride forth against the heathen who were laying waste a distant part of his realm. Then, as all the castle rang with the clash of armour and the trampling of steeds, Sir Ewayne drew his new-made wife aside and took her by the hand, and spoke gently thus:

"Sweet lady, my life and joy, there is a thing I would pray thee, for my honour and thine."

"Truly, sir, fear not but I will do all your wish," said the lady, smiling; yet her countenance changed when she heard that she must let her husband follow the king.

"Well thou knowest how loath I am to part from thee; but think how men will blame me if I leave all my knighthood, and dwell idly at home. Nay, what good wife would love her lord better if he cared only to lie in her arms? Give me leave, then, to ride forth for a twelve-month, and win worship in deeds of arms."

"Sad should I be to grieve thee!" she cried, though she was sore unwilling to let him go. "I give my leave; but, Sir Ewayne, promise, by the love thou owest me, to come again ere a year be gone. This is the eve of St. John. Look that thou comest by this day twelvemonth, else shalt thou lose my love for ever."

"Lady," said he, kissing her, "if I might have my will I would never leave thee, and now naught shall hinder me from keeping the day thou hast set. Fear not for my life. The love of thee will be a charm to strengthen thy true knight against every foe."

Gladly, then, Sir Ewayne let his squire do on his armour, dinted in many a fray. Lightly he leaped upon his horse among that band of goodly knights, while his lady held the king's stirrup and bade him good speed. But the tears trickled down her cheek; and when her husband lingered behind to give her one more kiss, she whispered in his ear, beseeching him again not to fail to keep his day.

II

Far rode King Arthur and his knights, and fiercely warred they with the heathen foe. Sir Ewayne, as of old, was first in every fight, yet escaped from all unhurt. When the war was over, he did not go homewards, for the love of knighthood was strong on him, and too lightly he forgot the love of his lady; but he rode with his brothers-in-arms to jousts and tournaments held here and there in honour of Arthur's knights. Wherever doughty deeds were done, Sir Ewayne still bore himself among the best, and won prizes in all the lists, so that his fame went forth over the land.

Thus the twelvemonth passed away, and so greedy of renown was the knight that still he stayed from his lady, and minded not the pledge he had given her. But one day, as he feasted at the king's table, and the queen spoke to him of his newly wed wife, he suddenly bethought him of her last words, and how he had promised to be with her by a day now some time past. Sorrowful and ashamed, he rose from the table, and would have saddled his horse to ride home that hour, so that even yet he might mend his fault; but before he could take leave of the king and queen, there came hastily into the hall a damsel, who knelt before Arthur, and said:

"Sir king, heaven save thee! My lady greets thee by me, and the good Sir Lancelot, and the courteous Sir Gawayne, and all thy knights, save only one. Sir Ewayne has deceived my lady, and it were shame to call so false a man a knight. She weened she had his heart, and truly he made great boast of his love, but all was treason and treachery, for now he has broken the term that was set between them, and thought nothing of her grief. He cannot be come of noble blood that so soon forgets his wife who loved him better than herself! Therefore, unkind and untrue man, she will see thee no more. Deliver me my lady's ring!"

With this she stepped up to Sir Ewayne, and, as he stood astonished, tore from his hand the ring his wife had given him, hurried from the hall, leaped upon her palfrey, and went her way without another word. Neither squire nor groom rode with her, and no man knew where she had gone.

Sir Ewayne stood still awhile, as overwhelmed by the news of his lady's anger; then rushed after the damsel, and would have followed her on foot. But nowhere could he see her, for she had ridden into a great forest.

Yet he ceased not to seek her, wandering through the
forest, wild with grief, crying out angrily against his own
folly and forgetfulness.

"Alas for the day I was born!   Have I thus lost my
love? Would, then, that I might die!" he cried loud
and often, and in his despair tore up the trees and broke
his sword against the rocks, till, breathless and exhausted,
he fell on the grass.   He rose again, and again fury took
him, and now he threw away his armour, helmet and
shield, and mail of proof, rent his vest and shirt to shreds,
flung them to the winds, running naked like a wild beast
through the deepest thickets. His men sought him far
and near, but found only his armour, which they brought
back to the king, and took their master for dead. The
news went abroad, and all men mourned for the brave
Sir Ewayne, his lady most of all, for she repented of her
anger when she knew that he had lost his wits for sorrow
and love of her.

But Ewayne was alive in the forest, sleeping on the
bare ground, and living on roots and berries. His madness waxed greater from day to day. Once he came
upon a savage hunting in the woods. He wrested his bow
and arrows from him, and was gone before the savage
could raise his club. Henceforth he could kill wild
beasts, and have raw flesh for his daily food, and drink
warm blood. Still he fled the sight of all men; his hair
and nails grew; he was frightful to behold, as he roamed
about, murmuring to himself the name of his wife, and
from time to time taken by a fit of fury, in which he
would tear up all around him, or try to dash himself to
pieces upon the rocks. To such a plight had this good
knight come, who stood once in so great honour and
renown.

Save himself, the only dweller in this forest was a

hermit, who had built a little cell in the midst of a bushy glade. When the hermit saw a naked man armed with bow and arrows, he fled hastily out of his way. But soon he knew Ewayne for a madman, and took pity on him, and set barley bread and water out at the window of his hermitage for him. Ewayne's wits were not so far gone but that he knew the hermit meant kindly by him, and every day he would steal up to take the food thus provided, though he never saw or spoke with the holy man. Every day, too, he would leave in return at the door of the cell the carcass of a deer, or some other beast, which he had killed; and when he was gone, the hermit would bring it in, and cook the venison, and set out part of that also for the hunter. Thus both of them fared better for their friendship, yet neither of them knew so much as the other's name. But by Ewayne's looks and bearing, and by the scars of his wounds, the hermit believed him to be a gentle knight, from whom some great sorrow had taken away his wits. Then he carried the skins of the slain beasts to the nearest town and sold them, and with the money bought clothes and arms, such as beseemed a knight, and medicines, for this hermit was skilled in healing, and hoped yet to cure the wild man of his madness.

So a year went by, while Ewayne still dwelt in the forest, and, but for that old man's kindness, would have led the life of the beasts. But now his fury was passed away. He began to bethink him who he was, and to remember what had gone before. Then he lay for hours on the ground sighing and weeping. His sorrow became so great that he cared not to eat, and he could no longer hunt for food. His strength left him; often he swooned away; he desired nothing but to die. The hermit always left out bread and water for him, but the poor man seldom came for them now. At last, when seven days had passed, and the food was untouched, the hermit, fearing he must be dead, set out one morning through the forest in search of him.

Before long he came upon Ewayne lying under a tree all pale and worn and senseless. But his heart still beat, and the good old man made haste to help him. He ran to his hermitage, and quickly brought back the clothes and arms which he had provided. These he laid by the side of the sleeping knight, then anointed his body above the heart with a precious ointment, of which the virtues were known to him alone. This done, he stole away and left Ewayne still sleeping.

When the sun came to noon, and its beams fell on his face, he awoke, and rose, and was astonished; for lo! his sickness and his madness had left him, and he stood up a whole man, in mind and body, though how he came by this cure he knew not. And there lay at his side clothes, and armour, and a good sword, such as he had cast away from him in his frenzy a year ago. That year now seemed nothing but a frightful dream; and yet, as Ewayne beheld himself in a clear fountain hard by, he knew that he had, indeed, been living like a savage man, and feared that all would fly from the sight of him. He bathed himself in the fountain, and, though at first too weak to stand upright, he was soon able to put on his clothes and armour, and found that he could still draw a sword. Then he knelt and thanked heaven for this deliverance, vowing never to use his sword save to succour the helpless and the oppressed.

III

Slowly he now took his way through the forest, stiff of limb and heavy of heart; and, though his madness had passed away, thought ever with sorrow on the lady whose love he had lost.   Thus many an hour and many a mile he wandered, but met no living thing.   But towards evening he heard a dreadful noise in a thicket close at hand, and when he hastened thither by the nearest way, he saw a fearsome sight.   A lion and a dragon were struggling together with all the fury of their kind.   The dragon, breathing out fire from its nostrils, twining round the body of its enemy, and driving its fangs deep into the flesh, had almost slain the lion, when Sir Ewayne, moved by his knighthood to take the part of the weaker, ran up to its rescue.   He held his shield before his face to keep off the monster's fiery breath; he raised his sword; for a moment the old might came back to his arm; and with one stroke he clave the dragon's body in two.

The lion, thus set free, rose to its feet, and shook its bloody mane, and roared so that all the forest echoed back the sound.   Quickly Ewayne stood upon his guard, for he thought he must now have to do with this other fierce beast.   But the lion had no mind to assail its preserver; it crept up to him, crouching on the ground, fawning upon him, and licking his feet, and in all ways tried to let the knight know its gratitude.   Ewayne spoke kindly to the beast, and dressed its wounds as best he could.   Then, when he went on his way, the lion would not leave him, but followed or strode by his side.   Soon it came to understand his commands, and obey his voice like a dog.   Never knight had such a faithful friend as this savage creature.

SIR EWAYNE SLAYS THE DRAGON

THE GREEN KNIGHT RIDES INTO KING ARTHUR'S HALL

At nightfall, when they halted, Ewayne broke down boughs, and made a rude lodge in which to pass the night. Meanwhile the lion went a little way off and killed a deer, the carcass of which it brought to its master, who with flint and steel lit a fire of moss and dry branches, and on a spit roasted the flesh for supper. But not a morsel would the lion touch till the knight had eaten; and when, after this simple meal, he lay down to sleep with his head upon his shield, the grateful beast prowled round, and spent the night in watching over its preserver.

Next morning, Ewayne rose betimes and set forward, knowing not nor heeding where he went, till at evening, as before, the lion brought him his prey, and they supped together and spent the night. Many days thus he journeyed on, with the lion by his side, through this great forest, and at last came upon a wide plain of rich meadows, in the midst of which stood a many-towered castle. Towards this the knight took his way, and reached the gate at sunset.

Men came out and let down the drawbridge, but suddenly they fled at the sight of the strange squire Sir Ewayne had with him. And the porter said:

"Sir, it behoves thee to leave that beast without."

"Nay," replied Ewayne, "my lion and I are not to be parted; we must either come in together, or else will go hence."

The porter still grumbled, but thereon came the lord of the castle, who bade that Ewayne and his lion should be both admitted, and he hastened to meet and welcome his guest.

The knight was now courteously led into a chamber, where the ladies of the castle unarmed him, and brought him clothes of rich silk, and showed him all kindness.

But to Sir Ewayne it seemed that they were sad at heart, though they tried to look glad of his coming. When he came into the hall, and supper was served, he still might see that some affliction had fallen upon all the inhabitants of the castle. His host made a fair show for his sake, but he could scarcely speak for sorrow, and the ladies would ever and again break out weeping and sighing as they waited on him, and none ate a morsel from the plenteous board. The knight wondered greatly, and when supper was done, he asked the lord of the castle the cause of their trouble.

"Sir, if it is your will, I would fain know why you make such ill cheer?"

"Alas," was the answer, "we would make joy, as becomes us, since we have you as our guest; but we cannot but grieve when we think of what shall be done to-morrow! Know that in this country dwells a proud and cruel giant, by name Harpins of the Mountain, who is the terror of our lives, for no man here living can say him nay. And oh, sir, I had four goodly sons that he has taken prisoner, as they strove to rid the land of such a pest! Two of them he has slain before my eyes, and each day must another be put to death, unless I deliver him my daughter. Because she would not be his wife, he has sworn to marry her to the meanest of his servants, so morning by morning he comes before my castle demanding her, and I must see all my children undone, unless I can find a champion to fight this monster. What wonder, then, if we be full of woe!"

"Methinks it strange," said Ewayne, when he had listened to this tale, "that you have not ere this sought help and counsel from the king. For in all this wide world there is no man of so great might, but King Arthur has knights at his Round Table who would be

full glad and willing to meet with such a man, and try
their strength against him."

"Sir, I have indeed sent to the king's court, but
there are no knights there, save the best, who can stand
against this giant.   And Sir Lancelot and all the best
knights have gone to rescue the queen, who has been
stolen away, they say, by a certain felon knight.   Till
they come back, and bring the queen safe again, I can
have no help."

"Help you shall have!" cried Ewayne.   "I know
Sir Lancelot well, and for his sake and the maiden's
I will undertake this battle and fight with the giant,
let him come as soon as he will."

"Heaven reward thee!" prayed the knight, and the
lady of the castle and her daughter came and knelt before
Ewayne, thanking him with tears and many words.   But
he declared that no lady should kneel to him, and raised
them up, and spoke kindly to them, and bid them be of
good cheer, for he would avenge them on their oppressor.
Then they and all in the castle took courage, thinking
that he must be a knight of strength and renown who
had a lion thus at his command, and so blithely promised
to meet this fell giant.

That night Sir Ewayne slept once more upon a bed,
and the lion lay beside, so that no man durst come near
his chamber.   In the morning he rose early, and before
he did any other thing, was going to the chapel of the
castle to hear mass, when a servant came running to say
that the giant was at hand.   All in the castle hurried to
the walls, and now Sir Ewayne saw a piteous sight.   With
huge strides the giant came on, a shaggy monster, whose
hair hung to his waist, dressed in bullskins, and bearing
no weapon but a great club of iron; in his other hand he
had a cruel scourge of ten cords, with which he furiously

beat his two captives, as he drove them before him almost naked, half-starved with cold and hunger, and having their hands bound behind their backs. At every blow the blood ran down their defenceless bodies, and their cries were heard throughout the castle, so that all rued the fate of these gentle youths, and their father and mother wept to behold them. Pale and trembling stood their sister, as the giant came beneath the walls roaring out in the ears of them all:

"If thou wilt have thy sons alive, deliver me that damsel, that I may give her to the foulest knave that eats my bread."

"Fear not," said Sir Ewayne, as the weeping ladies did on his armour. "This giant is full fierce and cruel of his words, but either he shall kill me, or I will deliver this maiden from the dread of him; for, certes, it were pity that such a foul hap should ever befall such a fair lady."

"Oh, sir," said the father, "do as you say, and I will give you this castle and half my land!"

"Nay, heaven forbid that a true knight should take reward for succouring a damsel!" said Sir Ewayne, and bid them let down the drawbridge.

Forth he rushed, with his lion at his heels, while all the people in the castle fell on their knees to pray for this gallant knight. When the giant saw him he gave over lashing his captives, and turned upon their champion with mocking and boastful words.

"What fiend made thee so bold to come out against a man like me? Whoever sent thee here loved thee full little, and shall soon be rid of thee!"

"Do thy best!" cried Sir Ewayne, and without more ado hurled his spear so straight and strong that it pierced the bullhide, and sank deep into the giant's hairy breast.

As the blood gushed out, the hideous monster gave a roar, and, brandishing his iron club, rushed upon the knight, as if he would crush him to the earth. But he deftly caught the blow upon his shield, and with his keen sword rained strokes upon the bull-hide, that could not turn its edge. Cries of surprise, fear, and pity rose all around. Again and again the knight seemed to be already a dead man, but ever he escaped the iron club, and gave back blow for blow, till all wondered, and said that this could be no other than Sir Lancelot or Sir Gawayne, that fought thus against such a foe.

But, ah! his strength began to fail him; he struck wildly in the air; he stumbled; his shield fell from his hands. The white maiden on the walls clasped her hands, and would have cried out, but she could not move her lips for terror. The giant gave a shout that went to every heart, he raised his club, one moment more and the knight was lost. Then suddenly the lion raised its head as it saw its master in such a strait. With a bound and a roar it sprang upon the giant, and tore his flesh so that the bones could be seen beneath. In vain he strove to use his club; the beast leaped aside from every stroke; then before, behind, on either side, it flew upon him afresh and mangled him till he bellowed for pain, and at last, blinded by the blood which flowed into his eyes, he overreached himself, falling on the ground like a heavy tree.

By now Sir Ewayne had taken breath; he ran up to the fallen monster, and with one mighty stroke cut off his right arm. Next moment he drove his good blade into the wicked heart. The trembling captives wept for joy. Their sister swooned away upon the walls. The castle gates were flung open, and all within ran forth to hail the victor.

Who can tell their gladness when they saw that cruel oppressor lie lifeless on the ground!   The lord and lady of the castle fell on the neck of their champion, and prayed him earnestly to stay with them and take all they had for his.

"Nay," said Sir Ewayne, "I will have naught of ye but it were a horse, on which to go my way as becomes a knight."

"Sir," said his host, "the best steed in my stalls is yours freely; but I would give you back what is dearest of all to me, my daughter, that you have given to me this day.   Well are ye worthy to wed her, and she is not to be despised by any in the land."

"Take it for no despite if I may not wed her or any other maiden," answered Ewayne.   "She is indeed fair and gentle, and in all the world there is no king or emperor or man of so great honour that he might not gladly have so sweet a lady for his wife.   But I have a wife, and, alas! I have none.   Courteous sir, entreat me no further, but let me go hence."

"And if any ask us what knight has done so doughty a deed, how shall we name thee?"

"Call me the Knight of the Lion," said Ewayne, and would tell them no more.

Long they pressed him to stay with them, but when they saw that his will might not be moved, they said farewell, and sent him forth upon a gallant steed, fit for such a good knight.

Sir Ewayne gave his horse the rein, and rode on wherever it bore him, with the faithful lion at his side. Well pleased was he to be sure that his sword had not forgotten its ancient sharpness; yet grief ever seized him as he thought of the lady to whom it should have been devoted.   Was she dead?   Was she married again, believing him dead? He cared not to know, since she loved him no more. He could do nothing for her but obey her request, never to seek to see her face, or let her hear his name.

IV

Before many months had passed, the land began to ring with the fame of this fearless champion, who was known only as the Knight of the Lion. Foul caitiff and fell tyrant shook at that name, for well they knew that the oppressed and helpless had no surer friend. All who were in misfortune had but to repair to him, and might then bless the day on which he was born, for they were not more ready to beseech than he was to succour, and he fought for no cause in which he did not conquer. Wherever he went the people came forth from the towns to greet him, and when he departed convoyed him out of the gates with prayers that no harm might befall so gallant a champion. These prayers were as a magic armour, against which the strongest weapons could not prevail, and for years this knight passed through all perils unhurt, achieving adventures in which all others had fallen.

" Never have men seen such a knight since the brave Sir Ewayne was alive," said King Arthur among his knights at Camelot, as the news came thither of fresh exploits done by this stranger. " Methinks he were well worthy to sit at our Round Table. Is there none of my knights who will go forth and find him, and bring him hither, by force or by his own goodwill ?"

The king's knights were nowise loath to do his will, for they envied the fame of the Knight of the Lion, and jealously desired to try their might against him. Sir Lancelot, Sir Gawayne, and Sir Kay the boaster sought

this quest, and Arthur sent forth all three, bidding them
not return without the unknown knight as courteous
friend or vanquished foe.

So these three took divers ways, and rode far and
wide, asking all they met for news of a knight who led
a lion with him wherever he went. All had heard of
this knight, all bore witness that he helped in word and
deed whoever had ne d of him, but no man could say
where he might be found. The three knights rode on by
hill and dale, by castle and town, but still could hear no
tidings of the Knight of the Lion. Yet Lancelot and
Gawayne ceased not to seek him. Only Sir Kay left the
quest, and rode back to tell the king that this knight
must be dead or held fast in some dungeon.

But now, as he rode, it chanced he met with him, and
perceived by the lion that this was the knight he sought.
Because his vizor was down, he knew not it was Sir
Ewayne, but Ewayne knew him well for Sir Kay, the
steward of the king, who ever railed and boasted himself,
but whose words were greater than his deeds.

"Hold, Sir Knight of the Lion!" he cried loudly.
"I have sworn to bring thee to King Arthur as friend
or foe."

"Sir Steward," answered Ewayne sadly, "I have no
friends, and I am foe to no good man. Have it as thou
wilt."

"Then sit firm in thy saddle," said the boaster.
"But first send thy lion away, or bind him, if thou wilt
not yield thee. Thyself shall fight with me alone."

"Let the lion not make thee aghast. It is neither
right nor custom to have aid against a single knight,"
and with that Sir Ewayne bade his lion lie down, and the
faithful beast obeyed him, nor would it ever move till it
saw its master in danger.

Scant courtesy passed between these two. Without more ado, they ran together with their sharp lances, and at the first onset Sir Ewayne hurled Sir Kay out of his saddle, and cast him on the ground a spear's length behind his horse, and with such force that his helm smote a foot deep into the ground. No other harm would he do him, because he knew him of old, but he left the steward discomfited on the ground, and thus took farewell of him.

"Go back to the king and tell him that the Knight of the Lion is not worthy to be his friend, and that knights such as thou are unworthy to be my foes."

He turned his rein and rode away with heavy heart, leading beside him the horse of the fallen knight. It was not in him to be proud of such a victory, and the sight of Sir Kay had set him thinking of the days gone by, when he fought and feasted among the princes of Arthur's court, and knew not of the sorrow that should come upon him. Then all his life was full of pride and joy; now his only hope was in death, and death came not to him who was sick of life. At times it seemed that his madness was about to return upon him; the best he could look for would be to die like a wild beast, un-known and unpitied, bereft of himself as he had been of his wife and his friends. Then the lion came and licked his hand, and with tears in his eyes he raised his head.

And lo! now, as he looked around, he knew well the place in which he was. There was a great leafless thorn tree above a trickling well, and, hard by, a little chapel built upon a rock. It was under this thorn that first he met his lady many years ago; it was in this chapel that they had plighted their troth. At the sight that dauntless knight grew white and trembled like a woman, then, overcome with sudden weakness, fell from his horse.

He rose to his feet, and wild thoughts rushed into his mind. In the fall his sword had escaped from the sheath. He seized it, he thrust the hilt into the ground, he placed the point against his throat, he would have slain himself on the spot, when a voice of distress reached his ear. In the chapel there was one weeping and complaining. Sir Ewayne paused to ask:

"Who art thou that mournest there?"

"Ah! well-away!" answered the voice, "I am the sorriest wight that ever lived, and as yet I have lived but seven years."

"Nay," said the knight, "by all the saints, there is no sorrow like mine for seven years past, nor any alive that might make such dole. I was a man and now am none, nor worthy to be seen of men. Once I was a noble knight and a lord of might and renown; I had knights and squires in my train, and riches and lands in plenty, and all I lost through my folly. But the greatest sorrow is yet to tell: I lost my lady that was full dear to me, and that loved me better than her life. I have naught to do but to slay myself by whom I was undone."

"Alas! mine is a more sorrowful case. I am but a little maiden seven years old; my father, they say, died before I was born, and left my mother in grief and fear. Many strong lords have sought her to wife, yet, though she lived alone, with none to protect her, she ever sent them away, and wept for her own good knight who is dead these seven years. Ah, sir! there is a felon knight called Sir Salados, who dwells near at hand, and of whom all this country is in dread. He has sore vexed my mother, and has robbed her of all her lands when she would not give them with her goodwill. And to-day this wicked knight came at the hour of prime, and has taken her captive in her own castle, and there, for she

will not marry him, she must starve in a dungeon if I
bring not some champion to her succour. Fain am I to
seek the Knight of the Lion, who, as men say, slew the
giant Harpins, and never fails ladies that are in need; for
certain he would fight this cruel man. But none know
where he may be found, and I am weak and tender of
age, and, alas! alas! my mother must die."

"Nay, dear maiden, she shall not die while I live!"
cried Ewayne, forgetting his own grief at this pitiful tale.
"Thank heaven that has brought to thee him thou
seekest. I am he whom men call Knight of the Lion,
and I will fight this felon while breath is in me. Come
forth and lead me to where he is, and be of good cheer."

Forth ran the little maiden with a cry of joy. But
on the threshold of the chapel she paused and shook
for fear, and pointed with her hand.

"Ah, see! There he comes, riding on a black horse,
and here in this meadow he is wont to defy all that fear
not to try his might!"

Sir Ewayne looked, and saw, riding furiously towards
him on a coal-black steed, a tall knight in black armour
from head to foot, with a black shield and a black pennon
on his lance, and the trappings of his horse were of black
velvet.

"'Tis well," he said, placing the child upon Sir Kay's
horse, and bade her not be afraid of the lion, for it would
do no maiden harm, and bade it watch by her while he
dealt with this black knight. Then he drew tight his
girths, took his spear in hand, leaped into the saddle, and
flew forth like an arrow, crying:

"Ho! Sir Salados, false knight and robber of ladies,
the time is come when thou shalt be well paid for all thy
villainy."

The black knight spoke not a word, but, with a scorn-

ful laugh, put his lance in rest and spurred upon Ewayne.
And now, as they rushed together, a loud peal of thunder
burst above their heads, and a heavy storm of rain and
hail poured down around them, so that the knights were
almost hid from sight. With a mighty shock they met
midway. Both lances splintered to the handle, but
neither was shaken in his seat. Out flashed their bright
swords, and deadly were the strokes dealt between them.
It was no Sir Kay with whom the Knight of the Lion
had now to do. Sparks flew from helmet and hauberk;
the armour crashed and gaped beneath the blows; the
blood poured down upon the field. Still each sat stiffly
upon his horse, and neither would yield a foot; it was a
battle for life or death. At last the black knight's strokes
seemed to wax faint; but Sir Ewayne gathered all his
strength and smote a blow which cleft helm and brainpan,
and made Sir Salados reel and give back as if he would
have fallen. For a moment Ewayne held his hand, deem-
ing that his foe would beg for mercy; then, of a sudden,
the black knight turned and fled for his life.

With all his main he sped away, and the Knight of
the Lion rode hard behind him, sword in hand. Like
the wind they rode, for now the beaten knight could see
his castle walls, and Ewayne would kill his horse but he
would take him dead or alive. The storm raged around
them, and the hail blinded their eyes, but with loosened
bridle and blood-stained spurs they urged their panting
steeds, and swiftly neared the castle gate. And now the
flying man gains the moat; three strides and he has crossed
the drawbridge; he is hidden within the walls. Fast
follows Ewayne, heedless of a warning cry. His good
steed bounds forward, and already he is within the gate-
way, when with a clang the portcullis falls from above,
smiting through saddle and horse, shearing the spurs

from the heels of the knight, and by a hairbreadth leaving him unhurt, but amazed, dismounted, and alone in the house of his enemy, which was no other than the house that had once been his.

In all haste he gained his feet and stood on guard with his back to the gate. But the sword had almost dropped from his hand when he saw no one in the courtyard save a lady weeping and wringing her hands. That lady was his wife, who seven long years ago had bid him see her no more.

"Alas! alas!" she cried; "what do you here? This is a den of robbers and murderers into which you have come, and I am an unhappy lady who must here lose my life."

"Then I shall lose mine own first, for my life is not so dear to me as thine."

The voice went to her heart. She looked earnestly upon the closed vizor of the knight, and was about to speak, when Sir Salados, all covered with blood, and brandishing a huge axe, burst forth through a door in the wall, a band of armed men at his heels.

Now Sir Ewayne was lost, unless some enchanter should come to his aid, or he might have wings to fly. Yet the good knight did not quail. He drew the lady to him and stood before her with his drawn sword, as on rushed the black knight and his treacherous rabble. But ere the sharp steel clashed, a sound was heard that made them hold and look round in dread.

It was the roar of the lion, that now came raging without the gate, and when it saw its master's peril, dashed against the steel bars and tore up the earth beneath, and with all its might strove to win to his side. Small wonder that these caitiffs shook at the sight, and drew back a space.

"Would ye fear a caged beast?" cried their felon lord, and led them once more against Sir Ewayne.

Alas! what could his single arm do against so many. They closed upon him; the lady shrieked and fell; his sword gleamed like light, and it was wondrous to see how he stood firm among such mighty blows. Then, as they bore him down, and the black knight's axe was raised above his head, the crowd gave a cry, and a crash was heard above the din, for the lion had burst through the bars to spring among them with bristling mane and open jaws. The heavy blow fell upon its head; but never struck Sir Salados another stroke. Hurled to the ground, he lay with his neck broken, and his craven crew turned and fled on every side, melted like snow before the hot breath of the lion, which chased them fiercely into the inner courts of the castle.

V

Breathless, but unwounded, Sir Ewayne sprang to his feet and looked around. He was alone with the lady, who knelt before him and thanked him full humbly. He would have spoken, but his tongue clove to his mouth. Then was heard the trampling of hoofs without, and two knights rode up, and the little maiden by their side on Sir Kay's horse. Ewayne made clear the entry to let them pass, and forthwith he knew them for Sir Lancelot and Sir Gawayne.

Much they marvelled to see him safe from such a fray, and fain were they, when the lady had told the tale, to learn the name of her deliverer.

"Surely," said Sir Lancelot, "there is no knight save him of the Lion who could thus succour a lady; and this knight have we sought these many days."

"Ah me," cried the lady, "there was once such a knight who took me for his wife! By my own sinful pride I drove him from me, or else I had never wanted succour against robbers and traitors. But all that I have and hope would I give to see him again for a moment's space, that I might pray him to pardon me, and die in peace."

"Fair lady," said Gawayne the courteous, "that may not be. Thou wert wedded to our fellow Sir Ewayne, and he is dead these seven years. Would, indeed, that he were alive!"

"He is alive!" spoke a voice that all knew well of old. "Sirs, I am him you seek. Lady, I am him you loved."

He raised his vizor, and, amazed, they saw Ewayne stand before them. The two knights made the sign of the cross; the lady gave a cry.

"Oh, my wife, it is your forgiveness that I should pray for on my knees!"

He could speak no more, and she could not hear for joy. Each of them would fain be the first to forgive. They fell upon one another's necks, and in one kiss forgot all the sorrows of these seven years.

SIR GAWAYNE AND THE
GREEN KNIGHT

At Camelot, in all mirth and jollity, King Arthur kept Christmas with his knights of the Round Table. When they sat down to dinner on New Year's Day, the king, looking round upon that goodly brotherhood, was moved to wish aloud that soon they might hear of some marvellous adventure to spice their feast. Scarcely had he spoken, when, as the first course was served, there rode into the hall a knight unknown to the eyes turned upon him in astonishment.

He was the tallest man anyone there had ever beheld, and the strangest in guise and looks. His face was as fierce as his limbs were stalwart; his red eyes glowed out of a shock of bristly hair; and over his broad breast hung a beard big as a bush. From head to foot he was dressed in green, coat, hood, and hose, only his spurs being of bright gold. His horse, too, was green as grass, its mane knotted with gold threads, its tail tied with a jewelled green band, its green trappings hung with golden bells. He wore no armour, and bore neither spear nor shield, but in one hand a green holly bough, in the other a huge axe, sharp as a razor, its handle and its head richly chased in gold and green. Never before had been seen at Arthur's court such a man, nor such a steed. All sat dumbfounded, as he gazed around as if asking who might be the chief of the company. Then Arthur was first to address him courteously.

"Light down from horse, sir, and sit with us at our feast, if so please thee."

"I came not to feast, nor to tarry," answered he, "but to prove the courage of this famous fellowship."

"If it be battle ye seek, there is many a one here will take your challenge," quoth the king, at which the stranger laughed loud and long.

"Had I come here to fight, I should not have left my arms at home! Here I see but beardless children to match the like of me. I come to try them with a Christmas sport. Is any of ye bold enough to fetch one blow at me with this axe, on condition that next New Year's Day he shall stand a stroke from my hand?"

All the knights were silent, as the green giant rolled his eyes and bent his brows first on one, then on another; but no one cared to offer himself for such an exchange of blows.

"And this is the Round Table and Arthur's court, of which mighty boasts are made!" he sneered, so that the king was stung by shame and wrath to take the defiance on himself, for the honour of his knighthood.

"Give me the axe, and have at thy head!" he cried. "Thou shalt see if we fear thy broad steel any more than thy big words."

The Green Knight sprang from his horse, and put the axe into Arthur's hands; but now the others held him back, saying that this was no adventure for their king.

"Grant me the chance!" begged his nephew, Sir Gawayne, youngest of all his knights; and the rest backed him up, holding that game more seemly for a young man to play.

"So be it!" said Arthur, unwillingly yielding him

the axe. "But see thou puttest such heart and hand into thy stroke, that he shall never pay thee back."

The Green Knight smiled grimly, asking the name of him with whom he should swap blows. And when he heard it was Gawayne, he said:

"It likes me well to take a blow at Sir Gawayne's hand. But first he must swear to seek me out within a twelvemonth and a day hence, that I keep next New Year by giving back what I got from him."

"I swear; but where shall I seek thee?"

"When thou hast struck thy blow, I will tell where to find me. If I speak not, so much the better for thee. Now do thy best!"

With this the giant made ready to stand a stroke. Turning his back on Gawayne, he drew down his collar and pushed aside his long hair, so as to unbare his neck to the axe, then, stroking his bushy beard, with unmoved countenance he awaited what should come.

The young knight grasped that heavy axe, heaved it on high, measured his blow with steady eye, and delivered it with all the strength of his arm. Down it came on the brawny neck, shearing through skin and bone, so that the hairy head fell on the floor, and the green garments were dabbled with blood. The giant had stood firm without flinching or saying a word; now, before anyone could stir, he picked up his own head, sprang on his horse, and rode from the hall. The king called out, the queen screamed, the knights stared. Then, as the green one passed out of sight, the head in his hand moved its eyes upon Gawayne, and opened its mouth to say:

"I have thy word. At the Green Chapel, next New Year's Day, we meet again, that I may do unto thee as thou hast done to me. Look that thou fail not, or be for ever stained as a recreant knight!"

"Here is an adventure indeed, such as well beseems Christmastide!" spoke Arthur, turning to cheer his dismayed queen.

The rest of the company knew not whether to laugh or to shudder over the prodigy they had beheld. It made talk for their banquet, and through all the revels of the season. Many pitied Gawayne, who next New Year must keep such a promise to one who could live with his head stricken off. Then, by and by, the wonder, out of sight, began to go out of mind.

But Gawayne did not forget, who had to fear that but one more year was his to live. For him the months passed by too quickly. After Christmas came Lent, bringing showers to brighten the grass and swell the buds, among which birds sang for joy of the summer at hand. Next the warm sun kissed out flowers shining with dewdrops; then leafy trees and yellow harvests mantled the earth's dusty nakedness. But with Michaelmas the leaves began to fall, and the ripe fruit to grow rotten, and the green grass to go grey; and soon winter was back again, when Gawayne should hold himself ready for that dread tryst. The king was first to remind him that he must not fail to keep his day; and at All Hallows he made a feast for his nephew, whose friends and kinsmen now took farewell of him as one they might never see again.

Since he knew not where the Green Chapel might be, it behoved him to start betimes in search of it. On his good horse Gringalet, in full armour, and wearing his richest attire, he rode out alone from Camelot. Much warm water, says the minstrel, poured out of fair eyes for so gallant a youth going forth a victim to that man of such unearthly strength.

Far and wide rode Gawayne, through England and

Wales, asking here and there after the Green Knight and
his Green Chapel, but no man could tell him where they
might be found. Many a hill he climbed, many a ford
he crossed, many a miry marsh; and at bridge or pass he
must often do battle with some knight who held it against
all comers. Often, too, he was in peril from wild bulls
and boars, and wolves and serpents, and savage men; but
through all he won his way unhurt. Worst was the
sharp winter cold, when he must sleep in his armour
on naked rocks, pelted by sleet and rain. Had he not
been hardy and hearty as few, he would never have come
so far safe and sound. But when he had thus travelled
for weeks, still he could hear no word of that Green
Chapel; and the dark year was drawing to an end.

On Christmas Eve, he found himself lost in a great
wood of hoary and mossy trees, where no paths could be
seen and no voices heard but the birds piping for cold
upon leafless branches. Of the Virgin Mary he prayed
this boon, that before nightfall he might be guided to
some dwelling of men, among whom to hear mass and
keep the holy season as beseemed. And lo! as he raised
his eyes, through an opening of the wood, he was aware
of a noble castle set on a hill, so that it stood out brightly
against the glow of the setting sun.

Spurring his weary horse, he reached the gate before
it was dark. The drawbridge being let down, Gawayne
bid the porter tell his lord that a wayfarer besought lodging for one night. There was no want of hearty welcome. The lord of the castle, a tall and sturdy knight,
came out to greet the guest, and with him his fair lady.
Squires took Gawayne's horse to stable, while his host
led him to a tapestried chamber and sent a page to undo
his armour. When he had washed and attired himself
in his best, he went down into the hall, where a goodly

Christmas company was gathered. Great honour and kindness they showed the stranger, the more when he named himself as of Arthur's Round Table, which over all the land was famed for courteous manners and noble knighthood. He was set down beside the lovesome young mistress, all smiles for such a guest; and to the other end of the board the lord led an aged, wrinkled crone, whom Gawayne marvelled to see made much of above many a beautiful and richly clad dame. That night he feasted choicely and slept softly, as he had not fared since he left Camelot on his dolorous quest.

In the morning, the lord and lady would by no means let him leave them, to keep Christmas among bears and wolves. For three days Gawayne stayed in their hospitable castle, feasting with all mirth and good cheer, before he began to ask his road to the Green Chapel, declaring that he was bound to be there on New Year's Day, but on what errand he kept to himself. If that were so, his host told him, he might stay three days longer, for the Green Chapel was close at hand, to which he himself would put him on the way. The knight was well pleased to know his journey so near an end, and gladly agreed to repose here for the rest of the week. Then this jovial host, taking him to be wearied by long travel, bid him lie at home all day, while he went out to hunt; and he proposed a strange bargain between them.

"Whatever you get each day shall be mine in exchange for what I win in the woods."

"So be it!" agreed Gawayne, falling in with his humour; and they pledged themselves to that compact in a friendly cup.

Next morning, then, the lord of the castle went out before daybreak, with hounds and huntsmen, while

Gawayne took his ease in his chamber. Here he was visited by the hostess, before whom he in vain feigned to be asleep, when, making eyes at him and rallying him on his sluggishness, she did not hide that her heart was given to this handsome young man.

"I am unworthy of such favour," pleaded the good knight; and when she mocked at his modesty, he let her know plainly how he might offer her no service but what a knight owed to all ladies; he durst not be untrue to his honour by deceiving a trustful host; and the errand he came on was one that quenched all thoughts of love. But the sportive dame, laughing at his scruples, did not go without giving him a kiss; then he could rise and banish temptation by hearing mass in the castle chapel. The rest of the day he spent with the ladies, well pleased to have the company of that aged crone, before whom the young mistress must sure bear herself discreetly.

Back came the lord at evening with his quarry of venison, which he bestowed on Gawayne, according to their agreement; and in return the guest embraced him with a kiss as all he had got at home.

"Ha! and who gave it thee?" demanded his host; but Gawayne laughed off that question as not in their bond. Then they sat down to supper the best of friends.

When the cock had crowed thrice next morning, the hunter again set out for the woods. Again, in his absence, Gawayne was visited by the wileful dame, who could not shake his fidelity to virtue; but this time gave him two kisses before she ceased to play the temptress. Her husband at night brought home a boar as game due to his guest, who this time had two kisses to give him in return, but did not confess where he had gotten them. Now he would have taken leave for next morning, but the hearty host would not hear of his going, and promised that on New Year's Day he should be at the Green Chapel betimes.

The third day dawned cold and clear, and the lord had gone off to hunt when his wife once more came wooing her guest to sinful dalliance, having awakened him from a dream of his sore ordeal at the Green Chapel. Again he minded her of her duty and his own, but for all his resolution not to be a traitor to hospitality she gave him three kisses, and would have him take from her a gold ring as parting gift. The knight, blushing for kisses given him behind a husband's back, refused on the score that he had nothing to give her in return; but next she offered him the girdle she wore, braided with green silk and fringed with gold.

"Thou dost wrong to scorn it for a poor gift," said she when he would have still denied her. "Know that this girdle, simple as it seems, hath power to make any weapon harmless against whoever wears it."

Since her gift was so well worth having, Gawayne let himself be overcome by love of life. He took the girdle, promising to keep it a secret between them two. Yet his conscience pricked him; so, after hearing mass, he got himself shrived by the priest that he might be clear from sin when on the morrow he had to deal with that fearsome Green Knight. Still was he ill at ease to find the dim eyes of the aged lady bent on him with a cunning smile, as if she well knew what he had to hide. As he looked hard at her, it seemed to him that this crone took airs of youth and beauty, till he asked himself if it were not she who had tempted him in a dream.

This last evening the hunter brought home no more than the skin of a "foul fox", which he called a poor reward for the three kisses Gawayne had been lucky enough to get, and duly bestowed, but said not a word of the girdle he had hidden about him. As before they sat down to meat, spending the hours in carols and jollity as merry as if the guest were not bound next day to depart, but on what an errand he would not tell.

Through the night Gawayne slept ill, and heard every cock crow that brought in a cold and stormy New Year's Day. He rose and arrayed himself, taking good care to belt twice round him that green girdle said to have such magic power. His heart somewhat misgave him, yet he bore himself gallantly as he bade farewell to his hosts, thanking them for their good entertainment. Then he mounted his horse Gringalet, and rode away through snow and wind, a servant being sent with him as guide to the Green Chapel. They went in the twilight by rugged cliffs and dark moors, where every hilltop wore a cap and cloak of cloud. As the sun rose, the guide stopped short at the head of a dale winding into the snow-dappled heights.

"Hence ye must fare alone," said he. "This is the road that will bring thee too soon to the Green Chapel. But, good sir, take thought, for one dwells there that lets none pass without deadly scaith. The best knight in Arthur's court could not be safe from him. Let him be, and go some other way: for my part I swear to tell no man how ye shunned so perilous an encounter."

"It were a coward's part for me to turn back, having come so far to find this Green Chapel," answered Gawayne.

"Well, if ye list to be done with life, ride down the path to the bottom of the dale, and there on the left look for the place and the man ye seek. For all the gold on earth I would not go nearer."

With this he turned back; but the knight fared on, commending himself to heaven. The dale was shut in by steep banks, where, look as he might, he saw nothing like a chapel, till in a crag on the left opened the mouth of a dark cave, all overgrown by weeds and grass, so that he had almost passed it by. Tying his horse to a tree, he climbed up the rocks to peer into the cave.

"If this be the Green Knight's oratory, it is the most unblessed church I ever saw," quoth he; and his voice was echoed back by a fearsome din, like a clattering of rocks, and a grinding of scythes, and the whirr of a mill wheel all at once.

"Who dwells here?" cried Gawayne, bearing himself stoutly, spear in hand. "And what would he with me?"

"Stand still," replied a voice above his head, "and have now what ye come for!"

From among the rocks strode forth a huge figure bearing a mighty axe. It was the Green Knight, his hairy head sound as ever on his body, who met Gawayne with this greeting:

"Welcome to my abode! Rightly have ye timed your travel and honestly kept tryst. Now to make good our bargain! Down with spear and doff helmet, to stand the blow I have owed thee since last New Year's Day!"

"I am ready," said Gawayne, unlacing his helmet and leaning forward so as to offer his bare neck to the steel without any sign of fear.

But as the Green Knight swung the axe aloft to bring it down, the other could not help shrinking his shoulders a little when he thought the stroke about to fall.

"Ha! is this the brave Sir Gawayne that flinches before he is hurt?" bawled the big man. "I bore thy blow better when my head rolled on the ground."

"If my head comes off I cannot put it back," said Gawayne. "But I give my word not to flinch again."

A second time the axe was brandished over his head;

and now he stood like a stone, waiting for the blow that did not come.

"Hit on and have done!" exclaimed he, as the axe whizzed harmlessly through the air.

"So bold!" jeered his foeman. "Then I must make an end."

With both hands he heaved the axe, frowning so fiercely and planting his feet so firmly that Gawayne gave up his head for lost. Down swung the blow, and this time the knight did not move a jot as the sharp edge struck his neck, cutting through the skin; yet but for the smart and a few drops of blood sprinkled on the snow beneath him, he stood none the worse.

Half-stunned with amazement, as soon as he felt the head fast on his shoulders, he drew his sword to face the Green Knight, crying:

"One stroke have I taken, and that was all our covenant. Hast thou more to give, I can now pay thee fairly back!"

The giant-like fellow leant on his axe, turning to Gawayne a friendlier face, which he soon remembered as that of his late host, the lord of the castle, strangely disguised by those green trappings and by the bushy beard.

"Brave knight, ye need not be wroth," said he. "I could have dealt with thee better or worse, an I would. The three blows I fetched at thee were for my wife's kisses given behind my back—nay, take no shame! I set her to try thee, and found thee true in faith and honour, as beseemed a knight. Yet love of life tempted thee to hide from me the gift of her girdle. For that fault I let thee feel how much sorer I might have struck. Was it well thus to come short of the truth?"

Gawayne stood confounded by his own weakness and by the generosity of him with whom he had to do.

"Cursed be the cowardice that made me false to my word!" he exclaimed, unclasping the green girdle to give it back to his host, who laughingly refused it.

"Thou hast confessed so clear, and done such penance under my axe, that I hold thee for absolved. Keep the green girdle as a token of thy adventure at the Green Chapel with the Green Knight, to whom thou hast worthily paid thy debt; and each owes either naught on this New Year's Day."

"Ah," said Gawayne, "had I done worse, I should but have been like our forefather Adam, and Samson and Solomon, and many another man that let himself be beguiled by women! But heaven reward thee for the girdle, which I shall wear to mind me how I failed through cowardice, and a look at it shall avail to abate my pride if ever I forget. And now, sir, tell me thy name ere we part."

The Green Knight told him that he was called Sir Bernlake, and how in his house lived the mighty Morgan-le-fay, no other than the ill-favoured crone Gawayne had wondered to see held in such honour. She it was that had endowed him with those magic charms and set him on to trouble Arthur's court out of hatred to Queen Guinevere. After what was past and gone, he bid Gawayne return with him to the castle, and be made better known to the fairy, who, as Arthur's sister, was his own aunt.

But Gawayne had no mind for dealings with his uncanny kinswoman. Taking leave of Sir Bernlake, like old friends, he rode homewards through thick and thin, and never stopped till he came to Camelot, to be welcomed with joy as one from the dead.

The cut on his neck had quickly healed, but there was the scar to witness the tale he had to tell; and he showed the green girdle, which he wore in penance for his faintheartedness. That one fault he confessed with shame; but Arthur comforted him, saying that the bravest man alive might well shrink from lonely death. And all the brotherhood of the Round Table agreed for Gawayne's sake to wear such a green belt as he brought back in token of his adventure with the Green Knight.

SIR LANVAL

At King Arthur's court was a knight of foreign birth, by name Sir Lanval, who, even among that famed brotherhood of the Round Table, excelled in knightly graces and virtues. Sir Lancelot, Sir Percival, Sir Gawayne, the bravest of his companions in battle and the wisest in council, knew well the worth of this stranger, and were proud to call him friend; and, when his name was spoken, the bitter Sir Kay himself forbore to sneer. By the poor, as well as by his own attendants, he was much beloved, for his kindness and generosity were unbounded, and he gave freely to all in need, so that his purse would have been always empty but for the rich rewards which the king was wont to bestow on those who served him faithfully.

Thus all went well with him till Arthur wedded the false and fair Guinevere. Henceforth Lanval had one enemy at the court, and that an all-powerful one. Once the new queen had loved this knight, but when she found her love unreturned, it changed to bitter hatred, and she set her mind on working his ruin.

It is an old tale, how the greatest heroes have shown themselves weak to the wiles of a woman. The noble Arthur too easily listened to and too blindly confided in his unworthy wife. She soon took occasion to poison his mind by false charges against Lanval, so that the king began to look coldly on his good knight; nor was

it long before Lanval felt the ill effects of this disfavour.
When, after a successful war, distribution was made of
honours and rewards, he alone found himself passed over,
though none had less deserved to be thus slighted.

Right well knew he to whom he owed such neglect,
but he was too loyal to let any word pass his lips that
might assail the name of his master's queen. Patiently
he bore himself under the king's displeasure, and made
no complaint of the troubles which soon came upon him.
His liberality had always kept him poor, and now that
the just recompense of his services was withheld, he
found himself falling into arrant want. No longer could
he indulge his disposition by feeding the hungry and
clothing the naked. It began to be a question with
him how he might maintain himself and his household.

He lodged in the house of a burgher, who, now that
he was without money, seemed to grudge him entertainment. Pride drove him to conceal his poverty, and he
was fain to keep his chamber day and night. He could
no more appear at tournaments in gallant array; his
friends ceased to invite him to feasts; he could not even
go to church for want of decent clothes. One by one, he
had parted with his servants, his chargers, his equipments, till at last there was nothing left him but an old
baggage horse, a torn saddle, and a rusty bridle. For
three days he had not tasted meat or drink. Having
come to this, he saw nothing for it but to leave the court
of Arthur, and seek his fortune elsewhere.

So one day, while his brother knights were holding
high festival at the castle, he mounted his sorry steed,
and rode forth in such a plight that the people he met
hooted and laughed as he urged on the stumbling beast,
dreading to be seen by any who had known him in the

days of his prosperity. Having thus stealthily left the town, he hid himself in the nearest wood, then rode through it till he came to a rich plain, across which ran a clear sparkling river. Here the unfortunate knight dismounted, to let his horse feed at will, and, wrapping himself in his tattered cloak, lay down beneath the wide branches of an oak that overshadowed the stream.

But now, when he would have given himself up to his sorrowful thoughts, he raised his eyes for a moment from the ground, and was aware of two damsels advancing towards him on the shady bank. As they drew near, and he stood up to salute them, he saw that they were strangely fair and richly attired. The one bore a gold basin, the other a silk napkin, with which they came to Lanval and offered to serve him, saying:

"Speed thee, Sir Knight! Our lady greets thee, and prays thee, if it be thy will, to speak with her."

"Lead me whither ye please," answered Lanval courteously. "Whichever way ye go, there I gladly follow, for never saw I fairer damsels."

"Nay, but you have yet to see our mistress," said they, smiling, and forthwith led him to a blooming meadow, where was set a magnificent pavilion covered with rich hangings and ornaments of gold and dazzling jewels, such as no queen on earth could call her own.

Within, all was alike costly and bright, but Sir Lanval had eyes only for the mistress of the place, a lady pure as the lilies of May and sweet as the roses of June, with hair shining like threads of gold, and eyes of enchanting radiance. At the first glance this marvellous beauty made all charms he had ever beheld or dreamed of seem as naught. And when she rose to give him friendly welcome, the knight felt that his heart had already gone into slavery after his eyes; he could love no other woman in the world, now that he had once seen this image of perfect loveliness.

"Gentle sir," she began in tones that thrilled him with delight, "think not that you are a stranger to me. I have long seen your worth, and now I have sent for you to ask if you may deem me worthy of your love."

"Oh, lady, command me in all things!" faltered the knight, scarce able to believe his senses. "What more might man hope than to serve such a peerless dame? But I am poor—friendless—despised."

"I know all," said the lady. "But so you will freely and truly give me your heart, I can make you richer than any emperor, for I have wealth at will, and nothing shall be wanting to him who is my knight."

For answer, Sir Lanval could only throw himself speechless at her feet. Need she ask if he loved her? She gave him her hand and made him sit down by her side, all ragged and rusty as he was; then short time served for his misery to be lost in a happiness too great for words.

The two damsels now appeared, covering a table with exquisite viands, of which neither the half-starved knight nor his fair hostess cared to eat. Long and lovingly they held converse together, and the hours flew by like minutes. Fain would Lanval have lingered in that charmed spot for ever, if the lady herself had not bid him return to Arthur's court, where she promised he should have means of putting to shame all who had scorned him.

At parting she gave him noble gifts—a suit of white armour such as the most cunning smith might have been proud to claim for his handiwork; a curiously worked purse which, she told him, he would always find full of

gold, let him spend as he pleased; and, best of all, the
assurance that he should see her again.

"One thing only I require of you," was her last
word, "that you take heed not to boast of my love. Call
me when and where you please, so it be in some secret
place, and I will come; but you must never speak of
me to mortal ears, on pain of seeing me no more on
earth."

Sir Lanval kissed her hand, and vowed by his knighthood that her wishes should be obeyed. Then they
took tender leave, promising each other that it was not
for long.

Without, a gallant white charger was awaiting the
knight, and bore him like the wind to his lodging in the
town. There sumptuous furniture and apparel now
abounded where he had left bareness and signs of
poverty. At the door he was met by a retinue of servants, well provided with new liveries and everything
needful for a wealthy household. Astonished, he perceived that he had to do with a queen of fairyland.
And when he opened her purse, he found that it verily
held an endless supply of gold. The more he took out,
the less it ever seemed to be empty.

Lanval rejoiced that he was now able to place no
stint on his open-handedness. He hastened to search
out all who might be in want or distress, and abundantly
relieved them. He feasted the poor; he gave alms
to pilgrims; he ransomed prisoners; he became the
bountiful patron of minstrels; he heaped rich gifts on
his friends and rewards on his followers. Once more
his name was everywhere spoken with gratitude and
affection, and he held his head high among his fellows
at the court. The white armour that had been given
him was enchanted against every weapon; so, mounted

on his matchless courser, he still overthrew all comers in tourney or battle. But his greatest joy was in seeing his fairy princess; for as often as he repaired to a solitary spot, and called upon her, she would appear, to bestow on him a wealth of bright glances and sweet words that could have made the most wretched of men forget his woes.

One alone grudged the young knight's good fortune. This was the queen, who had brought him to such a point of poverty that he might be fain to sue humbly for her favour. She was sore at heart to see him more and more generous and beloved; and she cast about for new means of venting her ill will upon him.

On the feast of St. John the knights and ladies had gathered to sport and dance in a meadow, whither came also the queen with her maidens. And when she saw that Sir Lanval joined not in the diversions of the others, but walked apart, thinking ever of his mistress, she turned aside to him and spoke scornfully, saying that he was not fit to be in the king's service, since he loved no woman, and no woman found him worthy of her love. At this the knight's pride took fire; forgetting the command that had been laid upon him, as well as the reverence due to the queen, he cried:

"Nay, madam; for know that I am beloved by the most beautiful lady in the world!"

"Who dares speak to my face of one more fair than me?" exclaimed the queen with kindling eyes.

"Aye, the least of her maidens is fairer than you," answered Lanval hotly; but, as he spoke, his spotless white armour turned black as coal, and he remembered with dismay how the fairy had bid him tell of her to no mortal ears.

And these words filled up the cup of Guinevere's

hatred. Furiously she broke away from him and hurried
to her chamber, where she shut herself, weeping for
shame and rage, till Arthur returned from hunting; then
she presented herself before him with red eyes and di-
shevelled hair, making loud complaint of the insult she
had received that day, and demanding that a heavy
punishment should be dealt out to the presumptuous
knight who had so set at naught his duty and her
charms. And other false and shameful things she laid
to his charge, trying to provoke her husband's utmost
vengeance. Nor was Arthur unmoved by the dishonour
done to his queen. Wrathfully he bid four of his
sergeants seek out Sir Lanval, and bring him to answer
for what he had said.

Little did Lanval heed this displeasure; a heavier
misfortune had fallen upon him, beside which the king's
displeasure seemed but a light matter. When Guinevere
left him, what would he not have given to recall his
rash words? But nothing had he now to give. No
sooner had he disobeyed the commands of his mistress
than all her gifts melted away like snow. His magic
purse was empty; he found his lodging bare as before;
his servants had disappeared. He hurried to the wood
where they had been wont to meet, and loudly and often
called upon the fairy, but only the echoes mocked him.
She came not; the charm was broken, and his love was
lost for ever.

Bitterly he reproached himself and cursed his folly,
but little could this avail him now. Beating his breast
and tearing his hair, he fell on the ground as in a swoon,
and thus Arthur's officers found him.

"Thou traitor," said the king, when Lanval was
brought bound into his presence, "how hast thou stained
thy loyalty! What boasts be these that thy mistress is

fairer than my queen ? Speak and justify thyself, if thou wouldst not be hanged like a thief."

But Sir Lanval's eye quailed not, as he bent before the king and spoke: "My lord, so have I said, and what I have said is true, though I should die for it."

"Now, falsely hast thou spoken, and sorely shalt rue it!" vowed the king, and named twelve lords who should be sworn to sit in judgment on the accused knight.

All were sorry for him, and the noblest champions of the Round Table came forward to offer themselves as sureties that he should appear before the court on the day of trial. But Lanval heeded little what might now be his fate. If he could no longer live in the love of his lady, he could at least expiate his fault by death for her sake.

The day came, and the judges assembled. Some few of them, wishing to make court to the queen, were for condemning the poor knight forthwith; but the most part, knowing her falseness, thought it pity that such a brave man should thus be lost, and were willing to find cause for acquitting him, or at least for changing his sentence from death to banishment. And one of the oldest of the lords spoke thus, careless of Guinevere's frowns.

"Sir Lanval is arraigned because he has boasted his lady to be fairer than the queen. It is right that we have knowledge of the crime, and, therefore, let him be required to bring this lady here that so we may judge whether or no he have spoken truth."

To this all readily agreed; but Sir Lanval shook his head, knowing that he could not call his lady there, or even speak her name; and men murmured that he must die the death.

But as the judges still deliberated, there came to the

castle two damsels robed in rich samite, and riding upon
royally caparisoned mules. Dismounting before the king,
they let him know how a great princess was approaching,
who desired him to receive her. Arthur declared that
their mistress should have all courteous entertainment,
ordering certain of his knights to attend upon the
damsels. Then he bid the trial proceed, for the queen
was urgent to have that proud traitor condemned without
more ado.

The lords were at last about to give sentence when
a great cry was heard without, announcing the arrival of
the mistress of the two damsels. Clad in a wondrous
robe of silver sheen, over which was a purple mantle
bordered with ermine, and crowned with a circlet of gold
and gems, she rode upon a milk-white steed, the housings
of which were worth an earldom. On her wrist sat a
falcon that marked her high birth, and behind her ran
two gallant greyhounds of the purest breed. All in the
town, old and young, gentle and simple, had come forth
to see her pass, and now, as she entered the hall of the
castle, the whole assembly rose to do her honour. Every
eye could not but gaze upon her, for such a wonder of
beauty and loveliness had never before been seen in
Arthur's land. And well Sir Lanval knew her.

"O lady, I forget all my troubles since I have seen
thee once again!" he cried, stretching his hands towards
her; but she answered him not a word, and passed proudly
on to where the king waited to greet her. Then she
mounted the dais on which sat Guinevere among her
maidens, whose beauty grew pale before hers, as the
moon and stars before the sun. Standing beside the
queen and throwing off her mantle, this marvellous
stranger turned herself to address the judges.

"Sirs, ye do wrong to this good knight, and may

well see that he is unjustly accused. I loved him; he hath called me; I am here. Judge for yourselves which of us two be the fairer."

With one voice all exclaimed that she was fairer than any lady upon earth. It was in vain for Guinevere to frown and weep; the king himself exclaimed that she was no peer of this unknown dame. Lanval had but spoken the truth.

So amidst loud acclamations the knight was justified and let go free. But little recked he, since his love, taking leave of none present, after throwing one scornful glance upon the false queen, had strode from the dais and was already remounting her steed at the gate of the castle, without a word or a look for him.

"Oh, have pity on me!" he cried in vain. "Why give me my life when, without thee, it were more bitter than death?"

Still she answered him not, nor so much as turned her head, but rode away with her attendant damsels. Sir Lanval's horse stood by the castle gate. In despair he leaped upon its back and spurred wildly after her, none staying him.

By field and forest he followed her, ever crying piteously and beseeching her to speak to him if it were but one word. But in silence she rode swiftly on, till she reached the river bank on which they had first met. There she dismounted and plunged into the deep and rapid stream. The knight, all in mail as he was, did the same, stretching out his arms and trying to seize and hold her. Deeper and deeper she made her way into the water, and on he pressed after her, though the current was strong, and he had much ado to keep his footing. Still deaf to his entreaties, she disappeared below the surface; whereon Lanval, throwing himself forward with

SIR LANVAL'S LADY APPEALS TO THE JUDGES

THE PILGRIM AT THE CASTLE GATE

a last effort to snatch at her shining robe, was carried away, sank, lost sight and hearing, and gave himself up for dead.

But as the waters closed round his helpless form the lady turned and caught him and bore him with her. And when he came to himself he was lying on a flowery bank, his love bending over him, while, with a radiant smile, she told him that he was forgiven, and that they never more should be parted.

Never again was Sir Lanval seen by mortal eyes. But men tell how, with his bride, he dwells for ever in fairyland. His gallant steed — so the story goes — has ever since roamed riderless through the country. Often has it been seen by peasants and travellers, but it will suffer itself to be approached by none. Every year, on the day when it lost its master, it still comes to the river bank and stands long, neighing loudly and tearing up the ground with its hoofs by the place where Sir Lanval disappeared.

GUY OF WARWICK

I

WHO in all the land was like Rohand, Earl of Warwick, that peerless champion and powerful lord, rich and generous, honoured and feared from one end of the kingdom to another? Many a strong castle and famous city were his; many a brave knight followed his banner; gold and silver had he in plenty; but of all his treasures none was dearer to him than his only daughter, the fair Felice, as wise as she was beautiful, and as beautiful as she was proud. The minstrels were never done singing her praises. As a rare prize her hand had been sought by lords and knights of the noblest lineage, not only in England but from far beyond the seas; yet the best and bravest failed to move her heart, and she remained the flower of all maidens of her time.

Not a little of Rohand's wealth he owed to his prudent and faithful steward Segard, whose son Guy served from boyhood among the earl's pages. A handsome, courteous, and modest lad was Guy; he had the good word of all who knew him, high and low; and, as much for his own merits as his father's, became a favourite with their master, whom he waited upon as cupbearer, while it so beseemed his youth. Withal the stripling was bold and hardy, diligently exercising himself in all knightly arts, so that none of his fellows could better back a steed or wield a sword. Right glad were his father and all his kindred to see him growing up to be so goodly a man.

Now it befell at Whitsuntide, when trees are green and birds begin to sing, and youths and maidens smile upon their lovers, that Earl Rohand, as his custom was, held a great feast, whereat Guy, all in holiday garb of silk, was bid wait upon Felice and her ladies. There were few of them that did not cast a kindly eye upon the graceful squire, but he had eyes only for his young mistress; and as he knelt before her, serving the cup, his heart was strangely moved, so that he knew not what had come to him.

It was love, and hopeless love, as well might seem, since she stood so far above him. Guy strove to cast it out from his heart, but all in vain. It had taken hold of him like a burning fire, and raged the fiercer the more he would have extinguished it, as in duty bound to his lord. He could not rest night nor day; he lost all his old cheerfulness; he grew pale and weak. His father grieved to see this change, but could not learn the cause; so too did the earl pity him; and at last the fair Felice herself, seeing his woeful state, asked what ailed him. Then he took courage to tell her of his love. But at the first word she flushed with angry pride and turned away, bidding him hold his peace.

Guy, thus left in despair, grew worse from day to day. Everyone was sorry for him, none more than Rohand, who sent the most skilful leeches to cure him if they might; but what salves knew they for wounds like his? The poor youth had neither hope nor care to live in such hopeless pangs. Yet once more he sought out Felice, as she was walking in a garden, and, falling on his knees, besought her to have mercy upon him.

"Upon thee, forsooth!" she cried wrathfully. "Art thou not the son of my father's steward? Who made thee so foolhardy as to talk to me of love? Out of my sight, or I will betray thee to my father; then thou shalt die for such rashness."

"Ah," cried Guy, "better to die than to live, if men might say that I died for the love of such a lady!"

"A foolish speech!" said she, and would have left him; but when she saw how he fell to the ground, well-nigh out of his senses with sorrow, she turned again, bidding her damsel see to him. The damsel's heart had been won by the sight of so true love, and she said to her mistress:

"If my father were a king or an emperor, and I were the fairest maiden that ever lived, and he loved me so dearly, I should not scorn him thus."

And Felice herself was moved by the squire's sore distress, for anon she spoke to him, saying:

"Rise up, and take comfort, for there is no maiden in the land, and no lady, however high, but thou shalt have her at will for thy wife. This I promise in my father's name."

"Lady," he answered, "in all the land there is but one maiden for me."

His looks, his sighs, his very boldness began to win upon the proud Felice.

"Hear me," she said. "I have sent away earls and dukes, all famous men and well-tried knights, who sought my hand. What, then, should men say of me, if I granted my love to a young squire without lands or rank or name? When thou art dubbed a knight, and able to win honour for thy lady, then may I listen to such a one."

With this she left him, and he rose a new man, these

few words of hope having proved a cordial to his sickness. Now he had cause to live; the red came back to his cheek and the light to his eye, and all were glad to see him once more in health. But the sports and pleasures and tastes of his boyhood no more delighted him, for all his thoughts were on deeds of arms. The first time that he could get speech of the earl he prayed to be made knight at his hands, to which Rohand willingly consented, saying that none was more worthy.

So, upon a set day, Guy with some score of other goodly squires went into the chapel, all walking barefoot, dressed in white with purple mantles, and each one carrying by the point a maiden sword with new gilt spurs hanging upon the hilt. Till midnight they knelt in prayer before the altar, and kept watch over their armour till dawn. Then came the earl, before whom, when their spurs were buckled on and their swords girt about them, they knelt humbly, and with a stroke of his sword he dubbed them all, bidding them show themselves brave and loyal.

In honour of these new knights a great feast was held in the hall of the castle, but Guy hastened away from the banquet, eager to present himself, in his knightly array, to the fair Felice, reminding her of her promise.

" 'Tis well," said she, " but it is not all. The sword and the spurs do not make a knight. Go now and prove thy valour; then will we talk of love."

Guy asked no better. Pressing her hand to his lips he took leave of her, to seek his father's blessing and the earl's permission to depart. The old father would have held him longer at home, since he was yet so young and all unused to war. But the youth besought him not to speak of delay, and Rohand was well pleased that he should go forth in quest of honour, not letting his bright armour rust in idleness. All in the castle bid him godspeed as he rode forth with three companions. Ere long they took ship and left England to seek adventures in foreign lands.

II

For years now was Guy wandering with his companions in arms from country to country, wherever they could hear of perils to be encountered or glory to be won. It would fill a great book to tell of all the battles, the tournaments, the gallant feats of arms in which he took part. Enough to say that he made himself known for such a knight as there was none better in Christendom. Many a prize of valour, the spoils of captive foes, and other trophies of his prowess, did he send home to be laid before the fair Felice in token that his love was still the same, and that he was proving himself worthy of her.

When the first year had passed, indeed, he came back to claim her promise. The proud lady smiled on him, but she answered:

"Truly, Sir Guy, you have shown yourself a good knight, yet if I grant your wish now, you would think of ease and pleasure rather than renown; and it were shame that you should lose a great name for love of me. Go forth again, and come not till all men know you for the flower of knighthood. Then can you fitly be my husband."

"Lady," he said, "your will is mine. Whether I can be the best knight in the world, heaven only knows, but no knight can have such hope to spur him on. I go, and if I come not again, remember that I died for love of you."

With this he hastened away, after greeting his parents, who vainly would have kept him at home. Once more he travelled into far-off lands and did countless deeds of valour, so that his fame rose higher and higher, and Felice lived ever a maiden for his sake, though many another rich suitor still sought to woo her.

At the end of seven years Guy came back again to England. Landing in the north, he rode first to York, where King Athelstan held his court. The young knight was welcomed by the king as beseemed his renown; then while he stayed at the court, taking part in games and joustings and revelries, there came news of a fearsome dragon which was ravaging all Northumberland. The poor country people had sent to pray for help against this monstrous thing, and Guy willingly offered to undertake the adventure.

"It shall be thine," said the king; "but take with thee some of my best knights to make thee surer."

"Nay," said Guy; "I am not one to go out with such a company against a beast alone. Have no dread of the dragon, sir, for I will bring you his head before long, and the country shall have peace."

Without more ado he put on his armour, and rode forth towards the haunts of the dragon. All along the way he met men and women and children flying from it in terror, and they bid him turn back, since no man could stand before its fiery breath and live.

"That shall be seen," cried Guy, and rode on till he came in sight of the monster. A grisly, gruesome beast it was, all covered, as in armour, with horrid black scales; it had claws like a lion and wings like an eagle; its eyes shone fiery red, and smoke belched forth from its mouth, when, on the approach of the knight and his attendants, it gave a roar that echoed for miles around, and lashed with its huge tail till the ground shook as in an earth-quake. Sir Guy had never feared the face of any foe in man's shape, nor now did he quail, yet he silently prayed that heaven would aid his arm, and with unwonted care looked to his harness and weapons. Then, bidding his squires hold themselves at a distance, he spurred towards the dragon, spear in rest.

With another frightful roar the dragon uncoiled its coal-black folds and opened its burning mouth, awaiting this bold assailant. Dreadful was the shock of his onset. The tough spear shivered upon the scaly hide as if it had been a rock of adamant, while horse and man reeled back, wellnigh stifled by the creature's poisonous breath. It made a mighty spring, hurling Guy to the ground. Swiftly he rose to his feet; deftly he drew his sword, and struck mighty blows like a storm of hail. But the good blade ever glanced off these foul scales; nowhere could he find a spot at which to pierce the snaky folds. He was overthrown; the dragon coiled its vast length about his body, crushing his armour and holding him fast in a deadly grip.

The watching squires raised a cry, and gave their master up for lost. The knight himself had hardly hoped to save his life, yet, gathering all his strength for one last blow, he thrust his sword down the mon-ster's open jaws. At once he felt its grasp loosened, so that he could again draw breath. Wrenching himself free, as it would have flown away he pierced its body beneath the wings, where the scales did not cover it, and drove his sword up to the hilt. With a shriek the dragon dropped on the ground, drenched by its black blood. For a minute more it writhed in agony, then lay dead, a hideous sight, filling the air with smoke and noisome stench.

This desperate combat over, Guy, all spent with the struggle, stood leaning on his sword, till his squires ran joyfully up to assist him. When he had rested a time, he hacked off the dragon's head, which was carried before him on his way back to York, greeted, as he rode, by the thanks and praises of the poor people, who might now return to their homes in peace. At the news of his approach King Athelstan came out to meet him with the whole court, and none else than Guy was now thought worthy to ride on the king's right hand, when this great train entered the city with the dragon's head borne high on a spear for all to see.

After such an exploit all England rang with the fame of Sir Guy of Warwick. The king would fain have kept so good a knight by his own side, offering him honours and rewards without stint, even to the hand of his daughter; but Guy's heart was elsewhere. Taking courteous leave of Athelstan he rode homewards, to learn that his father and mother had both been long dead. Nothing then kept him from Earl Rohand, who made the young champion right welcome.

No guest had ever before been received at Warwick with so much honour and such goodwill of all. But to Guy nothing seemed dear unless he could have the smile of his lady. To her alone he told all his adventures; how he had fared in foreign lands; how he had sped in a hundred encounters; how he might have married many a king's daughter, yea, the emperor's herself with all her wealth.

"But all I forsook for thy sake, Felice," he said.

"And I, too," said she, "might have had many a goodly husband, but all my love was gone with you, and I can be none but yours."

A happy man was Guy as he kissed this fair lady,

who at length for love had laid aside her pride. It remained to seek the consent of Rohand: would he not grudge the hand of his peerless daughter to a vassal's son? But the earl had not failed to see what was toward, and it pleased him well. Before long, one day as they were hunting together, he asked Guy when he thought of taking a wife.

"Sir," replied the knight in confusion, "there is only one maid in the world that I can wed."

"Hear me, Guy," said the earl. "I have one daughter, and no heir but her. Where shall I find a nobler husband to guard her and hers when I am gone. I give her thee with all my heart, and thou shalt be lord of these fair lands."

"Oh, sir," cried Guy, out of himself for joy, "I would rather have your daughter, if she were the poorest maiden, than any princess with the richest dowry!"

So all now was well with the lovers. The earl would have no delay, nor were Guy and Felice unwilling. In a week they were married at Warwick with the most sumptuous bridal that had ever been seen there. That wedding feast lasted for many days, and not only the lordly guests, but the poorest in the city had their fill. Minstrels there were in plenty to sing the glories of the bridegroom and the beauty of the bride. Guy gave great gifts to all in the castle; and for many miles around there was none who had not cause to rejoice with the newly wedded pair, for whom all men wished a long, happy, and prosperous life.

III

Behold Sir Guy now lord of all that the heart of man could desire. Who would not envy him in the love of his beautiful wife and the rich possessions granted him by her father? Yet at the very height of fortune he found sorrow, when now he was at ease to bethink himself of his past life.

Before the summer was ended it befell that, coming back one day from hunting, Guy mounted the tower of his castle and looked upon the fair scene around. He saw far and wide the lands, the towns, the stately mansions that called him master, all bright in the summer sun; but as he gazed a dark thought, like a thundercloud, rose within him. He thought how much had been given him, and how little he had deserved; how vainly men spoke well of him, since all his famous deeds had been for woman's love, and not for the service of his Lord. No longer might he take pleasure and pride in these great possessions. At once he vowed to change his life, if it were not too late. Renouncing worldly things, all his mind must henceforth be bent on making his peace with heaven.

The knight's heart was now as full of sadness as ever it had been of joy; he had no more delight even in the love of his wife. She was not slow to see his altered mood, and earnestly sought to know what so troubled him. Then, taking her by the hand, he spoke thus:

"Felice, all my manhood I have sorrowed for thee, but now I sorrow for myself. There never was knight that laboured and suffered as I; with this hand I have slain many a man, burned many a city, wrought woe to many, and all for thy sake, while I have done nothing for God, to whom I owe all. But since He hath brought me to a better mind, I have vowed to forsake thee for a time, and do penance as a pilgrim in the Holy Land."

"What is this!" she cried in grief and anger. "Dost thou hold me so light? Thou hast some other lady in distant lands to whom thou wouldst fain go, and come here no more. Alas, that ever I was born if I must be forsaken thus!"

"Not so, love," he said, taking her tenderly in his arms. "For my soul's health I leave thee. Dwell thou here among thy friends, and let thy father comfort thee, and make good cheer while I am gone, for thus only canst thou do me pleasure in this sorrow."

"Better were it for me to die!" she answered, weeping. "Oh, my lord, why this strange design? Hear my counsel. Stay at home, and build an abbey where holy men may pray for thee day and night, and thus save thy soul from peril."

"Nay," he said, "thou lovest me not truly, if thou wouldst have me break my vow. Evil have I wrought with my own body, and with my body must I do penance."

Thereupon, seeing his will not to be shaken, she would have fallen to the ground in a swoon, but he held her up, trying to comfort her.

"Dearest," he said, "grieve not, for I shall come again. Or if not—take my good sword!—we have prayed heaven that a son may be born to us—give him this sword, there is none better in the world, and let him know what manner of man was his father."

"And take this ring, if my tears cannot move thee. Let it be a token between us, for at the sight of it will I hasten over land and seas to thy side."

Guy could speak no more; his heart was too full. Placing the ring on his finger, he kissed Felice and was gone. In a pilgrim's garb he left the castle forthwith, telling no man of his intent.

His wife, thus left alone, remained mad with sorrow, wringing her hands, tearing her hair, and exclaiming against her unhappy fate. The proud Felice no longer

cared to live. She drew Guy's sword out of the sheath
and put the point to her heart, thinking to kill herself.
But she shrank from the deed when she remembered the
child that should be born of her, and bethought herself,
moreover, that were she found slain with Guy's sword,
and he gone, men would surely lay the crime on him.
In spite of all she loved him too well for this, therefore
put away the bright blade. All night Felice was like
a wild beast for despair; and with the break of day she
hastened to seek comfort from her father.

Rohand wondered to see his newly wedded daughter
all white and tearful and in mourning garments, still
more to learn how Guy had forsaken her.

"Think it not," he said, "that a man would leave
thee long to go thus into exile. He hath but done it
to prove thee, if thy love be true to him."

"Nay," said she, knowing her husband better. "He
spoke the truth; I fear never to see him more."

Still the earl could not believe this strange tale of
his son-in-law quitting wife and lands and all to wander
no man knew where or why. He sent out messengers to
the nearest cities in quest of Guy, and when they could
hear no news of him he sent all over England, and then
into foreign countries, but neither in England, France,
Germany, Burgundy, nor Lombardy was the Knight of
Warwick to be found.

Felice had small hope to see him again. In time
a son was born to her, whom she cherished tenderly,
having in him the likeness of his father, and he was her
only comfort; but the best joy was gone out of life for
her. Henceforth she gave herself up to devotion and
good works; she built churches, she fed the hungry,
she clothed the naked; her charity became as well known
as once had been her beauty, and for the sighs of gallant

knights she had now the blessings of the poor.   Never
was she seen to smile since the day her husband left
her.   And thus time passed on.

Meanwhile Guy wended his way as a pilgrim to
Jerusalem and did penance, alone and unknown, for
seven long years.

'Twere long to tell of all his sufferings and adventures: how it behoved him again to put on knightly
armour against the proud infidel, how he succoured the
distressed, how he humbled the caitiff oppressor, how
he passed unscathed through terrible combats, how he
bore himself so that men said there had never been such
a champion since Guy of Warwick, whom all now took
for dead.

Once more he came back to England to deliver
Athelstan from a foreign foe by slaying the terrible giant
Colbrand.   But the king's thanks and rewards were lost
upon him.   He stole away from the court as suddenly
as he had come, nor ever rested till in pilgrim's weeds
he stood at last before the gate of his own castle.   No
one knew him when, with a hood drawn over his face,
he joined the crowd of poor men who every day had
alms here from the lady's own hands.   Mingling among
them he heard their talk of Felice's piety and charity;
and he gave thanks to heaven that this sorrow had been
thus blessed to her.

At noon the gate was opened, and the pale lady came
forth, all robed in black, a fair child by her side, the sight
of whom stirred Guy's heart within him.   He could not
but know his own son.   And ah! how the fair Felice
was changed.   Humbly she moved among the crowd,
giving a piece of money to each, with the words:

"Kind man, pray for my husband, and for me that I
may see him again before I die."

But when she came to Guy she looked hard upon him, saying gently:

"All pilgrims are welcome here for the sake of one."

He bowed his head in silence, and she passed on. His heart was too full for speech. Yet when his son came by, gazing up wonderingly at the face of this traveller from far-off lands, he could no longer contain himself. He threw himself on the boy and kissed him.

"Dear child," he cried, with tears, "may the Lord give ye grace to do that which is pleasing in His eyes!"

Another moment and he must have revealed himself, but he hastily turned away. The lady had marked his wan looks and travel-worn form, and when she had ministered her bounty to all present she bid a damsel seek out this pilgrim to offer him food and rest within the castle. But the pilgrim was gone.

In a solitary spot the strong knight was weeping for joy and sorrow. With one word all his affliction might now be at an end, and yet he doubted whether it were well to speak the word. In prosperity and happiness he might once more fall into sin, for which he had already suffered so bitterly. Since Felice, as well as himself, had learned how to seek peace which the world cannot give, he feared for her the dangers of earthly love. Better for them both to live out their lives in holy grief, that after a few short years they might meet for ever in heaven! The love of wife and child, the pride of power and riches, he would fling them away like the fetters of some baffled foe, and thus it should be well with their souls.

In this design he made himself a hermitage beneath a wooded cliff near Warwick, and there spent the rest of his days in prayer and penance, reverenced by the country people around. Felice, among the rest, heard of this holy man, and sent alms to him, but he would take nothing more than bread, which, with the water of a spring, was his only sustenance. Thus the good knight wore away his life with fasting and vigils, and none knew his true name, while Felice never ceased to pray for her absent lord.

When in time he found himself at the point of death, he sent her the ring which she had given him on his departure for the Holy Land. What a cry she raised to see that token after so many years! Joyful and yet troubled, she hastened to the hermitage in the wood, to find her husband lying already like a dead man. He opened his eyes once as she clasped his hand, then with a faint smile drew his last breath.

"Woe is me!" she wept, throwing herself on the body, known now too late for that of the pilgrim to whom she had given alms. "I saw my husband at his own doors and knew him not! And thou didst kiss thy son, but not a word to me! Oh, what hast thou done? Guy, Guy, shall I never hear thy voice again? Let me die with thee, then, since there is no more hope in life."

In vain her attendants would have led her away from the spot. She hung over her husband, speechless for grief, and would take neither food nor drink, till upon his body she died of a broken heart. Both were buried side by side in a lordly tomb, whereon were carved their name and their fame, to be remembered for ages. Such was the end of the brave Sir Guy of Warwick and his lady, the fair Felice.

ROLAND AND OLIVER

The city of Vienne is closely besieged, for Duke Girard, its lord, is at feud with his sovereign, Charles, the great king of France. Fiercely have they quarrelled over a wager at chess, and Girard must fly from the court to call around him his kinsmen and vassals. Now they bravely defend the walls round which lies the mighty host of Charles. The twelve peers of France are there, Archbishop Turpin, the wise Duke Naymes, Ganilon the traitor, Lambert of Bourges, Ogier the Dane, Richard of Normandy, and many another knight renowned in song and story. Great feats of arms are done on either side, but all the land grieves for this war between those that should be at peace.

For two years the siege lasted, during which Charles remained before the city, unable to take it, and unwilling to retreat. The knights and squires were wont to pass much of their time in hunting and in the sports of chivalry. One day Oliver, Duke Girard's nephew, upon whose chin the beard was beginning to grow, had stolen forth from the city alone, without arms or signs of rank, and, passing fearlessly through the king's men, essayed his skill among a band of youths playing at the quintain. All were astonished at the strength and grace of this young stranger, who far surpassed even Roland, the nephew of Charles, at the game in which, hitherto, he

had always borne away the prize. Suddenly there rose
a murmur that this was one of the enemy who had found
his way into the camp.

"Seize him!" was the cry, and a score of mailed hands
were laid on Oliver. He shook them off; he snatched
up a tent stake and laid his assailants on the ground; he
sprang upon a swift horse, and flew towards the town.
The king's men followed hard and fast, and young
Roland rode foremost of them all. Already he was close
upon the fugitive; he had raised his sword to strike,
when he heard a cry from the walls. He looked up, and
there was the fair Alda, Oliver's sister, clasping her hands
and raising her blue eyes to heaven, as she saw her
brother's danger. The arm of Roland dropped to his
side. He reined his steed, and let Oliver ride on unharmed. Those who beheld him thought he had been
wounded by an arrow from the walls. The shaft had
gone to his heart.

Night and day Roland henceforth thought of the fair
Alda, and no longer cared to prove his courage in assaults
against the city of her kinsmen. There were times of
truce, too, when the ladies of Vienne rode freely through
the king's camp; then the youth might feast his eyes
on her beauty. The day came for him to be dubbed
knight; and before ever he had dinted his bright shield,
he sought speech of this lady, and said:

"I dare not ask of thee to accept me as thy knight;
but I trust that all the deeds of my life will prove how
there is none more faithful and devoted to thy service."

"Ah, sir," replied the blushing maiden, "I wish well
that we might be friends, but this may not be while thy
house is at feud with mine!"

From that day Roland strove to win his uncle's
mind to peace; and in like wise counselled Duke Naymes

and the bravest of the peers. But Charles frowned, saying bitterly that he had expected other things from the new-made knight, and the false Ganilon whispered doubts and sneers, for Ganilon hated Roland ever since the young knight had disabled him in his first tourney. These whispers came to Roland's ears, making his blood burn to show himself worthy of his spurs and to shame the slanderers.

Before long he had his wish. Now arrayed in rich furs and goodly mantle, as beseemed a knight, came Oliver to the king's tent to treat for peace. Before all the barons and knights he told his errand, but the king's brow was stern as he answered:

"Peace Duke Girard shall not have, till he come with a saddle on his back to sue for it."

"Nay, my lord king," answered Oliver, "he were unworthy to be a peer of France if he thus debased himself."

"We have here the nephew in our hands," spoke the false-hearted Ganilon. "Let us hang him over against the gates, and thus teach the proud uncle to rebel against his king."

The eyes of Roland shone with anger, and he felled that traitor to the earth.

"It were shame to us," he cried, "if a messenger might not come and go freely, and speak all his will!"

"I have done my errand," said Oliver. "If the king will remove his host, and seek no more to harm us, Duke Girard and all his men will henceforth serve him faithfully in all things. If not, ye know well how we can defend ourselves."

The wise Duke Naymes whispered in his master's ear, counselling him to fair words that might end unworthy strife. But Charles sat silent with the cloud on his brow. Long had he stayed round this rebellious town, and he was loath to depart till it had yielded to his mercy, or till not a soul within it should be left alive. Then suddenly Oliver turned to Roland, and cried:

"Shall thy uncle and mine be ever at war? Say, young knight, wilt thou meet me, and fight out this quarrel in single combat?"

"Aye, that will I, for France and the king!" answered Roland eagerly.

"So be it!" said Charles, rising from his seat. "These two are of like age and strength, and it behoves them to win their spurs. Go back to the duke, young sir, and offer him this covenant: that if thou be vanquished, he shall leave the town forthwith; but if my nephew fall, I will raise the siege and let him live in peace."

Willingly all the peers raised their voices in assent, for they were wearied of the long war, and loved not to shed the blood of their countrymen. Thus it was agreed, and the combat was appointed to take place next day on a little island in the stream that rolled between the duke's castle and the camp of the king.

That night King Charles had a troubled dream. He dreamed that a falcon and a hawk fought fiercely together; but before he might know which overcame the other he awoke, and could sleep no more. Anxious, he vowed a pilgrimage to Jerusalem if Roland should have the victory. Meanwhile the fair Alda spent the night on her knees in the chapel of the castle. If Oliver were slain on the morrow, she would become a nun. And yet she could not pray that Roland might fall by his hands. As she did on her brother's armour she wept, dreading both victory and defeat.

Now the hour of the combat had come. The bank

of the river was thronged with spectators. The besieged
covered the walls, and high above all sat the Lady Alda
with eager eyes. Opposite stood the mailed host of the
king. From either bank the young knights were rowed
across, and left together on the island. Oliver was
equipped in rich arms a good Jew had given him when
he was made knight. Roland had the famed sword
Durandal, that could not be bent or broken, and the
shield, with its red and white quarterings, the Saracen
was to know so well. Courteously they saluted each
other and forthwith the fight began.

Brightly shone their swords in the morning sun.
Fiercely the young champions closed for life or death.
Loud echoed the blows from the castle walls. The rivets
flew from their armour, and splinters of steel fell into
the river on either hand. All who beheld marvelled
to see such strokes, at each of which it seemed that
one of the fighters must fall. Blood and sweat poured
down their bodies; they panted for breath; they exhausted
their strength, but neither would yield an inch.

It was a good blade that Girard's nephew had from
the Jew, but no steel could withstand the matchless
Durandal. At last Oliver's sword broke in his hand.
He was forced to his knees; already he almost felt the
enemy's steel in his heart; he closed his eyes and thought
of heaven, and his sister's despairing cry rang in his ears.

But Roland flung away his weapon.

"Rise!" he said; "I am the nephew of the King of
France. I slay not unarmed men."

Oliver rose to his feet, and they faced each other with
naked hands. They tore up two saplings, and with them
struck mighty blows till these were broken. Then they
locked their bodies together, and wrestled like lions, till
both at the same moment came to the ground.

When they stood up breathless, the king saw them unlace their helmets and embrace.

"Ha, is my nephew tired of the fight!" he cried; and Ganilon whispered into his ear that Roland was betraying him for love of that lady upon the castle walls.

"Nay," said the wise Duke Naymes, "I will go through the fire, or fight a Saracen giant, if Roland be false;" and so spoke all the peers whose own hearts were loyal.

In friendly converse the youths reposed throughout the noonday heat. Another sword was brought to Oliver from the castle, and a great gold flagon of wine, from which they both drank to the Lady Alda, and pledged each other.

"Right glad am I," said Oliver, "to have to do with so good a man."

"And sad am I," thought Roland, "to grieve so fair a lady."

They aided one another to lace on their helmets, and with fresh strength renewed the battle. The hot sun went down towards the west, but still they fought on, and the two hosts watched them, now with hope and now with fear. Again and again they paused to take breath; then crossed their swords once more. Would the day not see the end of this struggle?

Now it was Roland who lowered his blade.

"Hold!" he said. "I am fevered and weak, and if it please thee, I would fain lie down and rest a time."

"With all my heart," replied Oliver. "It were no honour to vanquish a knight through faintness. Rest and fear not; I myself will watch over thee."

Roland undid his helmet, and stretched himself on the earth. Then Oliver brought a great stone, and put

THE FIGHT BETWEEN ROLAND AND OLIVER

"OGIER STOOD WITH HIS BLADE HELD ON HIGH"

it beneath his head to give him ease, and fanned his face, and fetched water in his own helmet.

"Ah, he yields; he is overcome!" cried the king, and Alda had great pity of the fallen knight.

But the king's nephew stood up and laughed.

"Nay, I did but feign, to try thy faith. I could fight on for days and nights, if need were. But, courteous sir, since ye use me thus, I would right willingly call thee my brother. And if I live I will marry no lady but thy fair sister."

"And if I live, she shall marry no man but thee," said Oliver.

The sun went down as again they closed in desperate encounter. All that day had they fought with all their might, and neither could boast of victory. Again the good blades clashed, and the blows resounded over the water. The shades gathered round and hid them from sight. The anxious watchers could see but the sparks struck from helm and hauberk. And at last the darkness came between them, and the sounds of strife ceased.

They had fallen into each other's arms, and vowed lifelong friendship, since neither might prevail over the other as a foe. Roland undertook to make Girard's peace with his uncle. Oliver promised him the hand of his sister. Henceforth, as brothers, they should share wealth, and honour, and love, and never again draw sword, unless it were fighting side by side.

That night a great uproar arose in the camp. News had come that the Saracens were invading France. Gladly now both king and duke heard their nephews' entreaty for peace, and willingly they agreed to turn their arms against the infidel.

The reconciliation was sealed by Roland's betrothal to Alda. All the land rejoiced that this long strife should thus be brought to an end, and with high hearts the united host marched to that great war in which Charles and his twelve peers won such renown. But, in friendship and war, none were more renowned than Roland and Oliver, who lived together henceforth as brothers, and died together on the field of Roncesvalles.

OGIER THE DANÈ

I

WITH a great host of knights and barons, and the twelve famous peers of France, Charlemagne marched against Godfrey of Denmark, the only prince in Christendom that still defied his power. Godfrey summoned his vassals and made all preparations for a desperate war, but he might as well have striven to withstand the waves of the sea. His territories were overrun, his castles captured, his armies scattered, till at last the haughty foe was fain to sue for peace. This was granted him on condition that next Easter he should present himself at Paris, and do homage to the emperor for his lands. Meanwhile his son Ogier was taken as a hostage, and followed in the train of Charlemagne on his return to France.

Ogier, a manly and handsome youth, was little sorry to quit his home, since he left there a stepmother who did all she could to set his father against him ; and he asked nothing better than a chance of distinguishing himself at the renowned court of France. Nor was his captivity a harsh one. Charlemagne gave him over to the keeping of Duke Naymes of Bavaria, his own uncle; and he lodged him in one of his castles, which the fair eyes of Belisande, the governor's daughter, made a pleasant prison. So there he spent the time in sport and gallantry, and all kinds of knightly exercises, nor ever wished to go back to Denmark.

But when the feast of Easter came, his father did not appear to do homage, as had been agreed, for the wicked stepmother had persuaded him to break his promise, hoping that Ogier would suffer for it, and that her own son would succeed to Denmark.   Nay, more, when Charlemagne sent messengers to remind him of his plighted word, Godfrey insulted and ill-used them: with their beards shaved and their heads tonsured like monks they brought back to their master an answer of defiance, bidding him do his worst, so heedless was the rude king what might befall his own eldest son in the hands of the enemy.

Right wroth was the emperor when this scornful message came to his ears.   In the first outburst of his fury he ordered Ogier to be brought before him.

"Am I to be set free!   Has my father come!" asked the young hostage, as he gaily took leave of bright-eyed Belisande, promising to be with her again before long, and no more as a captive but as a princely wooer.   But his heart sank to see the angry countenance of the emperor, and to hear the tale of his messengers, loudly demanding vengeance for the shameful usage they had met.

"For a time the father may escape my vengeance," cried Charlemagne, "but the son shall feel it before another hour be passed!"

"Ah, sire, I am innocent of all this!" pled Ogier, falling on his knees.   "It is an enemy of mine, as of thine, that has thus provoked thee.   But if my father refuses due service and homage, I, his heir, freely acknowledge thee as my liege lord.   Great emperor, receive me among thy humblest and most faithful servants."

"No more!   Cut off his head forthwith!" raged the emperor.

But now arose a murmuring among the barons and

peers, many of whom were the youth's kinsmen, and all were loath to see him die thus untimely; and the wise Duke Naymes whispered in his master's ear:

"Nay, sire, do not provoke so many proud lords whose swords you may need ere long. Let the youth serve under your banner, as he so desires; there will be time enough to talk of vengeance on his father. Or, if you will slay him, give me leave to go, and find some other councillor," he added bluntly.

In vain! The emperor would listen to no pleadings. Ogier, seized and bound, was already about to kneel beneath the axe of the executioner, when suddenly the crowd of pitying spectators parted right and left to let a breathless messenger come before Charlemagne with news that made every sword leap in its scabbard.

The Saracen host had once more burst upon the south. The warlike Soldan, with a hundred thousand turbaned infidels, was ravaging the fair plains of Italy, burning and slaughtering as he went, and even now would be almost at the gates of Rome. All was lost unless the champion of Christendom at once took the field.

"To Rome! To Rome!" shouted all the barons and peers of France when they heard this message sent by the Pope; and Charlemagne did not delay to set out to the aid of the true faith. On the spot he gave orders for the assembling and advance of his army. Then, as his eye fell upon Ogier, he bid his bonds be removed, for he durst not risk offending the peers and paladins at a time when all hearts should be one, and every sword drawn against the common foe. The young Dane was once more delivered to Duke Naymes, who promised to answer for his safekeeping.

He followed in the rear of the army, which now marched with all speed across the Alps, and before the

gates of Rome, not a day too soon, came face to face
with the pagan host.   Both leaders drew out their forces
for a great battle; and, if his arms were victorious, Charlemagne vowed to himself that he would hang Ogier on the
field, for still the despite done him by Godfrey rankled in
his heart.

Among a crowd of squires and servants the youth
looked down from a hill behind the Christian ranks, and
eagerly beheld the two hosts approaching to the encounter.
Never had he seen such a sight!   The plain was covered
with dazzling armour and waving pennons; the earth
shook beneath the tread of myriads of war steeds; the
shouts and trumpet blasts pealed through the air loud
as a tempest; on either side the lances rose like a forest
around the oriflamme of France and the green banner
of the Prophet.   Ogier's heart beat high, and he cried:

"Oh, for at least a sharpened stake that I might rush
into the fray!   Better to fall fighting among knights than
to die as a captive!"

With strained eyes he watched the lines close and the
mailed warriors mingle in deadly fight.   But what does
he see?   In the very centre of the battle the Christians
give way—the infidels rush on—the flower of the French
chivalry are surrounded!   Charlemagne himself spurs
into the thick of the combat; he is lost as in a thunder
cloud, and his war-cry is drowned in the exulting shouts
of the foe.   For Allory, the Lombard lord who at the
emperor's right hand bears the oriflamme, has turned and
fled—shame upon him!   With the white standard trailing
in the dust, he gallops wildly towards that hill where a
crowd of squires stand overlooking the field.

"All is lost!   The emperor is taken!" gasped Allory,
and would have spurred past them, but Ogier barred the
way.

"Craven, you lie; it is you that have failed him in the battle!" he said, and with a blow of his fist brought Allory to the ground.

In hot haste he stripped the fugitive of sword and shield and helmet; with which quickly arming himself, he vaulted upon Allory's horse, and waving the oriflamme on high, cried: "Who will follow me, and carry the standard back to the front of the fight?"

The squires and pages answered with a shout. Whoever had no better weapon seized a stake or a branch; they leaped upon hackneys and sumpter mules, or on foot charged down the hill, with the brave Ogier at their head. Once they had gained the corpse-strewn field there was no lack of arms and steeds for all. Like boars they rushed into the Saracen ranks.

"Allory! Allory!" was the cry among the French knights, as they rallied round the oriflamme, and now the infidels began to turn their backs.

Many a turbaned Turk bit the dust before Ogier, as he made his way to the spot where Charlemagne, unhorsed and bareheaded, was still fighting amidst a crowd of the living and the dead.

"Fair France is mine! The banner of the Prophet shall wave over Paris!" boasted the Soldan, as he swung his battleaxe above the emperor's broken sword; but next instant the weapon was dashed from his hand, and he himself was hurled down.

"I shall live!" cried Charlemagne, springing upon a fresh horse brought by his deliverer—"I shall live to see France again, and to punish Godfrey of Denmark and all my foes."

The emperor being once more on horseback, with that proud standard borne at his right hand, the Christians took fresh courage, and the Saracens, in their turn, were swept backwards. They lost heart and gave way on every hand; ere long their whole host were in shameful rout, hotly pursued by the triumphant chivalry of Christendom.

The battle was over, and Charlemagne turned to the champion that had brought him such timely succour.

"Valiant Allory," he said, "how can I thank you for what you have done this day?"

"Nay, sire, this is not Allory," said one who stood by. "He played the coward and fled from the fight."

"Who art thou, then, and what shall be thy reward?" asked Charlemagne, astonished.

In answer, the young man silently raised his visor and knelt before him, crying: "Oh, great emperor, pardon for Godfrey of Denmark! Let his son make amends for his offence by devoting himself to thy service."

"Gentle stranger, right glad am I that I spared thy life," quoth the emperor. "My good sword, Joyeuse, broken and hacked with all the blows of this day, never touched the shoulder of a braver man. Rise and embrace me, Sir Ogier!"

Lightly the new-made knight sprang to his feet, and, with tears of joy and pride, rushed into Charlemagne's arms, vowing that every drop of his blood would not be too dear a price for such an honour at the hands of the lord of Christendom. His kinsmen, and all the barons and peers, flocked round him, wishing him joy. Only Charlot, the emperor's youngest son, stood aloof, for he was jealous of the glory that Ogier had won, and ever whispered in his father's ear, bidding him not forget his hatred of Godfrey and all the race of Denmark.

II

The war ended gloriously, the Saracens being driven beyond the sea; and no knight won more honour than young Ogier, who henceforth became known as one of the great champions of France, every day giving the emperor good reason to be thankful that he had not put him to an ignominious death.

But now, while the army was returning in triumph to Paris, it went ill with Godfrey of Denmark. A horde of northern savages had burst upon him, and soon, in spite of his utmost efforts, became masters of all his dominions, except one town in which they held him besieged. In these straits his wife counselled him to send to Charlemagne, once more humbling himself before the emperor, praying him to take pity on a suppliant vassal and come to his aid. Godfrey refused to stoop thus before his great enemy; but she, caring less for honour than for safety, wrote a letter to the court of France in her husband's name, and sealed it with his seal; then sent it off unknown to him. This letter met Charlemagne on his return to Paris.

The proud emperor smiled bitterly when he heard it read aloud; there was no pity in his heart for the man who had defied him. Then, turning to Ogier, who, he thought, would have little will to aid such an unkind father, he asked:

"Say, shall I send you on this errand?"

"Sire, I obey your commands," said Ogier, "and never more willingly than in this."

"What! you go to succour him who has cared so little for you?"

"Oh, sire, if my father were to beat me every day, it would be my part to take it all in patience; and my place is where he lies in danger! That man is worthy of the love neither of heaven nor of his fellow men who does not ever place his father above all. Yes, I will go, and without an hour's delay."

"I forbid you not," said Charlemagne in surprise; "but at least you must go alone. None of my knights shall ride in the service of a rebel."

Forthwith Ogier set out with a few friends and followers, and rode night and day till he came to the town where Godfrey was besieged. But he came too late, entering it only in time to meet the funeral of his father, killed in an encounter outside the walls. There was little time for mourning. As soon as the body was buried the young prince placed himself at the head of his men, sallied forth, defeated the enemy with great slaughter, freed the country from them, and was joyfully recognized as the lord of Denmark.

This done, and his malicious stepmother being banished from the land, he returned to Charlemagne and paid homage to him for all his states. He married the fair Belisande, and for many years lived happily, growing always in fame and in favour with the emperor, and in friendship with his brother knights. He became one of the twelve peers of France, of whom, next to Roland and Oliver, none was more famous than he who bore a red eagle on a black shield. All men spoke well of him, all but Charlot, the ungentle son of Charlemagne, who was of his own age, and had often been his comrade in battle, but never could he forgive this stranger for having won honour and goodwill of which he himself was not worthy.

The court of Charlemagne was then the most illustrious in Christendom. The greatest paladins and champions resorted to it, and kings sent their sons there to be trained in chivalry. A hundred knights, with a naked

sword in one hand and a burning torch in the other,
watched round the emperor's bed while he slept; when
he went out to hunt, a hundred barons rode by his side.
Countless were the lords and ladies who sat down to
banquet every day in the hall; and all day long, all
kinds of sports and pleasures were going forward about
the palace, where, says the minstrel—

> Some men joust with spear and shield,
>   And some men carol and sing good songs;
> Some shoot with darts in the field,
>   And some playen at chess among.

But, alas! the evil deed of one man was to bring grief
and hatred amid all this right royal magnificence.

In time, Belisande died, after giving birth to one child,
a boy, christened Baldwin. He grew to be a tall, comely
lad, the pride of his father, whom he much resembled in
looks, and bid fair to equal him in knightly graces and
accomplishments. There were few knights and ladies
about the court who did not look kindly on the boy,
for his father's sake and his own; the greatest of them
took pleasure in talking with him and joining in his
youthful sports; the emperor himself had him for a
page, and promised to see to his advancement.

One day Charlot, having nothing else to do, invited
young Baldwin to play at chess. The lad willingly consented, ran for the chessboard, all of solid gold, inlaid
with silver, got out the ivory pieces, and the game began.

Charlot prided himself on his skill at chess; but, to tell
the truth, it was not great, and he soon found that he had
met more than his match. The boy Baldwin moved his
pieces so skilfully that before long he had taken a knight
and given check to Charlot, who began to lose his temper.

"Aha, my lord, you are going to be checkmated!" cried the boy, clapping his hands and laughing.

"Have done with your laughing, young sir, or you will repent it," replied Charlot with a frown.

"Why should I not laugh? The game is worth nothing without laughing."

"Do you mean to mock me, you little knave?"

"No, but to beat you."

Charlot castled his king, and saw his second knight taken. Hastily, then, he moved his queen, which was at once taken by a bishop. He played wildly at random, growing too angry to think what he was doing. When, after a few more moves, he found himself checkmated, he started up from the table, seized the golden chessboard with both hands, and struck the boy over the forehead with it so violently that he fell dead on the marble pavement.

When Ogier came back from hunting that day his fair-haired darling did not run out to take his falcon and to lead away his horse. No one durst tell him what had happened. What was his horror to see Baldwin lying bathed in blood, and his fury when he learned by whose hands the boy had been killed! He knelt over the cold, lifeless body, covering it with kisses; and strong men that stood by could not restrain their tears at the sight.

"Ah, Charlot, this is not the first injury you have done me, but it shall be the last!" he cried, starting to his feet, and flying through the palace in search of the murderer, wild as a beast robbed of its young.

Charlot had hidden himself at the first news of his approach, and it was in vain that Ogier rushed from chamber to chamber, calling on the slayer of his son to come forth and meet him, that one of the two might die before another hour was past. At last he burst raging

into the presence of the emperor, who came to meet him,
and said:

"Ogier, I would have given half my kingdom that
this should not have befallen. But since it is done, and
without remedy, be appeased. I will spare nothing to
make amends."

"Amends!" cried Ogier madly. "The only amends
I seek is to meet that miscreant of thine hand to hand.
Blood for blood, and son for son. While he lives, speak
not to me of peace."

"Nay, be not so fierce," replied Charlemagne, ever
desirous, like many another foolish father, to screen the
faults of an unworthy son. "Such speech becomes not
a vassal. If you will not be at peace with me and mine,
you must quit my kingdom and find amends as you
can."

In his fury, scarcely knowing what he did, Ogier drew
his sword and sprang upon the emperor. If a squire had
not thrown himself between them, blood would have been
shed. But at once all the knights and lords closed round
them. Some bore Ogier away, beseeching him to be
patient. Some strove to appease the wrath of Charlemagne, who loudly bid them seize the presumptuous
knight that had dared thus to beard him in his own halls.
Great was the uproar and commotion, but through the
midst of it pressed Ogier, with his bare sword in his
hand, and his kinsmen favoured his flight. He gained
the door, sprang down the steps, mounted his horse, with
a curse on the house of Charlemagne to gallop away.

The emperor vowed for his part never to forgive this
insult, and by his command a band of well-mounted
knights made haste to follow Ogier, with orders to lead
him to prison. But his matchless steed, Broiffort, which
he had won in the Saracen wars, soon bore him out of

their reach. Plunging into a deep and broad stream, he swam across, and from the farther bank shook his gauntlet at the pursuers, then rode swiftly on, neither knowing nor caring whither he went.

III

And now for years was Ogier an exile and a wanderer. He could not return to Denmark, for all the roads were held by his enemies. No prince durst harbour long the man who lay under the emperor's wrath, and he scorned anywhere to conceal his name and the cause of his flight. He went from country to country, and from city to city, but could find no rest. Everywhere he was hunted by the forces that Charlemagne sent out to take him. Many a sharp encounter he had with his old comrades in arms. Often he had almost been betrayed into the hands of his pursuers, but always he was able to baffle them. More than one good lord tried to plead for him with Charlemagne, but the emperor would not forgo his anger in all these years, and vowed never to forgive the man that should befriend the Danish knight. On his part, Ogier vowed not to sue for peace till Charlot should be delivered to him.

At last was he driven to bay in a strong castle near the Rhone. The emperor surrounded it with a great army, declaring that he would not end the siege till Ogier was a captive in his hands, and the castle razed to the ground. Few of his knights but were loath to serve him in such a cause, for all had pity on the brave Dane ; yet they would not disobey their liege lord, so the siege went on till the moat of the castle might have been filled with the good blood spilt on both sides. Charlemagne caused engines to be made to batter

down the walls; he threw Greek fire upon the gates
and towers; he led his bravest men once and again to
the assault; but again and again they were beaten back.
The castle held out stoutly against all his efforts, and
many of the best knights of France fell in the sallies
made by the garrison.

But Ogier's case grew to be desperate, though he
kept a good face towards the enemy. Food began to
fail him. All his faithful followers were killed one
by one. The rest, hireling men-at-arms as they were,
plotted to overpower him and open the gates to the
emperor. He discovered their plot, and slew every
one of them through the night with his own hands.
In their place he set up carved figures of wood, arrayed
in the helms and hauberks of the dead men, with beards
of horsehair, and battleaxes in their hands.

When Charlemagne saw these wooden sentinels upon
the walls, he marvelled whence Ogier had got so many
fresh men. Riding up to the moat, he addressed them,
promising them rich rewards if they would betray their
master, and threatening them with tortures if they still
resisted; but they answered not a word. In anger, he
called on his crossbowmen to shoot, and the arrows
rattled terribly on the walls; but not one of the warders
stirred, though it seemed to the emperor as if they shook
their great battleaxes at him in token of defiance.

"What manner of men are these that have so little
fear?" he cried; yet he would not listen when his councillors, and even Charlot, begged of him to raise the
siege.

Ogier was now alone in the donjon keep; the rest of
his castle had been burned or battered down. All his
men lay dead about him, and the horses had all been
eaten, save Broiffort, his own good steed. For days he

had not tasted food nor lain down to rest; he must watch in his armour night and day, and he could see the foemen making long ladders to scale the walls, and bringing piles of brushwood to fill up the ditch. Though they lay round him in thousands, and he stood but one half-famished man against all, even yet he proved terrible to them. And Charlot drew near the walls to seek a parley with him, saying:

"Ogier, I come to confess my crime. I was young when I killed Baldwin, and never a day since but I have had rage and bitterness in my heart because of it. In proof of my penitence, I will kneel before thee bare-headed and in my shirt, to beseech thy pardon. More-over, I will make amends, as thy kinsmen shall judge, and all thy heritage shall be restored to thee; then, this done, I will go a pilgrimage to the Holy Sepulchre to do penance."

Ogier looked grimly over the walls and answered with a loud voice:

"Heaven pardon me for all the blood that I have shed to reach thee, Charlot; but may I beg my bread from door to door if ever I pardon the slayer of my son!"

And Charlot, returning to the camp, set a guard round his tent, so great was his fear of that relentless foe; for certain squires of his who had crept to the edge of the moat to gather grass for their horses, told him how they had heard Ogier within the walls speak-ing to Broiffort and saying:

"Horse, never was beast so good and true as thou, and many a time hast thou stood me in good stead. Now canst thou help me when I have no other friend? Can thy swiftness save me again as often before; or shall we seek death in yonder camp? Ah, then, sound will Charlot sleep if we do not arouse him!"

The brave horse neighed and stamped with his fore foot, as if he understood his master and promised to serve him to the last gasp.

One man truly, however brave, could not longer hold the castle with his single hand. At the dead of night Ogier saddled his noble steed, let down the drawbridge, and suddenly spurred forth. Like a whirlwind he rode through the sleeping camp of Charlemagne, and before any of the watchers could stay him was lost in the darkness.

On he rode, making for Denmark, and had soon left the pursuers far behind. Then, when horse and man could do no more, he dismounted to rest in a pleasant grassy spot beside a sparkling fountain. Here, letting Broiffort graze, he stretched himself beneath the shadow of a chestnut tree and fell asleep, with his sword, shield, and helmet lying beside him.

And here he was found by his kinsman, Archbishop Turpin, one of the twelve peers, who came riding by with a company of knights and squires. Sorry was Turpin that this chance had befallen him, for he would fain have had Ogier go free. But Charlemagne had forced on the peers an oath to make him prisoner, wherever or however they could. So the archbishop had no choice but to bid his attendants seize the sleeping knight.

Full cautiously they mastered his horse and stole away his arms; then a crowd of them suddenly sprang upon him. Aroused, he struggled like a madman, and strove to lay hand on a sword, and felled more than one of them with the stirrups of his saddle: this was as they had feared, for they guessed well he would rather die than fall into the hands of Charlemagne. But, in the end, overpowered by numbers, he was bound and fastened on a horse, and the archbishop carried him to his own prison at Rheims.

Joyful news came to Charlemagne that this insolent rebel lay at last in his power. The longer Ogier had held out against him, the greater waxed the emperor's wrath; and now he was minded to have him brought to Paris and torn in pieces by wild horses. But he feared the friends of Ogier, who were urgent with him to be merciful; and Charlot himself begged the Dane's life.

"Take this time to make peace with him," counselled Archbishop Turpin, "for it were shame and scandal that such a man, the mirror of knighthood, and the praise of all France, a more valiant warrior than Hector of Troy, or Arthur of Britain, should be put to death before the people."

"That were but a villainous end for one of my race," said another of his kinsmen, "and be sure there are a hundred knights at your court that would die rather than suffer it."

"And bethink you, sire," said the wise Duke Naymes, "that if his death become known the infidels may take heart for another onset."

"Ah, father, France has suffered enough for my sin!" said Charlot.

Moved by such counsels and warnings, Charlemagne restrained his hatred, and contented himself by making the archbishop promise to keep Ogier in close prison, feeding him daily with only half a loaf, and one morsel of flesh, and one cup of wine mixed with water. On such a pittance the emperor trusted that the stalwart knight's strength would soon waste away, and he must die in prison, or at least that men might forget him.

So the good archbishop promised, and so he did.

But the loaf of which he gave Ogier half every day was baked of a whole bushel of flour; and the piece of flesh was the quarter of an ox or of a sheep; and his cup held well nigh a gallon of wine. The prisoner throve on this fare, and had no lack of company; for the ladies and burgesses of Rheims came daily to visit him, and his cousin and jailer, the archbishop, would often sit in his dungeon to play chess with him. Nor was he forgotten by his friends, and they were many.

But Charlemagne would hear no prayers for his release, and gave orders that none, on pain of his head, should so much as speak of Ogier before him. So time went on, and most men knew not but that the Danish knight was dead.

IV

Seven years Ogier lay in prison, and meanwhile year by year the glory of Charlemagne's arms was on the wane. Roland and Oliver and all the best of the peers of France had fallen on the field of Roncesvalles; the old emperor himself was no longer the doughty knight he had been, nor could his sons take the place of the great champions of Christendom that had passed away. The infidel became more and more insolent; and now, in the seventh year, an army of Saracens invaded France, led by the Emir Bruhier, one of their most renowned warriors.

The French were beaten and driven back at every encounter, till the emperor had nothing for it but to betake himself to the walls of Rheims. There he lay, not daring to risk a battle, while the Saracen host encamped over against him and desolated all the country round, so that daily he could see the smoke of his towns and castles arising on every side.

But Bruhier thirsted to win honour with his own hand in battle with the Christian knights. He was a right warlike chief, fierce, proud, and boastful, and gigantic in stature. Never yet, such was his boast, had he met his match; and his astrologers had foretold that he never should be slain but by Ogier the Dane, whom he believed to be dead. So he sent a herald to Charlemagne, offering to meet him or any of his champions in single combat; then, if he should be overthrown, he pledged himself to retire with all his people and do no further harm to fair France.

The herald who brought this challenge did not fail to sound the praises of his master's strength and prowess, declaring that he scorned all the knights of France, and feared no man on earth but Ogier the Dane, whom the emperor had starved to death in prison. Charlemagne was furious to hear the forbidden name again spoken in his presence, and his knights were stung to proud anger by this insult. Four of them, one by one, rode out to humble the haughty Emir, who, in a bower of branches which he had caused to be erected in a valley midway between the two armies, was awaiting the answer to his summons. But, one by one, all four met such a handling from the Saracen that they never cared to look him in the face again, and no fifth durst risk the same discomfiture.

"Have ye no good knight for me to deal with? It is but pastime for me to unhorse weaklings like these!" Such was the contemptuous message which he sent by the mouth of a prisoner.

Sorely disheartened were the French. All thought of one man, and the emperor also thought of him with shame and bitterness, for he knew that the very Saracens cried out upon him for the dungeon with which he had rewarded his best knight; and as he saw those about him whispering to each other, he could well guess what word was upon their lips. When he asked Duke Naymes, his wisest counsellor, where to seek a remedy for the perilous state of his affairs, the old lord shook his head, and answered:

" Sire, I have no counsel for you but to seek aid from one whose name I may not utter."

Charlemagne frowned and was silent. But as day after day the Saracen still came before the walls, defying them and exulting over them, the French lords grew bold with rage and despair, and sought in secret if none could be found to risk his head by speaking the forbidden name. A certain poor knight consented to undertake the dangerous task on the promise of a rich reward from the rest, who also pledged themselves to do all in their power to protect him against the emperor's displeasure. Moreover, he provided a swift horse to stand ready saddled at the door before he entered the monarch's presence, and addressed him curtly:

" My lord, you will lose your crown if you do not send against Bruhier the only man who can save it. His name is——"

Before the word was spoken, Charlemagne sprang up in fury, and would have fallen on the bold knight with his own sword, but he fled like an arrow, the crowd quickly opening to let him pass, and so gained the door, leaped on his horse, and galloped out of reach of the wrathful emperor.

None of those at the court could find heart to make the same trial again. But the lords consulted once more, and fell upon a device to brave their prince's gloomy mood. They gathered together their children and those of their servants, two or three hundred in number, who, coming in a crowd before the emperor, as he sat brooding over his trouble, suddenly shouted out with one voice:

"Ogier! Ogier! Ogier!"

"The very children cry out for him!" exclaimed Charlemagne, putting his hands to his head.

"From the mouth of children, sire, you may learn wisdom," replied Duke Naymes.

He hid his face, and for a time stayed in thought; then, looking up, called his lords round him, and said bitterly:

"Let it be as you will. Bring forth the Dane from his dungeon, and send him against Bruhier. Whatever he demands shall be granted if he will but be reconciled to me and mine, since the stars have so decreed."

This command was received with shouts of applause; joy and hope spread throughout the city when it was known that Charlemagne had granted what was the hearty wish of all but himself.

As quickly as if his limbs were still young, old Naymes sped to the prison. Calling through the bars, he offered freedom and pardon on the part of the emperor if Ogier would consent to be their champion against this mighty Saracen.

"Pardon!" quoth the captive. "Pardon for all the evil he has done me, forsooth!"

"Nay then, he would be friends with thee as of old."

"Aye, when he hath need of me; else I might have lain here long before he bethought him of our old friendship. Well, this lord of yours knows the condition on which I am, as I have ever been, willing to make friends with him: that Charlot be delivered, bound hand and foot, to my will. Without this will I not don breastplate nor draw sword in his cause."

"Good Ogier, forget thy vengeance and ask some other thing!" besought the duke.

"You have my answer," said Ogier sternly. "I will have my demand, or spend the rest of my days in prison."

With this reply Duke Naymes went back to Charlemagne, who, when he heard it, wept for grief, crying:

"Alas! what sins have I done that I should be the slave of my vassal, and must deliver my son to his mercy? Which of you has the heart to counsel me to such a sacrifice?"

"Better, sire, that one man die than thousands," said the duke.

All the others murmured assent, while Charlot himself knelt before the emperor, entreating him no longer to deny Ogier's wish.

"It is through my fault that all these evils have befallen; let me, then, suffer, and let France be safe. My father, had young Baldwin—woe on the day that I slew him!—been your son, you would have felt and done like his father; yet he was a noble boy, and I am unworthy to live."

"Thou, too, against me?" cried Charlemagne, embracing his favourite son; then, turning away to hide the sorrow that unmanned him, he bade Naymes tell the captive that his demand should be granted.

Once more the old duke hastened to the prison, the doors of which were soon flung open, and forth came Ogier amid a crowd pressing forward to see and welcome him with as much reverence as if he had been a saint. In those seven years his hair had grown white, and his beard reached his girdle; but his limbs were stout and his looks comely as ever, and the old fire shone in his eye as he stepped forth, looking proudly around him.

"My horse! my arms!" he cried, stretching himself

for gladness to feel the fresh air once more on his brow. "Not an hour shall pass ere I seek this haughty foe."

They fetched his armour from the vault where it had been lying. All battered and rusty as it was, he buckled it on, and fastened to his side the good sword that had served him in so many a fight. Then there was led to him the emperor's best charger, but he bade them take it away, and asked where was his own trusty steed, Broiffort, for on no other would he ride to battle.

Where was Broiffort? Most of the bystanders declared that he must be dead, and if so, Ogier declared that he would rather go against the Saracens on foot than trust any strange steed. Then a priest came forward, telling how the archbishop had given Broiffort to a company of masons who were building the cathedral; he himself that very day had seen the good horse dragging great blocks of marble in a cart. Ogier's brow grew dark when he heard to what base employment the noble beast had been set for those long years.

Men ran in haste and brought Broiffort from the cart in which he was found drawing a double load of lime and stone. Thin and ill-groomed was he, his sides galled by the shafts, and his tail shorn to the stump, but as soon as he heard his old master's voice he snorted and neighed for joy, and pawed the ground and tossed his head in the air like a true warhorse. And Ogier's heart was ready to burst, as he brushed the dust from his bare flanks, and picked a mouldy straw from his nostrils, saying:

"Broiffort, faithful friend, our enemies have had their will of us both for seven years. But bear me to-day as thou hast borne me many a day, and no man shall again put fetters and burdens upon us."

For answer, the good horse stiffened his neck, and you would have said that his eye spoke back, bidding the knight fear not that he would fail him. A golden bit was put into his mouth, and his sides were covered with a rich housing; then wonderful was it to see how he pranced and bounded when he felt Ogier on his back. The gates were thrown open, the people shouted, and man and horse went forth in right warlike guise to the encounter that awaited them.

V

All within the city, great and small, thronged the walls to see Ogier ride down into the valley and approach the Saracen emir's pavilion of boughs. Bruhier, weary of showing himself before the gates to repeat his challenge, was lying asleep when his squire woke him to say that a knight who bore a red eagle on a black shield was coming forth to do battle with him. Still did he not stir till he heard the clang of the knight's lance striking his shield that hung by the door of the pavilion. Then he called for his helmet, and went out to see who this might be that durst accept his challenge. He was taller by a head than Ogier, and his mighty limbs were encased in rich mail.

"Ho, Christian, com'st thou alone?" said he, scornfully surveying Ogier's rusty armour. "'Twas not worth while to wake me for this; I need ten such knights to measure myself with since Ogier the Dane is dead."

"Get to horse, and we shall see if you can measure yourself with Ogier or another."

"So thou thinkest to overthrow me, and to gain the prize with which Charlemagne rewards his champions," quoth the Saracen, laughing loudly. "Well, better for thee to die by the hand of a man like me than to starve to death in prison like the good Ogier."

"Enough! I did not come here to spend words on thee, but blows!" cried Ogier impatiently.

A magnificent black Arab courser was now brought to Bruhier, on which he sprang without touching the stirrup, and snatched his lance from the hands of his squire. Then, wheeling about to take ground, both knights made ready for the encounter.

Broiffort gathered all his strength for the charge, but at the first shock the good horse dropped dead, though he had borne his master so well that Bruhier also was dismounted. Since the death of Baldwin, Ogier had not felt such a pang as when he saw that his old steed would never rise again; but it was neither place nor time for grief.

"I will have thy horse for mine!" he cried, and the two knights sprang up and fell upon each other with their swords.

It was terrible to see how they hacked and hewed, and how splinters and sparks of fire flew from their armour. The Saracen was the stronger man, but Ogier showed himself the more skilful of fence; and thus they fought, as it seemed to the anxious spectators, for hours, and neither could gain the advantage. At last, exhausted by their efforts, they agreed to a short truce.

Now came a contest of courtesy between them: each unlaced the other's helmet, and offered his aid to bind up his enemy's wounds. When the emir threw his vast bulk on the ground, Ogier, perceiving him to lie uneasily, fetched a great stone and put it beneath his head for a pillow. Bruhier, on his part, desired the Dane to make use of a sovereign cordial which he carried at his saddle bow, but Ogier replied that he would have nothing of his till he had won it of him with steel.

Having thus rested a time, they stood up and went

to it again. And still Ogier fought so well that his adversary was astonished, and, lowering his sword, asked:

"Who art thou, knight of the red eagle! By Mahomet, I had thought there was none of Charlemagne's knights, save Ogier, that could have so long withstood me."

"Infidel, I am Ogier the Dane, and never more shalt thou boast thyself over the Christian knights."

"Ogier!" cried the emir, and a chill ran to his heart as he recalled the prediction of his astrologer. "Men said you were dead in prison; but if you are truly that good knight, it were better for you to serve a more grateful prince. Come! abjure your faith, and follow the standard of the Prophet. I will not only grant you your life, but my sister in marriage, and you shall lack no honours or rewards, such as you have well deserved."

"Nay, abjure you, or prepare for death, since you have tempted Ogier to treason and blasphemy."

Once more their swords crossed, and now Bruhier no longer doubted that he had to do with none but Ogier, that knight by whose hand, as he believed, he was fated to fall. In desperation, as he felt his strength failing him, he threw down his sword and rushed wildly on, brandishing a great brazen mace, and trying to overwhelm the Dane with his heavy shield. But Ogier stepped back; then his keen blade clove the shield in two, and what was the joy of the French to see the Saracen's weapon forced from his hand and his huge body brought tottering to the ground!

"Ogier, spare me!" he cried, embracing the victor's knees. "I will abjure my faith, I will receive baptism and become thy brother in arms—only grant me my life."

The Christian champion, suspecting no disloyalty, sheathed his sword, threw down his shield, and bid

Bruhier rise. But no sooner was the wily Saracen on his feet than he raised up the great stone on which he had rested his head, and heaved it at Ogier, who, for the moment, was looking away, and would have been crushed to death if a cry of warning from the city walls had not reached his ears just in time. He sprang aside, and drew his sword quick as lightning. It was in vain for Bruhier now to beseech mercy. The bright steel flashed in the air, and was buried to its hilt in the false emir's heart.

At this sight loud shouts arose on either side, of triumph and thankfulness among the followers of Charlemagne, but of horror and despair among the Saracens, who, panic-stricken by the fall of their leader, broke up their camp in confusion, and fled so hastily that when the sun set not one of them was to be seen. Ogier stayed only to take the spoils of the foe, then, mounting Bruhier's black steed, with one sorrowful look at poor Broiffort's stiffening limbs he rode back to the gate of the city.

A great crowd ran out to meet and welcome him, and Charlemagne himself held the stirrup as the knight dismounted amid a din of acclamations. The emperor's heart was divided between fear and joy—joy that he had been delivered from the enemy, and fear for his darling son, whom he must now put at the disposal of Baldwin's avenger.

"Charlemagne, on the faith of a prince, I demand the fulfilment of your promise. I have slain Bruhier; give me Charlot!"

In vain the emperor sought delay; in vain he offered cities, provinces, kingdoms, in ransom for his son's life. Ogier appealed to his nobles that the bargain which they had witnessed might not be broken.

Bound and disarmed, the miserable Charlot was led

forward.   He fell at Ogier's feet, all pale and trembling, silently praying that heaven would soften his heart, and loudly beseeching him to have pity.

"Pardon my offence, or at least doom me to exile in place of death.   I will leave France, and will never return to it so long as thou livest.   All my possessions shall be thine, as all I would freely give that Baldwin might be alive this day."

But Ogier did not answer him a word.   With his left hand grasping the craven wretch's hair, in his right he raised the great sword, red with Bruhier's blood, above his head.   Charlemagne uttered a cry of agony, and turned away, hiding his face in his mantle, that he might not see the fatal blow.   Every other look was fixed on Ogier, who stood with his blade held on high for a minute, during which his victim tasted the bitterness of death a hundred times.

A crowd of mingled thoughts rushed through the mind of the knight as in a vision he saw all the brave men who had fallen in this quarrel, and his eyes swam with tears; next arose before him the fair face of young Baldwin bathed in blood, and his heart swelled with fierce rage; then, lo! it seemed that the boy took the form of an angel, stretching out his hands towards him with a gentle smile as if to stay the swordstroke, and pleading like a messenger from heaven for mercy and forgiveness.

Suddenly he hurled down his sword, and let Charlot sink to the earth, fainting with terror.

"Sire," he cried, "you know now what it costs a father to lose his son!   I give you back yours!   Ah, would to God he could give me back mine!"

"Oh, Ogier, generous as brave!" exclaimed Charlemagne, falling on his neck with tears of gratitude, "how shall I pay all the debt I owe thee, and how canst thou pardon me for all the wrong that my house has done to thine?"

"Nay, thank not me, but Him who hath given me grace to bridle my heart and to reverence the sorrow of thy grey hairs," said Ogier, embracing the emperor with a kiss of peace.

Thus were they reconciled before all the peers and paladins of the Christian army. But never again did Ogier ride by the side of Charlemagne. He turned his back on France, and spent the rest of his life warring against the infidel in the Holy Land.

RONCESVALLES

I

SEVEN years had the great Charles warred in Spain, and never could the Saracens stand before the onset of his peers. No castle, no walled city, withstood him save Saragossa, where the King Marsilius still held out, but daily trembled to look for the Christian banners borne against his last stronghold. In this plight he called a council of his chiefs; and with one voice they urged him to send gifts and hostages to the invincible Frank, praying that he should depart from the land on good terms of peace. There seemed no help but in submission, so the proud Moor chose Blancandrin, wisest and bravest of his councillors, to head an embassy to the emperor's camp.

There Charles sat at ease, like a conqueror who had naught to dread; and round him his peers played chess or draughts, or the young lords exercised themselves at feats of arms, when the Saracen envoys came riding on mules, with olive branches waved aloft as sign of their mission.

In their train were camels and cars loaded with golden besants, also bears, lions, and other wild beasts brought in chains as offerings to the great king. The French knights crowded around in wonder as the strangers made their way to Charles's throne, before which Blancandrin alighted with lowly obeisance, and thus spoke his errand:

" Great emperor of the Franks, my lord Marsilius

greets thee with these gifts, praying thee to leave his land in peace. So thou wilt depart beyond the mountains, he pledges himself to follow to thy court at Aix and there to receive the Christian faith, since heaven fights against the Crescent. Thereafter he will hold his kingdom as vassal of France."

"He speaks fair and well," answered Charles; and, ordering courteous entertainment for the messengers, he called his peers and barons together, of whom he asked: "Does he speak true?"

"Trust not the infidel!" quoth Roland, ever first in word as in deed. "Seven years we have fought him and found him false as dastard. It is vengeance and not peace for which so much kindly blood still cries from Spanish ground."

Charles sat silent awhile, stroking his white beard as he looked from one to another of the lords; but none made haste to speak, till Ganilon rose, frowning askance at the stepson he had never loved.

"Listen not, sire, to rash braggarts," was his counsel. "Since the pagan king offers to be baptized and to do homage, what more have we to gain in courting death. It would be a sin not to have done with this long war; so every wise man must think with me."

The eldest and sagest of the peers murmured assent; and Charles bowed his head.

"Peace let it be, since peace is begged!" he declared. "Whom, then, of you all shall I send back to treat with the Saracen?"

"Me, if you will," offered Roland. "I would fain beard that proud Paynim in his hall, since ever he shuns my sword in battle."

"Nay!" cried Oliver with a smile. "We know thee too hot for quarrel to be fit messenger of peace."

"Loath am I," said Charles, "that any of my peers should risk his head in a lion's den. But choose amongst yourselves who best can do my errand to Marsilius."

"Choose my stepsire Ganilon, since he is so prudent and such a lover of peace!" cried Roland mockingly.

"He is the man!" agreed all the peers; and for shame's sake Ganilon durst not say them nay; yet it was with no goodwill he undertook the perilous mission. "If heaven grant me to come back safe, I will pay thee for this," he muttered to his stepson.

"With the king's will I am ready to go in thy place," answered Roland lightly, and laughed in his scowling face.

"Give me the message, sire. Since go I must there shall be no delay!" Ganilon spoke with bold looks, but it was with inward grudge that he made ready for the journey; and the peers took leave of him as one they might never see again.

Charles gave him letters to Marsilius, also his staff and glove as tokens; but in taking the glove Ganilon let it drop, in which men saw an ill omen of his errand. Then he set out for Saragossa with Blancandrin; and on the way the wily Saracen spoke thus:

"What a marvellous king this of thine, that wars with so many nations and is never tired of victory! Yet methinks his dukes and counts do him great wrong in counselling him to endless strife."

"For that," quoth Ganilon, "his nephew Roland is alone to blame, whose pride daily seeks death. Were he to find it we should all have peace."

"So it were well!" said Blancandrin, and more they said to each other as they rode towards Saragossa.

Ganilon had good cause to fear when he gave the Moorish king the letter that let him know he must yield up half his kingdom or else be taken in chains to Aix and there put to a villainous death. The proud pagan, red with rage, caught up a dart to throw at the messenger, who clapped his hand to his sword-hilt. But the Saracen chiefs restrained their king; and Blancandrin whispered in his ear, bidding him listen to the Frank, who had that to say that were well for him to hear. So Marsilius mastered his wrath, and took Ganilon aside to ask how he might have peace.

"Never while his nephew lives, Roland, to whom he will give half the kingdom. Were he and his friend Oliver dead, Charles would have no more lust for conquest; and thus might we all live at ease."

"Good sir," said Marsilius, "how might I rid me of this Roland?"

"Do this and thou shalt do well. Make peace now with Charles, that he may lead his host back into France. So proud is Roland that he must be the last to leave Spain. He and Oliver will command the rearguard; then, as they go slow and wearied through the pass of Roncesvalles, let thousands of thy men fall on them from an ambush. With him Charles will lose his right arm, and, his nephew dead, there will be none to spur him into war."

At this counsel the king was full glad, and threw his arms round Ganilon with a kiss. He gave him gold and jewels from his treasury, and spake him fair words; and so was made a secret pact between them to betray Roland to his death.

II

Back came Ganilon to the camp of Charles, bringing fresh offerings of tribute and this message:

"You may trust, sire, the pagan king. Not a month

will pass before he follows you into France, to do you homage and hold from you the kingdom of Spain."

"'Tis good," said the emperor. "Thou hast done thy mission right well."

He gave command, and through the camp a thousand trumpets sounded the news that the war was at an end. With joy the warriors broke up their camp and made haste to load the beasts of burden, eager to set out for sweet France they had not seen for seven long years. Proudly the emperor mounted his horse to lead them homewards with their rich spoil. But ere they marched away he spoke to the peers.

"Which of you shall I name to command the rear, and guard the army as it threads the narrow passes of the mountains?"

"Roland, my stepson, is the man," quoth the treacherous Ganilon. "You have no leader so brave."

"None, forsooth!" said the emperor. "With thee, nephew, I leave the flower of my chivalry, sure that our passage will thus be made safe."

"Sire, since you appoint me to this task," said Roland, "be sure that you will lose neither palfrey nor sumpter mule but it shall be paid dear by my sword."

"I will stay with thee!" cried Oliver, and so said all the peers; and it was the best of the French knights that shared with Roland his perilous post of honour.

They, then, held back on Spanish ground to guard the mouth of the pass, while the rest of the host rode away through dark valleys and grey crests and chill gorges, where the eagle and the vulture dwelt alone upon cloudy peaks. But now, so loud was the trampling and the clatter of their march, it might be heard for leagues around; and for once the gloomy rocks were gay with fluttering pennons and shining armour. A hard road and a long they took; but every heart beat high in hope to see the native land in which they had left lordly home and loving wife and child. And when at last from the topmost ridge their eyes looked once more down on fair France, there was none but filled with tears of joy. Only Charles wore a look of care, when he thought of his nephew and all the gallant knights that might never see France again.

Slowly, far in the rear, came that brave band, turning ever backward to watch for the foe, then warily advancing from point to point, where the vulture and the eagle hung over their way, marked by dead horses and abandoned baggage; but for a time they saw no sign of living man. They knew not how Marsilius, with thousands of his warriors, went stealing on before them by secret paths, nor how twelve of his fiercest chiefs had vowed to slay Roland before they should return to Saragossa; least of all did true knights deem that they had been sold by a traitor to the infidel.

All day they marched and all night, till at dawn they entered the narrow gorge of Roncesvalles. When it was full daylight, Oliver rode up a hill to spy around, before, behind, and either side. And well might he rub his eyes, for they fell upon dark woods that under the beams of the rising sun began to glitter with arms; and the rocky slopes, no longer silent, now echoed the neighing and tramp of horses. A moment he stood amazed; then a moment more showed him the banners of the foe, and hotly he spurred back to let Roland know what a multitude of Saracens was closing upon them, through whom they must fight their way to France.

" Heaven grant it ! " cried Roland, his face lit with the flush of battle.

" They are twenty to one, and by treason do they

take us at odds in this narrow pass. Sound thy horn, my brother, that Charles may hear from afar and turn back to our aid."

So said Oliver, and so said the rest of the peers; but Roland answered proudly:

"Nay, that were shame on us. It shall not be told in France that we called for aid against all the might Marsilius can bring. The more they come, the more shall fall before us; and if it be our time to die, men will say that ours were the swords of noble knights."

"Ganilon hath sold us to the Moor," murmured one and another.

"Then dear shall he buy his bargain!" vowed Roland, and his eyes shone like a lion's or a tiger's on its prey.

For by now the Saracens came to open view, topping ridge after ridge as they moved down from their ambush to shut the Frenchmen within a hedge of steel. Quickly and keenly the knights looked to their harness and their arms. For a moment they knelt on the ground, while Archbishop Turpin, upraised upon a hillock, stretched his arms over them in absolution and benediction; and for penance he enjoined them to strike stoutly upon the shields of the infidel. Then, mounting their horses, they spurred on with the warcry of " Monjoye!"

Never had the mountain pass resounded to such a swelling cry and such a din of arms. Terrible was the shock of the encounter. Many a horse and man went down; many a lance was splintered; many a helm was cloven; many a bright pennon trailed in the dust. Three times the French knights drove their enemies before them like chaff; but always came upon them a fresh crowd of dark-skinned warriors; and these fearless champions were overborne among so many. One by one they fell upon heaps of slain, while the rest still battled on with hacked swords and the broken truncheons of their spears. Roland, ever foremost, did prodigies of valour; Oliver bore himself bravely at his side; and the good Archbishop Turpin, too, struck many a doughty blow. But for one they slew, ten Saracens rose as from the ground; and long ere they had won through the pass no more than threescore of the Christian knights still fought on, wounded and weary.

"Yield, Frenchmen! since ye are betrayed into out hands by one who should have fought beside you. Ill has your king done in leaving you to perish among the mountains; but now shall he lose his right arm and the flower of his knights."

So boasted the chief that led on the Saracen warriors; but before his boasts were ended Roland clove him to the chine.

"Pagan, you have lied!" was his word. "Yielding we know not; and at the worst our king will avenge us twenty for one." And to Oliver he said: "I am fain now to sound my horn that Charles may hear across the mountains."

"So I bade you do when you scorned my bidding," answered Oliver hotly. "Now it is too late, and you have undone us all by your rash pride. True courage is not folly like thine. Out upon thee, Roland, who has lost to the king the best of his peers!"

"This from thee!" cried Roland. "No other man alive durst thus rebuke me."

When the good archbishop heard their voices loud in quarrel, he spurred between these two, bidding them save their breath for the enemy.

"Yet sound the horn," was his counsel, "that Charles may hear and turn back; and if he come not in time to save our lives, he will save our bodies from dogs and

THE STRUGGLE IN THE PASS OF RONCESVALLES

HUON PRESENTS THE CONQUERED GIANT TO THE EMIR

vultures, and bear us to be buried in Christian soil, with honour and mourning among our own."

"You say well," answered Roland, putting the ivory horn to his lips. "I sound not for succour, but for vengeance!"

He blew once, and the blast rang loud and clear over the mountains, bringing the Saracen onset to a stand in dismay. He blew twice, and the eagles flew screaming from their nests as if driven before a storm wind. A third time he blew, and louder yet, till the veins of his temples burst and blood gushed out from his mouth to mingle with the gore that besmeared all his armour. Then he fainted and fell from his horse; but he knew that Charles must have heard, were he ever so far on the way.

Far across the mountains, leagues and leagues ahead, the king's anxious ears caught that sound, and all the French host knew that it was Roland's horn.

"Never would he blow thus but in battle," said Charles.

"Nay," said the traitor Ganilon, "he is but hunting the hare, or he sounds it in jest and play. Let us halt not, with France already in sight!"

But others of the peers shook their heads, and the wise Duke Naymes told the king:

"Roland is in distress. He who would deny it deceives you, sire. Let us turn back to succour our brethren. Hark again!"

Again came the sound, like a cry of distress.

"Such a blast is not blown but for hunting of men!" cried Charles, ill at ease, for he had dreamt an evil dream, and it misgave him that all was not well. Still the false Ganilon counselled to pay no heed; but when his king looked him in the face, the traitor's eyes fell, and angrily the peers murmured that there had been treason.

"If so, the traitor shall dearly pay it!" cried Charles, and gave Ganilon prisoner to the kitchen servants who followed in his train, till it should be shown if he were felon knight or no.

A third time rang out Roland's horn, louder and clearer, and for answer Charles bid all the trumpets of his army sound together, in sign that he heard and heeded. Forthwith he gave order to return, and through the gloomy ravines, and over the rapid torrents the host spurred back towards Spain, praying that they might yet be in time to succour Roland in his need.

III

Roland rose from his swoon and looked around him to see the blood-stained ground strewn with the bodies of his comrades; but for every French knight there lay ten of the foe.

"Alas, brothers-in-arms," he wept over them, "ye die by my fault, and I shall die of grief for you if now I meet not death!"

It was no time for tears. Again the Saracens came on, and again the little band faced them so hotly that they drew back as before. But what availed such bravery against a host that flowed like the waves of the sea! Those who durst not press forward assailed the Christians with slings and arrows from overhead, or rolled down huge rocks to crush them in the narrow pass. At last but three comrades stood upright: Roland, Oliver, and Archbishop Turpin, who had fought like a warrior that day. When the Moors saw so few to withstand them, and these so sore wounded, there rushed on amain a troop blacker and fiercer than any that had yet charged; and once more they closed in mortal strife.

"Roland, help me!" cried Oliver faintly, as he felt himself hurt to death.

Roland rushed to his side and drove away like flies the Saracens that beset them; then, reeling on his saddle and blinded by blood, Oliver struck wildly around him, so that he clove through Roland's helm and unwittingly gave him a deadly wound.

"What dost thou, Oliver?" exclaimed he. "I am Roland, who loves thee; and thou hast stricken me to death."

"Ah," murmured Oliver, "I hear thy voice, but I see thee not! God forgive me, and Roland pardon me if I have done him harm."

With this he fell from his horse, Roland leaping down to hold him in his arms.

"Many a year we have been together; and now thou art dead, I care not to live!" was his farewell; but Oliver spoke no more.

Roland dragged himself into the shadow of a lonely pine tree, where his own good steed Veillantif was writhing in its death throes, and near him the archbishop lay bleeding out his life. Once more he looked around on the corpses of his friends, and at that sight he wept bitter tears mingled with blood.

"*Mea culpa!*" he cried; then with his last breath Archbishop Turpin gave him absolution, before crossing his own hands on breast as he turned his dim eyes to heaven.

Once more Roland sounded his horn till it burst; but now across the hills it was echoed back by a thousand clarions. When he knew himself not forsaken by his king, with a smile he laid his head upon his horse as on a pillow. Beside him fell from his weak hand the sword Durandal, that had spilt so much pagan blood, and never had it failed him till now.

As he lay thus to die, there crept up to him a bold Saracen, who would have carried off the good sword as a trophy, had not Roland opened his eyes. He raised himself, and with the horn, which his hand still grasped, dealt the fellow such a blow as broke helmet and skull; and the ivory horn, too, was broken in fragments.

Never, he vowed, should Durandal, with holy relics set in its hilt, be wielded by pagan hand. He gathered his last strength; he stood upon his feet; he reared himself upright, and with both hands swung the sword to dash it on a mass of brown rock at his back. But the steel did not splinter; it was the rock that burst in twain; and there to this day men show the breach cleft by Roland's last blow.

With that he fell dead over his horse under the drooping pine tree, his face turned to the foeman's land. Thus Charles the king found him when be rode up at the head of the army, hastening in vain.

"Roland! Oliver! Turpin!" he cried, and called on all his peers by name; but there was no voice to answer save the croak of the vulture and the scream of the eagle. Wherever he looked, he saw not a rood nor a yard of ground but it was hidden beneath the corpses of Frenchmen and of Saracen, ten for one.

Bitter was the grief of Charles at such a woeful sight, and terrible his wrath. Bidding Duke Naymes stay to watch the battlefield, that no wild beast or robber should touch the slain, he sounded his trumpets once again and set on in pursuit of the Saracens, flying before the first flutter of his banners. Men tell how that day a miracle was wrought through the king's prayers, for the sun stood still over mountain and valley, while the French host smote the heathen all along their craven flight; and those that fell not by sword or spear were driven into the Ebro to be drowned, their false god helping them not against the avengers of Roland's blood.

IV

The great Charles stayed in Spain but long enough to destroy the walls of Saragossa, and to slay Marsilius with every Moor that refused to be baptized and to do homage. Then he came back to the battlefield gilded by the blood of his peers, and there he made woeful moan, loudest and bitterest for his nephew Roland.

"Ah, best of kinsmen," he cried, "I shall have no good day in my life now thou art dead! The Saxons, the Huns, the Romans will rebel once more, and all those nations conquered for me by thy sword. Would I had died before I brought back such heavy news to France!"

With solemn chant and prayer he bid bury the bodies where they lay. But those of Roland, Oliver, and the good Archbishop Turpin he had embalmed in spices and wine, and wrapt in white cereclothes, that he might carry them over the mountains to be laid under marble tombs in their own land.

Through France marched the sorrowful convoy, and the emperor never halted till he saw his palace at Aix. Here first came to meet him the fair Lady Alda, she to whom Roland had plighted his troth; and when she met naught but silent and downcast looks, her first word was :

"Where is Roland, my love? Where have you left Oliver, my brother?"

Charles bowed his head, and awhile could not answer

her for tears. Then he took her by the hand to say
gently:

"Dear maiden, you ask after the dead. Roland can
never be thine, since God hath taken him; but in his
place I will give thee my son Louis, the heir to my
kingdom."

"How can I live to wed another if Roland be in
heaven!" she cried, and fell lifeless at the king's feet,
to lie with her lover in the grave.

When the dead were nobly buried, one deed remained to do. The traitor Ganilon must be brought
to trial before the king and his peers. He did not deny
his guilt, but would have brazened it out.

"I served the king no less than my stepson Roland,
but ever he hated me. He had me sent on a perilous
mission; then I saved myself by my wit, and I did by
Roland as he would have done by me. That was vengeance but no treason."

With black looks the king and the peers heard his
plea, for it had come to be known how he sold Roland
to that faithless Moor. None stood by him but his
own kinsmen, among whom he chose out Pinabel as the
doughtiest knight, and on his body he demanded the
ordeal by combat.

"Methinks that few will care to give me the lie!"
quoth Pinabel, as he threw down his gauntlet; and in
sooth, now that Roland and Oliver were gone, it was
hard to find another champion bold enough to risk himself against such a one.

Knights and barons sat silent, none daring to accept
the challenge, so that Ganilon seemed like to go free
for want of a respondent, till who but Thierry of Anjou,
youngest of the peers, sprang forward to snatch up the
glove, crying:

"Since no better offers himself, for Roland's sake and the king's honour I take on me to prove Ganilon false vassal and felon knight!"

So it was to be. The champions, having prayed and confessed themselves and given great gifts to holy shrines, rode into the lists arrayed in their choicest armour, before the court of Charles.

Lords and all ladies pitied Thierry, so slender and graceful that they feared to see him borne down by the huge bulk of his adversary. None prayed for Pinabel but Ganilon, whose wicked heart misgave him, for all that he had such a defender.

"Heaven speed the right!" cried Charles, giving the signal to engage.

And so it happed, for at the first shock the young knight's lance bore Pinabel from his saddle, and he lay like a fallen tower in the dust, never more to strike stroke or to speak word of defiance.

Thus heaven had given judgment; and now none could gainsay the guilt of that accused felon. Forthwith Ganilon was torn in pieces by four wild horses, and all the kinsmen were hanged who had pledged themselves for his cause. So perished the traitor, leaving a name ever hateful among men, who remember Roland as the trustiest and bravest warrior of the great Charles.

HUON'S QUEST

I

A CHRISTIAN knight had lost his way in the glades of a Syrian forest. For three days he wandered at a venture without meeting any man, and finding no food but berries and wild honey. On the third day the blows of an axe guided him to a clearing, where he saw a tall figure, half-naked, but almost covered with grizzled hair. So uncouth seemed he, and so sturdily he swung his axe, that the knight's first thought was to rein in his steed and lay hand to his sword. For a time they looked hard upon each other; then suddenly the wild man flung down his axe, and rushed forward to throw himself on his knees, exclaiming:

"Sir Huon of Bordeaux, my good lord!"

"Who art thou?" cried the knight, amazed to hear himself called by name, and his native tongue in this paynim land.

"Who but Geraume, brother of the Mayor of Bordeaux!"

"The most faithful vassal of my father's house! But how comes a Christian here?"

"Years ago, fighting by your good father's side, I was made slave to the Saracens, who in vain sought to turn me from the true faith, till after many sufferings at their hands I broke my chains and escaped to the wilderness. Here I have since lived as a hermit, little hoping ever again to see a kindly face. But say, my lord, what brings a knight of France so far from home?"

"That were a long tale for a hungry mouth," said Huon; whereon Geraume led him to his hut hard by, and set before him such poor fare as he had to offer.

When refreshed, the knight told at length how he had fallen under the displeasure of Charlemagne, his sovereign lord. In defence of his own brother he had slain Charlot, the king's spiteful son. In vain he knelt at the father's knees, imploring pardon for a chance blow in a quarrel forced upon him. When Charlot's body was brought in, Charlemagne grew so furious that he would have slain Huon forthwith, had not the twelve peers joined to denounce his injustice. In the end the angry king was moved to spare his life, but only on condition of his undertaking a desperate enterprise. He must go alone to the city of Babylon, where reigned the Emir Gaudisse, from whom Charlemagne had already demanded homage by fifteen messengers, one after another, but not one of them had come back. There, sword in hand, he must haughtily call on the emir to pay tribute, and, as proof of obedience, take from him certain tokens, without which Huon durst not return to France.

"You are sending him to his death!" the peers had cried with one voice; and Charlot's wrathful father did not say them nay.

Learning thus on what a perilous errand the knight was bound, Geraume asked no better than to accompany him as guide and squire; and Huon gladly consented, since the country was as strange to him as its speech. Two ways led to Babylon, the old man told him: the one, safe and easy, making a year's journey; the other much shorter, but full of perils. The bold knight did not hesitate to choose the latter, though Geraume warned him that it led at once through an enchanted forest, haunt of Oberon, the fairy king, who had power to turn them both into monstrous beasts.

"His enchantments have no power over me," quoth Huon, "for I come newly from Rome, armed with the blessing of the Holy Father."

They set out, then, and at nightfall found the forest growing thicker and darker about them, where strange shapes of beasts and birds flitted across their way. A storm of wind and thunder broke out, roaring through the fearsome shades, lit up by flashes of lightning. All at once Huon's horse started aside, rearing in terror, as there glided forth an unearthly figure, a young child in stature, but wrinkled and grey with age, magnificently attired in a jewelled robe that shone like daylight, and round his neck was hung an ivory horn.

"The saints defend us! 'Tis Oberon!" whispered Geraume, and seized his master's bridle to drag him back; but Huon, making the sign of the cross, looked steadfastly on the fairy prince.

"Nay, Sir Huon of Bordeaux, fear me not," spoke the dwarf in mild and benevolent tones, as if reading his thoughts.

"Thou knowest me, then?"

"And wish thee well! In me see one that, unknown to thee, has watched over thy welfare from the cradle. Now am I here to aid thee in the perilous enterprise on which thou art bound. Trust me; dismount; and my goodwill shall be proved."

For a moment the knight hesitated; then he leaped from his steed. Oberon waved his wand. Instantly the darkness became dazzling light, and with the sound of

entrancing music there sprang up around them, like
vapour, such a magnificent palace as no king in Christendom could boast. One moment Sir Huon stood on
the ground damp with rain, where the storm wind roared
above his head among dripping branches, the next he
found himself in a lofty hall, where the walls were of
glittering crystal and the pillars of gold, and the roof
was starred with gems of every hue. On a carpet of
blooming flowers stood a table loaded with sumptuous
dishes, at the head of which Oberon sat on a golden
throne. The knight's horse was led away, as if by
spirits of the air; unseen hands held before him a
jewelled basin of perfumed water; the same invisible
attendants relieved him of his armour, throwing around
him a robe of embroidered silk. Then, before he had
fully recovered from his amazement, the enchanter mo-
tioned him to a seat by his side, and the invisible hands
served them with meat and drink. The guest at that
banquet had only to form a wish, then it seemed that
a spirit stood beside him who knew and obeyed his
slightest thought. Oberon did not eat, but while Huon
satisfied his appetite, he pledged him in a cup of wine,
and spoke thus:

"I have vowed friendship and protection to thy
house; nothing that concerns them is hid from me. I
know the purpose of this journey and the charge laid
upon thee. For slaying the king's son in a chance fray,
a good knight is doomed to do penance after strange
fashion. He must ride alone to the palace of Gaudisse,
the Emir of Babylon, and present himself in the hall
while that miscreant shall be sitting at meat among his
vassals and friends. Before speaking a word, he must
cut off the head of whomever he finds sitting at the
emir's right hand, must then kiss his fair daughter

Esclarmonde thrice, and must take from Gaudisse a handful of his beard and four of his great teeth. Having further made the emir swear to be tributary to the crown of France, he is to return with these trophies, or expect no welcome but a shameful death. Say I not truly, and art not thou this luckless knight?"

"Marvellous sage, it is even as thou hast said!" replied Huon. "All this am I bound to do, who would liefer die by Saracen swords than on the gallows!"

"Fear not, Huon, thou shalt not die, if thou art a worthy son of my friend thy father, and wilt but accept my aid and obey my directions."

"Noble Oberon, I will obey thee in all things," vowed Huon, as with a benignant smile the enchanter placed in his hands a crystal goblet and an ivory horn.

"Take these gifts, and learn their value. The goblet will, at the wish of any good man, fill with meat or drink; while in the hands of the treacherous and base it remains for ever empty. When assailed by numbers, let this horn be thy defence. Sound it softly if the danger be slight, and watch what befalls; but in utmost need blow loudly, and I myself will appear with all the host of fairyland. Yet, remember, these charms serve only him whose heart is true and his honour pure; no summons from the coward or the liar will reach my ear."

"May I never prove unworthy of thy protection!"

"Beware, also, of rashness. I foresee too surely that the hot blood of youth will carry thee into perils where my aid may be of no avail. Above all, take heed to shun the tower of Angoulafre, the ruthless giant of whom all these countries are in dread. His enchantments are even stronger than mine, and he can be slain only by him who wears a coat of magic mail stolen from me years ago."

" Show me the way to that tower ! " was Huon's eager reply.

" Said I not well ?   Thy imprudence is too strong for good counsel."

" Nay, friendly enchanter, the imprudence is thine, to let me know this danger that may be sought and overcome.   If I am destined to leave my bones in the tower of Angoulafre, so be it ; but it shall never be said that Huon heard of a perilous achievement and passed it by."

" Thy task is already a full hard one," said Oberon, and sighed to think of the misfortunes that might yet lie before this gallant knight.

But now the morning began to break, when at the first beam of the rising sun the enchanted palace vanished away like a dream, and Huon found himself again in the heart of the forest.   The fairy prince conducted him to the verge of it, and gave directions as to the way he must now follow.   Then, earnestly repeating his injunctions, he took leave of him with all good wishes.

II

For several days the bold knight and his squire travelled over a barren desert, where they might have starved but for the magic goblet that never failed to fill in Huon's hands, furnishing them with whatever meat or drink they desired ; while they met no enemy on whom to test the virtue of Oberon's horn.

At last they came upon a richer country, where the road led them to a Saracen city named Tormont.   At the gate, Geraume begged his master not to enter it; and when the knight laughed his fear to scorn, he added:

" Know that the lord of this paynim stronghold is no other than thine own uncle."

"My uncle—lord among the unbelievers!" exclaimed Huon in astonishment.

"Even so, to the shame and sorrow of all his kin. Carried away captive by pirates, Sir Eudes, thy father's brother, was sold to the Emir of Babylon; then to save his life, he denied the Cross and turned infidel. Thus he gained that master's favour, who married him to his own niece and made him ruler of this city. Now he hates the Christians, so that he hangs or imprisons all who fall into his hands."

"It is my duty to visit so heartless a renegade!" declared Huon. "Before one of his own blood he cannot but blush for the cowardice that made him deny his father's faith."

"Alas! you know him not. Hardened by debauchery and power, he is past repentance, and will answer such reproaches by a cruel death."

But Huon was not to be moved from his purpose. He entered the city and took lodging at an inn, where he called together all the poor to entertain them by meat and drink out of his magic cup. The news of such liberality soon came to the ears of Eudes, and he sent to summon the knight to his palace.

That renegade's surprise was not less than his displeasure to find in this stranger his own nephew. Yet he feigned to meet him with joy, while secretly plotting to rid himself of so unwelcome a visitor. Huon, for his part, burned with indignation to see Eudes wearing a green turban crowned by a crescent of gems. It was all he could do to bridle his tongue, awaiting a favourable moment for denouncing the uncle's apostasy. But he, as if divining the nephew's mind, cunningly avoided being alone with him. The whole morning they spent among the train of courtiers and attendants in examining the palace and its gardens, till the hour of dinner sounded and the sultan gave Huon his hand to lead him to the hall. Now the young man could no longer restrain his impatience.

"Oh, my uncle!" he whispered in his ear; "oh, prince, brother of my father, in what a hateful disguise have I the grief and shame to find thee!"

Eudes secretly gnashed his teeth; but he pretended to be moved by this reproach; he gently pressed his kinsman's hand, and replied in the same tone:

"Silence for the present, dear nephew! To-morrow morning I will explain all."

Huon, deceived by his uncle's air, calmed himself and sat down by his side with a lighter heart. The muftis, the cadis, and the other officers of the court took their places; there were also some dervishes present, upon whom, like a good Catholic, our knight looked with the greatest contempt and abhorrence. As for Geraume, he remained without, and kept a watchful eye on what was doing in the palace. He began to suspect treachery, and his suspicions were increased when he saw armed men mustering about the hall. But before he could warn his master, what he dreaded had already come about.

At first Huon addressed himself to do honour to the feast, eating with the appetite of youth and a good conscience. All kinds of rich meats were served to him, but, according to the law of the Prophet, no wine appeared on the table. So, after a time, he drew from his bosom the magic goblet, which, at his wish, was at once filled with red and sparkling wine. At this sight the Saracens frowned and stroked their beards, but, feigning not to observe these signs of displeasure, he courteously handed the cup to Eudes, saying:

"Dear uncle, pledge me in this goblet. It is excellent wine of your own native province, and will remind you of your mother's milk."

Eudes often drank the juice of the grape in secret, though before others he made pretence of abhorring it. Not for long had he tasted the good wine for which his birthplace was famed; the very name of it made his mouth water; surely for once he might transgress the law: so, forgetting what watchful eyes were upon him, he stretched out his hand towards the crystal goblet in which the liquor glowed like a heap of rubies. He felt a thrill of delight as he already thought to taste the delicious flavour, when lo! the cup was empty at his lips, the contents disappearing as if by enchantment. Huon could not restrain a laugh at his confusion and disappointment, yet he drew back from the uncle whose falsity was thus revealed.

"Insolent!" cried Eudes, as soon as surprise allowed him to speak. "Do you dare to mock me in the midst of my court? Ho! without there!"

And he hurled the goblet at Huon, who, catching it in his hand, replied by tearing the sultan's jewelled turban from his head, and trampling it on the floor. The cadis, agas, dervishes, and muftis rose from the table, uttering cries of horror at this insult. At the same moment the doors of the hall were flung open on every side, and a crowd of soldiers and eunuchs, armed to the teeth, rushed in, running upon the young knight in such haste that the foremost of them tripped and fell in a struggling heap before him.

This gave Huon a moment's respite. He stepped back while his assailants were picking themselves up, and did not even take the trouble to draw his sword, but brought out the ivory horn of Oberon, on which he began to blow gently. Immediately the effects were seen. At the first soft and melodious notes every Saracen stood upright, then fell a-trembling in all his limbs, and, as the sound continued, had, willy-nilly, to break into a dance. The music of the horn was heard over all the palace, and each note thrilled through every limb. The dervishes whirled themselves into the middle of the hall; the eunuchs gambolled like kids; their weapons dropped from the hands of the soldiers, staggering as if they were drunk; the grave muftis and cadis flung their turbans on the floor, and spun round among the crowd; even their lord himself, after stamping and wriggling in a vain effort to keep his dignity, was forced to caper with the rest; and soon all the assembly was one wild reel.

Standing at the head of the hall, Huon blew faster and faster, and the dancers were hurried round and round with more and more vehemence. Howling, leaping, tumbling, tottering, skipping, tripping over their long garments, panting, perspiring, frantically clinging to chairs and tables, and even to each other's beards, dashing their heads against the walls, kicking their slippers up to the ceiling, raging, crying, entreating, struggling, they whirled on, and kept up the dance till they could neither stand nor speak, but still their limbs must jerk like a child's toy, of which the enchanter did not cease to pull the string. At last Huon had pity on this wretched rout. He suddenly took the horn from his lips, then in one moment every Saracen fell flat on the ground, breathless and exhausted.

Seeing that they were no longer able to do him harm, the knight made his way through the piles of helpless bodies, and sought out the inn, where his prudent squire was already saddling their horses for immediate departure.

III

Before one of the Saracens had recovered strength to move hand or foot, Huon and Geraume left the city and took the road to Babylon. Again they journeyed on without meeting any hindrance, till they arrived upon a plain in the midst of which a huge tower reared itself, losing its battlements in the clouds.

"It is the tower of Angoulafre!" cried Huon.

"Do not approach it!" begged Geraume, not so eager for adventures as his master. "Call to mind the warnings of Oberon. Back, if you love your life!"

But the knight feigned not to hear his squire's advice. He was determined at any cost to visit this appallingly mysterious tower. As they drew nearer, they perceived that the wall was pierced here and there with deep windows that resembled human eyes, but through which no human being could be seen. All without and within was dark, silent, and threatening. Round the whole pile ran a wide, deep ditch, crossed by a drawbridge but three feet wide, leading to a gate even narrower. The gate was defended by two tall brazen statues, that whirled round long flails of the same metal, like the arms of a windmill; so broad were these flails and so rapid was their motion, that not even a bird could pass between them without being crushed to pieces.

The more he saw of this fearsome place, the more Geraume urged his master to hold back from it. But Huon was only tempted on by these desperate obstacles. At a little distance from the tower he dismounted, bade his companion remain with the horses, and advanced alone and on foot towards the entrance, where hung a great basin of brass, as large as a shield. He struck it

with the hilt of his sword, and the brass gave forth a
deep, dreadful clang, echoed throughout the tower.

"Now we shall see who lives here," said Huon to
himself; and a sorrowful cry made him turn his eyes
upwards to the loophole above the gate, through which
he caught a glimpse of the face of a young and beautiful
lady. Before a minute had passed, the whirling arms of
the statues suddenly ceased their motion, and the lady
appeared at the wicket.

"Rash man, what do you here?" she cried, all pale
and shuddering, as Huon ran lightly across the drawbridge. "You are but hastening upon your death."

"Nay; what harm can await me in the abode of such
a fair one?" said Huon gallantly.

"Alas," replied she, casting looks of compassion upon
him, "it is not me ye have to fear, but the cruel tyrant
that holds me as his prisoner!"

"The giant Angoulafre?"

"No other. At this moment, happily for you, he
sleeps. Had he awakened, you were surely lost! When
I heard the noise you made, I gave you up for lost; then,
perceiving the cross which adorns your shield, I judged
that you must be a Christian knight, and would save your
life if I could. Now you are warned; oh, fly while there
is yet time!"

"Noble and beautiful damsel, I have not come here
to fly. And now that I have seen you, and know you to
be the captive of this monster, I am more than ever eager
to combat him for your deliverance. But tell me, lady,
before I seek the giant, who are you, and how came you
into his power?"

"Ah! the tale of my misfortunes is soon told. My
name is Sibille. I came with my noble father, Guerin
of Guienne, on a pilgrimage to the Holy Land; then,

returning, would have sailed to France, where a good
knight, nephew of Ogier the Dane, waited to make me
his wife. But a furious tempest threw us upon this hateful coast; Angoulafre discovered and attacked us; my
father and all his knights were slain, and I became his
prisoner. For three years have I pined in this house
of horror, and now for the first time I hear my native
tongue and see the face of a countryman."

"Nay, fair Sibille, of a kinsman! Know that I am
Huon of Bordeaux, the eldest son of your father's brother, and therefore your cousin, and doubly bound to
deliver you from this wicked giant. Lead me to him
forthwith, and let me deal with the robber of ladies!"

"But ah! he is strong and fierce and——"

"Say no more. Am I not one of the peers of
France?"

Sibille, scarcely able to suppress her exclamations of
joy, no longer delayed to admit this welcome kinsman;
and, walking on tiptoe, led the way to the chamber from
which the monster's snoring could be heard all over the
tower.

There he lay on his back, a hideous form, seventeen
feet long, with such a fierce countenance as even in sleep
would have made most men shudder. Huon stood over
him and raised his sword; his first impulse was to bury
it to the hilt in the giant's throat. But he bethought
him that he was a knight, and must in no case attack
an enemy who could not defend himself. Moreover, he
fortunately remembered that this monster could not be
slain except by the man wearing that enchanted coat of
mail of which Oberon had spoken; and, while Angoulafre
still slept heavily, the knight and his cousin searched for
it throughout the tower. It was soon discovered in
a cedar coffer that stood in one of the next apartments.

Huon seized it, put it on, and was rejoiced to find that it fitted him marvellously well.

"Now, fair cousin," he said gaily, "excuse me if I leave you here for a little. I am going to awake Angoulafre, and put him to the death he deserves."

But it was no easy task to rouse the giant from his nap. Not till Huon had shaken him, and struck him, and shouted in his ear, and pulled his beard, and tweaked his nose, did he begin to move, and slowly raised his head, gaping and rubbing his bloodshot eyes. Then, as he caught sight of this unexpected visitor, he stared wildly, with a bellow that shook all the walls, and sent Sibille, anxiously watching without, to her knees.

"Puny creature, what madness has brought you here to your death? Miserable wretch, tell me your name before I crush you with one blow, and you be never more heard of on earth!"

"Odious monster, my name is Huon of Bordeaux, and I am come to punish you for all your evil deeds. Arm, and prepare for the combat."

Angoulafre might well be astonished at this bold language. He regarded the knight with attention, and was still more astonished to see him encased in the magic coat of mail.

"By Mahomet," he said, "it was generous of you not to have slain me in my sleep, as you might well have done. Come, I pardon you; it would cost me too much trouble to take your life. Only give up that armour, and on this condition I will let you go free and unharmed."

"Nay, give you up this tower, and the princess whom you hold captive in it; and, moreover, consent to renounce Mahomet, and to follow me to the court of the Emir of Babylon, where I have a certain errand to do; on these conditions will I spare your life."

The giant laughed loudly, making a gesture of scorn.

"Fool, if I let you go, you could not come at the Emir of Babylon without my aid. He is my vassal, and this golden ring betokens the respect due to me by him and all his. Four gates guard his palace, each of which will fly open at the sight of my ring. Without it you cannot hope to pass. At the first gate they would cut off your right hand, at the second your left, at the third one of your feet, at the fourth another, and when thus you reached the hall it would be but a moment before your head were shorn from your shoulders. Be wise, then; take this ring, and return my armour."

"Ring, and armour, and all that you have is already mine," quoth the bold Huon. "We but waste our time; arm, and let me slay thee without more to-do."

Seeing that he could by no persuasion win back from Huon the enchanted mail, Angoulafre withdrew to prepare for the combat. In a short time he returned, covered from head to foot with massive armour, and wielding a huge scythe in both his brawny hands.

"I am ready to fight if you are ready to die!" he roared, brandishing this terrific weapon over Huon's head.

"Look to thyself, pagan," replied Huon, deftly escaping the blow.

The scythe, swung with all the giant's strength, struck against a pillar, and sank into it to the depth of three feet. Angoulafre made desperate efforts to draw it out; but before he could succeed, Huon rushed forward and cut off both his hands at the wrists. The giant, uttering a hideous howl of pain, turned to fly. He hurled himself into the chamber where the pale Sibille was trembling for the result of this combat, but, missing his footing, fell headlong, and his huge bulk rolled at her feet. She screamed out; but Huon was close at his heels; one good blow of the keen sword ended the cruel monster's life, and the cousins threw themselves into each other's arms.

When Huon had drawn the giant's ring from his finger, they hastened to leave this gloomy abode, and Geraume rejoiced to see his master come back safe. To him the knight confided the care of Sibille, directing him to take her to the nearest seaport and put her on board a ship bound for France, while he himself was achieving his enterprise. So they parted with all good wishes, and Huon pursued his journey alone with the ring of Angoulafre, the enchanted coat of mail, the wonderful goblet and horn, and his own good sword to be his guide.

IV

A few days more brought Huon in sight of the rich and beautiful city of Babylon, where upon a high hill rose the marble palace of Gaudisse, the emir, or admiral of that country. Glad to arrive at the end of this long journey, Huon left his horse at the foot of the hill, to climb impatiently up its steep side, wondering whether Gaudisse would easily comply with the requests he had to make, and if his daughter Esclarmonde were indeed of such surpassing beauty as fame reported her.

As a loud flourish of trumpets announced that the emir and his guests were sitting down to dinner, Huon presented himself at the outermost gate of the palace, and demanded admission. That same hour Oberon was dining in fairyland, when suddenly he rose and uttered a cry of pain.

"Alas!" cried the enchanter; "the brave knight whom I loved so well is at this moment perjuring himself basely, and thus deprives me of both the power and the will to succour him."

It was too true. Huon had just been asked by the guard whether he belonged to their religion, this day being a high festival among the Saracens, in which none might take part who were not faithful followers of the Prophet. The knight had thoughtlessly answered "Yea", and was at once allowed to enter without further question. But he no sooner found himself within the precincts of the palace, than his conscience began to smite him for having thus spoken a falsehood and denied his faith. He would have given much to be able to recall the words, but it was now too late. He could only determine not again to be guilty of the like weakness. And when he had advanced as far as the second gate, which was closed and guarded like the first, he drew his sword and called out at the height of his voice:

"Infidel dogs! I command ye to open to a Christian knight!"

The guards sprang to their arms. The barrier bristled with spears and sword-points, and in another moment a cloud of darts would have been hurled upon this rash intruder. But the captain of the guard caught sight of the giant's ring upon the stranger's hand, and called out:

"Forbear! Know ye not the ring of Angoulafre, to whom our lord owes tribute and homage?"

Instantly the weapons were lowered, the gate was flung open, and as the knight passed through, looking sternly around him, the guards fell upon their knees, and the captain, bowing low, conducted him across a courtyard to the third barrier that must be passed.

Here Huon bethought him of again trying the effect of the giant's ring.

"Behold," he cried, "the sign before which you must tremble and fall at my feet!"

Again the effect was magical. At this gate, as also at the fourth, he was received with every mark of profound respect. Then, crossing the last court, Huon made his way into the great hall where the banquet was being served, and found himself face to face with the personages upon whom he was to perform his strange mission.

At the head of the board sat the turbaned emir in all his pomp. On his right was the King of Hircania, a cruel tyrant, of whom all the neighbouring lands stood in dread. On the left of Gaudisse was his daughter Esclarmonde, the most beautiful princess of the East, her fair face pale and her bright eyes red with weeping. Sore against her will she had just been betrothed to this hateful king, and in honour of the betrothal was gathered a brilliant assembly of warriors and chiefs, both of Babylon and Hircania, who filled the hall, placed according to their rank. The King of Hircania was rising to kiss his destined bride at the moment when Huon entered; but now every eye turned upon the knight, as, with open visor and naked sword, he marched up the hall amid such a silence of amazement that no sound could be heard but the trampling of his mailed feet and the clattering of his scabbard.

The attendants shrank right and left out of his way, and, thus unopposed, Huon reached the emir's seat. Then, before a word was spoken, he swung his sword, with one mighty blow to hew off the head of the King of Hircania, and it rolled at the emir's feet. Esclarmonde uttered a cry. The feasters sprang up in confusion. Gaudisse, all bespattered by the blood of his guest, and speechless from surprise, gazed openmouthed upon the audacious stranger. What was his amazement to see him calmly walk up to the princess, who, half-terrified, half-rejoiced at the fate of her unwelcome suitor, stood as if spellbound and did not shrink while the handsome knight stooped and saluted her coral lips once, twice, thrice, before all the bewildered beholders! With the last kiss her father found words to express his feelings.

"Madman! Who are you, and in the name of the Prophet, what would you here?"

Huon did not concern himself to reply till he had courteously bowed to the blushing lady. Then he turned to the emir, and said in a clear voice that could be heard in the farthest corner of the hall:

"My name is Huon of Bordeaux, and I am sent hither by Charles, the great king, to do as I have done; and, furthermore, to have from thee a handful of that grizzled beard and four of thy strongest teeth, as tokens of the tribute owed him. Be pleased to do me this favour without delay."

"This to my face!" bellowed Gaudisse, stamping, and choking, and glowing like a live coal. "My friend! My beard! My daughter! My teeth! Am I alive to hear such things! Impossible! Outrageous! Irreverence! Audacity! Madness! Never! Ho, my guards, my slaves, my vassals——"

Suddenly the emir checked himself as Huon raised his hand, and displayed the ring of Angoulafre.

"The ring of my sovereign lord, to whom I owe homage and tribute! Stranger, I am bound to hear the man that bears this token. But, speak the truth, how came you by it, and where last saw you the mighty Angoulafre?"

The knight had too well repented of one falsehood to tell another.

"Pagan, thy sovereign lord is no longer to be feared even by such as thou! This arm has ended his wicked life. Think no more of him, but prepare to obey the commands of my king."

"Angoulafre dead!" exclaimed the emir, and now cared not to restrain his wrath. "Then, robber and murderer and insolent fool, prepare to meet thy death. My beard and teeth, forsooth! What next? Cowards, how long will ye suffer him to insult your prince. Seize him! Bind him! Off with his head! Tear him in pieces!"

At the first word out leaped the scimitars of the Saracens, and a score of warriors rushed furiously upon the dauntless knight. He stepped back quickly and loudly blew his horn, looking round in confident expectation. But, alas! the charm was broken. The offended enchanter did not regard the summons, and the knight must defend himself alone. The hall rang with the clash of weapons, and above all rose the furious voice of Gaudisse, bidding his men take the intruder dead or alive. The fair Esclarmonde clasped her hands and wept to see the fray. The indignation she should have felt against her father's enemy was lost in regard for this daring youth; and despite of filial duty she could not but wish for his escape.

But wishes were in vain, when one stood against so many. Huon's shield was covered with darts; his sword was forced from his hand; the Saracens rushed in and threw themselves upon him. He was seized, dragged away, loaded with chains, and hurled into the emir's darkest and deepest dungeon, with the assurance that he might expect no better fate than to be flayed alive.

Exhausted from loss of blood, he lay insensible on the cold stones; and when at last he came to himself

his condition was most pitiable.   He could scarcely
move for pain; the emir's dreadful threats rang in his
ears; in all that country he had no friend to speak a
word or shed a tear for him; and, worst of all, it was
by his own fault that he had come into such misfortune.
Bitterly he reproached himself for the falsehood by which
he had forfeited the favour of Oberon, but for which he
might now have been reigning a victor where he pined
in fetters, and might have sought the hand of that beautiful princess whose charms had at first sight made such an
impression on his heart.

All night long he was tormented by these sad reflections, and the day brought no ray of light to his gloomy
prison.   He began to feel the want of food; his magic
goblet as well as his horn had been torn from him in
the struggle, and no one had come near him since he
entered the dungeon.   Was it the intention of his enemies
to reduce his strength by starvation before bringing him
to the torture, that they might have the satisfaction of
seeing a Christian knight die with unmanly weakness?
A burning thirst also distressed him.   Thus he passed
that day in anguish of mind and body, thinking sorrow-
fully of fair France and the gallant comrades in arms he
should never see more.   The death of Charlot was indeed
avenged, and his unjust king might well be satisfied.

At last, towards evening, he heard footsteps without.
The bolts were drawn back; the key grated in the door
of the dungeon.   The knight summoned all his fortitude,
and prepared to meet his executioners.   The door opened
softly to let pass a veiled figure bearing in one hand a
lamp and in the other a basket.   Huon strove to rise, but
could not for the weight of his fetters.   The figure advanced slowly towards him; the veil was drawn back, the
lamp raised, and he saw the pitiful face of Esclarmonde.

V

When some weeks had gone by, a stranger arrived at the court of Babylon, who spoke the language of the country well, and made believe to be heir of one of the great sultans of the East. Such a guest the emir received with open arms, hoping to find in him a husband for his daughter to take the place of the King of Hircania. A great feast was held in his honour, and, as they sat at dinner, the stranger spoke of the death of Angoulafre, with which all the country rang, and asked for news of the Christian knight who had slain him.

"That knight will do no more murders," said Gaudisse grimly. "Long ere this he has starved in my dungeons."

"Dead!" exclaimed the stranger in such tones that Esclarmonde eagerly fixed her eyes upon him and caught a meaning in his words that her father perceived not.

"Aye, dead, and too soon to get all his deserts," said emir. "Know you not how that madman came here, and how he fared?"

The stranger was not unaware of Esclarmonde's glances, and as her father told his tale at full length, he, as if thoughtlessly, drew aside his robe and let her see a rosary that hung beneath this disguise. At the sight of it she started and blushed, and he knew he had not been deceived.

When the Emir had ended his story and gone to sleep, the stranger sought private speech of the princess, then, as soon as they were alone, he fell on his knees, crying: "Lady, tell me the truth, for you can and will. I am come to seek out my dear master, Sir Huon of Bordeaux."

"You are his faithful squire, Geraume, of whom he has so often spoken to me?"

"I am no other. But say, does he live? Is he in health? Where may I see him?"

"Follow me," replied the princess, and led the way to a dungeon below the palace. She drew back the bolts, and in another moment the knight and his squire were embracing each other with mutual joy.

Soon now Huon's tale was told, while Esclarmonde stood by, the darkness hiding how her cheeks glowed as she heard him speak of her part in his deliverance. His courage, as well as his misfortunes, had so moved her heart that she could not rest for thinking of his unhappy lot. Overcoming all scruples, she persuaded his jailer to let her visit the prisoner and supply him with food. The more she saw of this knight, the more she was grateful to have been delivered from the hateful King of Hircania. Deserted by the enchanter, Huon now found himself succoured by the powerful magic of love. She secretly restored to him his goblet and ivory horn; and when her father ordered the captive to be led forth to the most cruel death that could be devised, she bribed the jailer to say that he was already dead of hunger, and in proof to exhibit the emaciated body of a prisoner who had really died that very day.

The emir, wrathful to see his vengeance thus escape him, had the jailer executed forthwith, and tried to gratify his hatred by inflicting all imaginable tortures on the senseless corpse believed to be that of his enemy. Esclarmonde shuddered at the horrors from which she had preserved Huon, who became dearer to her day by day. She was easily persuaded of the errors of her faith; she consented to be baptized as soon as possible, and asked nothing better than to be allowed to fly with her lover to his native land, abandoning gladly for his sake her friends, her rank, and her religion.

With the aid of Geraume, they now began to concert measures for escape. It soon seemed that there was need of haste, for the approach was announced of the giant Agrapard, King of Nubia and brother of Angoulafre, who, the emir understood, was coming to seek his daughter's hand. Esclarmonde grew pale at the thought, but Gaudisse exulted in the prospect of such a match, and forthwith began to look coldly on Geraume. He, without exciting suspicion, took his leave and hurried to the seacoast, where it was agreed that he should have a vessel in readiness, while Huon and Esclarmonde watched for the first favourable moment of escape.

But as Agrapard drew nearer the city it appeared that he had come intent on far other thoughts than those of love. He sent a herald before him to reproach Gaudisse with having lost a single day in avenging his brother's death, and to defy him to mortal combat, or to demand a tribute which would exhaust his revenues.

The emir was in despair; vainly through all his host he sought a warrior bold enough to accept the challenge of this terrible giant; and, when there seemed to be no hope for him but in submission, he cursed his gods and shed tears of rage before his daughter, who seized the moment to make him regret the loss of the vanquisher of Angoulafre.

"Ah," cried the emir, "I let him starve to death, and now it repents me to have lost such a champion! He alone could save me from this monster. Willingly would I give half my state to bring him to life."

"Learn," said Esclarmonde joyfully, "that he of whom you speak is not dead."

"Not dead? But no—1 saw his corpse! Do you mock me, child?"

"It was the corpse of another. The brave knight, Huon, is still alive, and, if you are willing, will maintain your cause against the giant."

Gaudisse was astonished, but this was not a time to ask questions. He desired that Huon should be sent for, and was surprised to find him as stout and vigorous as the day on which he was thrown into chains. This must be explained when the present danger was overpast; in the meantime he welcomed the knight and declared what was required of him.

"The brother of the giant whom you slew so doughtily is under our walls, full of threats and fury. As you conquered Angoulafre, so must you conquer Agrapard. Go forth, brave youth, and if you rid me of this foe I promise to give you my daughter and to obey the wishes of your king."

Huon replied by demanding his armour. It was brought forth to him all rusty and battered, and his sword notched with many a blow. Right glad was he to find himself again harnessed like a warrior. They brought him the best horse in the emir's stables, and after taking a tender leave of Esclarmonde, and assuring her father that there need now be no fear of the giant, he mounted and rode forth to defy Agrapard without the walls.

The combat was long and desperate. For hours Esclarmonde's heart was torn with anxiety, and the emir remained trembling in the middle of his army, till a great shouting announced the victory of their champion, and soon Huon appeared leading the humbled giant bound to his saddle and covered with blood. He brought him thus to the feet of the emir, sitting

on the terrace of the palace, and after he had lovingly
embraced his lady he turned to her father and said,
while Agrapard was being dragged to the dungeon he
himself had lately quitted:

"Behold, I have kept my promise. Now it is for
thee to perform thine."

"My promise?" answered the wily Saracen. "What
promise? Thou art still alive: what ask ye more?"

"Emir, the commands of my king are still unfulfilled.
Make haste to give me your teeth and beard; and, moreover, you must renounce the law of your false prophet
that has taught you thus to lie."

"Dog of a Christian, I would perish a thousand times
rather than consent to such insolent demands. Now will
I load thee with ten times heavier chains, from which this
time none shall set thee free."

Esclarmonde screamed and clung to her father's
knees, begging for mercy, till she swooned away from
terror. Huon ran to support her with the cry:

"Ungrateful miscreant, as well threaten the winds!
I grant you one moment to obey me, or else fear my
wrath."

"Seize him! Slay him! Away with them both to
the dungeon!" replied Gaudisse, waving his scimitar
and shouting to his men; but he held back, not caring
to measure himself with the knight that came from proving his strength upon Agrapard.

The guards rushed forward. Huon smiled and
drew forth his horn. Rightly he judged that now the
enchanter must be appeased by his repentance and his
sufferings. He gave one blast so loud that all the walls
of the palace quivered, and lo! in a moment Oberon was
by his side, and the ground shook with the trampling of
invisible horses and the tread of marching men.

The emir's soldiers could not stand against such a foe. As they paused and looked round, to ask each other whence came these martial sounds v ith which the air was filled, the host of fairyland fell upon them. The dwarf waved his enchanting wand and their arms were struck from their hands; their leaders were seized and dragged away before their eyes; horses and men rolled in the dust; the blood flowed from the wounds of phantom steel; whole troops were laid low, as trees by a hurricane; destruction swept through the ranks like a thunderbolt, and the terror-stricken Saracens turned to fly in wild confusion, without being able to see a single one of their assailants.

Gaudisse beheld this rout of his army with dismay; but what were his feelings when he found himself in the grasp of invisible hands, and loaded with the very chains he had ordered for Huon! Before he could beg for mercy, the irresistible hands had plucked the beard from his chin; he opened his mouth to roar in agony, and four of his largest teeth were torn from his jaws.

"Be this the fate of all cruel and unbelieving princes!" said Oberon, and gave the beard and the teeth to Huon. "Take now these tokens; return to the King of France; salute him from me, and say that, through my aid and thine own stout heart, thou hast performed the task, and mayst well be forgiven. Take, too, this fair lady to be thy bride, and, so long as ye are loving and true, Oberon the Enchanter will be your friend."

Thus made master of Babylon, Huon bestowed it as a reward upon his faithful squire. Gaudisse and Agrapard he sent to be kept in prison in the tower of Angoulafre. He loaded the emir's treasures upon camels, and set forth homewards, not forgetting to take

with him the most precious treasure of all, the fair
Esclarmonde. Arriving at the seacoast, they embarked
in the ship which Geraume had provided, and, after many
more perilous adventures, reached the city of Rome.
There Esclarmonde was christened by the Pope and married to Huon; after which they repaired to France, and
the knight, presenting the tokens of his success, was in
due time restored to the king's favour. So ends this
ancient, honourable, famous, and delightful history of
Huon of Bordeaux.

VIVIEN

I

GARIN, brother of William of Orange, had fallen captive
to the unbelievers. While out hunting he was taken in
an ambush and carried off to the enemy's city, Luiserne
by the sea. In vain he offered the Saracen chief as ransom all his gold, all his horses, all his lands.

"Thy freedom will I grant but for one price," answered the grim pagan. "Let thy son Vivien be given
up in the stead of his father!"

"Vivien is but seven years old! What would ye
with a child?"

"His death, if it please me. The younger the victim,
the sweeter my revenge for all the ill wrought me by thee
and thine."

News came to Garin's wife, daughter of Duke
Naymes, that her lord pined in a Saracen dungeon, sore
wounded, and threatened with a cruel death unless Vivien
were yielded as his ransom. Bitterly she wept, and loath
was she to part with her darling. But the noble boy
willingly offered himself to save his father; and his stern
uncle, William, declared this to be no more than the duty
of a good son. So, torn from his mother's arms, Vivien
was sent to Luiserne that Garin might go free.

"It is as if I had strangled him with my own hands!"
cried the unhappy father, when he saw his son in the

power of so ruthless men; but soon they were dragged
apart.

Vivien had shrunk from the first sight of those
swarthy faces, yet he overcame his childish terror, and
steeled himself as became his birth to bear what might be
done to him. They bound his hands; they dragged him
by the hair to be chained at a stake; and round it they
heaped faggots and dry branches.

"Christian, thou shalt die in torment!" exulted their
chief, to whom the boy answered, looking him dauntlessly
in the face:

"Nay, I shall live, to be the avenger of my kinsman
Roland!"

At the name of Roland the Saracens cried out for
rage, and they made haste to light the pile. But scarcely
had it begun to crackle and glow when all other sounds
were drowned in a din of alarm. A crew of pirates,
landing at Luiserne, had burst upon the Saracens, taking
them by surprise. The assailants came in time to dash
out the fire before a hair of Vivien's head had been
singed. Thus they saved the boy from death but not
from bondage, for they carried him across the sea with
the rest of the booty made in that sudden raid.

When, in a foreign city, they put up to sale their
captives and other spoils, a good woman was so taken by
Vivien's looks that she bought him for a hundred marks;
then he sang for joy to be out of the hands of Saracens
and pirates. And soon he found that he had gained a
kind mistress. She was wife of a merchant named
Godfrey, who had gone on a long journey that kept him
seven years from home. In his absence she had lost
a son of Vivien's age, and she soon grew so fond of the
young captive as to adopt him in that child's place.
Nay, when her husband came home, she even presented

the boy to him as their own son. Godfrey was not less
pleased to have such a handsome and sturdy heir, and
at once proposed to bring him up betimes to his trade as
a merchant.

"Thou shalt go with me to fairs and markets, to sell
corn and cloth, and pepper and cumin. It is the best life
in the world!"

"I should like better to be a knight," quoth Vivien.

"Fie! a poor business that, and little to be gained
at it but getting knocked on the head, and dying out of
the way of priest or sacrament! I will teach thee weights
and measures, and the course of money-changing. Forthwith thou shalt be fitted out with warm clothes and big
boots for our travelling."

"I would liefer have a horse and a sword," laughed
Vivien.

"And what wouldst thou do with them?"

"Would I not hew the pagans in pieces!" cried the
boy; but his new father only laughed at him, promising
to show him a safer way of getting on in the world.

The first time this apprentice had any money of his
own he spent it on a falcon, which his supposed father
took for sheer waste.

"No profit in idle birds that eat and kill!" the merchant instructed him. "You must learn, my boy, to
lay out your money better if you mean to be rich. I
myself began with six farthings, and see what I am
now!"

But, to give Vivien another chance, he sent him to
market with a hundred bright marks in his pouch. What
did the lad buy with so much money? Nothing but a
horse; and such a horse—a lean, stumbling, half-blind
beast, belonging to a wounded squire, who was glad to
get rid of this bag of skin and bones. At the sight of it

the merchant cried out, and louder still when he heard what it cost.

"You might have had it for one-tenth of the price!" was what vexed him most. "The beast is not fit to carry its own provender. Had I spent my money so ill, I should be begging on the roads to-day!"

Yet once more he trusted Vivien with charge of a booth at a fair. There the lad paid little heed to his instructions, and managed as ill as might be. He forgot the price of his goods; he sold everything for what was offered; he gave double measure and took half-price; but if anyone tried to rob him, he laid the fellow on the ground. Then the whole fair was in an uproar, and while Vivien was fighting with those who would have wronged him, the booth came to be plundered by slyer thieves. His gains were no more than bought a couple of hounds, which he brought home as all he had to show for the day's work. This time Godfrey was full wroth, and beat the boy sorely, crying:

"My money! My money! What have you done with my goods? What can I do with these useless curs?"

"Not useless," sobbed Vivien; "they can catch hares for us."

That beating set him ready to run away; but his kind mistress soothed him and made his peace with her husband. The stripling grew up in their house, tall, strong, and winsome; and they loved him well, though every day Godfrey lamented that he would never learn to be a good merchant.

But when Vivien came to years of manhood, the worthy man, who still took him for his own son, put him to one more trial of what he was fit for. He gathered a great train of horses, mules, and wagons, loaded with merchandise, with hundreds of his servants to guard it, and in charge of this company he sent Vivien to Luiserne, the city where he had been captured by pirates.

Promising to do his best with what was entrusted to him, Vivien set out gaily, glad to see the world and to have a chance of adventures. His high spirits pleased Godfrey's men, who declared themselves ready to go anywhere under leadership of such a gallant youth, riding proudly like a king at the head of his army.

And before they reached Luiserne their road led them by the coast, where that pirate crew were landing to plunder after their wicked way. Vivien hid his men among the rocks, armed with sticks, stones, knives, and whatever came to hand. Then, as the pirates lay heedlessly at ease, feasting along the shore, he rushed upon them with his company to take them by surprise, killing or setting to flight the whole crew, and capturing their ship before they could push it off.

The ship was loaded with gold and silver, which the young conqueror forthwith sent home to Godfrey; so that he, at the sight of such wealth, began to think his son no such useless idler after all. But on board also was found a store of arms and armour, in which Vivien equipped his men, hiding coats of mail under their cloaks and jerkins, and stowing swords, daggers, and axes among bales of goods. So they came to Luiserne, to be admitted within the walls as peaceful traders and brought before the Saracen lord of that city.

"Who are ye?" he asked; "and what brings you here?"

"We come to pay the price of blood," cried their leader. "I am Vivien, son of Garin the captive, whom ye would have burned at the stake, but I live to avenge Roland!"

Out flashed sharp steel, and before the astonished
Saracen could speak a word his head rolled at his feet.
At once the rest of the band flung off their mantles,
drew forth their hidden weapons, and fell to plying them
on the infidels. They ran through the streets, hacking
and hewing at every turbaned foe, Vivien ever foremost
in the fight that raged all day; but before the sun set
he had mastered the city, driven out all the Saracens
left alive, and shut the gates in their black faces.

Recovering from their dismay, the Saracens soon
gathered an army that besieged Luiserne, and made
many fierce assaults, but always were repulsed by Vivien
and his followers, so quickly turned into men of war.
The siege lasted long, and the brave garrison began to
fail for victuals. News of their plight came to the town
where Godfrey lived; then grieved was the good merchant to hear how his son and his men stood in peril,
and still more heartily grieved his wife. In her sorrow
she now owned to her husband that this was no child of
theirs, but the son of a great lord of France, ransomed
by her from pirates.

Yet still Godfrey loved and pitied the lad, so that
he set out forthwith for the court of Louis to beg him
to send succour to Vivien against the Saracens, ere it
should be too late. That faint-hearted emperor loved
peace well, and was loath to stir from his idle throne.
But when William of Orange and his kin waxed so
wroth and threatened so proudly that Louis was fain
to consent, all the peerage of France were mustered to
march for Luiserne.

They came in sight of the city not a day too soon.
Vivien and his brave comrades had eaten up their horses,
and now were starving to death when from the walls
they saw the fierce besiegers scattered like foam before

the cry of *Montjoye!* Up rolled, wave after wave, the warriors of the Cross. The gates were thrown open, and Vivien, hardly able to stand for faintness, fell into the arms of his uncle, who led him to Garin as a son of whom he might be proud.

When he had embraced his true father, the youth turned to Godfrey, standing modestly back among the knights and lords; and him, too, he greeted kindly.

"I have caused thee many a trouble to whom I owe so much. Now I ask thy pardon, and will make amends for all."

He made the merchant governor of Luiserne, which he had won by his arms. All there was joy, then triumphantly the Christian knights rode back to France. When Vivien came home to his mother, after many years, the bells rang, the priests sang, the jugglers danced, and all his father's people laughed and wept together to see their young lord delivered from the paynim foe.

II

It was Easter, and on this high festival Vivien was to be dubbed knight by his uncle, William of Orange, France's sword and shield against the Saracens. With him knelt a hundred noble youths to receive the accolade from that hero. Then Vivien, flushed and eager, rose to his feet with a cry:

"Good uncle, may I never dishonour the sword you have girded to my side. Before you and your peers I vow to heaven that, once I have donned my hauberk and laced on my helm, I shall never give ground before the infidels, were they a thousand to one!"

"Nay, nephew," said the well-tried warrior, "to keep that vow will cut thy life full short. There is no cham-

"VIVIEN FELL INTO THE ARMS OF HIS UNCLE"

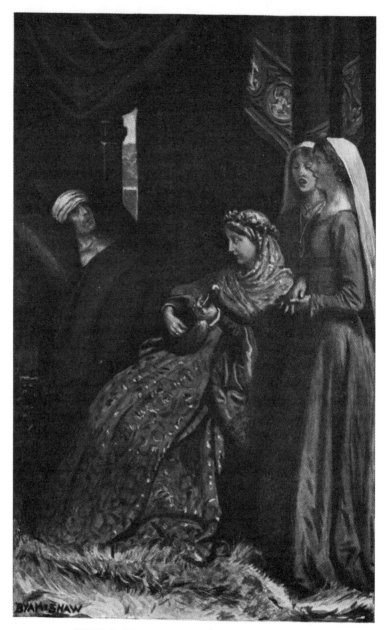

"THE LADY PLAYED TO HIM ON A LUTE"

pion so valiant or so renowned but that in battle he may need to draw back when overcome by numbers, unless he have a mind rather to die. Thou art young, but be not rash. Let him who has to fly, fly fast and come back quickly as he can."

"Uncle," repeated Vivien, "I swear never to yield a foot before Turk or Saracen."

"Then, nephew," quoth William, "the Saracens will give thee a short life of it, and all thy kin may soon have to mourn."

But the daring youth would not listen to counsel. With his band of new-made knights he set out for the south; and ere long all Christendom rang with his deeds against the unbelievers. Not a day passed without his watering the ground with heathen blood, for he would take neither ransom nor homage from the enemies of his faith. The cry of the conquered went up to the Moorish king Desramé, at Cordoba, till he tore his beard for grief and rage, and swore by Mohammed to have that young champion's head. To all peoples ruled by the Crescent he sent for succour, and soon had gathered such a host that he made sure not only of slaying Vivien, but of capturing Orange and winning the whole land of France. There were thirty emirs and all their Moorish horsemen who took ship to land at Alischans.

Here, one bright spring day, from the heights above, Vivien was aware of the sea covered so thickly with sails and banners that the waves were hidden beneath them, and like a storm rose the cries of the men and the clanging of horns and cymbals as the ships drew to shore.

"Ha! The Saracens are upon us!" he cried to his followers. "To-day we must prove our mettle, as never before."

But while he spoke so proudly, they beheld with dismay the multitude of the foe.

"Vivien," said one of his cousins, "the miscreants are too strong for us. Send for help to our uncle at Orange, while yet we can."

Others murmured that they would do wisely to retreat before an enemy that outnumbered them seventy to one. But their leader scorned such faint-heartedness.

"Are we not young and strong? Have we not good steeds and sharp swords? Will not heaven fight on our side? For me, I have sworn never to draw back before these pagans, dead or alive. Nor will I send for help to Orange, so long as I can strike a blow. But you, sirs, if you fear to die with me, turn back an ye will, and leave Vivien alone to keep his vow."

With tears in their eyes they refused to desert him, if every one of them should be cut in pieces. Vivien himself, reviewing his troop, could not but feel concerned to see it so small before the numbers of the enemy; and he was moved to mutter a prayer as he did on his armour.

When hauberks had been buckled and helmets laced tight, they rode forward to charge upon the Saracens before these could bring their horses on shore and form their ranks. A deafening shout went up from the paynim warriors as they saw the young chief so dreaded and hated by all Moslem warriors. Their king swore not to take off his helmet till that champion were dead or captive.

"*Montjoye!*" was the thundering cry with which the French knights burst among the dark-skinned host, their swords flashing like lightning, and at every stroke a turbaned head rolled in the dust. But that little band too went down one by one, overwhelmed by odds, on a shore so crowded that the foemen could not turn to fly. Ten Moors fell for one Frenchman, but there were a hundred to take the place of each dead unbeliever. Vivien in vain searched out the king, who as vainly charged his doughtiest champions to rid him of such an enemy. By his own hand had already fallen all the chiefs sent against him. But when he had broken through to the centre of the host, he saw that he was followed by not half his men to a space cleared for them among the dismayed Saracens, where, as from an island, he saw around fresh waves upon waves crested with steel. Bleeding himself from several wounds, he wept bitter tears under his visor to know that this multitude was too many for him.

"Ah, mine uncle, bad news will come to Orange!" he exclaimed, and was overheard by his cousin, who reproached him with not having taken good counsel in time.

"That which is done, is done," Vivien gave him back. "If the worst come to the worst, we keep our honour in death. And all is not yet lost. My vow forbids me to turn my back. But see there before us yon strong castle by the sea! Behind its walls we may defend ourselves, since we cannot hold the field."

"But how can we reach it through thousands of Saracens standing between, bristling like a forest?"

"To be hewn down by our swords!" cried Vivien. "Follow me!"

He blew his horn so mightily that his wounds began to bleed afresh; then, as he set spurs to his horse, the Christians rallied round him, and with the fierceness of despair they cleft their way through thousands to the gate of that castle. Once within the walls, and the drawbridge raised, the survivors of such an onslaught could draw breath for a time, hardly one of them able to stand for wounds and weariness.

The walls were strong, the towers were high, the moat was deep; and they might hope here to hold out against ten times their number. But, alas! in this empty castle they found no provisions, and must live upon their horses, butchered by their own swords.

The fear of hunger dismayed these men more than the swords of the foe, and once again they called on Vivien to send a messenger to William of Orange.

"So be it!" he gave consent. "Our uncle will at least be in time to bury the bones of loyal kinsmen."

His cousin Girard offered himself for the perilous errand, since he spoke the language of the Saracens. Disguised like one of them, at nightfall he rode out among their tents, and passed without notice till challenged by a watch post. When they bid him stand and name himself, he answered:

"I am the Emir of Nubia, steward to King Desramé."

"So you lie foully," cried the guard, "for that chief was to-day slain by the terrible Vivien. A spy! Upon him!"

The whole body rushed at Girard, who had nothing for it but to turn back and ride for his life into the castle, amid a widespread clamour of alarm.

"What! Have you found our uncle already?" was his scornful greeting from Vivien. "Or is it that you are afraid?"

"Sir," said Girard, "you are unjust. The bravest man in the world could not pass through the Saracen camp, so well is it guarded."

Yet, stung by his cousin's taunt, he ventured another trial, if it should cost him his life. Making the sign of the cross, he spurred out again, and rode for a mile in the darkness before being once more stopped by sentinels.

"Who goes there?"

"I am the Emir of Saragossa, sent on a charge from the king."

"You speak falsely, for that chief lies sore hurt in his tent. Seize the traitor!" they cried, as out came their scimitars.

But Girard dashed on to cleave the head of the first that offered to stay him, and broke through the rest of the band, whose darts hurtled idly upon his shield and helmet. By daybreak he was spurring freely along the road to Orange.

III

For weary weeks the garrison of that castle by the sea had no news how it fared with their messenger. Daily the heathen swarmed to the assault, only to roll back like the waves of the tide that bore ever more ships to their aid. Still William of Orange did not come. The besieged had eaten up almost all their horses, starved to skin and bone like themselves. A day more and food would altogether fail them.

Then one morning at daybreak they were roused by a clang of trumpets, and from their towers saw the sun glittering on the arms and the pennons of ten thousand knights.

"I knew William would come to our aid!" cried Vivien. "It is for us now to sally forth and win to his side."

The gate was thrown open, the drawbridge let down, and at the head of his little band Vivien rode out, lance in rest, on the one horse left to them. They charged into the midst of the Saracens, who closed round them

as the sea swallows up a rock. One by one the famished
Christians went down, each selling his life dearly. Upon
them was the whole force of the foe, who as yet knew
not how they were attacked in rear, since they took
William's knights to be friends come to their aid.

But Vivien ever pressed on through the turbaned
ranks. Once only he drew back the length of his lance,
on confronting a band of black heathen, so hideous to
behold that he took them for fiends, and, in amazement,
forgot his vow, when his steed too was scared by the
sight and by the shouts of such barbarous men. But
quickly the young knight recovered himself, spurring
forward to shear off the black-bearded heads like thistles.
Wherever his sword flashed an infidel fell to the earth;
and not all their loud exultation could drown the death-
cries that winged his charge.

Over all the din rang out the trumpets of Orange.
Ere he could cut through to William, Vivien felt his
horse staggering beneath him, not less sorely wounded
than himself. When now the foe left a way clear before
him, he sank to the ground, and thought his last hour
had come. Faint from hunger and loss of blood, he
could no longer see; but he heard a fresh outcry where
the Saracens were drawn away to meet the attack of their
new assailants, by whom he hoped to be avenged.

He was left alone for a time among the corpses of his
comrades. Then through clouds of dust came the hot
gallop of a warhorse, on which his dim eyes caught sight
of a tall champion bearing down upon him. Taking this
for a Saracen, Vivien swung his sword, and put all his
strength into a blow which the other caught on his shield.

"By my faith, since Charlemagne made me knight,
I have never felt such a blow!" exclaimed the horseman,
brandishing his own blade to pay it back; but Vivien

knew the voice, and fell fainting before him with the cry:

"Alas for my blindness! Do you not know me? I am your nephew."

William of Orange, for it was he, sprang from his horse and raised Vivien in his arms, lamenting over the miserable state in which he found him.

"We are not women, and tears cannot avail us," murmured the young knight. "I am dying without remedy. Do me one last kindness. Raise me into my saddle, put the sword in my hand, and turn my horse to where the foe press hottest; then shall I die like the nephew of such a peer!"

The uncle did as he desired, leading him by the bridle into the thick of the fray; but soon they were separated, and William never thought to see his nephew again. Before long he had to fear that none of them would come alive out of so fierce a fight. He and his men did prodigies of valour, cutting down the Saracens like ears of corn; but so many were they it would have taken a month to reap that harvest. Though the field ran with blood around them, the Christians, too, fell fast, buried beneath the heaps of their slain. When at last William fought wellnigh alone, he saw nothing for it but flight, if ever he would see Orange again.

He turned his rein, and the Saracens at first forebore to pursue him. Spurring over the field of battle, he came to a pond by the side of which lay Vivien, to all seeming dead. He had closed his eyes when he no longer heard the French warcry pealing above the din; but at William's voice he half-opened them. Kneeling over him, his uncle felt the heart faintly beating.

"Ah, Vivien," he cried, "are courage, comeliness, and nobleness come to this? A lion could not be more brave; yet was this no proud boaster, but as gentle as brave. He never gave back a single foot from the foe; he, the best knight of France, who now must die in the flower of his youth, after killing more infidels than any man alive!"

Kissing his brow for the last time, the uncle saw how he feebly moved his hands as if to beat his breast, asking pardon of heaven for some sin.

"Nephew," he said, "where there is no holy man to hear thy confession, I, as thy nearest of kin, take the place of a priest to absolve thee. Open thy heart to me, thy godfather in this baptism of blood."

Therewith he tenderly raised the young man in his arms, who gasped out:

"The day I was made knight I vowed before my peers never to draw back a foot before the heathen foe. But to-day a troop of demons in human form scared me into giving ground, I know not how far, and thus I fear to have broken my vow. God forgive me; the saints receive me!"

These were his last words; his eyes fell dim as the uncle made the sign of the cross on his brow. William would fain have placed the body on his horse to carry it away for Christian burial; but now the Saracens came up too close upon him, and he knew that his tired steed could not bear a double burden—well if it could speed himself out of the enemy's reach! He laid out Vivien in his blood-stained armour, and covered him as best he could beneath his shield. Then he rode for his own life from that fatal field, hoping for the day when it should be avenged upon the unbelievers.

THE FORBIDDEN ISLAND

I

In the land of Bealm dwelt Bragas, a powerful earl, whose banner was followed to war by many a knight, none braver and truer than Sir Edgar and Sir Grahame. These two were inseparable friends from youth; they shared the same chamber; they had no secrets from one another; each held the life and honour of his brother-in-arms dear as his own; moreover, they were alike in form and features as if they had been brothers by birth.

But in time a stronger passion than friendship took hold on Edgar's heart. He loved Winlayne, Earl Bragas's daughter, that proud damsel looking on none but a matchless champion as worthy of her hand. Since Sir Edgar had never yet been overthrown, she was willing to be called his ladylove, so she might hold her head high above the mistresses of less manful heroes. Then he, not content to be the best knight in all that land, was greedy of greater fame to lay at the feet of his haughty fair one, and took on him an adventure in which many the bravest had fallen.

Beyond the bounds of Bealm lay an island known as The Forbidden Country, because it had long been kept against all comers by Sir Grey-Steel, dreaded as a warrior of more than human strength. Again and again had doughty knights set out in hope to humble his pride, but few who entered The Forbidden Country had ever returned, or if they did, it was with a woeful tale of how its grim lord had overthrown and wounded them at the first onset, then had cut off the little finger of their hands before sending them back, to be a warning to others that might covet the same fate. Sir Edgar knew well these tales, yet none the less was he bent on matching himself against Sir Grey-Steel, thus to prove to Winlayne beyond doubt that there was no knight so worthy of her love. Secretly he set out from Bealm and rode towards the scene of this great achievement.

Away he rode, till he came in sight of a deep river, beyond which lay the dark moors and forests of The Forbidden Island. Before long he found a ford by which he crossed to the other side, and struck through the wood in search of this country's stern lord. He had not far to seek, for Sir Grey-Steel kept watchers on foot to rouse him with news that a new adventurer had come to the ordeal of battle.

"He shall not go home till he leave a pledge behind him," quoth the tyrant, calling for his armour.

So full soon Sir Edgar saw a huge horseman riding forth against him all armed in red, with red shield and red spear, whom he knew to be no other than the adversary he had come to challenge. Without a word of greeting they put their lances in rest and bore down upon each other. And now Sir Edgar felt that for once he had met his match. At the first charge Sir Grey-Steel hurled him to the ground from the horse slain beneath him. The young knight sprang up and drew his sword. In vain! His blows fell on the blood-red mail as on a rock, while Sir Grey-Steel's blade shore through helmet and hauberk as through a shirt of silk. Sore wounded, Sir Edgar still strove to defend himself. But his strength

failed; the blood flowing down his face blinded him; he
sank to the ground and swooned at the feet of the red
knight.

When Sir Edgar came to himself, he was lying alone
by the dead body of his horse.   He crept to a brook
hard by; he washed the blood from his face; he looked
about him and examined his hurts.   He found his arms
gone, as well as the little finger of his right hand, cut off
by the conqueror as a trophy.   Weak from loss of blood,
he could hardly stir; and his first thought was to lament
that Sir Grey-Steel had not slain him outright.   Near at
hand he came upon the dead body of another knight who
had been treated in the same fashion; and by its side a
lean and sorry horse stood grazing on weeds and thistles.
Painfully Sir Edgar mounted this half-starved beast to
ride away, woeful and ashamed.   How could he meet
his proud mistress, and in what words tell her the tale
of his disgrace?   Better far to have died than thus to
live a beaten man.

With such gloomy thoughts he left the Forbidden
Island, recrossing the ford, then slowly his stumbling
steed carried him all the rest of that day, till at nightfall he came in sight of a castle overlooking a goodly
garden.   Into the garden he turned aside, thinking to
rest here unseen.   But before he had lain long on the
grass he was aware of a lady, richly attired and noble
of bearing, at sight of whom, weak as he was, he stood
up to greet her.

"Sir," said she, seeing his sorry plight, "methinks
you have need of better lodging than the bare ground;
but my father's door is never shut to any good knight."

"Courteous lady," quoth he, "far have I come and
glad would I be of a bed, and of a stable for this steed,
though it is none of mine.   But you see before you the

most miserable of men, in sooth no fit guest for lordly hall."

Nevertheless, she would not be denied; she called her maidens, one of whom led away his horse, while two more supported the wounded knight into the castle, where they refreshed him with meat and drink, unbuckled his gory armour, and brought water to wash his hands. Then the lady of the castle marked how the little finger of the right hand was newly gone, and she heaved a grievous sigh, for well she wot with whom he had had to do, when he brought away such mark of his misfortune. She had him laid in a soft bed, and played to him on a lute, while her maidens sang a sweet, mournful song, watching by his side till he fell asleep. Full often had they sung that song for knights that had met worse hap from the lord of the Forbidden Island.

Next morning, when Edgar awoke, the gentle leech was ready to salve his wounds afresh, and she would have had him remain where he was till they should be healed. But, finding him bent on home as soon as might be, she did not hinder his going. She had his horse brought forth with his armour bound to the saddle. Before he mounted it she bound up the wounded hand with one of her own silken kerchiefs, and she gave him a cordial which seemed to put new blood into his veins. Grateful for all her kindness, but with the scornful Winlayne's image ever in his mind, the beaten knight took leave of her and rode homewards without even asking the name of the lady of the castle.

But the strength of the cordial passed away, and faintness began to come upon him again, tormented as he was by the thought of Winlayne's pride and his own shame. When he had almost reached Earl Bragas's castle his wounds burst out bleeding afresh ; he swooned and fell from his horse. On coming to his senses, the sorry beast having strayed away, he had to rise and drag himself to the castle on foot. Secretly as he had set out, hoping to return in triumph, so now he came back, seeking to hide his disgrace from all but his brother-in-arms. At nightfall he crept unseen into their chamber, where Sir Grahame was amazed to receive him in such a plight—pale, befouled by blood, scarcely able to stand, arms and armour gone, all but an empty scabbard and the broken truncheon of his lance. Sir Edgar sank down on the bed; then, as soon as he had strength to speak, poured into his friend's ears the whole tale of his misfortunes.

"I went to win honour and I have bought dishonour dear!" was his bitter lament.

Sir Graham pitied that downfallen brother with all his heart, but he strove to put on a cheerful face and to raise his spirits.

"You grieve more than is meet," he said, "for never was man so doughty of heart or hand but he may be put in such a case as he is as like to lose as to win. I warned you that Sir Grey-Steel was the strongest knight in any land, by whom it is no shame to be beaten. Only let us take heed that the lady Winlayne knows not what has befallen thee."

Well wished Edgar that it might be so; but, alas! she already knew. At the news of the knight's return, eager to learn where he had been and how he had fared, she hastened to his chamber, and there, pausing at the open door unseen, had heard from his own lips the story of his overthrow. With anger and scorn in her heart she turned back; then as Grahame spoke her name he caught the sound of her footsteps that drew him out to see her flitting away, and he guessed how she had overheard all. But this he hid from Edgar, feigning it was a dog that had made a stir at their door, for he feared that if his friend knew himself despised by Winlayne there would be little hope of his life.

The surgeons who bound up Edgar's wounds said he must die; for nine days indeed he lay in a state more like death than life, and already Earl Bragas and all the castle mourned over that flower of knighthood. All but Winlayne, who, while her lover lay in such danger, came never near his bed, and spoke coldly of him, saying:

"He might full well have stayed at home, since he got so little honour abroad. He has left one finger behind; next time he may leave his whole hand."

Such cruel words, too, Grahame hid from his friend, and made excuses for her keeping aloof from him, not yet daring to let him know that he had lost her love. And to Winlayne he said, trying to call forth her pity:

"You know how Sir Edgar has been defeated, and you may well know how he is eager to meet the same foe again. But he is sore wounded; it were good if you bade him stay; he will do more, methinks, for you than for me."

"Let him do as he will," answered Winlayne, hard and proud. "While Sir Edgar won in every fight I scorned for him many of his betters; but now will I neither bid him ride forth nor stay at home."

In hot indignation Sir Grahame turned his back on her; and at the sick knight's bedside he no longer laboured to conceal from him the faithlessness of his lady love.

"Ah! what have I done to offend one for whom I would gladly die?" exclaimed his friend; but at heart he knew what disaster it was that had robbed him of her love. From that moment, however, he began to amend, strengthened by the very violence of his passion, and by the hope of being able to wipe off the stain of his defeat in another battle with Sir Grey-Steel.

"If you will do after my counsel, I warrant that you yet may marry the lady within a month," said the pitiful Sir Grahame.

"How may that be?"

"Let me feign to be sick for a time, and see no man. Pallyas, my brother, will tend you, while, under your name, and wearing your arms, I go to the Forbidden Island and fetch the hand of Sir Grey-Steel, or leave my life there."

"Nay!" said Edgar. "If I lie here seven months, no man shall take my matter in hand till I am able to avenge myself."

But Grahame's generous devotion was not to be denied, who pressed Edgar so hard that at length he consented to that device, sorely unwilling to put his friend's life in peril, yet unable to bear the thought that while he lay thus helpless Winlayne might wed some other, as the gossip already went. He agreed to let Grahame go in his stead against Sir Grey-Steel, and, moreover, asked him to visit the lady of the castle who had so kindly harboured him, taking, as a token, the blood-stained kerchief she had lent him on his departure.

The plan was carried out, so that all in the castle were deceived. Sir Grahame pretended to be confined to bed for a few days under the care of his brother, Sir Pallyas, who had been taken into their secret. Sir Edgar, now able to rise, showed himself in court and hall and announced his intention of setting out for the Forbidden Island.

On the appointed morning, he sat reading a romance at the window of his chamber, so that all might see him.

Then, fully armed, he went down to take leave of the earl and his family; and only Winlayne gave him cold greeting. All the rest wished him godspeed, yet pitied him and feared for him, seeing how unfit he was to face such a foe.

"Farewell, my lady fair!" said the knight, hoping against hope for one kind word.

"Heaven keep you better than before," was all her answer, as she turned away without giving him even her hand to kiss.

As his horse was led forth, Sir Edgar slipped back to his chamber and took his friend's place in bed, while Sir Grahame came forth, with closed visor, armed and equipped like the other, to ride off before the eyes of many.

Winlayne, though she spoke so coldly, could not altogether be heedless of her knight. Unseen, from behind the battlements of the castle, she watched him, as she thought, till he was out of sight; then she went to the chamber shared by Edgar and Grahame. Here she found the curtains of the bed drawn close, and Pallyas by its side, who told her that his brother was too ill to bear the light. He courteously set a chair for the lady, and she, supposing herself heard by Sir Grahame, began at once to rail at his absent friend.

"I have been on the walls to see him ride off as fiercely as a raging lion. He makes great boast and noise when there is no foe before him, but when it is man to man, and steed to steed, then will he be not so ready to prove his manhood."

At this Sir Edgar, remembering how often he had fought and conquered to win her smile, could scarcely keep himself from starting up to reproach her with such cruel injustice, had not Pallyas held him down by the

shoulders. He himself undertook to rebuke the heartless lady, bidding her own how the youth whom she
slandered was acknowledged the noblest knight in the
land, and how he had overcome such and such a champion, and how the king had offered him the hand of
his daughter, which he had refused for her sake. But
still Winlayne looked scornful, and would have it that
Sir Edgar was sure to come back like a beaten hound.

II

Into the country of Gallias rode Sir Grahame, making
first for the castle where his friend had been entertained.
It was not hard to find, since all the countryfolk gave
him ready guidance and furthering when they knew how
his errand was to overthrow that dreaded tyrant of the
Forbidden Island. They told him how Gorius, the lord
of that castle, went all his life in fear and trouble for Sir
Grey-Steel, who had cruelly slain both the brother and the
betrothed husband of his only daughter, Loosepayne by
name. Well then might their house give welcome to any
champion set forth on so perilous quest.

As he rode up to the castle, in the garden Sir Grahame
saw the lady Loosepayne among her maidens, herself
known by her surpassing stature and beauty, as Sir Edgar
had described. It had been agreed between them that he
should feign to be his friend; so, kneeling before her, he
greeted the lady as one who was no stranger.

"Sir, you must hold me excused; I never saw you
till now," said she, looking hard at him; but she smiled
at the sight of her own blood-stained kerchief; nor did
she frown on the gifts of gold and jewels which he
brought forth, professing to be the grateful knight whose
wound she had bound up; and for a moment she was

deceived, so like indeed in face and form were these two friends.

Right glad to see him so well healed, she welcomed him with a kiss, and with that kiss strong love entered into the heart of Sir Grahame, filling it so that he forgot all else in the joy of her countenance, fair as a rose after rain. So entranced was he, that he thoughtlessly drew off his glove and exposed his right hand. Then, as her eye fell upon it, she drew back exclaiming:

"Sir, it is plain why at first you hid your hand, for there are no leeches in all this world that can set on a finger shorn away. What jest is this? Surely that knight never sent thee to mock me thus."

In anger she threw down his presents and turned to leave him. But as she was going, Sir Grahame caught her by the hand, crying eagerly:

"I beseech you, lady, hearken to me a word or two, and I will tell you how the matter is."

Overcome by her anger, he no longer tried to act another part, but forthwith told her his own name and blurted out all the truth: how his friend pined for the love of a lady who scorned him as a beaten knight; how he still lay weak from his wounds, and unable to clear his honour; how he himself had come to encounter Sir Grey-Steel in Edgar's stead.

"Ye seem a gentle knight that answer a lady so and that will do such service to a friend," smiled she, all her displeasure melting before his tale; yet once more her eyes flashed at the name of Grey-Steel.

Courteously she bade him stay at the castle that night to refresh himself for the perilous task of to-morrow. Her old father, she told him, saw no guests, having never left his chamber since her brother was slain by Sir Grey-Steel. When these two went to supper, she could not eat for pity of such a gallant guest, nor he for love of so fair a host. He sat by the lady's side in silence, devouring her looks with eager eyes, and in her sad smiles cheering his heart to do battle with that ruthless foe of her house. Only it repented him that, bound as he was to fight in Edgar's name, he could not lay the trophies of his victory at her feet.

After supper the lady led the knight to the same bed on which his friend had lain, and would have lulled him to sleep with music, weeping as she played sweetly on her lute, while her maidens sang a sorrowful song and wrung their hands for grief. But Sir Grahame could not sleep, so great was his love and so strong his desire to know who this lady might be that was so fair and yet so sad, and what the sorrow that told itself in such a song.

"Lady," he was moved to say, "of one thing I have great marvel: never heard I such sweet music and such sore weeping."

"Sir knight," she answered, "I can never be joyful while Sir Grey-Steel lives; for he slew my love and made me a widow before ever I was wed. My brother sought to avenge him, but he, too, was slain. And a hundred other knights have fallen by that cruel hand. But if thou fear him not, heaven be thy speed!"

She wept afresh, but her tears no longer grieved Sir Grahame, since now he might hope to dry them with the hand that had avenged her betrothed. He sprang from his couch, vowing that, with the help of heaven and his good sword, Sir Grey-Steel had but one more day to live. Ah, how often had she heard the same boast from lips that now were cold!

All night Sir Grahame would have continued in such converse, had not Loosepayne, minding his need of rest, retired with her maidens. But there was no rest for the eager knight. He lay wakesome, longing for the dawn, tossing and turning in fevered visions, now of the fair one he hoped to win, now of the fell foeman he trusted to behold at his feet.

At last came the welcome day and the glad chirping of birds. Sir Grahame was in such haste to set forth that he could hardly be persuaded to break his fast; but Loosepayne would not let him go without meat and drink. Pledging her in a cup of wine, he begged of her a favour he might wear in the battle, and she bound upon his helmet the same kerchief he had brought back from Sir Edgar. Then, as he mounted to horse, she gave him counsel by which he might hope to overcome their fell foe.

"I know him well, alas! none better. His might is given him by enchantment; from midnight to noon he waxeth stronger every hour, and ever abateth from noon till midnight. Moreover, he is better on horseback than on foot. You must aim, above all, to unhorse him, then press on, and think of your lady love."

"Lady, thy lightest word I would bear well in mind," he thanked her, and with a farewell greeting spurred towards the river that guarded the Forbidden Island.

When he was out of sight, Loosepayne went to her chamber, and all day lamented over him, fearing that she should see him no more. Many a knight had ridden forth from her in the same pride and strength, promising before evening to bid her rejoice over the death of Sir Grey-Steel, but not one had ever brought back good news; and of all who thus went to their fate she had seen none whom she pitied so much as this generous stranger. The day passed wearily on; the night fell, and he came not; by this time, no doubt, he must have perished, like so many another.

She had supper set in readiness for him, if by any chance he should escape alive; but she herself could not eat a morsel, ever thinking on Sir Grahame, and murmuring:

"Last night I led him to his chamber; to-night, Grey-Steel has made his bed. Sore pity is it, for he is a goodly and gentle youth, and woe is me for his love in his own country!" Then she thought of her own slain lover, and her tears flowed freely.

But, as she wept, there came a clatter of arms at the gate and a cheerful shout. Who but that good knight rushed into the hall, covered with blood and dust, yet with proud joy sparkling in his eyes! She rose, she sprang to meet him, she flung her arms round his neck, and kissed him again and again, eagerly demanding how he had fared.

"Full well, my lady. I have taken surety that none shall fear Sir Grey-Steel more," he told her, and in proof displayed a huge hand encased in a blood-red gauntlet.

The sight of that gory hand, by which so many had fallen, was a key opening her heart to love for the knight that had at last achieved such an adventure. Nothing in the castle was too good to be set before him who had rid the land of its oppressor. She unlaced his armour to search his wounds, with joy to find them but slight, while he told her how the hard battle had gone, and how at last, over the body of her foe, bleeding into his blood-red armour and clutching at roots and grass in his death throes, he had drunk to her in the wine with which she provided him. Having made him all good cheer, her next thought was to carry the news to her father.

She found old Gorius pacing backwards and forwards in his chamber, brooding over vain projects of revenge on Sir Grey-Steel, as was his wont. Thus had he kept himself aloof from strangers for many a day, none of his friends or retainers daring to break upon the gloomy mood that had possessed him ever since the death of his son. Great was the amazement of those who sat silent beside him, when Loosepayne burst in with a cry, flinging down the huge gauntlet:

"I bring you tidings you will like right well. Our enemy is slain!"

All started up, staring at that trophy; but the lord would not raise his dull eyes.

"Nay," he replied bitterly; "never was man born of woman that could kill Sir Grey-Steel."

But when he saw the gory hand in its gauntlet, and heard how the slayer of Grey-Steel was within his walls, Gorius could no longer refuse to believe. Thanking heaven that he had lived to see that day, he seized his daughter by the hand and hastened with her to greet a so-valiant champion.

No praises were loud enough to be showered upon Sir Grahame, and no reward seemed below his desert, who had conquered where so many had failed.

"All that is mine is thine!" cried the father. "Ask what you will that is in my power to give."

"Then, my lord," said the knight, kneeling before him, "I ask this lady; let her hand be my wages!"

The looks of the daughter did not say him nay. Gladly Gorius gave his consent, and blushingly Loosepayne took the hand of him whom she loved better than any man she had seen since the death of her betrothed knight. Before Sir Grahame left the castle they were plighted to each other, and the day of the marriage was set. They would scarcely let him depart, but he urged his covenant with his friend, and set off for the castle of Bragas, promising to return as soon as might be.

Proudly he sped homewards with Grey-Steel's helmet, gauntlet, and armour fastened to his saddlebow. These spoils he left with his horse in a wood near the castle, and, having entered it secretly, passed unseen to his friend's chamber.

Blithe was Sir Edgar to welcome him back and to hear how he had accomplished his perilous quest. There could be no jealousy between these two brothers. Nor was the one unconcerned to know how the other also had gained for himself a prize in the lists of love. Now all would be well.

But the plot had yet to be carried out to the end. Edgar, having stolen out of the castle to bring in the horse and spoils of Grey-Steel, next morning Grahame rose and appeared in the hall, feigning now to be restored to health.

"But sick am I in mind," he said aloud, "for my brother, Sir Edgar. Seven days have come and gone since he rode forth weak from his wounds, and now I fear me he will never return. The pride of Lady Winlayne drove him into this peril. Alas, that she was ever born, if for her the best knight in the world should be lost!"

Then, as the earl and countess, with all their followers, were coming from church, they saw a knight riding towards them, and when he drew near it was seen to be no other than Edgar. First of all, Grahame sprang forward to welcome him, and the rest came crowding round, all eyes for his trophies and all ears for his tale that the adventure of The Forbidden Island was at last achieved. The earl gave him his hand, the countess kissed him, and Winlayne would have done the like; but he, acting on the counsel of his friend, turned away from her, saying coldly:

"Old friends cannot be called back again."

Sorely mortified was the earl's daughter to find her own disdain returned upon herself; and as her triumphant lover entered the castle, stretching her arms to him in vain she fell back in a swoon with his name upon her lips.

Grahame had rightly gauged this haughty heart. He now took pains to spread a report that the vanquisher of Grey-Steel was about to leave the castle to marry a beautiful lady who had favoured him in his adventure. When this news came to her, Winlayne's pride was humbled to the dust. Tearfully she sought out her lover, on her knees praying him to forgive her. The earl, her father, joined his entreaties to hers; then be sure how Edgar had no mind to deny them! With little asking he declared himself willing to accept her hand, and, as his friend had promised, he led her to the altar within a month. Sir Grahame stood as groom to his brother-in-arms; then, as soon as the wedding-feast was over, they hastened away to the castle of Gorius, again to play different parts in a like ceremony. Thus both were married to the ladies of their love.

But they did not all live happy, if the tale be truly told. For not long after his marriage the good Sir Grahame fell in war; then, so bitter was Edgar's grief that over his friend's bier he could not refrain from confessing openly how to him rightly belonged the glory of that great adventure in the Forbidden Island. And when Winlayne knew what deceit had been practised upon her by these two, so hot was she in wrath and scorn that she vowed she would never again speak to a husband thus disclosed as no unbeaten knight. She hid her pride in a convent, and he saw her no more.

Caring not to live now that he had lost wife, and brother, and fame, Edgar went to the East to fight against the Saracens with such desperate valour that his exploits rang through all Christendom. But death ever flees from those that seek him; and after years the good knight came home unhealed in heart but sound in body, to find his wife dead, and Sir Grahame's widow still mourning over her spouse, the friend whom he also had never forgotten. Their tears flowed together; their hearts were one in the same sorrow; and ere long these two became man and wife, hoping thus with new love to sweeten the memory of the old.

BELTENEBROS

I

To the Firm Island came Amadis of Gaul, with his
brothers Galaor and Florestan, and his cousin Agraies,
prince of Scotland, all well-tried knights, but Amadis the
most famous of them when not yet twenty years old.
Secretly plighted to Oriana, daughter of Lisuarte, King
of Great Britain, whom he loved as truly as ever knight
loved lady, he had left her side to fulfil a promise of
restoring the Princess Briolania to her father's kingdom
and avenging that king's death upon a cruel oppressor.
This service done, Briolania would fain have had him for
husband as well as deliverer; and indeed what fair one
could look but with love on a face the more comely for
the scars that marred its youthful bloom? But Amadis
gave her to know that his heart was all Oriana's, and
with a sigh she forbore to shake his constancy. Had but
Oriana seen her lover with the eyes of this despairing
princess! For she mistook his readiness to serve Briolania, as behoved a knight never to deny the aid of his
arm to any damsel in distress. Love being quick to
suspect and cruel in tormenting itself, Oriana believed
that she was forsaken, and jealousy worked upon her till
she sent Amadis a letter which wrought long affliction for
them both. And he, all unconscious how he had dis-

pleased his lady, still tarried from her that he might try the enchantments of that famous island.

The greatest knight of his day had been Apollidon, who was also the sagest of enchanters, and had married Grimanesa, the most beautiful lady then alive. Rich and happy, these two had built for them a palace adorned with precious stones and costly woods from all quarters of the earth, set among gardens blooming the year round with the flowers and fruits of every country under the sun. Never had been seen such magnificence nor such marvels as the lord of this land gathered together by his wealth and by his magic arts. The retreat in which he looked to end his days bore the name of the Firm Island, yet was it no right island, being joined to the mainland by a narrow neck of ground. But in time Apollidon was called away to be crowned Emperor of Greece; then he left the Firm Island, with all its wonders, as a heritage to any knight who should prove as brave in arms as himself and as loyal in love to a lady not less fair and faithful than his own wife. To test the virtues of all aspirants, he laid mystic spells on the island, only to be broken by him who should be its lord. At the entrance to the gardens was an arch that could be safely passed by none but true lovers; and in the midst of them stood a Forbidden Chamber, fast closed to all but the knight and lady destined to achieve such great adventure.

A hundred years had passed since that spell was laid, and a hundred knights had vainly sought to break it, when Amadis came with his kinsmen to visit the Firm Island. There the governor received them with all honour, and showed them the wonders of the palace, outside of which they saw a hundred shields hung up, some higher than others. These, said the governor, had been left behind by the knights venturing their fortune, some of them winning farther than others, but not one had pressed on to enter the Forbidden Chamber; and when the strangers saw the arms of so many champions, known to them by name and fame, well might they doubt of success where such men had failed. Then they came to the Arch of True Lovers, over which stood a gigantic image in copper, holding a trumpet to its mouth. If any-one, they heard, who had been untrue to his love, sought to pass under it, the trumpet would belch out against him such a blast of smoke and flame that he must fall as if dead. But if he were true of heart he would pass through to the sound of music, as had been the lot of few.

Eager to prove his fidelity, Agraies advanced first to the ordeal.

"My love, if I have deserved thy heart, do not forget me!" he exclaimed, as he sped through the arch un-hindered, the trumpet giving forth sweet music and a gush of perfumes.

On the other side he came to statues of Apollidon and Grimanesa so artfully fashioned that he thought they smiled on him, and at their feet a table of jasper on which were carved the names of those knights who had come through aforetime. Now, while he read them, as if written by a sunbeam a fresh line appeared on the stone, where he saw with amazement his own name springing to view:

Agraies, son of Languines, King of Scotland.

When thus their cousin had passed safely, Amadis would have persuaded his brothers to follow. But Galaor and Florestan made excuse, for they knew them-selves too well; so the eldest went on alone, all his beat-ing heart fixed on Oriana.

He need not have feared, for as he came under the arch that trumpet poured down flowers upon him, as if giving shape and colour to its sweet breath. With music ringing in his ears he joined Agraies, and by his side saw his own name being carved by an invisible hand on the jasper record:

Amadis, son of Perion, King of Gaul, loyallest of lovers.

Side by side now these two walked through the enchanted gardens, talking to each other of their loves and admiring the leafy arbours, sparkling fountains, and statues that seemed as if alive, where every tree was astir with brightly plumaged or sweetly singing birds. But suddenly there arose a great clamour not far off; and up rushed Amadis's dwarf Ardian, screaming out:

"Help, sir, or your brothers are slain!"

Meanwhile Galaor and Florestan had asked the governor to bring them in by another gate, and to show them where the Forbidden Chamber lay. He, slyly smiling, pointed out how the way to it led first by a brazen, then by a marble pillar; the one, he said, harder to pass than the other.

"Shall we make trial?" asked Florestan.

"Nay," quoth Galaor; "for me, I meddle not with enchantments."

"Then await me here!" cried his brother, and, taking sword and shield in hand, dashed forward towards the brazen pillar.

But ere he had reached it he was seen to be fighting as if with the air. From all sides hailed upon him heavy blows dealt by invisible enemies, and when he struck back he felt his sword's edge turned upon ghostly weapons besetting him at every step. Bravely struggling and staggering on, he gained the brazen pillar; but there he fell senseless, and was hurled back to the feet of his brother, staring in astonishment.

"If the adventure be so perilous, I must take my share!" declared Galaor, drawing his sword; and, having given Florestan over to the care of their squires, he in turn advanced towards the pillars.

No sooner had he passed the threshold of the spell than he also felt the air full of spears and swords, and himself beaten down by blows and buffets such as he had never endured in any fight with mortal foes. But he fought his way manfully to the bronze pillar, and, clinging to it a moment for breath, he pushed on through the ever-thickening storm towards the marble pillar; then soon fell to the ground, and like his brother was cast forth as if dead.

Hereon ran up Amadis and Agraies to find the scared squires reviving their masters by throwing over them the water of a fountain. When he heard what had befallen, Agraies would take no warning, but sped sword in hand along the same way on which his cousins had fared so ill. And he fared little better, for, reeling and tottering like a tempest-stricken ship, he was seen to gain the marble pillar, but there to fall and be flung back like the rest, bruised and breathless.

"No knight in my time hath won so far," said the governor. "None can fight through this enchantment but the peer of Apollidon who devised it; and does such a man live?"

"Be that as it may, I must not spare my body what others have undergone," declared Amadis, and made ready for the trial.

In vain they all would have held him back. Commending himself to heaven, steeling his heart also by thoughts of Oriana, he charged forward upon those in-

visible perils. Never had he borne such a brunt of battle
as now closed upon him. It seemed as if he had to do
with a thousand knights at once; and so dreadful a din
filled his ears as if all the world were in arms against
him. Sometimes he had almost fallen; once he was
beaten to his knees; again his sword was struck from his
grasp so that it hung by a thong to his wrist. He feared
he could bear no more, when suddenly the door of the
Forbidden Chamber flew open, and from it came a hand
that seized his to lead him on; and as the tempest of
blows rose to its height, it suddenly fell calm before a
voice pealing over his head:

"Welcome, bravest of knights, who in love and war
surpassest the builder of what is henceforth thine."

Those who had watched his course from a distance
now rushed after him without hindrance, that strange
enchantment having melted out of the air, like snow-
flakes before the sun. They found the Forbidden
Chamber open, where within sat Amadis, his helmet laid
aside and his sword sheathed, showing no sign of what
he had endured. The governor and all fell on their
knees to kiss his hand as their lord; and great was his
brothers' joy to know one of their kin worthy of an
honour sought in vain for a hundred years.

At the rumour that Apollidon's spell was at last
broken, the people came flocking together to see this
peerless champion, whose name had already gone out
through the world, now to stand highest among knights
alive and dead. Such a great day must be given up to
feast and revel; and none guessed what a chilling shadow
would soon quench the glow of pride and rejoicing.

II

Amadis was about to enter the hall where the islanders should do their homage, when his squire and foster-brother Gandalin let him know how Oriana's friend Durin had brought a letter from London. Durin came to the island just as those ordeals were beginning, but, guessing the letter to be from Oriana, Gandalin had kept its bearer back, lest it should hinder his master in the great achievement. Now Durin gave him the letter, which Amadis would have kissed in rapture at first sight of his lady's handwriting, but had almost let it fall on reading the superscription:

"*To the false knight Amadis, from her whom he hath stabbed through the heart.*"

He looked again, hardly trusting his eyes. The blood fled from his cheeks, and for a little he could not bring his hands to break the seal. At last, finding courage to tear it open, with consternation and amazement he read these words, written, as it seemed to his fevered sight, in letters of blood, and in a broken voice he muttered them aloud:

"The madness of grief nerves my weak hand to declare the complaint of my woeful heart against the faithless and disloyal lover, through whom I am made the most miserable woman in the world; and great as was my love, so now great is my hatred. One vengeance lies in my power: I forbid thee ever again to appear before her whom thou hast deceived and deserted. Go, to cheat other poor ladies with such treacherous vows as befooled one too-trustful maid; and leave me to weep away the life thou hast made wretched for thy once loving   "ORIANA."

These cruel words struck Amadis to the heart like a poisoned dart. With faltering lips he asked Durin what

they meant, who could tell him no more than that Oriana
had bid him carry the letter with all speed, and that he
was straitly charged to bear back no answer.   Again
Amadis read it, like one in an evil dream; then, as if
thunderstruck, he fell on the ground.

"This message is my death; let it lie here that the
end come the sooner!" he moaned, placing the fatal letter
in his bosom.

For a time he gave way to tears of despair; but presently rose to bathe his eyes in a fountain, before calling
for Gandalin and the governor of the island.   In silent
astonishment they heard him order his horse to be
brought to a postern gate; and he made them promise
to keep his departure a secret from his brothers till next
day.   It was done as he bid; then at the gate he took
leave of them, as one they should never see again.

"Gandalin," he said, "we were nursed by the same
milk, and till now we have spent our lives together in
weal and woe.   Right well thou hast followed me in all
adventures.   I looked to make thee knight, but this one
of my brethren will do for me.   As soon as ye hear of
my death I leave this island as heritage to thy good
father, who reared me, and after him to thee, trustiest
of squires, to whom I now say farewell."

"But, sir," cried Gandalin, "never before was I
parted from you in any hour of trial!   If you die, I care
not to live.   I want no lordship nor honour but that of
serving the best knight on earth."

"It may not be!   This last dole I must dree alone.
I forbid all to follow me."

With these words, embracing Gandalin and commending him to heaven, Amadis mounted his horse to ride
away in such distraction that he left his arms behind him.
The woeful knight rode at a venture, neither knowing

nor caring where he went. His horse, for once unguided by rein or spur, took him among lonely hills, where at nightfall he found himself riding through a dark thicket. The branches, striking him on the face, roused him from his dream of misery; then, hoping to be here hidden, he tied the horse to a tree and sank down on the grass, weeping till for faintness he fell asleep.

But in spite of his commands he was followed by Gandalin, bearing his arms, and by Durin, who cursed himself that he had been the innocent bearer of so great affliction to such a knight. As, holding on his tracks by moonlight, they entered the wood, the steed of Amadis neighed in greeting to their horses; and so they stole warily forward till they found him lying asleep. All night they sat near, heedful not to disturb his restless slumber; but before daybreak Amadis awoke to pour out fresh lamentations.

"My birth, my victories, my lordship, my renown, what are they all beside the favour Oriana has withdrawn from me!"

So ran the burden of his complaint, that set these two hearers weeping for pity; and they did not venture to show themselves till by chance Amadis caught sight of Gandalin moving dimly in the dawn.

"Who goes there?" he cried, but knew Gandalin at once by his voice. "Darest thou follow me against my command?"

"Sir," said Gandalin, "I have brought your arms, of which you may stand in need."

"What need of arms when I have lost valour and strength and all in losing her who gave me heart and hath taken it away?"

Yet he took his arms and let Gandalin bring him his horse. Then, seeing Durin, he bade him return to the

court of Lisuarte, there to salute all his friends, and to
tell them how the proudest knight in the world was
become the most wretched, who henceforth sought
nothing but death.

With tears Durin turned back to do this errand; but
Gandalin would not quit his master, promising obedience
when Amadis enjoined him:

"If thou art set on coming with me, speak no word
to hinder whatever I may say or do, else thou must leave
me here."

These two mounted, and rode all day through the
mountains, Amadis speaking never a word unless to
himself. Nor would he eat, though Gandalin begged
him to taste a pasty he had brought in his wallet. So
often he murmured the name of Oriana that the good
squire could not but understand the cause of his forlorn
state. And when at nightfall they unsaddled by a stream,
Gandalin made bold to speak his mind.

"Sir, I have thought two things of that letter that
so strikes you to the heart. Either the lady Oriana has
given her love to another, or she feigns anger against
you to excuse her own fickleness; or, rather, may she
not have been deceived by some falsehood, which it is
for you to make known, that she may repent and forgive, and all shall yet be well?"

"Peace!" cried Amadis. "On pain of my hottest
displeasure, never say to me again that Oriana can do
wrong. Her love is so true that she knew well how the
loss of it was a command for me to perish."

He turned away in anger, striding up the stream that
echoed his troubled thoughts. When he came back he
found Gandalin asleep, overcome by weariness. Then,
hiding the squire's saddle and bridle among the bushes,
that he might not follow, Amadis took his own horse

and his arms and rode on alone through the night, still careless where he went.

When Gandalin awoke he bitterly reproached himself for having let his master slip away. It was long before he could catch his horse and find its hidden harness; then he pricked on, but now could nowhere come up with Amadis. After searching for days, beside a fountain shaded by tall trees he found the well-known shield and armour, but no other sign of the knight, who, without weapons, might well have fallen a prey to wild beasts. There was nothing for it but ruefully to carry back these tokens to his brothers. They also, once aware how Amadis had disappeared, were riding here and there on a bootless search. The new-made lord of the Firm Island had vanished so utterly that men feared he must be dead through the madness of his sorrow.

And indeed Amadis went longing for nothing so much as death. He had let his horse wander at will through the wildest valleys till he came to that fountain by which Gandalin lighted on his arms. As there the horse stopped to drink, Amadis was aware of a grey-haired priest or hermit, robed in goatskin, who had halted to water his ass. Dismounting and laying aside his arms, he knelt at the old man's feet, whom he desired to hear his confession.

"If these be tears of repentance, in a happy hour we meet!" answered the good father, raising him up and encouraging him to speak freely.

In his ear Amadis poured out the sins of his life; but what he most heavily laid to his own charge was having lost the love of a lady whom he declared to be all goodness.

"Meseemeth you make too much moan for what is as easily lost as won," said the greybeard, when he had heard all. "I know not who this lady may be that hath brought to such despair a brave and noble knight, but I counsel thee to leave so great folly as loving one who answers love by scorn; and thus shalt thou be free to serve God."

"Good sir," answered Amadis, "your counsel on this is neither asked nor needed. I can never cease loving till I die, and that will not be long. For my soul's sake I pray you to take me with you, else I perish like a beast among these mountains."

"My son," said the old man, "mine is a hard life in a sorry place. My name is Andalod, and I dwell in a hermitage on the top of a rock, sevèn leagues out at sea, to be reached by ships only in summer. Now for the first time my sister's burial has called me away from this desolate abode. Thirty years have I lived there, content to renounce the pleasures of the world; but for one like thee such solitude would be a living tomb."

"I seek no better!" cried Amadis. "Let me go with thee, good father, to dwell in penitence while I live, and to obey thee in all things."

The hermit wept tears on his hoary beard, for pity of this broken-hearted knight, so goodly of face and mien. He consented to take the stranger to his hermitage, and forthwith laid upon him a wholesome penance, that he should eat some bread and fish which the old man brought from his wallet. Amadis ate but little, and unwillingly, yet that was the first food he had tasted for days.

These two slept side by side at the fountain, where Amadis left his arms when next morning they fared on together to the seacoast. On their way he asked the old man a boon, that he would never breathe the name revealed to him under the seal of confession. The hermit might well ask how he should call this companion of his solitude; and the knight begged of him to name his humbled life anew. So, after reflection, the holy father christened him Beltenebros, or the Fair Forlorn, as fitting his noble aspect, all overclouded with grief. That name pleased Amadis well, and he vowed to bear it henceforth in poverty and obscurity.

On the seashore they found a bark to carry them over to the hermitage on an island called the Poor Rock. To the mariners Amadis gave his horse, getting in exchange such a coarse goatskin garment as the hermit wore. The wind blew fair, and ere nightfall they landed on the storm-beaten islet, where this despairing knight looked to end his days, forgotten by all men, since he was no longer beloved by Oriana.

III

To the court of Lisuarte came all at once great news good and bad. It was told here, as over the world, how Amadis had victoriously achieved the adventures of the Firm Island, as also how he had vanished from the ken of his friends. They brought to London his shield and his arms in proof of this strange story; and with them came Durin and Gandalin, the last to see him alive.

On news of his arrival Oriana made haste to send for her messenger. Sorely now she repented of that message, for she knew that no faithless knight could have passed under the Arch of True Lovers; nor could her jealousy be so abiding as her love. Eagerly she asked Durin if he had given her letter, and how Amadis had received it.

"Do not ask," answered Durin with tears in his eyes, "for never such wrong was done by lady to her lover."

"What say you?"

"I say," repeated he, "you have been the death of the best knight that ever was, and the truest to his love that ever will be. Would that death had stricken me before I had carried so cruel a letter to pierce so noble a heart!"

Then he told her all he knew; how Amadis at the height of his triumph had gone mad for sorrow, how he had fled into the mountains alone, and how none could learn what had become of him. Before the tale was told out, she began to call on death to take her also.

Still more bitterly did Gandalin reproach her for having distrusted one ready to bury himself alive at a word of her displeasure; and this faithful squire's laments wrung her heart sorest of all, so that she cried:

"Kill me, Gandalin, for I killed thy good master; and thou shouldst revenge his death as he would have revenged thine!"

Fainting away for shame and sorrow, long she lay like one dead, till her friends and ladies were able to rouse her from despair by hopes that Amadis might still be alive. On their advice she wrote another message to heal the heart she had so deeply wounded, and to call back the lover she had so cruelly driven away. Durin's sister, the Damsel of Denmark, who was her best friend among women, undertook to carry this letter over the world, till she should find Amadis, if he were anywhere to be found. Durin also devoted himself to the same quest, if haply he might help to undo the evil done through his means.

So the letter was written, as in Oriana's heart's blood, and sealed with her saltest tears. With it the Damsel of Denmark first took ship for Scotland, where Amadis had been brought up from childhood. But there his foster-parents knew nothing of his fate, nor had he been heard of in his father's court of Gaul. In vain search for him Durin travelled as far as Spain. But many as there were who would gladly have had good news of that great knight, none could tell where he might be. On the Firm Island, as in London and elsewhere, Amadis was heartily mourned for dead; but there was joy among the foes of the king he had served so well.

The kind Damsel of Denmark had wellnigh given up hope to find him, yet for long she durst not return, fearing lest her ill speed on this errand might be the death of Oriana. When at last she would have sailed for London a great storm arose that drove her ship out of its course. No land being in sight, the sailors gave themselves up for lost, till a bell sounding through the tempest guided them towards a rocky island, for which they steered and were able here to anchor in shelter. Some of them knew it as named the Poor Rock, inhabited only, they said, by the pious hermit, Andalod, whose chapel crowned its summit. Then, the storm being abated, the Damsel desired to be set on land, that she might offer thanks in that chapel for deliverance from so great danger, while the sailors repaired their shattered craft.

With her page, Enil, she reached the chapel as the hermit began to say mass. Behind him, in service of the altar, knelt his sole companion, so wan and wasted by sorrow and fasting, and so burned by the sun, that none who had known this acolyte in happier days would now have recognized him, even were his face not hidden by a goatskin hood. But when the holy rite was done, he turned round to cast eyes upon the lady, a sight that went to his heart, for he knew her well as Oriana's dearest friend. Hiding his face, he strove in vain to rise from his knees, and with a groan he fainted away on the floor.

The hermit got Enil's help to carry him into the

BELTENEBROS RECOGNIZES THE DAMSEL OF DENMARK

ESPLANDIAN RESCUES THE OLD KING

little hut hard by, which was his lodging; and when they had laid him there on a couch, the Damsel of Denmark asked:

"Good sir, who is this sharer of your solitude over whom you weep as if he were your own son?"

"Alas!" said the old man; "I know him as an unhappy knight named Beltenebros, whose choice is here to do such sore penance that he has not long to live."

"Maybe," said the damsel, "in the ship we have some remedy for his sickness."

"That is the last service you can do him," sighed the hermit. "I fear me his sickness has no remedy but death."

Yet the damsel sent to the ship for a cordial, with which she visited the sick man's bedside, saying gently:

"Sir, I learn from the holy father that you are a knight; and because we damsels are so beholden to good knights for what they do in our defence, it behoves us to visit and relieve all such in affliction."

But the poor man turned away from her, moaning so bitterly that she thought him about to yield up the ghost. Opening the shutter of the dark room, to give him air, she raised his head in her arms; then the sunlight fell on his face, so changed by suffering that she might not yet have known it but for a well-remembered scar on his brow.

"Amadis!" she exclaimed, as he feebly opened his eyes.

"Let that name be never again spoken," he murmured, "since it is no longer dear to one you know!"

"Nay, sir, she sends me to seek pity and pardon from you, since her injustice makes her own life worse than death. The hand that wounded you so deep can cure you. Behold what I have borne in search of you

far and wide! In this letter your lady bids you forget
the past, and hasten to forgive her if you are the same
Amadis she loved so well."

"Heart, take thy remedy!" cried Amadis, pressing
the letter on his lips; and when he tore it open, his
eyes lit up as they read:

"If the injuries of an enemy may claim pardon, when humbly
repented, how much more those that come from too much love!
She who writes confesses to deserving punishment for doubting
a faith that never failed her; but by thine own misery judge
of mine. Her friend that bears this letter will tell thee what
she endures, and how heartily she implores thy mercy, not as
merited, but as longed for by her who can have no other comfort
on earth. For thine own sake, as for hers, forgive the contrite

"ORIANA."

No cordial could have cheered Oriana's knight like
these blessed words, that sent the blood to his parched
face, and tears to his eyes, not now of sorrow but of
joy.

"You bring me back my life!" he cried to the
Damsel of Denmark.

"Then save her from despair that has wronged you
through too much love!" entreated she, who now easily
persuaded him to abandon his retreat, and go back with
her to where that lady was waiting to make amends for
her cruelty.

But his weakness so shamed him that it was agreed
between them to hide yet from all others his real name.
As Beltenebros she should carry him to Britain, on pretence that this was a sick man received on board the ship
for his health. He took leave of the hermit with warm
thanks, promising to show his gratitude by building a
monastery on the Firm Island and giving it to this good

man's charge. Nor did the greybeard seek to stay him, when he had heard how it was with his love.

"Farewell, my son! Solitude is blest but to withered hearts like mine, that have wearied of life's deceitful joys, and can await patiently the end of all its sorrows. Go back to the world, then, and may heaven protect thee as thy arm upholds the right!"

Kneeling before him on the shore, Beltenebros kissed the hand of this good father, whom he honoured like a son. His last sight of Andalod was with arms raised in blessing as the ship bore him away on a smooth sea from the island where he had spent such doleful days.

IV

Landed in Britain, Amadis felt as if new life came to him day by day, so that soon he began to hanker after the knightly weapons he had thought to lay aside for ever. Leaving him to rest at a nunnery, whence he might travel on at ease when he had got back his strength, the Damsel of Denmark hurried forward to break the good news to Oriana, who was at her castle of Miraflores, near London. Meanwhile, no one else should learn the real name of him who desired to be still known as Beltenebros. The good damsel gave him money to buy arms and armour; and she left with him Enil to be his squire, the youth well pleased to serve such a kindly master, whom he little guessed to be that knight famed above all others.

And ere long Beltenebros heard news to stir his blood. King Cildadan of Ireland had never forgiven the death of his brother Abies, slain by the hand of Amadis. Now, believing Amadis dead, he sent a challenge to Lisuarte to stake the tribute of his kingdom upon a battle of a hundred knights on either side. Leagued with Cildadan were gigantic warriors, such as the cruel Famongomadan, who sent on his own score a haughty demand that Oriana should be given over to him as handmaid to his daughter; for no other price would he grant peace. King Lisuarte declared himself ready to die rather than deliver his child to such a heathen wretch. Defiances were proudly exchanged, a day had been set for the battle, and now each party was gathering its hundred choicest champions.

Beltenebros was right wroth to hear how that caitiff would make Oriana a servant in his house, and he promised himself to undertake no adventure till he had chastised so great insolence. He sent Enil to the nearest town to buy a horse and arms, the armour all silver, and the shield thickly set with golden lions. Thus arrayed and mounted, he felt his old spirit welling up within him, as he managed his mettlesome steed to the admiration of the young squire.

"I know not, sir, what your prowess may be," said Enil, "but I never saw knight appear so well in arms."

"You have judged the one; you shall judge the other when put to the proof," quoth his master, as they turned their backs on the nunnery that had harboured them till now.

Beltenebros rode on with his helmet closed, that he might not be known; and the cognizance he had chosen for his new shield gave no hint who he was. By and by he came past some pavilions pitched by a riverside where ten knights and a bevy of damsels were sporting on the bank. The knights called out to him to stay and joust with them.

"Not now," said he, and would have ridden on,

though they jeered at him, saying that he feared to lose his horse if dismounted. "If so," he answered, "I had better not risk such a loss."

"You trust a smooth tongue for safety rather than a stout heart!" they cried after him.

"Think of me as you please; your words do not touch my worth, such as it is," he cried back, for he had no mind to fight with men he despised.

But before he reached the ford of the river a damsel came riding after him to say that in these pavilions was Leonoretta, the younger daughter of King Lisuarte, and that she and her ladies requested the stranger to joust for their pastime.

"I would rather do her service myself than couch a lance against her knights," quoth Beltenebros; "but be it as she will."

He turned about to take his ground, where, one by one, Leonoretta's ten knights rode against him, and, one by one, were overthrown; and he who had railed loudest at the stranger now lay groaning with broken bones. Enil, joyful to know himself squire to such a knight, took their horses as prize of the victor; but Beltenebros bade him lead them to the princess with a message that she should charge her knights either to be more courteous to strangers, or else to joust better, for some other adversary might choose to make them go on foot.

They were astonished by his generosity, as abashed by their downfall; and one said that the unknown had done as Amadis would have done had he been alive, to which another added:

"Would it were Amadis, then might our dishonour be the less."

Beltenebros rode on, well satisfied to be sure that

he had not lost his old skill in arms. When he had crossed the river, and gone some quarter of a league beyond, he saw near the road a chapel embowered among trees, and to this cool shade turned aside for rest and prayer, being wearied after jousting with all those knights. Then, as in a brook he washed away the dust and sweat, he was aware of a miserable clamour borne to his ears, and on the road which he had come he saw an appalling sight. Along it, drawn by twelve horses and driven by hideous dwarfs, came a wagon of wickerwork huge as a tower, in which were chained the very knights from whom he had just parted, and the damsels, with their mistress Leonoretta tearfully lamenting over the fate that had fallen upon them amid sport and play. Before and behind rode two gigantic figures, he in front on a tall black horse, himself glittering from head to foot in plates of steel, and he carried a boar spear whose point was longer than a man's arm. The good knight guessed well who these monsters were: that heathen giant Famongomadan that was wont in such a wagon to carry off captives for sacrifice to his idols; and he who rode behind must be his son Basagante. And when Amadis remembered how Famongomadan had demanded Oriana to be given him as serving-maid, he forgot his weariness in wrath, and called to Enil for his arms.

"Let these demons first pass by!" said the trembling squire.

"They shall not pass without my trying to redress their cruelty," declared his master.

"Ah, sir, have pity on your youth!" begged Enil. "Were the twenty bravest of Lisuarte's knights here, they would shrink from so fell an encounter."

"I must do my best, and thou shalt see my fortune.

'Tis a squire's part to obey, not to prate," said Beltenebros
in so stern a tone that the youth brought him his arms
without more ado, yet shed tears as if he never looked to
equip his lord for another fight.

All his old fire kindling in his heart when he thought
of Oriana, the knight spurred down to meet that sorrowful train, and with lance in rest loudly bade the dwarfs
halt, as they did. But the giant that rode on in front
charged upon him with an angry outcry, seeming to
smoke for wrath behind the bars of his helmet. Not
a whit dismayed, Beltenebros met the onset with so
true an aim that his lance pierced the giant's body
through his mail and hurled him, saddle and all, to the
ground, while the thrust of the huge boar spear went
amiss to maim the other's horse.

"Help, Basagante! I am overthrown!" bellowed the
fallen monster to his son; and up dashed that young
giant, brandishing a battleaxe as big as a breastplate.

The good knight had quickly leapt from his wounded
horse and drawn his sword, with which he struck at
Basagante's leg as he passed, cutting through the stirrup
leather and the sinews of his knee, a wound which the
giant did not feel in his fury. Wheeling round, with
his axe he would have cleft Beltenebros in two, but its
head stuck fast in the shield, beaten out of the knight's
hands, whose own sword broke upon the giant's armour.
He snatched at the huge axe which Basagante could not
pluck out of his shield; and in their struggle, the broken
stirrup leather giving way, the rider lost his balance and
fell over on the ground. He drew his sword as he tried
to rise, but the wound in his leg brought him down on
that knee. One mighty sweep he made with the long
sword to shear off the knight's head, yet only cut away
the crest of his helmet. Leonoretta and her ladies, looking

on from the wagon, raised a cry to heaven when such a blow fell upon their champion. But he kept his feet, and swinging the giant's battleaxe in both hands cleft him through the skull so that he never spoke again.

Meanwhile Famongomadan lay helpless, cursing in his agony, till Beltenebros ran back to stop his mouth by thrusting into it his own boar spear, to nail him to the earth. When both giants were dead, he broke the chains of their captives, joyful and thankful for such gallant rescue. In the wagon he packed the monstrous bodies of father and son, never more to afflict Christian souls. These trophies he prayed the knights and ladies to convey to King Lisuarte, with this message, that in the coming battle he would have two foes less to encounter and one more knight to fight on his side, ready to spill every drop of blood in his service.

"Beltenebros will not fail him on the appointed day!" was his parting promise, as he rode off on the black horse of Famongomadan, leaving the princess and her train loud in praise of such a doughty deliverer.

V

Amadis had no mind for further adventures to delay him on the way to Miraflores, where Oriana eagerly awaited his coming ever since it was announced by the Damsel of Denmark. Unknown to all others, he reached the castle; then who can tell, says the chronicler, what joy there was in embracing and kissing and the mingling of tears. Only true lovers may understand how these two exchanged forgiveness for the past, and vows for the future, and sighs and smiles over what both had suffered during their cruel separation. Enough to say that here the knight remained hidden for a week, each day going by in a too short dream of bliss.

Turn we now to the court of Lisuarte, as the day drew near for that great battle with Cildadan and his hundred champions. Leonoretta and her train had brought news of the prowess of Beltenebros, with the bodies of the two giants for proof; and well might the king rejoice in the promise of such a doughty helper. All the talk was of this unknown hero, whom men gave out as braver and stronger than Amadis himself. Such boasts hurt Galaor and Florestan, who had laid aside the search for their brother to take his place in the battle; and nothing but their pledge to undertake no other quarrel till it were fought hindered them from now seeking out and defying this Beltenebros to mortal combat, so enraged were they that any knight should be called the equal of the vanished Amadis.

As for Cildadan and his allies, the young knights made sure to have the better of them. But the old king knew the might of those foes; and his heart misgave him when, on the eve of the combat, he received a scroll from the enchantress Urganda, that sage guardian of his race. Thus the writing ran:

"To King Lisuarte of Great Britain, Urganda the Unknown foretells what shall befall in the battle with the King of Ireland. Perilous and cruel it will be; and in it Beltenebros, to whom thou trustest for victory, will lose his name and his fame. Thou thyself wilt be in danger of death, when the sword of Beltenebros sheds thy blood. And by his sword will the battle be won."

"How can that be?" thought Lisuarte in bewilderment. "Beltenebros is to win the battle, yet to shed my blood, and to lose his name. Ah, were Amadis alive, whose sword was worth a hundred! Sure he is dead, or he would not have failed me at this hour. I am old, and must soon die, by the hand of Beltenebros or another; but at least let me die as becomes a king who has so many brave knights at his command."

With this he put the warning out of mind and spoke of it to none, lest his followers should be disheartened. He, above all men, was bound now to bear a bold front to the enemy. Their galleys had already come to land, where the Irish king's knights were pitching their tents beside the plain marked out for the encounter. So stalwart and fierce appeared these strangers that king Lisuarte's people truly had need to pray heaven for their lord.

That one night there was truce, and men slept who would never see another sun go down. With dawn King Lisuarte mustered his hundred knights, among them one mounted on a huge black horse, in silver armour, with a shield full of golden lions, who announced himself as Beltenebros, the unknown yet so quickly famed. All beheld him with wonder for his deeds; only Galaor and Florestan looked on him askance through the bars of their helmets. Lisuarte welcomed this champion, whose aid he could not refuse, since he now got news how was lost to him one of his trustiest warriors, Arban of Wales. He had been made prisoner by the wife of Famongomadan in revenge for her husband's death, and was pining in that giant's dungeons till the king were able to deliver him. Beltenebros made up the tale of his party, all of them famous knights of their time. There were the brothers of Amadis, and his cousin Agraies of Scotland; and Gandalac, Galaor's foster-father, with his sons Gavus and Bramandil; and Nicoran, keeper of the Perilous Bridge, with Dragonis, and Palomir, and Pinorante; Giontes, the king's nephew; the renowned Sir

Bruneo of Bonamar, who, before Amadis, had achieved
the passage of the True Lovers' Arch; also his brother
Branfil; and Sir Guilan the Pensive; and good old Sir
Grumedan, who bore the king's banner in the centre
of the troop, and Ladasin, and Galvanes, and Olivas,
and many another whose name should not be forgotten.

On the adverse side, also, were chiefs of renown, and
some of gigantic stature, such as Cartadaque, Albadanzor,
and Gadancuriel, whom King Cildadan placed in the front
of his ranks. He missed that day Famongomadan and
his mighty son Basagante, laid low by Beltenebros on
their way to take part in the battle. But not less fearful
was the giant Mandanfabul, lord of the Isle of the Ver-
milion Tower, who with ten of his like were placed in
the rear on a hill, with orders not to engage till they saw
the enemy broken and weary, then to rush down upon
King Lisuarte and kill him or carry him off prisoner.

The trumpets gave the signal for both lines to close,
breaking upon each other like waves foaming with steel.
The ground shook under the crash of that onset, in which
many a man went down, and many a horse galloped away
without a rider. Soon all the field was hidden in clouds
of dust, where the fighters, panting for heat and rage,
were mixed in a confused struggle; and those who looked
on with throbbing hearts could not tell how it went with
friend or foe. But like a thunderbolt gleamed through
the medley that silver knight on a black horse, that kept
ever close to the old king, when, caring not to live unless
victorious, he threw himself into the hottest press. Nor
was King Cildadan behind him in desperate valour, who
would have encountered Lisuarte, but was met by Beltenebros and by his sword smitten to the ground, hurt almost
to death. Not far off, Galaor, for his part, did prodigies

to emulate that rival of Amadis, but he in turn was unhorsed and like to be slain.

By this time the battle had lasted half the day, and more than half the champions on either side had fallen. Still the rest fought on, faint with wounds as they were, their arms broken, their horses stiff and weary. And now through the thinned ranks swooped Mandanfabul with his band of fresh fighters, like kites upon their prey, and came charging towards the royal banner. The knights around Lisuarte fought gallantly to shield him, but the giant, beating down all who stood in his way, seized the old king by the neck, dragged him from his saddle by main strength, and was carrying him off locked helplessly under his brawny arm.

Beltenebros had just mounted a fresh horse brought him by his squire, when he saw the plight of Oriana's father. Spurring forward, he soon came up with Mandanfabul, and fetched him such a mighty blow as not only shore off the giant's right arm, but beneath it cut through Lisuarte's armour and drew his blood. Mandanfabul, losing control of his horse, was carried away bleeding to death; and Lisuarte fell to the ground, where Beltenebros held his shield over him till he got to horse again, for the wound was slight by which Urganda's prophecy had come true.

The king's banner had gone down, but the knight in silver was as a standard for all who still lived to fight on his side. Again and again he sped so recklessly into the thick of the foe that every moment Lisuarte feared to see his champion trampled in the dust. But Beltenebros seemed to bear a charmed life as he hurled down all that stood against him and gave their horses to dismounted knights of his own party. What inflamed him to put forth his full strength was the sight of his brother Galaor stretched upon a heap of the dead and wounded. Then over all the clang and clamour rang out his warcry:

"Gaul! Gaul! I am Amadis!"

"Amadis! Amadis!" was the cry echoed from both sides, here raised with exultation, there with dismay.

At the sound of that well-known voice the British knights took fresh heart to know that their hero was in the field. Round him they rallied for a last charge that drove the foemen to rout, scared by his very name. They fled for their ships, chased and slaughtered on land, or drowned in the water before they could get on board. There was nothing now to do but to tend the wounded, and gather up the bodies of the slain.

"Thus then hath Beltenebros lost name and fame!" cried the astonished king, when that unknown knight knelt before him, with visor raised, and was seen to be no other than Amadis, come back as from the dead.

Right heartily Lisuarte thanked him to whom, under one or another name, he owed the destruction of his enemies. But there was no pride or joy in the good knight's prowess like his lady's, who vowed that never again would she mistrust a love as steadfast as his valour. So leave we this happy pair, looking forward to the day when Amadis should lead Oriana through the Arch of True Lovers to take her place in the Forbidden Chamber as his happy bride.

ESPLANDIAN

I

THE wanderings and trials of Amadis de Gaul seemed at last to be at an end. Reconciled to his father-in-law, King Lisuarte of Great Britain, after a feud stirred up between them that should have been friends, and triumphant over his enemies, he now ruled in the Firm Island, publicly united to the incomparable princess, Oriana, who had long in secret been his bride. Archalaus, that wicked enchanter and implacable foe of his house, lay a prisoner, condemned to brood in solitary rage over idle schemes of evil.

But the sky of their happiness was not long unclouded for Amadis and Oriana. One day they were walking together on the shore, when a veiled woman in long black robes came to throw herself at their feet.

"My lord," she cried with a lamentable voice, "have pity on my unhappy lot! Never, they say, did lady appeal in vain to your generosity. No, sir, I will not rise from my knees till you have granted me a boon! And you, madam, do not fear; I seek nothing of your husband which will take him from your side. The gift is one within his power to grant by a single word, and I beseech you, by your love for him, to join your entreaties to mine that he will not deny me the favour I desire."

Oriana's tender heart was moved by the tears of this

afflicted lady. She joined in requesting Amadis to fulfil her petition, for which he, in his courtesy, needed little beseeching.

"Rise, madam," he said, taking her by the hand. "The boon you demand of me is already granted."

Then the lady rose, drew aside her black veil, and exclaimed exultingly:

"Amadis, do you know me? I am the wife of Archalaus, and my demand is that you let him go free."

Amadis and Oriana might well be indignant at the cunning and audacity with which this woman had beguiled them into granting her request. But the knight had promised, and his word was sacred.

"Follow me," he said, and led the way to the narrow iron cage in which her husband lay fettered.

His gigantic form was bent double; his hair and nails had grown to an enormous length; his eyes gleamed savagely; indeed he looked more like a beast than a man, and his first words showed that the wretch's disposition was not a whit changed.

"Archalaus, how would you thank me if, for the sake of your wife, I were to set you free?"

"By ceaseless hatred and vengeance," hissed out the malignant enchanter, gnashing his teeth, and glaring upon them so as to make Oriana shudder.

Amadis would waste no more time in parleying with this monster. He drew his trembling wife away, with orders that the prisoner should be at once released. This was done; then Archalaus and his companion made haste to leave the palace and to set sail from the shores of the Firm Island.

Its lord could no longer give himself up to enjoyment of the delights of his new abode, bestowed on him as the reward of valour and constancy. In the midst of all its magnificence Amadis was ill at ease, troubled by a presentiment that some evil would ere long come of his generosity. He could scarce look at the face of his beloved Oriana without thinking of what unknown calamity Archalaus might at that moment be preparing for her.

Too true proved his forebodings. Before many days had passed there were gathered together the sovereigns of the neighbouring countries and several of his old companions in arms, come to be present at the ceremony of knighting his son Esplandian. And as they sat at a banquet came news that King Lisuarte had, while hunting in the woods, been ensnared by three damsels and carried away into captivity, but none knew whither. Here could plainly be seen the hand of Archalaus, who as yet durst not strike a blow at Amadis himself, of whose power he had been made so well aware.

The guests hastened to condole with Oriana under her father's misfortune, and willingly offered her the help of their arms. Never had the world seen such a goodly band of knights as met now in that hall, taking earnest counsel for the discovery and deliverance of Lisuarte, when loud cries of wonder were heard without. Forth they ran, sword in hand, and hurried down to the beach, followed by Oriana, leaning on her son Esplandian. What did they behold?

A mountain of fire seemed to be swiftly advancing towards them over the calm surface of the sea; it sent forth neither smoke nor flame, but glowed throughout with a brilliance which dazzled every eye, even at a great distance. If it touched the shore the whole island must be burned to ashes. The heat could already be felt more scorching than that of the noonday sun, when the fiery mass burst open with a terrific crash; the two sides fell hissing into the sea, and disclosed what appeared to be a monstrous green serpent, which cleft the waves with its gleaming wings stretched out like banks of oars. The head of this prodigy stood out of the water higher than the mast of the largest ship, its throat vomiting forth streams of flame and thrilling cries. As it kept approaching, the knights upon the strand, for all their intrepidity, were on the point of drawing back, had the example of Amadis not constrained them to hold their ground.

Their astonishment was still greater when the marvellous thing, now close at hand, was seen to undergo a new transformation. Its wings beat furiously, sending up to the sky clouds of spray, amid which beamed a gilded ship with glistening sails. From stem to stern it was covered with rare flowers and precious gems, and on the snowy deck stood a band of nymphs, surrounding a queenly figure upon a throne of emerald, to fill the air with the music of golden flutes and harps that seemed to waft the stately vessel to shore.

" 'Tis Urganda the Unknown!" cried Amadis, hastening forward to meet his powerful and beneficent protectress, as soon as this recognition released him from the spell of surprise.

It was, indeed, the fairy Urganda. Her wont was to disclose herself under the most strange and often the most hideous forms, which could inspire nothing but terror. But now, coming amidst her friends, she appeared in her natural beauty, as a blooming maiden, uniting all the freshness of spring with all the richness of summer. Amadis and Esplandian gave her their hands to lead her on land; the assembled kings and knights pressed forward to salute her; and she, graciously embracing Oriana, spoke thus:

" Did I not promise that ye should see me again if ever ye were in need of my aid? I am come to let you know that Lisuarte is unharmed, and shall yet be set free. But, valiant and well-tried knights, in vain you will traverse sea and land to discover him; this achievement is reserved for one alone."

"For which of us all?" they cried in one breath.

"For him who is youngest among you, and must now enter upon the career that may prove him worthy of his illustrious birth."

"For me?" cried young Esplandian, starting forth from his mother's side with sparkling eyes.

Urganda smiled and beckoned to the fairy crew. Straightway her damsels began to play so marvellously upon their instruments that the sweet sounds fell like a spell upon the ears of all who heard. Their eyes softly closed; they gave themselves up to the entrancing music, and insensibly they sank into a deep sleep.

It was hours before they awoke. Urganda had sailed away, and no trace of the wonderful *Green Serpent* was to be seen on the horizon. Esplandian had gone from among them. In the hand of Amadis was a scroll bearing these words:

"Do you, kings and heroes, return to your own countries to dwell there in repose, leaving glory and the prize of arms to those who begin to climb the changeable round of Fortune, and contenting yourselves with the favour which she has hitherto shown you. And thou, Amadis of Gaul, who hast conquered so many fierce knights and cruel giants, let the honours already gained suffice thee; now taste the sweets and bitters of royal rule, and learn to be diligent in great affairs, as in thy young years thou hast so long and so faithfully done the duties of a knight errant. Rest henceforth in peace, knowing that a scion of thy race shall never be wanting to perpetuate thy renown! I have said. Too often have I proved my goodwill towards thee and thine that thou shouldst hesitate to trust thy unfailing friend

"URGANDA THE UNKNOWN".

II

Esplandian had been carried off upon the deck of the *Green Serpent*. To the youth it seemed as if the music bore him away in a delicious dream, and when he awoke he found himself alone, lying upon the shore of an island in the midst of the ocean.

He rose and looked around him. The island was nothing but a high, bare rock, rising steeply from the waves, and crowned by the ruins of a vast tower. There was no sign of life or vegetation upon its craggy sides, and no other land could be seen across the calm surface of the sea, nor was any sound heard in that solitude; even the water lapped silently upon the stony edge. It was a place to try the spirit of the bravest, but Esplandian did not fear. He felt certain that this was the first step in a glorious career of adventures to which his destiny was about to lead him, and his heart beat high as he began to climb the rock, making towards the ruined tower.

The way was long and steep, and it seemed as if he should never reach that tower to which the young knight toiled on undaunted. He found himself clad from head to foot in new and brilliant armour, yet without sword or other weapon; and before long he was aware of hissings and growlings within the deep caverns of the rocks, which told that there might be fierce beasts to be encountered. Still he turned not back. The rays of the noonday sun beat upon him till he had almost fainted from the heat, and often he was forced to halt and take breath; then, looking down, he saw that he had mounted to a dizzy height, while the summit appeared ever nearer the clouds. But, after hours of this laborious journeying, he stood at last upon the rocky platform from which rose the crumbling ruins of the tower, and amidst them a little temple of Hercules, which he now perceived for the first time.

This temple was one solid mass of granite, without window or other opening. Walls and roof were polished like a mirror, and there was no trace of chisel or mortar upon the smooth surface, which reflected back the sun so brightly as for a time to dazzle Esplandian's eyes. The entrance was by a double door, likewise of granite, the two sides of which were firmly closed by a great sword buried to its jewel-studded hilt in the thick stone. It seemed as if no mortal strength could force open that door or withdraw the blade that barred it.

Wellnigh exhausted, the youth advanced slowly towards the entrance of the temple. At the sight of the sparkling hilt he forgot his fatigue, and sprang eagerly forward with outstretched hand. But before he could reach it a dreadful din was heard echoing throughout the ruins, and an enormous dragon rushed forth.

Esplandian had scarce time to mark its red eyes and grizzly scales. In an instant it was upon him, weaponless as he was, hurling him to the ground, and winding its coils round his body. Half-choked, he struggled in the loathsome embrace, while the monster endeavoured in vain to tear his armour with its sharp claws. In vain, too, he tried to free himself; but the son of Amadis was no easy prey. He clung to its wings, he dug his nails into the flesh, he pulled it down with all his might; man and monster rolled upon the rock in desperate wrestle; he dragged it towards the door of the temple, and despair gave him energy to lay his hand on the hilt of the sword. To his joy the blade started out at the first touch, and with all the strength left him he drove it into the dragon's throat. At the same moment the gates of the temple flew open with a crash, and all the island shook as if an earthquake were upheaving it. So terrible was the commotion that, as he felt the dragon's grasp relax, his brain spun round, and he staggered to his feet only to fall senseless on the rock.

When he came to himself the shades of night had fallen, and the pale light of the rising moon showed the hideous form of the dragon lying motionless by his side. The temple was open, its interior brilliantly illuminated. He stepped across the threshold, and saw that the light came from a tomb in the centre, which shone with a splendour like that of the sun. Upon this tomb couched a gold lion, that in its claws held a rich scabbard, and before it was an inscription in letters of fire:

" *The sheath of the sword that can be drawn forth by none but him who is destined to surpass the renown of all knights now living*".

Esplandian eagerly laid his hand upon the sheath, which yielded to him as lightly as the sword had done. He could not now doubt his high destiny and the protection of the sage Urganda, and would not delay an hour in proceeding on the perilous adventure reserved for him.

He left the temple, the heavy doors of which closed behind him with a sound like thunder, and took his way down the side of the rock, following the same path by which he had ascended. In his hand he bore the drawn blade, which flashed so brightly as to guide his footsteps and light up the crevices on either side. He saw how they swarmed with venomous reptiles, which, now that the darkness had come on, stole forth and would have assailed him, but at the glare of the marvellous sword they fled back into their holes, and the youth went on unharmed, though all the air was filled with the angry hissing of the foul creatures, and he could feel their hot breath at every step.

The descent seemed as short as the ascent had been long. A few minutes brought him down to the edge of the sea, where he found a skiff moored, and in it an old man clad in uncouth garb.

"Who are you, and what do you here?" asked Esplandian; but the old man did not open his lips. By signs he gave the knight to understand that he was dumb, and in the same fashion invited him to enter the skiff.

As Esplandian stepped on board, the mute seized the oars, and pushed off the frail vessel, which shot forth like an arrow into the open sea.

III

The little bark carried the young knight and his dumb companion safely across the ocean, and at last brought them in sight of a rugged country covered with woods. Towards this the skiff was turned, and no sooner had Esplandian leaped on shore than it sped away, leaving him alone at the foot of a mountain, on which might be seen a great castle, fortified with strong walls and tall towers.

The youth could not think that chance alone had brought him to this spot. Full of confidence in the wise Urganda, and believing himself invincible with his magic sword, he followed the coast, seeking carefully among the rocks for a path which might lead him to the castle. After wandering for an hour he came upon a little hermitage, surmounted by a cross, and ran forward to find the inhabitant of this retreat.

The hermit was coming from a fountain which bubbled from the ground in the wood behind his hut. As he issued from the wood he was surprised to see an armed knight, who saluted him in his own language, and, kneeling before him, asked his blessing.

"For long," said he, "no inhabitant of this heathen land hath saluted me thus. Your speech, your arms, show you from the realm of King Lisuarte, like myself. But say, how come you here, where your life and liberty are in such danger?"

"Holy father, fear not for me," replied Esplandian. "I can punish whoever dares to attack me. It is fate that brings me here, and I burn with impatience to know what achievement it has decreed for me."

Then, believing that he might trust the hermit fully, he related to him what had happened on the Firm Island, how Archalaus had been set free, and how King Lisuarte had been entrapped and carried off.

"Alas," cried the old man, "your tale is but too true! You are now near the wicked enchanter's stronghold, to which yesterday he returned, and brought with him a captive, who is rumoured to be a great prince. This may be no other than the King of Great Britain."

"Would, then, that the sun were not near its setting! But to-morrow I will deliver him."

"My son," said the hermit, looking kindly on his youth and his comeliness, "beware of risking an enterprise so much above your strength. This castle, named the Forbidden Mountain, is wellnigh inaccessible, and the giants who guard it would suffice to put a whole army to flight. Besides, should this prisoner prove not to be Lisuarte, why would you imperil yourself for the sake of an unknown?"

"It is enough that he be an unfortunate prince: his

need and the laws of knighthood call me to his aid. Grant me only shelter for one night, and to-morrow at daybreak show me a path that will lead me to that robber's gates."

The hermit no longer attempted to dissuade this high-spirited stripling. He seized him by the hand, bid him welcome to his humble retreat, and shared with him his frugal provisions.

While Esplandian lay down to rest, the good old man spent the night in prayers for his success. At daybreak he awoke his guest, aided him to arm, and conducted him to a path cut out of the rock, by which alone the castle of Archalaus could be reached. There he took leave of the youth, giving him his blessing, and embracing him with tears, as one he scarce hoped to see again.

With a light heart Esplandian sprang up the steps that by a winding ascent led him to the brow of the mountain, where stood the grim castle, on one side hanging over the sea, and on the other enclosed by a deep and broad moat. A narrow bridge crossed it and led to the heavy iron door, which appeared to be the only entrance. Before this door was posted a gigantic sentinel, who advanced towards Esplandian with uplifted axe, shouting to him to give up his sword if he cared to escape death.

"It would be more to the purpose," replied Esplandian, "if you were to offer to lead me to your master, armed as I am. Go on; I am ready to follow."

"Ah, ah!" said the giant. "So you would play the babbler. Well, I am sorry to spoil your arms; they are new and handsome. For the last time: Are you willing to give them up peaceably? Then perhaps I may allow you the honour of serving me."

Without another word Esplandian impatiently rushed

upon him. The giant swung round his axe and brought it down, but the young knight caught the blow upon his shield.

"You should love well the shield that hast saved you from such a stroke!" cried the giant, and raised his ponderous weapon for another; but, before he could deliver it, Esplandian drove the magic blade through his armour and pierced him from side to side, leaping back to escape the torrent of blood which gushed from the wound.

With his last breath the fallen sentinel raised a cry of alarm; and as Esplandian sprang over his body, to rush through the gate sword in hand, he found himself confronted by a taller giant in green armour.

"Ah, wretch!" he cried in a voice of thunder. "How could the redoubtable Argantes have fallen under the arm of such a puny creature?"

"You shall know anon!" retorted the knight, as the portcullis crashed down behind him, and he found himself alone in the castle of the enemy, with no hope of escape but in victory. He ran towards the giant, who came on no less hotly, and the combat began with the utmost fury on either side. As the green armour reddened under the magic steel its wearer raged aloud against his foe Urganda; and Esplandian's heart thrilled to know that he had now to do with no less an adversary than Archalaus himself.

"Perfidious enchanter," he cried, with a stroke at every word, "learn that it is the son of Amadis whom heaven has sent to punish thy crimes!"

"Would that he were here himself! But at least on thee can I avenge myself for the long and harsh captivity which thy father forced me to undergo."

With this he whirled round his sword with both hands; but the mighty blow only cleft the air, for

Esplandian leapt aside, and in his turn smote the enchanter so surely that, uttering roars of pain, he reeled towards the archway which opened into the next court. The young knight followed hard upon him. Archalaus struck wildly in the air, and could not parry the keen point. Again and again it pierced the stout armour, till the enchanter fell expiring in his blood before the eyes of the people of the castle, as they brought forth chains to bind that audacious stranger.

"Furion! Furion!" Archalaus cried on his nephew, and a young giant, unarmed, ran up in time to unlace his casque and to receive his last words:

"Avenge my death upon Amadis and all his race!"

Esplandian, the generous, now lowered the point of his sword and drew back a few paces, unwilling to follow up his victory against an enemy whom he saw to be without defence. But he might not sheathe his blade. Furion, as soon as sure that his uncle was dead, hurried back into the hall, calling out for his arms to be brought to him. Esplandian did not attempt to pursue, but at the sight of an aged lady he took to be the mistress of the castle he advanced and addressed her respectfully as she came wringing her hands.

"It grieves me, madam, that those whose fate you lament have forced me to combat and put them to death. I do not know where I am, but I cannot doubt that a supernatural power has led me here to deliver a great king who is confined in your dungeons. Restore him to liberty and I will cease to trouble the place of your abode."

"Fool!" she exclaimed, kneeling by the body of her brother. "I hope yet to see you in a more pitiable case than even that king. The blood which you have shed calls out for your own. Know that Arcabone, mother

of Argantes and Furion, fears not the race of Amadis
as she hates it!"

Esplandian did not deign to reply to the furious
woman, and he passed into the next court to escape
her reproaches. Here a door was thrown open, whence
Furion issued forth covered with glittering armour, and
holding an enormous scimitar in his hand. The first
thing he did was to call his mother, and, kneeling before
her, he said:

"Soon shall you rejoice to see my uncle avenged.
But as I am determined that my arm alone shall sacrifice
this rash intruder, let me forbid that anyone enter this
court till the combat be ended."

With his own hand Furion then shut all the en-
trances, leaving open only the archway, from which his
mother might watch the fight; and Esplandian courteously
waited till these preparations were made. Then the two
adversaries flew at each other, and all the castle rang with
the clash of their weapons.

The young giant, who was at least eight feet high,
seemed like to have the advantage in the struggle; but
the armour which Esplandian had received from Urganda
resisted the most terrible blows, while the magic sword
shore through Furion's mail as if it had been silk, so
that his blood soon reddened the white pavement of the
court. He began to give ground, and still Esplandian,
unhurt and untired, followed him, till Arcabone trembled
for her son. She would have rushed forth to separate
the combatants, when to her horror and despair she saw
that it was too late. The mortal blow had been struck.
The boastful Furion gave one great cry, and fell lifeless
at the feet of his opponent.

At this the mother fainted away, and her damsels
came out to bear her into the castle. Esplandian, his

mind always set on the deliverance of Lisuarte, followed them at a little distance; but, respecting a mother's grief, halted upon the threshold till she should have recovered her senses.

"Cruel!" she cried, when she opened her eyes and saw him standing without all covered with the blood of her sons; "cruel knight, do you seek to put an end to the life which you have made miserable? What would you of me? I will give up my treasures and all the wealth of the castle."

"Nay, madam," replied Esplandian, "I seek nothing that is yours, and it grieves me to have caused your tears to flow; but release straightway the king whom you hold here in prison, and resist no longer the will of fate."

"Come hither, then," cried the treacherous enchantress. "I am ready to deliver thee the key of his prison."

Thus summoned, Esplandian stepped over the threshold. An enchantment had been laid upon it, so that no stranger could cross without falling senseless on the ground, and it was trusting to this spell that Arcabone had invited him to enter. But she knew not that the marvellous sword held him who bore it free from every enchantment. Without faltering, Esplandian passed over the charmed spot, and approached her fearlessly. Sore was her dismay to see that her wicked arts had no power over him.

"Ah, thou hast triumphed!" she cried; "or, rather, the power of my old enemy Urganda triumphs in thee! So be it! Follow me, and thyself shall break the chains of him whose captivity has cost me so dear."

With this, bidding her attendants remain, she led the way to a damp, slippery staircase, which brought them into a vast subterranean vault. Esplandian followed her cautiously along the tortuous windings of this gloomy place. Here, indeed, she might willingly have profited by the darkness to attempt some new treachery; but Esplandian's luminous steel lit up all the vault, so that, as plainly as in daylight, he saw the dripping walls and the floor strewn with bones, and the dagger which the enchantress had half drawn from her bosom. The light of this wondrous blade took away all her hope; she no longer tried to wreak her vengeance upon the knight, but led him straight to the cell where the unfortunate Lisuarte lay expecting and desiring nothing but death to end his sorrows.

"Who comes here to mock my misery?" he murmured, as the blaze of the sword burst upon him to dazzle his old eyes.

"One who in your cause, sire, would gladly shed half the blood he owes to you."

" 'Tis the voice of Esplandian!" cried the old king, stretching out his chained hands, and his grandson fell upon his neck, while Arcabone, unable for rage to witness the triumph of her enemies, hurried away to seek some champion who might yet discomfit this victorious knight.

IV

The joy may be imagined with which these two kinsmen now embraced each other. Esplandian hastened to relieve his grandsire from the enchanter's chains, which fell off like threads at the touch of the magic sword. Lisuarte thanked heaven for his deliverance, and wondered to hear how so young a scion of his house had overthrown those redoubtable giants. Then, as they eagerly conversed, communicating to each other what had befallen them since they parted on the Firm Island, a great noise of shouting was heard above, which reminded them that it was not well to tarry in this perilous part of the castle.

Esplandian took the old king's hand, leading him through the dark windings of the vault and up the broken stairs, till they came out into the light of day. They now found themselves in a hall the windows of which looked over the sea, where a large fleet of vessels had just cast anchor below the castle. This was the fleet of Matroco, the eldest of the sons of Arcabone. He had been absent on a piratical excursion to the neighbouring coast, and now returned to hear of his kinsmen's fate. With enormous strides he was hastening towards the gate of the castle, and Esplandian went down to await him in the court where Furion still lay bathed in his blood.

This Matroco was the tallest and strongest of his family, more courteous too than his brethren. A terrible outcry he raised when he found Argantes lying lifeless in the first doorway. What, then, was his rage and grief to see a little farther on the corpse of Archalaus! And he had scarcely shed a few tears over it before his mother ran up to show the body of his youngest brother in the next court.

"Is this thy work?" he cried, hurrying towards Esplandian, who awaited him with drawn sword. "Ah, would thou hadst more lives than one, that thou mightst pay me fully for all I have lost!"

But now Arcabone, wrath and fear struggling in her mind, gave way to womanly weakness, and threw herself before him with tearful entreaties.

"Oh, dearest of my sons, do not expose thyself in combat with the destroyer of our race, but think that thou alone art left me to console and protect my age!"

"Madam," replied Matroco, gently putting her aside,

"those whom you and I lament have died like brave men; their courage, if not my own, forbids me to shrink before their conqueror."

"Beware what you do," said Esplandian, willing to spare him. "Give heed to the tears of your mother. They that have fallen beneath my sword sought their own fate in attacking me. My adventure is achieved, since I have here the king whom I came to deliver. Take back, then, this castle; I abandon it to you freely. All that I require of you is to repent of the cruelty and oppression which have made your race so hateful, and to embrace the true faith, in the strength of which I have come here to punish Archalaus, to deliver Lisuarte, and to enlighten your heathen mind."

"I do not blame you," replied Matroco. "You have borne yourself like a brave knight, but you must not think to overcome me by empty words. Honour bids me avenge my kinsmen, and it is not at any man's bidding that I will change my faith. Shall a warrior of my might, hitherto victor in every combat, submit without a blow? No; it is for our arms to decide between us!"

With that he brandished his sword and ran upon Esplandian, who quickly put himself on his guard, and once more the clash of steel resounded from the walls.

Their first blows were more terrible than any which had been struck that day. Both were received upon their shields; but while Esplandian's was not even dinted, the magic sword carried away half the buckler of Matroco. No words can describe the fury of the combat which now ensued, and which lasted for more than an hour before either champion would yield an inch. Breathless and bleeding, they fought on, so that the onlookers were amazed, and it seemed as if there could be no end to the

battle till both fighters fell lifeless. In spite of the goodness of Esplandian's armour he was hurt in several
places; but Matroco was covered with wounds from head
to foot, his mail strewn in shreds all around. For the
first time he drew back, and leaned heavily upon the
hilt of his sword. The strength of that giant brood, men
said, was wont to be at its height at midday, and thereafter to decrease as the sun sank towards the west. It
was now long past noon, and the last nephew of Archalaus began to fear that his hour had come. Esplandian
was still full of heart and strength, but his generosity
forbade him to press upon the enfeebled foe.

"Pagan, see how your evil deeds are visited upon
you through my hands!" he exclaimed. "It is not to
me that I conjure you to submit yourself, but to heaven,
which you have too long offended by your pride and
perverseness."

Matroco trembled and sank upon his knees, crying:
"Christian, thou hast conquered! I repent me of all
I have done, and I would fain be instructed in thy
faith."

Joyful to see the change wrought in the giant's disposition, Esplandian held out to Matroco the hilt of his
sword, and said:

"Ah, worthy foe, take now my sword as a sign of the
victory thou hast gained over thyself!"

To this Matroco replied by desiring that a priest
should at once be sent for to receive his confession and
admit him into the true Church. He also gave orders
for the release of the Christian prisoners on board his
fleet. Lisuarte and Esplandian, perceiving that his
wounds could not be stanched, and that he was growing weaker every moment, took him up in their arms
to carry him gently into the chamber of his mother,

who followed, rending the air with her cries. The knight forgot his own wounds in attending to those of his enemy, but it was too plain that they were mortal.

The hermit arrived in haste, and, while he was shriving the wounded man, Esplandian went out to give directions for the burial of the slain. Before long he was summoned back by a bitter lamentation raised round the bed of Matroco, and entered in time to see the penitent giant expire with eyes lifted to heaven. His last words were to implore the holy man's blessing.

Lisuarte knelt by the bedside and wept to see this heathen come to such an edifying end. The old Arcabone, out of her senses with grief, as she beheld the death of her last and dearest son, snatched up his sword, and would have struck the king with all the strength of madness and despair. Esplandian seized her hand, not a moment too soon; they drew her away, and the hermit vainly endeavoured to calm her. With a piercing scream she rushed to the window, then, before a hand could be laid upon her, had hurled herself over the precipice into the waves rolling far beneath at its base.

The mariners of Matroco's fleet, seeing her fall, were launching their skiffs to rescue her. But now upon the horizon appeared a terrible mass of fire; already the beating of the gigantic wings could be heard; and the *Green Serpent*, Urganda's mysterious vessel, came swiftly towards the Forbidden Mountain. At the sight the sailors were horror-struck. Some hastened to seek safety on land, some cut the cables of their ships and tried to sail away. The whole fleet scattered like minnows at the approach of a strange monster, and the body of Arcabone floated lifeless and unheeded upon the water.

Thus perished all the race of Archalaus!

THE DRAGON OF RHODES

In old days, when the island of Rhodes was held by the Knights of St. John, a certain part of it suffered grievously from the depredations of a dragon, or, as some say, a gigantic serpent. The haunt of this monster was a rocky mountain overhanging a dismal marsh, and crowned by a chapel to which pilgrims came from far and near. Issuing forth morning and evening out of a dark cave in the side of the mountain, it not only made daily havoc among cattle and horses but often devoured the luckless country people and pilgrims on their way to the shrine, who were unable to fly for terror at the very sight of its dreadful fangs, or fell senseless to the ground overpowered by the venom of its fiery breath. One after another the bravest and most famous members of the order went forth against the dragon, but were never more seen by mortal man. The swords and spears that scattered Saracen hosts proved powerless upon the impenetrable scales of this creature. And when six of his best knights had thus been lost, the Grand Master gave command that no other should undertake such a fatal enterprise.

But in spite of this prohibition many still hoped that the slaughter of the dragon might be achieved, and none more earnestly than Theodore, a knight of Provence, youngest of the order, as yet untried in arms, but burning to do some deed of prowess that might emulate the old glories of his brotherhood. Many a time this youth watched the dragon from afar, and chafed against the command which forbade him to try his maiden sword upon its grisly scales. His mind was constantly filled with one thought; by night he dreamed of the combat, and by day he found no pleasure in life so long as this monster still ravaged the land. By dint of watching it, and considering how it could be overcome, he conceived a plan by which he believed that he might be more successful than his unfortunate companions in arms; and this plan he long revolved in his breast, communicating it to no one, lest some better-tried knight should be chosen to put it in execution. At last he could no longer restrain his impatient ardour; he resolved to kill the dragon or die in the attempt, disregarding the orders of the Grand Master and his own oath of obedience. He at once sought leave to return to his native country, and, obtaining it, embarked for France, where he spent three months in secretly preparing to carry out his plan, which brought skill to the aid of courage.

He found out a cunning artificer, and employed him to make a wooden figure which should exactly resemble the dragon in size, colour, and shape. Then he procured two bull dogs of the best breed, which he carefully trained to throw themselves upon this figure and hold it fast with their obstinate fangs, while he exercised his horse in riding boldly up to it; and when, by a mechanical contrivance, it was made to rear in the air, he aimed his lance with firm eye at the belly, the only part of its body unprotected by scales. The very likeness of the creature was so horrible that at first both horse and dogs would turn away from it in trembling; but, after several efforts, Theodore was able to bring them to face it, so in time they became accustomed to the appearance of the counterfeit monster. When they were thoroughly practised in the task which he designed for them, he left home as secretly as he had come, setting sail for Rhodes with his horse, his dogs, and two faithful squires.

They landed on the island at nightfall, and found the country people lamenting the death of some shepherds, who had that evening been slain and mangled by the dragon as they were driving their flocks home from the marsh. Hearing this, Theodore vowed that another sun should not set before he had done what in him lay to rid the country of this pest. Forthwith he took his way up the mountain with his attendants, and at midnight reached a little chapel which crowned its summit. While his squires watched without, he spent the night before the altar, recommending himself to the favour of heaven; then, as the dawn began to appear, he rose from his knees and equipped himself for the combat with a good heart. From head to foot he was encased in shining steel, over which he wore a red surcoat, embroidered before and behind with the silver cross of the order; his sword and spear were weapons of proof made by the best smith of his native land. When the beams of the rising sun touched the mountain, Sir Theodore sprang upon his gallant steed to ride towards the haunt of the dragon.

Before long he came in sight of the cave's mouth, and was aware of the monster lying rolled up on the ground as if asleep. At the hideous sight the hounds began to bay, whereon the dragon awoke, uncoiling its scaly folds, and made the rocks re-echo with its outcry. Then Theodore turned to his squires and said words that might be his last:

" Bide you here and watch; and if I fall, return home without delay, letting no man know my fate."

With this he drove the spurs into his horse, and rode

boldly forward, as the dragon rushed forth to meet him with dreadful din, shaking the ground with its tread, and breathing fire and venom from its gaping jaws. The knight hurled his spear. It struck the thick scales and rebounded as if it were but a twig. Undaunted, he drew his sword and urged on his steed; but the poor beast, terrified by the unaccustomed uproar and by the scorching breath of the dragon, swerved and turned in spite of all its rider's efforts. The monster was upon him. Nimbly he leapt from his saddle, and with his good sword dealt blow after blow. Alas, it might as well have been a straw which he held in his hand! With one stroke of its tail the dragon felled him to the earth, and the shuddering squires already gave up their master for lost, while his horse wildly scoured the plain.

But the faithful dogs had not so ill learned their lesson. Now they fell upon the dragon, seized it with their fangs from beneath, and all its furious struggles and horrible cries could not force them to loose their hold. The monster, maddened with the pain, reared its huge body in the air at the same moment that Theodore recovered himself and rose to his feet. With all his might he drove his sword to the hilt in its white belly, unprotected by scales such as covered its back. The squires uttered an exclamation, and what was their joy to see the hideous beast sinking on the ground! The point had reached its heart; a deluge of black blood gushed forth from the wound; the dragon gave one last scream, so horrible that men heard and trembled for leagues around; then it fell upon its conqueror, crushing him to the ground with the weight of its carcass.

The knight's attendants ran eagerly up, hastening to drag their master from beneath the dragon's body, which the bull dogs still held in their grip. He was stunned and bruised, but otherwise unhurt. When they had unlaced his helm and poured water on his face, he came to his senses; then, as soon as his eyes fell on the dead dragon, no other cordial was needed to bring back his strength. At last his hope was fulfilled in freeing Rhodes from this hitherto invulnerable enemy. Well might the youth be proud of such a deed, which so many old and famous knights had failed to do!

Scarcely was the dragon dead before rumours of the conflict began to fly over the island, and from all sides the people came flocking to learn if the good news were true. When they saw with their own eyes that they had no longer anything to fear from the monster, they could not restrain their joy and gratitude. Being rested and refreshed, Sir Theodore rode towards the city amid an increasing throng that struggled and pressed to come near him, and followed by his squires, drawing the dead body of the dragon behind them as proof of their master's prowess. When they came near the walls another crowd poured forth to meet them, eager to see the won-drous sight and welcome the victor. The whole popula-tion hurried out-of-doors to behold his triumphal entry, every voice raised in acclamation as the young knight rode through the streets and made his way among the shouting thousands to the council chamber, in which the knights of the order were wont to assemble.

Here were already gathered the noble brotherhood in their black hooded robes, with no other ornament than crosses of white linen. On either side of the stern Grand Master they took their places, and into their presence was brought the young knight, with a flush on his brow, as the rejoicing crowd, which surged into the hall behind him, proclaimed his victory and made the vaulted roof ring with his name, every eye fixed upon him in admiration and pride.

"Peace!" rang forth the deep voice of the Grand Master, and in a moment all was still. "We know your tale. The dragon is slain. 'Tis well."

Now the looks of all were turned upon him, and men waited to hear from his lips what should be the guerdon of this fearless champion.

"Rash youth," spoke the venerable Master, "thou hast indeed proved thy courage, but thou hast transgressed my commands! Say, what is the highest duty of our sacred order? Knowest thou to which virtue, above all, our vows have bound thee?"

The blood fled from Theodore's face as he replied, in a low voice that thrilled in every ear:

"Obedience."

"Even so. And what must be his doom who comes proudly to tell us that he has set his vows at naught?"

The youth bowed his head, making no answer. A murmur ran through the hall as if imploring pity. Once more the Grand Master commanded silence with upraised hand, and with knitted brow and sorrowful voice addressed the offender:

"Thy courage is but that of the infidel; nay, in this thou art no nobler than the monster thou hast slain. In thine own breast dwells the fellest foe, against whom it beseemed thee to make lifelong war. Better that every one of our brethren should have perished before the dragon than that one should have broken the bond by which, on the holy soil where our Lord gave us the example of humility, we have been consecrated to serve Him in conquering our rebellious hearts. He who forgets his vow and follows his own will in the hope of vain glory is no longer worthy to be a soldier of the cross.   We spare thy life, which thou hast not spared at our bidding.   But strip off these sacred emblems, these honourable arms.   Depart to our deepest dungeon, and be thy name forgotten from this hour."

All were silent.   Many a knight would have fallen on his knees to beg for mercy to the brave youth, but none durst question the decree of their chief.   Theodore himself prepared, without a word, to submit to his sentence.   Meekly he disrobed himself and put off his shining armour.   He took one last look at his sword, still stained with the dragon's blood, then laid all before the Grand Master's feet, and, reverently kissing the old man's hand, turned to depart from his presence.

With folded arms and downcast looks he moved towards the door, and the crowd, murmuring for pity, made way to let him pass.   The Master followed him with kindling eye; then, ere he was gone, a voice of joy and triumph rang through the hall.

"Return, my son!   'Tis enough: once more thou art worthy to wear the cross.   Thou hast conquered thyself, and mayst now receive the honour due to him who has vanquished the dragon.   Take back the sword that has earned thee a place henceforth among our bravest and best."

Before the eyes of all the old man fell on the youth's neck and embraced him with tears.   Now was Theodore's triumph fulfilled.   His fellow knights might crowd round to take his hand and praise him for his bravery.   Once more the people raised a shout of joy, and his name was on every lip.   The whole city spent the day in feasting and rejoicing.

Long was that day remembered in Rhodes.   They set up the head of the dragon above the city gates, where all that came thither might see and thank heaven for this deliverance. In time Sir Theodore became himself Grand Master of the Order, and his age was graced by wisdom as in youth he had proved his courage. When he died, full of years and honours, there was graven upon his tomb: HERE LIES THE VANQUISHER OF THE DRAGON.

PIERRE OF PROVENCE

I

An old Count of Provence and his lady had left to them
but one son, their joy and pride, and the hope of their
subjects, since he was the last of a well-loved race. This
boy, Pierre by name, grew up at home to the age at
which youths desire to go out into the world. When he
had been dubbed knight, and had already distinguished
himself among the chivalry of Provence, he chanced to
see a picture of Magdelona, the daughter of the King
of Naples. From that day he longed to see the lady
herself, and took no pleasure in life and gave his parents
no rest till he had gained their consent to going abroad
like other knights in search of adventures. To them he
spoke of winning honour at royal tournaments, but in
his heart it was the lists of love where he burned to try
his chance. Sorely unwilling they agreed in the end to
his wishes, and, having furnished him for the journey
as became his rank, sent him forth with many tears and
good counsels.

"Go then, but promise to return within a year," were
his mother's last words, as she placed a costly ring on his
finger, her parting gift.

Pierre promised and rode gaily away, thinking little
of his elders' sorrow, but much of glory and more of
Magdelona; such is the mind of youth.

He went straight to Naples, and arrived in time to take part in a great tournament which the king was holding to celebrate his daughter's birthday. Pierre eagerly presented himself in the lists, bearing as his cognizance a device of crossed silver keys in honour of his patron saint. Then so well did his strength and skill serve him that he was by all adjudged worthy of the prize of the tournament.

Therewith he won what in his eyes was the richest prize that any knight could desire. At first sight he told himself that the picture had deceived him, for the princess was a hundred times more beautiful than it represented her. And she, from the first, cast eyes of no less favour upon this young stranger. Their looks soon betrayed their hearts to each other. From looks they went to words, and from words to vows; and their lives became all bright with the sunshine of pure love.

But while Pierre still kept his happiness a secret, and durst not risk it by letting the King of Naples know his presumption, the emperor's son came to Naples to seek the hand of this great princess. Her parents were well pleased with such a wooer, and would have forced Magdelona to consent to his suit; but how could she listen to it? She had vowed never to wed any but the Knight of the Silver Keys, and they had exchanged pledges, she giving him a gold chain, and he giving her the most precious thing he had, the jewelled ring which his mother placed on his finger at parting.

Troubled by the ceaseless importunities of that unwelcome lover, as well as of her parents, Magdelona found courage to consent when her own knight urged her to fly with him from the kingdom of Naples, leaving all for his sake. At midnight she arose, dressed herself in haste, took her jewels, not forgetting the ring dearer to her than all the rest, and, wrapped in a mantle, stole through the silent halls of the palace. Light as a bird she passed across the garden, and opened a postern gate at which awaited her a knight holding two horses ready.

" Pierre! you are true?" she whispered.

" For ever, dearest!"

One fond embrace they took beneath the shadow of her father's gate; one tearful look she gave to the home where she could no longer be happy; then mounting their horses they galloped away in the moonlight, side by side.

All night the lovers rode swiftly, Sir Pierre on his good steed and Magdelona on a nimble palfrey, so by daybreak they found themselves many leagues from Naples. Yet fearing they might be pursued, the young knight thought well to lie hid through the day, and turned their course towards a wood which the sunrise showed them not far off. Having gained its shelter, he aided the princess to dismount, and let the horses graze, while they sat down on the thick grass beneath the shadow of a tree.

Alone in this solitary place these two had been in no want of endearing speeches to pass away the time. But Magdelona was fatigued by the hasty journey, during the latter part of which Pierre had held her with his strong arm to keep her from falling off the palfrey, she resting her head upon his shoulder. Now, as the heat of the day came on, and her bright eyes began to close for weariness, he strewed on the ground a couch of perfumed branches and soft herbs, rolled up his cloak to serve her as a pillow, and bid her lie down to rest.

" Sleep in peace, dearest," he said, " for be sure that no harm will come to you while I am by."

" Have I not trusted you with all my life?" she said,

thanking him by a smile. Then she lay down, and in
a few minutes was sleeping soundly as a tired child.

Pierre sat on the grass beside her, watching over the
safety of his treasure. Never had she been so dear to
him as now, when he thought of the perils and fatigues
to which this tender princess had exposed herself for
his sake! Never had she looked so beautiful as in this
happy sleep! He could have sat there all day, now
gazing on her sweet face, now listening to the birds
that in the branches overhead seemed to be singing of
hope and joy, now idly counting the links of the gold
chain that she had given him as a pledge of her love.

"Ah!" he exclaimed, "is not this a symbol of the
chain that shall bind my heart for ever while I live?
Nor is this gold purer than our happiness."

Once more he turned to look at his lady. She stirred,
smiling in her sleep, as if from some pleasant dream,
and her mantle fell on one side to let him see a small
bag of red velvet clasped round her neck, but now, as
it chanced, hanging loose from the folds of the dress.
What could be in the pouch which she thus wore near
her heart? He was seized with an irresistible impulse
of curiosity. Stooping over her, he gently unclasped
the bag and opened it. To his joyful surprise, he found
that this talisman, so carefully guarded, was no other
than the ring, his mother's parting gift, which he in turn
had given to Magdelona! He kissed the precious token
again and again, and, replacing it, laid its velvet case on
a mossy stone beside him, while he gazed once more at
her who held it dear for his sake.

"Is there any power on earth that can sunder loves
like ours?" he asked himself; but straightway was he
to learn how little man should reckon upon the abiding
of any earthly joy.

A raven, soaring overhead, had marked the red velvet bag upon the grass, and, taking it perhaps for a piece of flesh, suddenly swooped down upon it. Pierre gave a cry to scare the bird away, but too late. It had snatched up the bag in its beak, and flew off with ring and all, settling upon a tree full in sight. The knight hurried to rescue this precious thing from its grip. The raven at his approach flew away to another tree farther off. He followed it hotly from rock to rock and from bush to bush, always unable to catch it, when it lit from time to time as if to mock him, then took wing again to lead him on, till at last he came to the seashore, where the provoking bird perched itself upon a high point of rock.

Pierre was sorely at a loss; he had come so far from his beloved, and feared that any moment she might wake to find him absent. He shouted and gesticulated at the bird, hoping to make it let go its prize, which, however, it still held fast. Then he picked up a stone and threw it with such close aim that the raven made off, fluttering and croaking, and at the same time let the bag drop into the sea.

Pierre saw the red velvet floating among the waves, but it was far out of his reach when he had hastened down to the water's edge. He could not bear to think that Magdelona should lose this ring while he had undertaken to watch over her; but what was he to do? He had already begun to strip off his clothes, though he could not swim, and the bag was every moment being carried out into deeper and deeper water, when his eye fell upon an old broken skiff which a fisherman had left upon the shore. Joyfully he ran up to it, pushed it into the water, leaped on board, and rowed towards where he had last seen the stolen treasure.

But now he could see it no more, and to his dismay

he found himself embarked on a strong current which, in spite of his utmost efforts, was rapidly bearing him out to sea. Soon a violent wind struck the boat, whirling it faster and farther from the shore. It became quite unmanageable; the rotten oars broke in his hand, the water poured in through the leaky sides, and the frail craft seemed about to sink in the waves which broke over it and tossed it at their will.

Horror and despair fell upon the knight; yet at such a time, with death before his eyes, he had no care for himself.

"Oh," he cried, raising his hands to heaven, "save her and forgive me! What a base, untrue knight am I, who have taken this tender princess from her rich home to abandon her in a wilderness to beasts of prey or still more fierce men! Let me suffer as I have deserved, but pity and preserve her, so true, so innocent, so gentle—shield her from all evil when my arm can no longer protect her!"

II

By this time the flight of the princess had been discovered, and, the Knight of the Silver Keys being also missing, her father was at no loss to guess the truth. He at once sent out armed men to gallop along every road in search of the fugitives, charging them to bring back that knight alive to suffer a punishment of which all the world should hear. His men rode fast and far; for days they scoured the whole country, but to no purpose. Nothing could be heard of Pierre nor of Magdelona, and her parents remained in vain rage and grief over the loss of their daughter, whom they declared worthy of death for her disobedience, while trembling to think that she might indeed be dead.

All their anger must have changed to pity could they have seen poor Magdelona when she woke to find herself alone in the wood. In terror she called for Pierre, but he came not. Then her first thought was that he had deserted her, and this became confirmed when she missed the pouch containing his ring.

"Pierre, Pierre, come back! Wilt thou abandon me, who for thee have sacrificed parents, country, and all? What harm have I done to thee that thou shouldst leave me in this wild place to die a wretched death? Oh, my life and hope, where are those vows to which I listened so rashly? Come back to me, or I am the most miserable maiden upon earth!"

So she cried again and again, running wildly through the wood; but there was no answer save the neighing of their horses. She flew to the spot and found them both still fastened as Pierre had left them. This was a comfort to her, for if he had meant to desert her he would surely have ridden away.

"No," she cried, "he cannot have left me of his own will—how could I thus have distrusted my true knight! But, alas! where is he gone? What adventure has separated us? Is he dead? and, oh, then, that I were dead with him! Pierre! Pierre!"

Once more she ran backwards and forwards, here and there, vainly calling upon her love. She climbed a high tree, but could see nothing except the wild land and the raging sea near by. She went towards the shore—still no trace of Pierre! All the rest of the day she wandered about the wood, without food or drink, and when it grew dark she mounted another tree, among the branches of which she spent a miserable night, tormented by grief, anxiety, and the fear of wild beasts, whose roarings could be heard all round her in the darkness.

Morning came, but Pierre returned not with it. What must this poor princess do? She durst not go home to meet the anger of the king. She could not bear the thought of passing another night in this lonely place. Her lover must have been destroyed by some savage beast, or carried off by her father's men. She could think of nothing but to go out into the wide world to seek him, if he might still be found, or at least to learn news of his fate.

Descending from the tree she came to the place where the horses were fastened, and set them loose.

"Go where you will, since your master is lost to me," she said, stroking them with tears.

Then she took her way through the wood on foot, hardly knowing where she went. Before long she reached the highroad which led to Rome, and there met a poor woman returning home from a pilgrimage. She stopped this woman and asked her to make an exchange of clothes.

"Gracious lady," said the woman in astonishment, "you surely mock me. You are richly clad, and I wear a pilgrim's weeds, to be despised of all men for my sins' sake."

"Dear sister," replied Magdelona, "I pray you do not refuse me; I speak out of my heart, and will freely change with you."

The woman no longer hesitated, but took the rich robe of the princess, while she put on the other's humble gown, and drew the hood over her face so that no one should recognize her.

Thus attired, she fared on towards Rome, meeting by the way a troop of her father's men, who passed her without notice, never thinking that this poor pilgrim could be the princess they sought. It seemed to her that the hand of heaven had sent such woe to punish her disobedience to her parents, and that it behoved her to do penance for that sin. So when she reached the city she took up her abode in a hospital for pilgrims, and there lived in great lowliness, courting pains and privations to which she had been little used. Daily she went to St. Peter's Church to pray for herself and her lost lover with bitter tears. She prayed that they might yet be united in this world or the next, and every day that separated them she vowed to spend in succouring the poor, the sick, and the afflicted. It pleased her to offer her devotion in this church, for the very name was dear to her for the sake of Pierre of Provence.

One day, when leaving the church, she met her uncle, the Duke of Calabria, who had come to Rome in search of her; and though she hid herself behind a pillar, and escaped his eyes, this encounter determined her to seek some foreign land where she might live wholly unknown. She set out, then, for the coast, and embarked on board the first ship ready for sea, which landed her at a small town of Provence near the mouth of the Rhone.

Here she found kindly entertainment in the house of a pious widow, who took pleasure to hear of her pilgrimage to the holy city and of those countries through which she had passed. In return the widow told Magdelona of the land in which she now was, of the good count who ruled Provence with power and justice, how he held his subjects in peace, how kind his lady showed herself to the poor, and how they were both loved by high and low.

"But, alas!" said she, "they live now in sore trouble on account of their only son, who is called Pierre, a noble knight such as few. A year ago he went away on some knightly quest, and has never more been heard of, so his parents believe him to be dead."

As the widow spoke, Magdelona clasped her hands with a cry, and the good woman made sure that this pilgrim had a tender heart to weep so for the sorrow of the bereaved parents. She had not known till now that this was no other than the country of her Pierre; now she thanked Providence for having directed her hither, and resolved to go no farther, but to pass here the rest of her days, devoting herself to good works.

At the mouth of the harbour was a small island, frequented by mariners and merchants. It seemed to Magdelona well fitted for her abode, not only because she had pity on these sea folks, many of whom were put ashore to die uncared for of diseases brought on by their long toilsome voyages, but as hoping through them, as they came from all parts of the world, to hear some news of her Pierre. She had still preserved some costly jewels, which she now sold, and with the money built a hospital on this island.

Here she made welcome unfortunate persons of all nations; she cured the sick, she tended the infirm, she relieved the poor, and consoled the miserable with her gentle words and loving looks, so that they went thankfully away and spoke of her everywhere as nothing less than a saint. Her fame spread far and wide, till it reached the ears of the Count of Provence and his wife, who, coming to reside for a time at one of their castles in this neighbourhood, visited the island, to honour the pilgrim as her pious charity deserved.

They felt a warm friendship for her from the first, and how was the heart of Magdelona stirred to see this good pair, in whose features she well recognized those so deeply engraved on her memory! Yet she forced herself to be calm, and kept her precious secret locked within her breast. Nothing pleased her more than to hear the countess speak of her lost son; they mingled their tears together; and the mother found hope and comfort in the gentle words of that young stranger, whom she already loved as a daughter.

Before long they had both need of comfort. Some fishermen, having caught an enormous fish, brought it as a tribute to their lord, the count. When it came to be cut open in the kitchen of the castle the cook was astonished to find inside its belly a red velvet bag, which he at once carried to his master and mistress. Then, as soon as the countess opened the bag, she uttered a cry of anguish, recognizing the ring which she had given to her Pierre.

"Oh, my son, my son!" she cried. "He is dead—there can be no longer doubt! He has perished in the waves, and I shall never see him more!"

The old count tried to show more firmness, but the tears trickled down his cheeks in spite of himself. He, too, gave up all hope at the sight of this token from the sea. He ordered the rich tapestries of the castle to be taken down, and all the walls to be hung henceforth with black, and the servants obeyed him mournfully, grieving for the fate of their young lord.

The afflicted parents hastened to the island that they might share their sorrow with Magdelona. When she saw the ring she turned pale, and on hearing how it had been found, in her heart she gave up Pierre for lost; yet still she spoke cheerfully, for sorrow had taught her to be strong.

"Dear lady," she said, with eyes shining through their tears, "and you, my lord, do not give way to despair for such a cause. Let this be the ring which you have given to your son, he may yet have lost it or given it away to some other. Life is full of strange chances, but God is always good: trust then in heaven and hope!"

Never had she looked more lovely, more loving. The countess threw her arms round her neck, praying Magdelona to live with them always, taking the place of their lost son. But she sadly told them that it might not be so: her work lay here, and she was under a vow.

So she continued the care of her poor people, while the count and his lady went back to their chief town. But before quitting her they gave orders for a church to be built beside the hospital, and dedicated to St. Peter, as a monument of their lost son. This was done forthwith, and thenceforth whoever went from her cured or relieved Magdelona sought of him for all reward to enter this church and pray that the heir of Provence might yet return to those who loved him.

The foreign pilgrim and her hospital did not fail to be widely spoken of, and from all parts of that region good women came to assist her in this work of hers, which grew from day to day. Many gifts and offerings were made by those who had been cured, as well as by pious and charitable persons visiting the place, so that she was able to enlarge her hospital and increase the number of those who enjoyed its benefits. Among these gifts was a strange one, as might seem—several barrels of salt, which were sent her by the master of a ship touching at the port. They had, in fact, belonged to a certain passenger whom he had been forced to leave on shore; and not knowing how to deal with them honestly, he thought to quiet his conscience by presenting them to the hospital.

Before long, being in need of salt, Magdelona opened one of the barrels. Great was her amazement to find that below a covering of salt it was filled with silver!

She opened another, the contents of which, in like manner, proved to be gold coins. And so with all the barrels, which contained treasures of every kind hidden in salt.

"It is the gift of God!" cried Magdelona, heartily grateful for this blessing, which, as she thought, had thus been sent upon her work of charity.

What would she have said had she known that these riches belonged to none other than him to learn whose fate she would willingly have given all the wealth in the world!

III

Pierre, indeed, was all this time alive, though far away, and no day passed but he thought of and prayed for Magdelona, longing yet hardly hoping to see her again. As his frail boat was sinking in the waves there had borne down upon him a vessel carrying a green flag with the sign of the crescent, so dreaded on these coasts. It was a Saracen pirate, which lowered a boat and rescued him when at the very point of drowning. Brought on board the pirate ship, the rich gold chain he wore and his knightly spurs let the crew know that they had taken no common prize. They treated him well, and, carrying him to Alexandria, sold him to the sultan of that country.

Here Pierre's lot was better than that of most captives. The sultan, his master, took a liking to him and showed him no little favour. He used him more like a friend than a servant, appointing him his chamberlain and loading him with gifts. For his part Pierre tried to repay his master's goodness by faithful and diligent service, since fortune had ordered it so; and, the sultan's goodwill growing from day to day, the young knight became one of the chief persons at the court of Alex-

PIERRE IN THE HANDS OF PIRATES

andria, none more trusted and more honoured. Had he but been willing to abjure his faith, the sultan would have gladly adopted him as heir, so much had this Christian won upon his affections.

But Pierre himself could not be happy, for all these favours. He was ever gazing across the sea, thinking sadly of his native land and wondering how it fared with Magdelona, and with his poor parents who must be mourning him as dead. At times his heart was so heavy that he wished the pirates had left him to drown rather than he should live apart from all that was dear to him. He had much ado often to wear a cheerful countenance before the sultan, who took note that some secret trouble oppressed his favourite, and invited him to disclose it, saying:

"Fear not but I will grant any request you have to make. Often you ask for others; ask now for yourself."

"Great sultan," answered Pierre, with a sigh, "I have but one request and one wish: to go back to whence I came. I must always remember your goodness to me in the years I have served you; yet never can I forget my own country and those who love me there."

"Good friend, speak no more of this!" cried the sultan. "In no country can you find yourself so well loved as here, for I will make you the greatest man in all my dominions."

But Pierre fell on his knees and told him all his story, which touched the sultan's heart. At last, though unwillingly, he agreed to let him go in search of Magdelona, making him only promise to return if he could not find her within a year. Then Pierre's joy and gratitude knew no bounds. He spoke of a good ransom to be paid by his father; but of this the generous sultan would not hear. Nay more, at parting he presented his captive with gold, silver, jewels, garments, and other valuables, enough to make him the richest man in Provence; and they took leave of each other more like father and son than master and slave.

Fearing to be robbed or murdered for the sake of these treasures, Pierre hid them away in barrels which he filled up at the top and the bottom with salt. In the plain garb of a merchant he went down to the port to find a ship bound for Provence. He soon made a bargain with the captain of such a one for the conveyance of himself and his barrels; and next day they set sail with a fair wind. The good ship flew like a bird, yet not fast enough for the impatience of Pierre, who counted each day an age that still separated him from news of those he loved, and spent every hour on deck straining his eyes to catch the first glimpse of the coasts of Christendom.

All prospered with them till they had wellnigh reached the end of their voyage, when they were becalmed off a certain uninhabited island. Here some of the sailors went on shore to fetch fresh water, and Pierre accompanied them. While they were filling their casks, he strayed some way apart, led on by the beauty of the scenery. The brightness of the flowers, the greenness of the grass, the pleasant shade of the trees, the sweet singing of the birds, all charmed him with new force after his tiresome voyage. As wandering through the woods he came to a little valley filled with flowers and blossoms, he was reminded of the place where he had left his Magdelona. This remembrance took possession of him so powerfully that he forgot all else, and spent hour after hour in thinking of her, till, lying down in such a spot as she had made her resting-place on that doleful day, he insensibly fell into a deep sleep.

When he awoke it was evening. Rousing himself, he hurried back towards the shore to rejoin his companions. But now he could not find his way. He ascended a little hill to look around him, and the first sight that met his eyes was the masts of the ship vanishing on the horizon. During his sleep a wind had suddenly sprung up. The sailors had shouted to him in vain, and looked here and there for the missing man. Their captain waited some time; then, his passenger not returning, he had seen nothing for it but to sail without him while the wind still held fair.

Pierre was in despair to know himself thus abandoned. It was not his lost treasures he thought of, but the hope of reaching his own country that had been snatched from him just as it seemed to be already in his grasp. Now he must pine for months, years perhaps, in this lonely place, the charms of which were but a mockery to him so long as he remained in doubt as to her fate of whose beauty he took every lily, every rose, for a token.

All night he kept pacing up and down, making the rocks re-echo his lamentable cries; and by the morning he was lying on the sand of the shore, seized with a raging fever.

Thus he was found, helpless and senseless, by some fishermen who happened to come on shore at that spot. These good people had pity on him and took him away in their boat. Then, as he seemed at the point of death, one of them remembered the hospital of St. Peter and the pious woman by whom he himself had once been cured of a dangerous disease. They agreed to carry the stranger thither, and steered for that island on which could now be seen from far the spire of its newly built church rising like a beacon to guide all the unfortunate to a haven of hope.

Magdelona had just finished the prayers which she
never failed to make night and morning for the accom-
plishment of her heart's dearest wish; she was coming
out of the church when she learned that a new sufferer
had been brought for her care. She hastened to receive
him, as she had done so many others; but at the first
sight of the sick man she stood still, trembling from head
to foot. Fixing her eyes eagerly upon him, she scarcely
heard the fishermen's tale of how they had found him in
this plight. Worn and pale as he was, she knew him
and had almost cried out his name. Yet she mastered
herself so far as to do her usual kindly offices, washing
his hands and feet, placing him in a bed, and giving him
a cordial drink, while he showed no signs of life beyond
drawing his breath faintly. Then, leaving him to the care
of one of her companions, she flew back to the church,
threw herself before the altar, and poured out her heart
in tears of thankfulness.

IV

For many days Pierre lay between life and death,
watched ceaselessly, all unknown to him, by her whose
name he kept repeating in the ravings of his fevered lips.
Her loving care and skill were not thrown away. At last
the fever left him, and he came to his senses, wondering
what this place might be, and how he found himself so
kindly tended.

Weak and wasted, he was lying on a snow-white bed,
and beside him sat a woman wrapped from head to foot
in black, like some holy sister of mercy, as indeed she
was. The closely drawn veil hid her features, yet the
sight of this unknown woman recalled to Pierre her
who was all the world to him. With a heavy sigh

he let his head fall feebly on the pillow. Then he heard a low voice, full of compassion, murmuring in his ear :

"Are you, then, so unhappy, poor stranger?"

"So unhappy," answered he, "that my sorrow can only end with my life, which, did I not fear to offend heaven, I would often have sought to destroy and my misery with it."

"Rather trust in heaven's goodness, and hope that this sorrow may yet be turned into joy!" she said, and every word was strangely sweet to him.

"Ah, lady, it is pardon rather than hope I should demand! If you knew my guilt! I loved a great and beautiful princess. I stole her from the arms of her parents. I tore her from a house of which she was the pride and the joy; then by a most cruel fatality I left her to perish—how can I forgive myself, though truly I would have laid down my life for hers."

Now he heard this good sister utter a deep sigh from beneath her hood. Encouraged by her sympathy, he went on with his story, telling her how he left his love sleeping, how he had followed the raven, how he had been carried away, and how never since had he ceased to lament the suffering that he must have unwillingly brought upon her. As he spoke she bent her head over him, and he felt warm tears running down on his face.

"Tell me," she whispered through her tears, "do you still love this lady whom you believe to have left to destruction?"

"Do I love her? So truly that if she be no longer alive to grant me her forgiveness, I have no heart to live longer, but ending my wretched days in some hermitage of the desert."

"Pierre, Pierre! Look up and live to love her, thanking heaven that she lives and loves you still!"

She threw back her veil, she let fall her coarse robe, and stood before him dressed like a king's daughter as he had left her that fatal day, which now seemed as it were yesterday, and all that had passed between like the visions of a disordered brain.

"Magdelona!" he cried; then, speechless for joy, held out his feeble arms towards her, and she fell upon his heart.

Few more words are wanting to end the tale. With the smiles of his beloved for medicine Pierre soon grew strong. His parents, already sent for by Magdelona, arrived to welcome him as one from the dead. Nor did the King and Queen of Naples, when they learned that their daughter was still alive, refuse to forgive her freely, and to consent to her union with the knight who had suffered so long for her, as she for him.

THE RANSOM

SALADIN, the great Sultan of the East, was at the height of his power. Long had he afflicted the true faith, and made Christian blood to flow like water upon the soil of the Holy Land, where the knights of Christendom had joined to make a struggle against him. From all countries they came in arms, lords and heroes of renown, and if courage could have given victory the Sultan would have been overthrown. But heaven willed it otherwise; for in a great battle the best of the Christian champions were slain or taken captive.

Among the prisoners was Hugo of Tabarie, forced to yield when from loss of blood he could no longer hold the sword with which he had laid low many a turbaned infidel. Covered with wounds, he was brought into the presence of Saladin, right proud to have such a warrior in his power. And when he learned that this knight was a powerful prince in his own country, he asked him why he had not chosen to remain there in peace, rather than travel far across the seas to suffer hardships and affront death.

"Nay," said the Christian, "that were the part of the churl that cares not but to eat and sleep like the beasts of the field. Honour and religion constrain us who are vowed to knighthood; therefore, heedless of pains and dangers, we come to rescue the sacred sepulchre from your profane hands."

"On a vain errand, truly, ye have come," said the Sultan sternly. "And, since the fortune of battle is thus, ye shall not go lightly away. Thy ransom must be a hundred thousand golden bezants, a fit price for such a prince; or thou must pay for this rashness with thy head."

"So be it," replied Sir Hugo, unmoved. "I am ready to die, if need be; but as for the ransom, if I were to sell all my lands, I could not bring half the sum."

Saladin marked him well, and was pleased by his firmness and spirit.

"'Twere pity a brave knight should die for lack of gold. This much I grant thee: go freely back to thy friends and seek their aid, leaving me thy promise to return upon a set day. Surely the Christians will give much to save such a champion."

Sir Hugo thanked the Sultan, and gave the promise required of him. The day was appointed for his return, and as soon as his wounds would allow him to travel, he set forth from the camp of the infidels, to go among the Christians of Palestine seeking to borrow money for his ransom. But, alas! he could not gather half that great sum before the day on which he had promised to return. There was nothing for him but to die; so in his heart sadly bidding farewell to wife and children far over the sea, he came to deliver himself into the Sultan's power with the tale of his ill success.

"And I," said Saladin, "have sworn by the Prophet that thou shalt die unless the ransom be paid to the last bezant. Yet it grieves me to slay a man who has thus given himself to death rather than break his word. Many a one in such a strait would have thought less of my trust than of his own safety."

"The word of a knight is stronger than iron chains

and bars," said the captive proudly. "On the day when I was received into that sacred order I vowed to hold honour dearer than life, and he who doubts our good faith knows little of Christian chivalry."

"I would know more of this order and its vows," said the Sultan, leading his prisoner aside into his chamber. Hugo hesitated, not willing to speak freely on these things to an infidel, but at Saladin's earnest entreaty he consented to describe the ceremonies of dedication to knighthood, and the Saracen monarch listened with interest and growing respect.

This degree, he learned, is the noblest of earthly honours, beside which the pride of kingdoms, lordships, and wealth are as naught. The gentle youth who aspires to it, after worthily serving as page and squire, is duly prepared by vigil, fast, and prayer. Then Sir Hugo told how his hair is cut close, and how he is bathed in pure water, a type of that inward cleanness without which no candidate should dare to present himself. He is now laid upon a soft couch, that may remind him of the rest that in paradise awaits the faithful soldier of the cross. His limbs are covered with a shirt of spotless white, a symbol of the purity in which it ever behoves him to keep his body. Piece by piece his armour and habiliments are girded on, and the mystic meaning of each is explained. Over all is thrown a rich red robe, as a token that he must always be ready to shed his blood in every good cause. Now, bareheaded, he kneels lowly before the sovereign or warrior of renown at whose hands he is to be made knight, who strikes him on the shoulder with the flat of a sword, the last blow he may receive without dishonour. Lastly, his spurs and helmet are fastened on, and his sword is given him with a solemn charge.

"Henceforth," ended Sir Hugo, "he is bound to speak truth and to hate liars, to honour religion, to obey his king, to be courteous and helpful to all ladies, to sustain the right and to confound those that do wrong, to succour the oppressed in all the world, to despise hardships and death, and to fear the face of no man."

Saladin heard, and for a while sat in deep reflection. Then he rose and without a word led his prisoner into the hall, crowded with Saracen emirs and chiefs. Silence fell on all that assembly when they saw their great sovereign, and thus he addressed them:

"Behold a gallant enemy who must die for want of ransom. Which among you will give of your wealth to buy his life?"

The generous Saracens pressed forward, vying with each other who should offer most in such a cause. Freely they poured out their gold before the Sultan, and soon the sum required lay in a glittering heap. Saladin turned to the captive:

"See, thou art free! Accept this gold, which I give thee in return for the lesson thou hast taught me, and as a proof that there are noble minds in our host as well as among the Christian knights. Go back to tell through Christendom that Saladin can be as courteous to the vanquished as he is well known to be fierce on the field."

Overcome with surprise and gratitude, the knight could scarcely thank his generous conqueror. But when he found words, he prayed that with the gold he might be permitted to ransom some of his companions in captivity.

"'Tis well," replied the Sultan, "that I have a richer gift to offer thee, since gold is no meet guerdon for such a man. I set them all free—they are thine."

He kept his word. The Christian prisoners were set free forthwith, and spent several days in feasting and sport among their enemies, now for the nonce become friends. Then, loaded with presents, and attended by an honourable escort, they were conducted to the camp of the Crusaders, by whom, henceforth, the magnanimity of Saladin was known and esteemed no less than his prowess in war.

INDEX

NOTE.—In this Index the accent has been marked and the usual English pronunciation indicated, where it seemed necessary, by a respelling.

ā to be pronounced like *a* in *fate*; when unmarked, like *a* in *fat*, or in *far*.
ē like *e* in *me*; when unmarked, like *e* in *met*.
ī like *i* in *pine*; when unmarked, like *i* in *pin*.
ō like *o* in *dote*; when unmarked, like *o* in *dot*.
ū like *u* in *bull* or *pull*; unmarked, like *u* in *nut*.
c, followed by *e, i,* or *y,* soft like *s,* as in *cent*: hard like *k,* when followed by *a, o, u,* as in *cat,* &c.
g, soft like *j,* when followed by *e, i,* or *y,* as in *gem,* &c.; hard when followed by *a, o, u,* as in *gate, go,* &c. But *g* in the respelling is to be always pronounced hard.
ñ indicates the French nasal sound.